EUROPEAN IMPERIALISM AND THE THIRD WORLD

This book presents a comprehensive overview of the evolution of imperialism in Portugal, Spain, the Netherlands, France, and Great Britain. It delves into the background of colonialization and focuses on the nature of the motives of necessity, utility, religion, and exploration and the modus operandi of the establishment of the colonies which required a substantial amount of capital. The volume discusses a wide range of themes, including the role of Spain as a Muslim colony; rise and fall of Spain as an imperial power; Portuguese discoveries and colonialization; conquests of Dutch companies of East India and West Indies; the French company of the Indies; British colonies in Americas, Africa, and Australasia; and English East India Company to showcase a holistic history of European competition for trade through wars in North America, South America, Africa, Australia, New Zealand, and Asia.

This book will be of interest to general readers interested in the history of colonization, imperialism, Third World studies, post-colonial studies, international relations, defense and strategic studies, South Asian history, and European history.

Abdul Qayyum Khan is the author of *Understanding Afghanistan, History, Politics and the Economy*. He has published many articles in an international journal of Europe. He earned his PhD in Agricultural Economics from Colorado State University, USA, and received his Master's in Economics from Quaid-i-Azam University in Pakistan. He has worked as a Project Director at the University of Illinois at Urbana-Champaign (UIUC) and New Mexico State University. He has also worked with the United States Agency for International Development (USAID) and the Food and Agriculture Organization (FAO) of the United Nations.

EUROPEAN IMPERIALISM AND THE THIRD WORLD

Abdul Qayyum Khan

LONDON AND NEW YORK

Cover design: Shutterstock

First published 2023
by Routledge
4 Park Square, Milton Park, Abingdon, Oxon OX14 4RN

and by Routledge
605 Third Avenue, New York, NY 10158

Routledge is an imprint of the Taylor & Francis Group, an informa business

© 2023 Abdul Qayyum Khan

The right of Abdul Qayyum Khan to be identified as author of this work has been asserted in accordance with sections 77 and 78 of the Copyright, Designs and Patents Act 1988.

All rights reserved. No part of this book may be reprinted or reproduced or utilised in any form or by any electronic, mechanical, or other means, now known or hereafter invented, including photocopying and recording, or in any information storage or retrieval system, without permission in writing from the publishers.

Trademark notice: Product or corporate names may be trademarks or registered trademarks, and are used only for identification and explanation without intent to infringe.

British Library Cataloguing-in-Publication Data
A catalogue record for this book is available from the British Library

Library of Congress Cataloging-in-Publication Data
A catalog record has been requested for this book

ISBN: 978-1-032-43516-9 (hbk)
ISBN: 978-1-032-45593-8 (pbk)
ISBN: 978-1-003-37771-9 (ebk)

DOI: 10.4324/9781003377719

Typeset in Bembo
by Deanta Global Publishing Services, Chennai, India

To my sons Shahab and Zoraize,
to my daughter Naureen, to my wife Saeeda,
to my grandchildren Osman, Imran, and Umar
for their love and support throughout many years.

CONTENTS

List of figures   *viii*
Acknowledgments   *ix*
Chronology   *x*

   Introduction   1

1 The Muslims' Rule in Spain   5

2 Rise and Fall of Spain as an Imperial Power   55

3 The Portuguese Discoveries and Colonialization   82

4 The Conquests of the Dutch Companies of East India and the West Indies   106

5 The Conquests of the French Company of the Indies   122

6 The British Colonies in the Americas, Africa, and Australasia   129

7 The English East India Company   148

Index   *227*

FIGURES

6.1	British American colonies	136
6.2	British colonies in Canada, the West Indies, and South America	143
6.3	British colonies in Africa	144
7.1	British colonies in Asia and Australasia	223

ACKNOWLEDGMENTS

I am thankful to Shahab and Naureen for their continued encouragement for authoring a book on Imperialism, a topic so important for Naureen who has been discussing it with her students in the school. Shahab, who is a connoisseur of business, has eagerly supported me to know how the trade and wars in the third world built the European empires during the seventeenth and eighteenth centuries. I am deeply thankful to Shahab who has also helped me in the preparation of the maps and figures. Naureen has arranged the research materials that helped me to move on to this research project without any hindrance. On top of this, I am indebted to my wife Saeeda and my elder son Zoraize for their continued support during the implementation of this project.

I am also thankful to an anonymous reviewer of my manuscript who has provided me very thoughtful comments and critique.

CHRONOLOGY

711   Muslim conqueror Tariq ibn Ziyad crossed the Strait of Gibraltar and after defeating the Gothic forces led by King Roderic captured Toledo, Egica, and Cordoba.
712   Muslim conqueror Musa ibn Nasyeer captured Sidonia and Sevilla.
713   Muslims captured Merida and Lisbon, now a part of Portugal.
714   Tariq ibn Ziyad captured Zaragoza, Huesca, Lerida, Barcelona, Aragon, Leon, and Castile.
998   Muslims captured Zamora and Leon in northern Portugal.
1450   Arab navigator Ahmad ibn Majid discovered the Cape of Good Hope, while the Portuguese explorer Bartolomeu Dias arrived later at the Cape of Good Hope in 1488.
1456   Portuguese discovered the Cape de Verd islands, which remained under their control for 519 years.
1492   Granada fell to the Spanish, which ended the Muslim rule in al-Andalus.
1494   Columbus discovered Jamaica and Cuba.
1496   Spanish discovered Santo Domingo in Hispaniola, which had gold mines.
1498   Trinidad in the West Indies and Venezuela in South America became Spanish colonies.
1498   Portuguese explorer Vasco da Gama discovered the sea route between the East and the West by anchoring off Calicut in Kerala on the southwestern coast of India.
1500   Portuguese discovered Terra de Santa Cruz in South America, which later became Brazil.
1502   Gama captured a dhow named *Merri* near the Malabar Coast, which was carrying 380 Muslim pilgrims from Mecca, and plundered and burnt the dhow along with all the pilgrims including men, women, and children.

1508	Puerto Rico became a Spanish colony.
1509	The Spanish established settlements at Cartagena and Santa Marta, Columbia.
1510	The Portuguese conqueror Albuquerque, who dreamed of establishing an empire in India, conquered Goa seaport after a second attempt by defeating the Ottoman ruler Adil Shah.
1511	Albuquerque captured Malacca by defeating the Sultan of Malacca and built factory and fort.
1511	Cuba became a Spanish colony.
1519	The Spanish explorer Vasco Nunez de Balboa discovered Panama.
1521	The Spanish captured Mexico by defeating the Aztec ruler.
1532	The Spanish captured Peru by defeating the Inca ruler.
1598	The Dutch sailor Wybrant van Warwijck discovered the island of Mauritius.
1604	The Dutch established the first headquarter of the VOC at Bantam on the island of Java.
1607	The British established their first colony on the bank of James River and named it Jamestown, Virginia, in America.
1611	The Dutch established their trading factory at Batavia (Jakarta).
1612	The British captured Surat from the Portuguese and established their factory at Surat.
1613	The Mughal ruler granted the British the right to trade at Surat.
1640	The Dutch took over Malacca from the Portuguese.
1662	China expelled the Dutch from Taiwan.
1664	The British won New York from the Dutch in a war.
1673	The French took Pondicherry from Sher Khan Lodhi of Bijapur.
1710	The French took Mauritius from the Dutch, which was later taken by the British in 1810.
1746	The French captured Madras in India.
1748	The British got back Madras in exchange for Louisburg, which the British had taken from the French.
1759	The French surrendered Canada to the British.
1761	The French lost Pondicherry in India to the British.
1776	George Washington announced the Declaration of Independence of the United States of America after capturing the 13 states of America by defeating the British general Lord Cornwallis at Yorktown, Virginia.
1788	The colonialization of Australia began by establishing a British colony of New South Wales.
1795	The British captured Ceylon from the Dutch and made its colony for 153 years. The British also captured the Cape of Good Hope from the Dutch.
1796	The British took Guiana in South America.
1798	Honduras in Central America became a British colony.
1800	The British captured Malta from the French.

1802	The British took Trinidad from the Spaniards.
1803	The British captured Tobago in the West Indies from the French.
1812	The United States attacked Canada to humiliate the British.
1819	The British captured Singapore from a native Raja.
1838	The British captured Aden on the coast of Arabia.
1839	New Zealand was annexed to the British colony of New South Wales.
1842	The British captured Hong Kong islands.
1861	Lagos came under British control.
1882	The British invaded Egypt and captured it in the battle of Tel el Kebir.
1892	The British occupied Sudan.
1900	The British occupied Johannesburg and Pretoria.
1947	India and Pakistan got independence from the British.

INTRODUCTION

The ancient civilization of Rome had an agrarian-based economy that had sufficient domestic land to meet the needs of all the inhabitants. The land was distributed to the people for earning their livelihoods. Later due to an increase in population, the land changed hands through inheritance and sale and purchase activities. Most of the people became landless. The government introduced land reforms to limit the land holding to 350 acres, but that too did not work. Consequently, the land was concentrated in a few hands who did not till themselves. All the rich landlords purchased the slaves to cultivate their lands. The slaves just worked for their masters and did not have any freedom of opportunity to get empowered to compete. Even the manufacturing and trading activities were carried out by the slaves. When resources are concentrated in a few hands then it leads to an inequality of opportunity that breeds a revolution.

The ancient civilization of Rome needed additional land in the foreign territories. Their modus operandi of colonialization was to conquer the territory to satisfy the demand for lands and then settle its population to engage in economic activities. The settlers were granted lands in the colonies. The new Roman colonies in the conquered areas were allowed to make bylaws for their governance but mainly acted under the authority and guidance of their mother country. The Roman colonies were subjects to the home country. For the security of new colonies Roman garrisons were established in the conquered areas. The Roman colonialization not only satisfied the demand for land for its people but also discovered the opportunities of economic wealth which was later sent to their home country. Though the mechanism of the Roman and the Greeks colonialization was different, their motives for establishment of the colonies stemmed up either from the motives of the necessity or from the utility, or both. Some of the Roman colonies like Florence had grown, but their growth was not rapid because the colonies were being pillaged by their mother country. The colonies

DOI: 10.4324/9781003377719-1

were established in the conquered territories where the inhabitants were indifferent because they did not enjoy freedom to run their affairs as they liked.

Unlike the Roman concept of colonialization, the Greek concept of colonialization was just meant to leave the house in search of an opportunity to satisfy the necessity and the utility. This was necessitated by the fact that the increased population of Greek was unable to maintain within the limited land of their territory and finding the additional land in the neighboring hostile countries was not possible, it had therefore to target the distant territory. Dorians settled in Italy and Sicily where the inhabitants were unimproved and did not bother aliens' presence and this was well before Rome was born. Ionians settled in Asia Minor, Middle East, India, and southern Asia. The colonies were self-governed through enacting their own laws and made decisions without seeking approval or consent of the home government of Greece. The home government had no control and authority over the colonies and also had no intention of pillaging them. In return, the home government just expected respect and gratitude. Unlike the Roman colonies, the Greek colonies made rapid economic progress toward wealth and prosperity to such an extent that most of the colonies became either equal to or excelled even the home cities of Greece. The colonies had abundant land of good quality and welcomed the colonists. The colonies were at liberty to manage their affairs as they liked. The cities of Syracuse and Agrigentum in Sicily, Tarentum and Locri in Italy, and Ephesus and Miletus in Asia Minor emulated the cities of ancient Greek.

The European nations, that were getting the spices and exotic commodities through the Muslim traders, were unaware of the origins of these commodities. Based on the experiment of the Roman and the Greek colonies, the European nations also wanted to meet their necessity and to maximize their utility. The European nations were interested in the identification of geographical locations of the exotic commodities and the mode of transportation either by sea or by land to allow them to establish a network of commercial organizations to have access to these commodities.

In 1271, Marco Polo traveled through Turkey, Central Asian States, Iran, Afghanistan, Pakistan, India, and reached China via the silk route. From China he traveled through Sri Lanka, Burma, North Vietnam, and islands of Java and Sumatra. He not only studied the region's landscape, people, and their culture but also discovered some commodities which were not available in Europe. Marco's plan was expected to link Asia with Europe through trade in precious and profitable commodities. Asia was rich in commodities like pepper, nutmeg, spikenard, galangal, cubebs, indigo, cloves, ginger, cinnamon, and various other spices. Other precious commodities included the gold and the gems such as balas rubies, sapphires, and lapis lazuli of Sar-e-Sang Mountain of Badakhshan and diamond of Golkonda mines located around the Krishna River east of Hyderabad, India. These precious stones were also found in modern-day Burma and Sri Lanka.

Marco's book *The Travels of Marco Polo* influenced the Europeans through the knowledge of the region and its vastness and richness which provided an opportunity for establishment of the business relationships between the east and the west. Now the east had become accessible to the Europeans. As a sequel to the travels of Marco Polo, the traffic of the European merchants and missionaries started toward the east. The Franciscan John of Montecorvino reached Beijing and established a church in 1291. In 1340, an Italian merchant named Francesco Pegolotti visited the region and prepared a guide for the Europeans which said that the silk route from Crimea to Beijing was safe for travel. Marco Polo's travel was just exploratory rather than the consideration of necessity or utility. After Marco Polo, in 1325, a Muslim traveler and explorer, Ibn-Battuta from Tangier in Morocco, traveled through Muslim and non-Muslim countries, including Central Asia, Southwest Asia, South Asia, and China. Ibn-Battuta traveled three times the distance of the travel of Marco Polo, and his mission was just exploratory and not based on necessity or utility or business concerns.

During the fourteenth and the fifteenth centuries, the Venetians got engaged in a profitable trade in spices with the east. The Venetians purchased spices at low prices from Egypt under the Mamluks and distributed them among the European countries at higher prices, making considerable profits as these commodities were not available in Europe. The huge profits by the Venetians were envied by the Portuguese. During the fifteenth century, the Portuguese were looking for a way either through sea or through land to the countries from where the Moors brought them ivory and gold across the desert. The Portuguese discovered the islands of the Madeira, the Canary, the Azores, the Cape de Verd, the coast of Guinea, Congo, Angola, and the Cape of Good Hope.

In 1497, after about 200 years of Marco Polo's travel of the east, the Portuguese sent Vasco da Gama by sea to the land of spices. Portugal carried out the whole of trade with East India without an exclusive Company and did it for more than a century. Now the European countries jumped in the trade of spices by establishing the Dutch East India Company or VOC (1602), the Danish East India Company (1620–1777), the French East India Company (1664), and the English East India Company (1600). However, the poor countries of Europe like Sweden and Denmark neither sent a single ship nor established an exclusive company to trade with East India. These countries never thought of risking their small capital in the distant and uncertain adventure. Both Sweden and Denmark bought East India goods from other nations at higher prices. Christopher Columbus was influenced by the travels of Polo and started his voyage of reaching the east by sailing to the west.

This book has delved into the background of the colonialization and has focused on the nature of the motives of necessity, utility, religion and exploration and the modus operandi of the establishment of the colonies which required a substantial amount of capital. Capital facilitated discoveries which led to the colonies through violence. The colonies then provided return on the capital in the form of profits which further led to the establishment of empires. The empires were the product of war and trade. The wars were needed to acquire the right to trade and trade provided the profits to fight the wars. The trade and wars went side by side under imperialism. Chapter 1 discusses how an Islamic civilization, the jizya, and the sword come into being and how they extinguish by the baptism civilization and expulsion, pillage, and violence. Chapter 2 of this book discusses how Spain emerges from Muslim rule of 800 years to an imperial power by expanding its empire through violent and destructive colonialization of the Caribbean region; the North, Central, and South America; and Asia in the east. And how the naval wars happen among the Spaniards, the Portuguese, the Dutch, the French, and the English to acquire trading rights in the west and in the east.

Chapter 3 discusses in detail how Portugal, being neglected by the rest of Europe, discovers the route to the east and captures the spice trade and exotica from the Muslims in the eastern Archipelago and India and how it finally yields to the Dutch and the English. Chapter 4 discusses how the Dutch, through their behemoth shipping company Verenigde Oostundische Compagnie (VOC), breaks the monopoly of Portugal in the spice trade and exotica and successfully establishes a commercial network in the eastern Archipelago and India by capturing the posts of Spain, Portugal, and Britain. Chapter 5 discusses the details of the war between the French and the British simultaneously going on in America and India and how the British, through their supreme naval power, defeat the French in both places. Chapter 6 discusses how the English Virginia Company establishes its plantations in North and South America by challenging the Spanish, the Portuguese, the Dutch, and the French establishments; how the colonists become rich at the cost of the colonies through their policies of destruction, extraction, and displacement; and what happens to be the success factor for the British to overwhelm the other Europeans. Chapter 7 discusses a comprehensive history of the English East India Company from trading to building of an empire in India through killing of the natives, destruction, and pillage of the villages; how the British change their color from humble petitioners for the trading rights to violent terrorists duly getting approval by London; and how the British through intrigues and bribes subdue the local princes and rulers and destroy the old Mughal Empire stretching from Kabul to Carnatic but remain unsuccessful in taming Afghanistan.

ND# 1

THE MUSLIMS' RULE IN SPAIN

Spain is a country in the southwest of Europe in the Iberian Peninsula, and Portugal was a part of it before its independence in 1668. In the north it is separated from France through a range of mountains called the Pyrenees and in the south by the Strait of Gibraltar, north of Africa, and in the east and the southeast is limitrophe to the Mediterranean Sea and in the north and in the northwest and in the southwest with the Atlantic Ocean. Spain was home to all religions of the world. Christianity was prevalent in Spain during the second and third centuries that practiced Roman Catholicism through the teaching of St. Paul and St. Augustine.[1] Saint James, who was a fisherman, later joined Jesus as one of his 12 disciples and made a visit to Spain, where he preached the gospel before returning to Jerusalem. The Old Roman Center, named after Caesar Augustus in the Ebro Valley in Zaragoza province in Aragon, was the place "where Virgin Mary appeared to James the Apostle,[2] and where hundreds of the Christians faithful had been massacred on the orders of Emperor Diocletian", writes Lewis. Diocletian had proclaimed himself God which the Christians did not accept.[3] Many of the Christians were killed by the Romans in Sevilla, Cordoba, Barcelona, and Gerona.[4] On his return to Jerusalem, St. James was beheaded in 44 CE by King Herod-I Agrippa.[5] Saint James is buried at a place called Santiago de Compostela[6] in Galicia. Diocletian was succeeded by Constantine. Christianity was strengthened during the reign of Emperor Constantine who, in the fourth century, declared Christianity as the official religion of the Roman Empire and gave his name to the capital of his empire as Constantinople.[7] Christianity in Spain was a minority.

Spain was ruled by the Roman Empire as a colony between the third and fifth centuries. Romans had used Spain as a source of wealth to enrich Rome just like other Roman colonies. Later, the local Visigoth tribe rebelled against the Romans and expelled them from Spain (Romans called it Hispania). Visigoths

DOI: 10.4324/9781003377719-2

established their kingdom in Toulouse which included the northeastern part of Spain and ruled Spain until the arrival of the Muslims. A hundred years later they transferred their capital to Toledo and got control over most of the peninsula. Visigoths were Arian, the followers of "Arius, Presbyter of Alexandria (318–81)[8] who argued that Jesus the Son was created, and therefore not eternal and therefore not the equal of God the Father", writes Akram. This was close to the Muslims' version that Jesus was a man, a prophet, and a servant of God. The Arian doctrine, followed by the Visigoths, challenged the Roman Catholic orthodox dogma. Emperor Constantine called a meeting of the council of bishops at Nicaea in 325 for discussion on the principle. In this meeting the Christian orthodox dogma prevailed that the son was equal to God, the Father. At the Second Ecumenical Council held in Constantinople in 381, the Nicaea dogma was confirmed that two natures of the Son were of the same substance as the Father.[9] But this was not accepted by everybody. The controversy among the Visigoths and the Romans continued. In 580, King Leovigild accepted the dogma of Catholic relating to the Son that Christ the Son of God was equal with the Father, which was the main point between Catholicism and Arianism.[10] This acceptance was a radical one.

In the sixth century (586–601), Hispania was ruled by a Christian Visigoths king Reccared, son of Visigoths king Leovigild, who originally followed the Arian faith. King Reccared later in February 587 converted to Catholic by baptizing himself secretly. Before his conversion Reccared called a meeting of the Arian and Catholic bishops to find out the religious truth. In this meeting Reccared informed the participants how an Arian bishop failed to cure a blind man. Later, Reccared held a meeting with the Catholic bishops and announced his decision of conversion to Christianity. Reccared under an imperial fiat based on the recommendation of the Third Council of Toledo held in May 589 officially rejected the Arian faith and ended the division between the Visigoths and the Roman Christians. Catholicism now was the official religion of the Visigoth kingdom. Reccared lifted the ban on Catholic synod that was imposed by Agila and maintained by Athanagild, Liuva, and Leovigild, the Visigoth kings of Hispania.[11] Before Reccared's conversion to Christianity, the Visigoth kings were very tolerant toward the Catholics and never criticized their faith. Thompson reports King Agila as having said that "Speak not evil of the law which thou thyself observest not; as for us, though we believe not the things which ye believe, yet we do not speak evil of them, for the holding of this or that belief may not be imputed as a crime".[12] Later, Agila himself was forced to be baptized. Reccared suppressed the Arians' protest by banning them from employment in public service until they yielded and accepted the new orthodox Catholic dogma. Reccared, after his conversion to Catholicism, destroyed all the Arian existing documents.[13] The Arian churches and their properties were given to the Catholic churches. After conversion to Catholic, the Visigoths stopped the ritual of burying grave-goods with the dead. None of the Arianism existed in Iberia. The Arianism faith was finally defeated by the vox populi.

Now Jews were the only non-Catholic community in Hispania. In 70, Romans destroyed the Temple of Solomon[14] and tens of thousands of Jews were expelled from Jerusalem and were forced to emigrate to Hispania. In the late sixth century, slavery was at the apogee in Europe. In Islam, slavery was prohibited and the holy book Quran encouraged the Muslims to free the slaves. In the Iberian Peninsula, slaves were an important source of creation of wealth and were mostly owned by Jewish landlords. King Reccared looked at the Jewish and and their slaves with covetous eyes. The Christians, now well settled in Spain, despised Jews by considering them the killers of Jesus.[15] The Christians envied the richness of the Jews which they used to influence their benefits.

In consultation with Pope Gregory, King Reccared made a law against the Jews. Jews tried to bribe the king with a huge sum of money, but the king refused to be corrupted which was liked by the pope. According to the law, he forbade the Jews from buying a Christian slave or getting one as a gift. If a Jew circumcised a Christian slave, the slave was to be set free without any compensation to the owner and the owner would not only lose all his property but would also become a slave of the state.[16] Reccared died at Toledo in December 601 and was succeeded by his illegitimate son Liuva-II. Liuva died at the age of 20 after ruling for 18 months. Now Witteric ascended to the throne. He was a very harsh ruler, not a supporter of the church, and was assassinated in April 610. Witteric was succeeded by Gundemar, who was soft toward the church and died at Toledo in February or March 612 and was succeeded by Sisebut, who turned out to be a harsh ruler for the Jews and was deeply involved in the church affairs and reigned until February 621, when he died a natural death.

In 306, a church council of the bishops prohibited the Christians from marrying or working with the Jews. Christians continued despising Jews until 506, when the Council of Agde[17] (Agatha) even disallowed the Christians to eat with the Jews. In 612, King Sisebut (612–21), who was not satisfied with the effectiveness of the implementation of the laws of Reccared, promulgated a law that prohibited the Jews from owning Christian slaves. Consequently, the Jews had to sell the Christian slaves and their properties at throwaway prices. Failing to sell them, they had to set the slaves free. The timeline for implementation of the law was three months. At the end of three months, if any Jew was found having a Christian slave, half of his property would be confiscated and the slave would be set free. The law also provided that if a Jew proselytized any Christian to a Jewish faith, he would be punished to death and all of his properties would be confiscated.[18] Anyone who converted to Judaism and refused to return to Catholicism would be publicly whipped and would be made a slave of the state. In the case of prohibited mixed marriages, if a Jewish partner refused to return to Catholicism, he would be exiled permanently and those who had baptized would be allowed to keep the property and the slaves. The slaves born of the mixed marriages would be Christians and nothing else. The law was implemented in its true spirit, and the Jews suffered a lot. After this law, under another imperial fiat, the Jews were banned from public service employment,[19] civil or military, to make sure they would not be able to use their positions to harm the Christians. Jews were allowed to repair their synagogues but not to build a new one. If they built a new synagogue that would be converted to a Christian church and the builders would pay a fine of 50 lb. gold to the Treasury,[20] writes Thompson.

In 616, King Sisebut passed another law that required the Jews to convert to Christianity within one year. The Jews would remain as catechumens for eight months before they are baptized. After one year, if a Jew was found with his Jewish faith, he would be served 100 lashes and then would be expelled from Hispania and all of his properties would be confiscated. According to Dozy, "Under the influence of terror more than ninety-thousand Jews were baptized".[21] Although they ostensibly accepted Christianity, their spirit and hearts possessed their Jewish faith and they continued practicing circumcision of their children and observed their Sabbath and other Mosaic rites secretly.

The intermarriages between the Christians and the Jews were banned. The Fourth Council of Toledo reiterated the intermarriage ban with the punishment of public whipping in case of violation. The Jews and Christians who intermarried would be separated from their spouses and their children would be taken away from them to be raised as Christians.[22] Even when Jews married Jewish women, their children would be taken away from them to be brought up as Christians.[23] In 638, during the reign of King Chintila, all the baptized Jews were forced to renounce their Jewish faith and abandon their rites such as Sabbath, circumcision, and dietary rules. They themselves accepted the task of stoning to death any Jew who violated the pledge of adoption of the Catholic faith.[24] The irony was that the baptized Jews were not considered true Christians. King Sisebut died in February and was succeeded by his son Reccared II, who died after a few days and was succeeded by Chintila who had worked under Sisebut.

In 650, King Reccesuinth made ten laws against Jews by which no baptized Jew would leave the Christian faith. No Jew would marry by other than Christian rites, the practice of circumcision was banned, Jews would not care about their dietary rules, no Jew would testify against a Christian or a Christian slave, no Jew would give evidence in court. The punishment for violation would be death by stoning and burning by their own people. Now to be a Jew in Hispania was a capital offence.[25] In 655, at the Ninth Council of Toledo, all Jews were ordered to spend Christian feasts in the company of the local bishops who would certify their faith and any violation would be punished by whipping.

After his death on September 1, 672, King Reccesuinth was succeeded by King Wamba, who ruled until his death in 683. His death was caused by a poisoning drink that Erwig gave him who later became the king. Erwig drafted 28 laws against the Jews. The new king Erwig ordered that no Jew would possess and read any book that goes against the Christian faith, which carried a punishment of 100 lashes. Even a child above the age of ten years was required to follow this rule strictly. He further ordered that both the persons involved, one who is being circumcised and the other who performs the circumcision, would have their genitals cut off as well as confiscation of their property. In case of a woman doing this, it would have her nose amputated.[26] Erwig made baptism obligatory in the kingdom and those who failed to do so would be exiled and their properties would be confiscated. Erwig instructed all the bishops to call the Jewish community to the Catholic church and explain them the law. During his reign, Arab invasion of the kingdom started. On November 14, 687, on his deathbed he nominated Egica instead of one of his sons. King Egica (687–701) continued the practice of his predecessors and attacked the economic roots of the Jews by banning them from the harbors for trading activities with the Christians and overseas trade with the rest of the world. All the properties and businesses that the Jews had purchased from the Christians would be taken back by the state at the prices decided unilaterally by the state.[27] Later, all the Jews were stripped of all their properties and businesses in Toledo, Tarragona, Merida, Baetica, and Catalonia. The Jews, their spouses, and children were taken away from their homes and made permanent slaves. Egica died in 702.[28]

In 704, the rulers of North Africa pledged allegiance to the fifth Umayyad caliph Abdul Malik bin Marwan (685–705), and thus Ifriqia (Province of Eastern Roman Empire), Libya, and Morocco became part of the Dar-al-Islam. By 691, Abdul Malik built the hexagonal Dome of the Rock at the site of the Temple of Solomon. The success of Maghreb was largely due to the Umayyad Generals Tariq bin Ziad and Musa bin Nasyeer, who brought the Berbers into the fold of Islam.

In 700, Egica appointed his son Wittiza as a co-king just to get the experience of ruling the country. The last Visigoth king Wittiza died in 710 after ruling for a period of eight years.[29] Wittiza had three sons, namely, Akhila, Olmondo, and Ardabasto. Wittiza appointed Akhila as the Duke of Terraconesis, the northeastern province of Spain, with the idea to gain experience to succeed Wittiza. Wittiza was succeeded by his son Akhila. Akhila was overthrown by another tribe led by usurper Roderic who had served Wittiza as commander of the Goth cavalry and was also the Duke of Baetica, southern province of Spain. With the support of nobles, bishops, and officials, he became the king of Spain in 710.

Soon after his accession to the throne, Roderic was confronted with the story of an enchanted house in Toledo. This was a house that cast a spell over the people of Spain and every time a new king visited this house and just locked it. So far 26 locks had been placed on this house. Now the people asked the new king Roderic to visit and lock the house because it was good for the people and the country. Roderic refused to do so and said he would not lock it until he has seen what it is. The people requested Roderic not to do so because it would not be good for his kingdom and the people. Roderic was unshakable. He was determined to see it at any cost.

Roderic along with the people went to the house, broke the locks, and entered the house. There he found a locked urn. He broke the locks of the urn and found a scroll of parchment. Roderic unfolded it and read the manuscript written on parchment which said that the people shown in this picture look like

Arab warriors dressed in animal skins, mounted on the Arabian steeds armed with swords and bows slung across their shoulders and the standards raised in their hands shall invade and conquer Andalus,[30] write Gayangos and Akram.

On seeing the picture and the manuscript, Roderic became sad and regretted he should have not done this. The people were terrified now. Roderic immediately ordered the replacement of the locks and ordered guards to stand at the house. From now onward, Roderic remained mentally disturbed all the time.

In 711, Musa bin Nasyeer, the viceroy of Maghreb, known as northwest Africa including the countries of Algeria, Morocco. Tunisia, Libya, and Mauretania ordered the governor of Tangier, Tariq bin Ziyad, to cross the nine-mile stretch of the strait of Gibraltar that connects the Atlantic Ocean to the Mediterranean Sea and separates the two continents of Europe and Africa. Tangier was a very old entrepôt used by the Greeks and Phoenicians along the eastern end of the coast of the Mediterranean Sea where now-modern Turkey, Lebanon, Syria, and Israel are located. Tariq bin Ziyad[31] became Musa's general, who captured Tangier and was appointed its governor. Tariq was a convert from a Berber tribe of Luwata, and the mission was to carry the message of the Holy Prophet to Europe. Tariq was a good horseman and a capable administrator with the knowledge of Maghreb; that is why Musa appointed him as the governor of Tangier. The viceroy of Afriqia, Musa bin Nasyeer, directly reported to the sixth Umayyad Caliph al-Waleed bin Abdul Malik at Damascus.

Another support to the Muslims came from Julian (or Ilyàn as reported by Gayangos), the governor of Ceuta, who was married to the daughter of King Wittiza of Spain. Julian received a message that his daughter Florinda was disgraced by King Roderic. Instead of taking an immediate reaction, Julian thought it appropriate to first get his daughter back from Toledo and then deal with Roderic. Normally Julian used to visit King Roderic in the summer, but this time he made it earlier. When Julian reached the court, Roderic was surprised to see him at an unexpected time. Roderic asked Julian what brought him over here at an unusual time. Roderic became suspicious. Julian told Roderic that his wife was on a deathbed and that she loved her daughter very much. She wanted to see her before her death. Roderic agreed. Roderic reminded Julian of bringing some African hawks for him. Julian told Roderic that certainly he would get the African hawks that he would remember forever. Julian took Florinda and came back to Ceuta.

Julian was very furious and was determined to take revenge for the disgrace of his daughter Florinda that he loved too much. According to Gayangos,[32] Julian swore that he would destroy Roderic's throne and dominion with the help of the Muslims from Africa. Julian visited Tariq bin Ziyad in Tangier and Musa bin Nasyeer in Qayrawan and invited the Muslims of the Maghreb to invade Spain and in that case, he would provide key information about the weakness of the kingdom and necessary logistical support and would personally participate in this invasion. Count Julian's invitation to Musa to invade Spain was considered in Spain as "inviting the wolf into the sheep pen to help out with some entirely local matter", writes Hopkins.[33]. Messages were exchanged between Ceuta, Tangier, and Qayrawan, and the terms were agreed upon. According to the agreement, Julian invaded the coast of Spain and killed many Spaniards, collected the spoils, and made a sizeable number of coastal Spaniards as captives. The raid was successful, and the raiding forces returned to Ceuta with booty. Julian again visited Qayrawan and explained the success of his campaign and showed the booty that was collected. The Muslims were surprised to see the nature of the booty. Now Julian had demonstrated his loyalty to the Muslims and his enmity to the Spanish king.

Musa wrote to Caliph Al-Waleed in Damascus and explained the details of Julian's raid of coastal Spain and the richness of the area and requested the caliph's permission for invasion of the Gothic kingdom. The caliph wrote that instead of putting Muslims' life at risk, it was better first to conduct a reconnaissance mission to have more information. Caliph Al-Waleed gave permission subject to the execution of a reconnaissance mission. The reconnaissance mission was carried out by Tarif bin Talib al-Mu'afire who, in 710, with 400 Berbers, visited Iberia by landing at a place known as al-Andalus. The Christians fled instead of resisting the Muslims. After a few weeks, the Muslims came back to Morocco laden with booty and women and narrated the stories of the richness of Iberia which were waiting for the Muslims' picking.

Musa, after getting the secret information from Count Julian, that Roderic is engaged with Basques and Franks, immediately ordered Tariq to invade Spain. In April 711, Tariq and 20 Arab officers with an army of 7,000 Berbers[34] reached the Ceuta port, where they were received by the governor of Ceuta, Count Julian, who assured the Muslims complete support and provided valuable information about disunity among the Visigoths. Julian and his forces joined Tariq's forces. Julian provided his four vessels for the transportation of the Muslims' army to the coast of Spain. The crossing on Julian's vessels was done at night starting on Tuesday, April 28, 711, so that no Spaniard was aware of the landing of the foreigners on the coasts of Spain. The army would raid the coastal areas and destroy the Spanish army that falls in their way and capture the territories as much as possible to generate the supplies for the forces away from home.

Tariq was on the first vessel crossing the strait, and during the voyage he slept for a while. During his brief sleep he dreamed of the Holy Prophet, Peace Be Upon Him, who was accompanied by his companions with swords in their hands and bows slung around their shoulders and walked on waters. When they passed the vessel, the Holy Prophet said, "Take courage, O Tariq! and accomplish what thou art destined to perform", writes Gayangos. The Holy Prophet and his companions continued walking on the water and reached Spain. Tariq woke up and narrated his dream to his soldiers, who were very delighted and said it was a happy omen. Tariq was now sure of the victory.[35] Tariq disembarked with his men and horses on the southwestern shore of the mountain called Mount Calpe which was regarded as one of the pillars of Hercules. At the foot of the mountain,

12 The Muslims' Rule in Spain

Tariq built a fort as a base camp for the continuation of further expeditions. The fort was known as Jabal-e-Tariq and later changed to Gibraltar.

Now, Tariq called for a woman who was famous for prognostication. The woman came and said that her husband used to prophesize and once he had said that a person, with a prominent forehead just like yours and a black mole on his left shoulder with hairs on it, would be the person who would conquer Spain. If you have a mole with hairs on your left shoulder, then you are that person. When Tariq got his left shoulder naked, everybody who was present at the moment saw a black mole with hairs just as described by the old woman,[36] writes Akram.

When Roderic was engaged in the north with the Basques and the Franks, he left the southern region under the control of Count Theodomir,[37] the Gothic governor of the southeastern province with its capital at Orihuela, now Murcia, writes Akram. Theodomir was a capable administrator and soldier to deal with the Muslims. On hearing the news of the arrival of the Muslims, "the passage from the Green Island to the mainland was at first defended by seventeen hundred Christian soldiers under the command of Theodomir",[38] writes Conde. To stop the Muslims, Theodomir took the control of Carteya;[39] the Muslims called it Cartagena, not the one located in the southeast of Spain. Carteya was a hurdle in the way of Muslims, and it had to be removed.

To secure a beachhead at Carteya, Tariq sent Mughith al-Rumi with a strong force that attacked the Goths and expelled them from the town of Carteya. The defeated Gothic Theodomir wrote to Roderic that he had failed to stop the Muslims. Now they are here. Theodomir wrote to Roderic that some forces from Africa, adverse to them, have come and he does not know whether they have dropped from the heaven or sprung up through the earth,[40] writes Conde. Tariq joined the forces at Carteya and then moved to a place on the coast called al-Jazeera-al-Khadra (Algeciras). The Muslims established their base at Algeciras. In July 711, Tariq led mounted forces from Costa de La Luz into the mountains. People saw the unknown invaders and informed Roderic at Toledo. The time of the invasion was not good for Roderic as he was already engulfed in problems with the Basques in the north and the rebellion of Duke Akhila and his brothers in the southeast. The local Jews, who were ostensibly converted to Christianity and whose properties were confiscated by the Visigoth ruler, also volunteered to support the Muslims against the Visigoths.

On receipt of information from Count Theodomir, Roderic became suspicious of the roles and involvement of Count Julian and Duke Akhila and thought that they were also part of the Muslims' operation. Roderic then made the right decision of stopping his engagement with the Basques and Franks and now concentrated on the preparation of his forces to face the Muslims aided by Count Julian and Duke Akhila. After leaving his north engagement, Roderic took a large army of one hundred thousand soldiers, far larger than the Muslims, and moved toward Cordoba. In order to stop the Muslims, Roderic sent a strong detachment, led by his nephew named Bencio, which moved from Cordoba southward by picking up the remnants of Theodomir's army on its way to face the Muslims. Theodomir also joined Bencio[41] with his army. In the meantime, the Muslims were raiding the towns to collect supplies including food and fodders for the armies to live long. The Muslims raided deep inside the districts of Algeciras and Sidonia. While the Muslims were busy collecting and bringing back cattle and sheep, Count Julian's agents were busy collecting information about the movement of the Gothic army. The petrified natives left their places and made the way clear for the invaders.

Tariq's forces came close to Bencio's larger forces across the plain stretching from the Rio Barbate to the Guadalete River. Both the Muslims and the Visigoth armies for the first time came across each other at a place called Shaduna, now Sidonia, a hilltop town in Cadiz province of Spain which is 25 miles inland from the Atlantic Ocean. Sidonia has the church of Los Santos, one of the holiest sites of Visigothic Hispania. Muslim forces moved back toward Algeciras. Bencio moved forward to engage the Muslims. A series of clashes took place where the Muslims dominated. Bencio and Enecon or Edico[42] were killed, and Theodomir fled to survive. The Visigothic forces withdrew toward the north, and some of their horses were captured by the Muslims and it was a good addition for them as they did not bring many horses from Africa. Muslims went after the fleeing Visigothic forces and followed them up to Cordoba. The Muslims dominated and prevailed in the southern part of Spain.

Roderic invited King Wittiza's sons Olmondo and Ardabasto to join his army against the Muslims. The princes joined him reluctantly, and Roderic marched southward. The princes' reservation about Roderic made other nobles think likewise. The nobles, though in minority, despised Roderic and thought that the coming of the Muslims was a blessing from God in that they would get them rid of this wretch and that the Muslims would not be a threat to the kingdom. The nobles were of the opinion that after the defeat of Roderic, the Muslims would just get what they wanted through booty and would go back instead of settling here and would hand over the empire to them. Then, "we can place on the throne him who most deserves it",[43] writes Gayangos. The noble thought that Roderic was a usurper and was not entitled to be the king as he was not from the family of the kings.

Tariq, at his new base camp at Tarifa, heard about the advancement of 100,000 Gothic army for which his army was of no match. Tariq wrote to Musa about the Gothic army's strength and their march toward the Muslims. To confront such a big force, Tariq asked Musa for help. Musa sent 5,000 Berbers under the command of Tarif ibn Talib al-Mu'afire to reinforce Tariq. Tarif crossed the strait and joined Tariq, making the total strength of the Berber army to 12,000 fighters.

Tariq was a devout fighter. When Tarif joined him at Tarifa, Tariq burnt all of his boats,[44] including the four vessels of Julian, to ensure that there would be no retreat from Spain, a stage set for a do-or-die in the conquest of Spain. This showed Tariq's dedication to embracing martyrdom for the cause of Islam as a holy devout Muslim warrior. Historians, including Gayangos and Conde, have confirmed that the event of burning the boats and vessels by Tariq bin Ziyad did happen.[45] Gayangos writes that "they have set fire to their vessels to destroy their last hope of escape". Tariq was the first commander in the history of military campaigns who burnt the boats to avoid retreat. After destroying his transportation fleet, Tariq now marched toward Medina-Sidonia along the coast and then turned to inland and stopped at the Pass of Facinas, a small village in the province of Cadiz, which was an ideal place for defense. The Muslims encamped here and took the advantage of hilly terrain which formed the basin of the River Barbate.

Roderic was in hurry to meet the invaders and did not wait for the Christian warriors who were on their way to join him. Roderic's army passed Medina-Sidonia and reached into the plains of the Barbate River. Near the town of Casas Viejas now Benalup de Sidonia, Roderic's forces encamped by the bank of the river. Roderic waited to learn about the Muslims' strength and intentions. Tariq now received information about the location and strength of the Gothic army. Tariq marched toward Casas Viejas and before reaching the town he crossed the River Celemin on his left and went to west and the foothills of the Sierra Momia on his right, and to the extreme left were the marshes of the Lagoon of Janda. Consequent upon the arrival of the Muslims in their camp, Roderic moved forward and crossed the Barbate River and encamped at the east bank of the river. The two armies got close to each other and were now ready to hit the battle. But before that, Roderic sent one sleuth on a reconnaissance mission to the Muslims' camp. The Muslims spotted him and took him into their camp and showed him everything. Tariq treated him well[46] as a guest and served him dinner. The sleuth returned to Roderic and reported that these people are the same whose picture you have seen on the scroll of the enchanted palace. Beware of them, writes Gayangos. They are not afraid of death. To avoid retreat, they have burnt their boats. Roderic did not bother about the report.

The Gothic army of 40,000[47] men, well equipped with swords, lances, bows, German battle-axe, and shields for defense, assembled between the foothills of the Sierra Momia and the Lagoon of Janda for battle with the Muslims. Roderic was high in appearance but not in spirit and took his place at the Centre of his army protected by the guards in front of him and behind him was a reserve force. The force also included many mules loaded with ropes to be used to tie up the Muslim captives.[48] The wings were commanded by Sisberto and Abba (Oppas),[49] the uncles of the princes. The young princes were not part of the battle.

On 28th Ramadhan, July 19, 711, the Muslims accompanied by Duke Akhila and Count Julian's forces met the Gothic forces at Jerez de la Frontera in Cadiz province. Roderic was the first to start action against the Muslims. Gothic forces did not find any weakness among the Muslims' fronts. During the first three days of fighting there were heavy losses on both sides. However, Roderic had the advantage of the reserves which he used to replace the losses, while Tariq could not do so because he did not have any reserve. The same men had to go day after day. The Muslim soldiers were tired as they did not have rest. Tariq went to the fronts and addressed his soldiers and exhorted them to fight gracefully. After praising Almighty Allah, Tariq said, "Oh my warriors, whither would you flee? Behind you is the sea, before you, the enemy",[50] writes Lewis. "If you demonstrate your courage, the booty will be yours. I shall be the first to set an example for you and you do what I do", writes Gayangos.[51] According to Gayangos, the soldiers responded, "we are ready to follow you, we will stand by you and fight for you and the victory will be our only hope of salvation".[52] The men forgot their fatigue and recharged themselves for the combat.

Now the good news came to Tariq. The sons of Wittiza had defected Roderic, as they thought, they had enough of battle. Actually, the sons of Wittiza did not want to deliver a victory to Roderic because that means the continuation of his cruel rule. The princes sent the message to the Muslims through Julian which, according to Akram, said, "Roderic is a dog from the dogs of our father, his follower and servant, who usurped the throne after his death".[53] The next morning the princes deserted Roderic with their army and joined the Muslims. In return, they sought Tariq's protection and handing over of the 3,000 farms of their father's estate which the usurper had taken. Tariq accepted these conditions.

On the fourth day of battle, the Muslims took the initiative which surprised Roderic. The Gothic wings bolted and left the Gothic flanks open. Roderic immediately brought his reserves to the wings that were vacated by the sons of Wittiza. Now Tariq attacked the Gothic front. Although many Gothics fell due to a fierce attack by the Muslims, its center continued resistance. The Muslim group pierced through the Gothic guards in front of King Roderic, who was sitting on the chariot. When Roderic saw these men, his eyes and head swam back to the picture that he saw at the enchanted house in Toledo. On seeing Roderic, Tariq shouted, "this is the tyrant of the enemy",[54] writes Akram. The Gothics disintegrated and bolted. The Muslims captured the horses of the fleeing Goths and now every Muslim soldier was mounted on a horse. Tariq crushed the Visigoth forces and killed Roderic near the banks of Barbate and found in a ditch his dead stallion, white horse, Orelia still saddled. One of Roderic's sandals studded with pearls and sapphires was found which was later sold for a hundred thousand dinars.[55]

The weeklong battle ended on July 26, 711. This was the bloodiest battle in the history of Spain in which the ablest general of the Visigoths was lost. Sisberto, brother of King Wittiza, was also killed. The Muslims took 10,000 Goths as prisoners who became slaves except those who accepted Islam and most of them did so later. The Muslims collected a huge amount of booty and after paying the state's share of one-fifth, the rest was distributed by Tariq in which everyone's share was equivalent to 250 gold dinars. The credit of this victory goes to the skills and leadership of Tariq who had put a small army against the behemoth Visigoth army. The severed heads of the Visigoths wrapped in camphor-soaked cloth along with bejeweled hilts and gold were sent to Damascus as proof of the Muslims' victory. Tariq's 3,000 men embraced martyrdom in the fiercest fighting against the Visigoths. The Muslims for the first time planted the flag of Islam on the soil of Spain that would flutter for eight centuries until the fall of Granada in 1492.

Tariq sent his messenger to Musa to inform him about the Muslims' victory in Spain. On hearing the news, Musa immediately prostrated and praised Allah for this victory. After the battle, the three sons of Wittiza, namely, Akhila, Olmondo, and Ardabasto visited Africa and met Musa and the caliph in Damascus and showed the agreement made with Tariq about the restoration of their father's estate. The caliph received the princes with great honor and confirmed the agreement made with Tariq. The princes returned to Spain and got their father's farms and each prince got 1,000 farms as his share. Olmando settled in Sevilla, Ardabasto in Cordoba, and Akhila in Toledo. After many years, Olmondo died and his farms were forcibly taken by his brother Ardabasto. Olmondo's beautiful daughter named Sara visited Damascus, met the caliph, and complained about the illegal occupation of her father's farms by her uncle Ardabasto. At Damascus, Sara got her father's farms back.

In early August 711, Tariq embarked on a new mission of Cordoba. Tariq crushed any resistance that came on his way. The first place on his way was Moron de la Frontera where the enemy soldiers did not resist. After Moron de la Frontera was subdued, Tariq moved toward the northeast to Ecija located on the bank of River Genil, a town in the province of Sevilla, and the Roman tradition has it that this place was visited by Saint Paul during his visit to Spain. Ecija in Roman was also known as Astigis and Arabs named it Istija. It is located on the main highway between Sevilla and Cordoba. Four miles from Ecija, Tariq encamped at a place known as Barrancas del Molinillo, later became known as Ain Tariq (Spring of Tariq). Tariq sent his scouts on a reconnaissance mission which reported back a big gathering of the Gothic army in front of the town of Ecija. It was the middle of August 711.

Tariq moved forward to confront the large Gothic army. The Goths retreated to the town, and the Muslims moved forward and laid a siege to Ecija. On the eastern side of Ecija was a Genil River, and the western side was protected by a high wall. It was difficult to break the fortification and the siege continued and would have continued for a long time, had the Commander General of Ecija not come to the river for bathing. Gothic General was spotted by the Muslims and then Tariq embarked on this adventure. Unaccompanied and unarmed Tariq went to the same river for a bath. Both the Gothic general and Tariq were swimming in the same river without knowing each other. Then all of a sudden, Tariq pounced and picked up the Gothic General above his shoulder and brought him to the Muslims' camp. In the camp it was revealed that the Gothic was in fact the Commander General of Ecija. The deal was negotiated, and the Gothic General thought it appropriate to surrender peacefully. The deal was sealed. Ecija opened the gates, and the Gothic garrison surrendered. There was no bloodshed and no plunder. Tariq freed the Gothic General. The Muslims captured Ecija, and the people agreed to pay jizya at the rate of two dinars per head and lived peacefully. After Barbate, this was the second victory of the Muslims.

At Ecija, Tariq received a letter from Musa which included the orders that he should stay where he was and wait for his arrival.[56] Such orders from a commander and a great military strategist were not expected at a time when the enemy's forces were shattered and were defenseless. Stopping Tariq from chasing the broken Gothic army would mean providing an opportunity for them to regroup and make preparation to stop the invaders. Tariq did not want to miss this opportunity. Tariq was non-stoppable. Tariq called a meeting of the Generals and shared Musa's letter with them. The generals were shocked and instantly disapproved the orders. Based on the ground realities Tariq ignored Musa's orders. Count Julian advised that it was high time to move against the Goths. Julian advised instead of marching toward Cordoba to move toward Toledo where the enemies were assembling and send their detachments in different directions. Julian's advice provided strength to Tariq's decision to ignore the commander's orders and move forward.

Tariq dispatched one detachment of 700 cavalrymen under the command of Mughith al-Rumi to capture Cordoba before the Gothic army was reorganized. The second detachment of the same size under the command of Zaid bin Qesadi was sent toward the south. Tariq led the main body of the Muslim force through Jaen toward Toledo which was 250 miles away from Ecija.

Zaid's operations were carried out in two districts of Reijo with its capital at Archidona and Elvira in southern Spain. Elvira was a small Roman town called Iliberri about ten miles from the site of Granada, as Granada did not exist at that time. Later Elvira was replaced by Granada. Zaid sent two small detachments to each district which were supported by Julian's guides. The detachment that raided the district of Reijo captured the important city of Malaga, and the people fled to the mountains. The Muslims occupied the entire district with its capital Archidona. The second detachment stormed Elvira and captured it, and after this the army spread throughout the Elvira district and subjugated the entire district. In all the big cities of Malaga, Archidona, and Elvira, the Muslims were welcomed by the Jews. After the subjugation of the districts, the administration of two districts was given to the Jews supported by a small group of the Muslim soldiers. After completion of the task, Zaid left southern Spain to join Tariq at Toledo.

Mughith's army marched towards Cordoba. Cordoba was an old Roman fortified city and the capital of Baetica province; it was located on the north bank of River Baetica, which the Muslims named the Shaquanda River, and later, after their settlement, they called it Wadi-ul-Kabeer, meaning the Great Valley. The river is now called Guadalquivir in Spanish. Cordoba, a walled city, had many gates, and two important gates were the Gate of Statue with a lion atop the gate, also called the Gate of Bridge because it faced the bridge across Guadalquivir and later was called the Gate of Algeciras. The second gate at the southwestern corner of the city was the Gate of Seville. Near the gate was the Church of San Acisclo, well respected by the Cordovans. On the north of it were the hills of the Sierra de Cordoba. The plain between the hills and Shaquanda is now known

18 The Muslims' Rule in Spain

as Campo de la Verdad, meaning the Field of Truth. In the south of Shaquanda, at a distance of one mile, there was a village called Tercial (Tarsail), which later became a farm known as Cortijo de los Torres, and in between these two places were the cedar forests.

In the third week of August 711, Mughith encamped in the forests between Shaquanda and Tercial. Mughith sent his scouts on a reconnaissance mission of Cordoba. The scouts saw the bridge dismantled by the Goth, and there was no way to cross the river other than swimming through the river with their horses. The scouts also found a shepherd who had information about the defenses of Cordoba. The shepherd informed the scouts that all the inhabitants had gone to Toledo and that the governor of Cordoba with his 400 soldiers was still in the city. The other people left behind in the city were poor people and were least interested in the fighting. The shepherd also informed that the wall along the river bank was strong enough and could not be breached. However, the wall on the Gate of Statue had a breach that could be exploited.

Now the problem was how to cross the river without the bridge. The distance between the wall and the bank was just 50 feet which was not enough for Mughith's 700 horses. Mughith now decided that two soldiers would be mounted on one horse. But the noise of the stamping of the horses' hooves would alert the guards in the battlements and the Muslims would be exposed and would be at the mercy of Gothic guards' arrows and javelins. Should they cross at night, they were mulling over it. Then the help from almighty Allah came in the form of storm, rain, and hailing. The sky was overcast, and before the fall of night a thunderous storm hit the city followed by heavy rains and hailing. At night, the Gothic guards left their parapets due to heavy rain and hailing.

The Muslims now moved to the south bank near the demolished Roman bridge facing the Gate of Statue. Two men mounted on one horse plunged into the river during the course of heavy rain and hailing. The crossing of the river was successful, and the Muslim cavalry assembled between the river's edge and the city wall. The shepherd now led the Muslims to the wall where there was a breach. The breach was not sufficient enough to let the Muslims get through. Now the Muslims were trapped on the far bank without any protection and were at risk of a Gothic attack.

Mughith now found a quick solution to the problem. He found a big fig tree near the gate. He ordered one of his soldiers to climb on the tree and from the top branches of the tree jump on the wall. The soldier successfully did it. Then Mughith opened his turban and threw it to the soldier up on the wall and then with the help of the turban the other soldiers managed to climb on the wall. When a group of the soldiers were up on the wall, Mughith ordered them now to get inside and attack. The soldiers attacked the guards inside the wall; some were killed and some managed to escape and raised the alarm. The Muslims broke the lock of the door, and the gate was open. The Muslims now entered the city with swords drawn in their hands. The Visigoth governor of Cordoba left the city, and the Muslims announced peace to those who surrendered and death to those who resisted. Mughith called the Jews and left them with the Christians and the Muslims together as in-charge of Cordoba defenses.

There was no fighting yet. The governor of the city of Cordoba decided to peacefully slip away with his 400 men through southwestern corner of the city to the Gate of Sevilla. The Goths went into the Church of San Acisclo which was fortified like a citadel for any sort of attack. The church had a secured water supply coming from a spring in the foothills outside Cordoba. The church was stocked with supplies that could last for a long period. The Muslims occupied the city and settled in the quarters. The people did not resist, and the Jews welcomed the invaders and offered their services to the Muslims. Mughith had the control of the city of Cordoba but did not reach the Church of San Acisclo inhabited by the governor and his 400 men. Mughith had no equipment to break the siege and just waited until the supply ran down.

The siege continued for two months, and Mughith, a restless person, lost his patience and decided to do something about it. Mughith thought that if he could get hold of one of the inhabitants of the church, he would be able to get some information that could help him to break the siege. For this purpose, Mughith picked up one of his slaves named Rabah equipped with brawn than brain. Mughith asked Rabah to secretly enter the orchard of the church and hide in the shrubs until a resident of the church becomes his prey.

Although Rabah was a strong person with a stout body, he did not have the intelligence for the task he was assigned to. Rabah waited for hours and he did not get any Goth. He was very hungry. He saw a fruit tree in the orchard and came out of the bushes and climbed up the tree to satisfy his hunger. He was spotted by the Goths and a few soldiers came and surrounded the tree and compelled him to come down. As Rabah came down, he was captured and made a captive. The soldiers had never seen a person of African race before. They thought he was painted in black. They planned to wash him with a brush to make sure his black color is gone and he turns out to be like one of them as Germanic people. The Goths continued scrubbing his body, and Rabah was feeling pain. Through his body language, Rabah was able to explain to his captors that he was a human being just like them but in a different color.

The Goths understood him that he was naturally black and stopped scrubbing him. They chained him and kept him at a place as a showpiece where the people came and saw for the first time, with their astonishment, a human being in black color, never heard of before. After a week, the Goths became disinterested in him and left him in chains under the control of guards. The strong muscled Rabah broke the chains, killed some of the guards, and successfully fled. Rabah came back to Mughith and explained his adventure and explained in detail the channel through which the water came to the church, the direction the water came from, and its depth.[57]

Mughith sent local engineers who discovered the source of the supply of water to the church and stopped it. No more water was coming to the church. Some water was stored in the cisterns. The Goths in the church were compelled to surrender. The Muslims offered them three words: Islam, the jizya, or the sword. They rejected the offer with disdain. The siege continued. The governor managed to escape leaving behind his family and soldiers at the mercy of the Muslims. When Mughith heard that the governor fled on his horse, Mughith immediately took his horse and chased the governor and caught him near the village of Talavera (Talbeera) located at some distance in the west of Cordoba. The village is now known as Ollerias.[58] When the governor saw the furious pursuer, he turned his horse toward the ditch which his horse was capable of crossing, but unfortunately, the governor fell in the middle of the ditch and broke his neck. Mughith captured him and brought him back to the city.

Mughith again offered peace in terms of Islam or the jizya, and again the offer was rejected by the defenders of the church. All of the 400 defenders of the church were killed, and the church became known as the Church of the Captives. The siege lasted for two and a half months, and by the end of October 711, the whole of Cordoba was under the Muslims' control. The Muslims, here again, asked the Jews to run the administration of Cordoba with the help of a small group of soldiers that the Muslims left behind. The Gothic women and the royal family of the governor, including his beautiful daughter, were taken as the prize of war. Mughith as commander of the force said he had the right to possess the beautiful girl, but the girl refused to be in his possession and was determined to die in the protection of her chastity rather than handing over her body to Mughith. Mughith praised the determination of the girl and let her be chaste. After this, Mughith left Cordoba to reunite with Tariq's forces at Toledo.

In the last week of August 711, Tariq left Ecija for Toledo with his force of 10,000 fighters. Tariq avoided the main road to Cordoba and arrived at Jaen and then turned to north and crossed the Guadalquivir at Menzibar and then took the main road to Toledo. On the way, Tariq's forces did not face any resistance, and by the middle of September, Tariq's forces arrived at Toledo, once called Toletum by the Romans, who had captured the fortified town in 193 BC. Later, it was captured by the Gothic king Theudis in the middle of the sixth century and remained the capital of the Visigoth kingdom of Spain. Toledo was protected by the Tagus River from the northeast, the east, the south, and the west. Toledo was deserted as the people fled to Guadalajara, also known as wadi al Hijara, a few miles from the village of Madrid. The remnants of the Gothic army who remained in Toledo after their defeats at Barbate and Ecija were not in a position to confront the Muslims.

When Tariq arrived at Toledo, he found all the gates closed. The only access to the town was from the north side. After crossing the Tagus River, Tariq encamped on the north side. The inhabitants believed that the defense against the Muslims was not an option and then asked for the terms of surrender. The terms that Tariq announced for them were very generous. According to the terms, the residents of Toledo would surrender their weapons and horses. Those who want to leave can do so without their possessions. If they want to stay, they would be free to live with peace and practice their religion, traditions, and their own laws for governing themselves. They would also enjoy the protection in return for payment of the jizya. The old men, women, and children would be exempt from the payment of the jizya. There would be no pillage, captivity, or slavery.

After the terms of surrender, the gates were opened and the Muslims entered the city. Tariq and his guards settled in the palace of the citadel, later known as Alcázar of Toledo. The soldiers took their quarters. Tariq's men collected the spoils. This was a victory without bloodshed and had big consequences as the Visigoths never rose against the Muslims. Tariq made the administrative arrangements to govern the city by the Jews with the help of a small detachment of the soldiers and ordered the rest of army to get ready for another campaign as it was September and the weather was good.

In the middle of October 711, Tariq's forces marched towards Wadi-ul-Hajara (Valley of Stones) which the Arabs called the ancient Roman town of Compluto and in Spanish as Guadalajara. The forces passed via Alcala de Henares through the hills which later were to be known as Fajj Tariq, meaning Pass of Tariq. On the way Tariq captured a town called Maya or Amaya, where the Gothic soldiers had taken refuge. He also took the city of Maida, now known as Almeida, in Malaga province south of Alcala de Henares where Tariq found the Table of Solomon. Tariq stopped further campaigns as the winter approached and the soldiers were also exhausted. Tariq returned to Toledo in the early weeks of November 711 and settled for the next orders from the commander-in-chief.

A huge amount of booty was collected at Toledo, and after paying a one-fifth share of the state at Damascus, the rest was distributed among the warriors. The booty included gold and silver and 25 crowns of gold embellished with pearls and precious stones, each one belonging to the Gothic kings who ruled Spain. There were 1,000 swords whose hilts were adorned with rubies and pearls. There were several vessels filled with rubies, emeralds, and pearls. There were many utensils of gold and silver. And there was the Table of Solomon.[59] Now after subduing south Spain, Zaid and his troops joined Tariq at Toledo. Almost all big cities of Spain in the south, Cordoba, and Toledo were conquered by Tariq and his operation was now over. Tariq's achievement was not the great amount of booty but most importantly the conquest of Spain with an army of 12,000 Berbers, which laid the foundation for the Muslims' rule in Spain to last for about 800 years. Tariq broke the power of the Gothics just in two battles. Berbers came from the modern-day countries of Libya, Tunisia, Algeria, Morocco, and Mauritania. When Mughith met Tariq at Toledo, Tariq asked him to deliver him to the prince of Cordoba so that he could keep him as a prize prisoner and then he would present him to Caliph Al-Waleed. Mughith refused to give the royal prize,[60] and this became the bone of contention between the commander and his subordinate. The Gothic prince of Cordoba was the most prized catch in the hands of Mughith. Mughith himself wanted to present the prince to Caliph Al-Waleed. Further campaigns would be led by the Commander-in-Chief Musa bin Nasyeer.

A year after Tariq's invasion, the second invasion of Spain in June 712 was carried out by Musa himself. Musa left his son Abdullah to act, in his absence, as governor of North Africa at Qayrawan. Musa's force included 18,000 Yemeni mounted warriors. Musa took a route different from Tariq by starting from Ceuta and landed at a point far away from Algeciras, and this point was known as Marsa Musa, meaning Harbor of Musa.[61] The hilly region around it was to be known as Jabal Musa, meaning hill of Musa or Mount Musa. From here, in July 712, Musa moved to Algeciras and encamped for his initial campaigns. Musa's son Abdul Aziz was second in command in his force. Musa took along a number of the venerated Muslims known as companions of the Holy Prophet. After the Holy Prophet, any Muslim who knew a companion was called a Tabi in Arabic. Musa himself was a Tabi. Musa had 25 Tabi'een in his group. Musa also took three sons along, named Abdul Aziz, Abdulla, and Marwan. Musa was also accompanied by Count Julian, who helped the Muslims to invade Spain.

Musa called a meeting of the Council of the war which was also attended by Count Julian who acted as an advisor. Julian told Musa that he would guide him on a path different from Tariq to the different rich cities which were never conquered by anyone and that he could conquer, if God wills it.[62] Musa wanted to take all of Spain, and he wanted to start with the southwestern part of the country. When Musa reached Vejer he turned toward north.

The first opposition that Musa met in the winter of 712–13 was Medina-Sidonia located on top of a hill which was 1,000 feet above the sea level in Cadiz province. Musa laid a siege to Sidonia and captured it. This was Musa's first battle and the first victory in Spain. After this Musa moved toward Sevilla. Before entering Sevilla, Musa handled two fortresses which acted as outposts. The first was Alcala de Guadaira, ten miles to the southeast, and the second was Carmona, 20 miles to the east of the city on the main road to Cordoba. Without conquering these two places, the conquest of Sevilla would not have been possible. Musa stormed Alcala de Guadaira and took it without any problem and left a small detachment for its control. Now Musa moved to the second outpost known as Carmona. Carmona outpost was built as a strong defense, and it was almost invincible.[63] Musa got close to the wall but was unable to enter the town. Musa sought an advice from Count Julian. The Christian allies told Musa there was no way to get into the town without playing a trick, and Musa was the master of stratagem.

A group of cavalry men reached the Carmona fortress and informed the gatekeepers that they were just coming back after fighting with the Muslims. They needed refuge against the Muslims. They were speaking the local language. They were in fact Count Julian's men. They were welcomed and entered the fortress. No one noticed the horses they were mounted on. At night the Muslim warriors reached the main gate known as the Gate of Cordoba, and Julian's men opened the gate and the Muslims mounted warriors entered the fortress and went to the center of the town where they crushed those who resisted. Those who surrendered were captured alive. Carmona was taken, and now the way to Sevilla was clear for the Muslims.

Sevilla has been an ancient city of Spain since the times of Phoenicians, Greeks, and Carthaginians. The man named Ishban[64] conquered the peninsula and named it Ishbania, from which Hispania (Spain) was evolved. Ishban also founded the city of Ishbeelya, which is called Sevilla in Arabic. To the western world it was known as Hispalis, conquered by the Romans in 205 BC and made the capital of their province Baetica. Since then, Sevilla remained a rich city and the religious center of Christian Spain. The fortified city is located on the left bank of Guadalquivir. Sevilla could only be attacked from the east and short places in the north and south, and it was protected from the west side by the river. In August 712, Musa laid a siege to Sevilla and later conquered it. The Christian warriors fled and crossed the river westward to Beja and Ocsonoba. The rest of the population surrendered and lived under the Muslims' rule peacefully. Musa asked the Jews to run Sevilla with the help of a small force of Muqatila (fighters).

After Sevilla, Abdul Aziz's forces captured Beja, a garrison town founded by Julius Caesar, which is now a district in Portugal. After Beja, the Muslims cleared the resistance in Murcia province and the people agreed to pay the jizya. The Muslims now marched toward Merida. Merida was an old city founded by Romans in 25 BC on the right bank of River Guadiana and was the capital of the southwestern province of Lusitania. The province then included part of Portugal's territory in the south of River Duero and the west central region of Spain. Merida had a big fort-like citadel with huge parapets. In November 712, the Muslims reached Merida, and to their surprise they saw a big army of Duke Sacarus which came, one mile out of the city, to confront the Muslims. They were determined to defeat the Muslims. Musa was happy to provide the Goths with an opportunity to fight it out. Musa attacked the Goths and drove them back to the fortified city. Muslims reached the gates of Merida, and Musa offered them the three words: Islam, the jizya, or the sword. Duke Sacarus chose the sword.

In November 712, Musa laid a siege to Merida. Musa divided his forces and deployed them on the northeastern side and south of the river to cover the bridge to stop supplies and reinforcement from reaching the town. There were many gates on the protective wall of Merida, and the fighting took place in front of these gates. Sometimes the Gothic sallied out from the fortress and the Muslims pushed them back inside the fort. Sometimes the Muslims attacked the gates to compel the Goths to fight. The major fighting took place on the north side which had a weak spot for the invaders to exploit. These activities continued on a daily basis, and Musa was not satisfied as he wanted the result immediately. Consequently, Musa carried out a reconnaissance of the area and designed his plan to fight with the Goths outside the city.

One night, Musa positioned one detachment of cavalry behind a low hill about half a mile away from the north gate. Next morning, the Muslims attacked the fort and when Goths came out to fight with them, the Muslims ostensibly

24 The Muslims' Rule in Spain

created a confusion of disintegration among themselves by running in different directions. This gave an opportunity to the Goths to move forward and fight it out. General Sacarus failed to understand the dangerous maneuver of Musa and thus fell into his trap. According to this stratagem, the Muslims continued falling back and the Goths continued moving forward to contact with the Muslims. In pursuing the Muslims, the Goths forgot that they were getting far away from the fortress. When the Goths reached near the hill, Musa gave the signal to the hiding cavalry for action. The retreating Muslims turned back on the Goths. At the same time the cavalry behind the hill attacked the Gothic flanks. Now the Goths found themselves attacked from the flanks and the front. Some of the Muslims got on the back of the Goths to cut their line of retreat. Now the bloody battle took place which is called the Battle of Merida. The intrepid Gothic soldiers gave what they had and finally succumbed to the pressure and were cut into pieces by the Muslims. A few of the Goths were able to get back to the city. The Muslims also suffered heavy losses in this fierce battle. In spite of the fierce battle, the siege to the city could not be broken and still the Goths were inside the fortress and Muslims were outside.

Now the winter was set in and the fighting was not expected. Musa now started working on the equipment including testudo that could be used to break the siege. During the winter, Musa sent some detachments to the different regions to bring peace to the conquered regions by destroying the rebellion wherever it occurred. Sevilla had rebelled and one detachment was sent there to fight it out. After a few months, Musa received a new reinforcement from North Africa. In May 713, the fighting resumed at Merida. Duke Sacarus was determined to fight and had no intention of giving up. Now the Goths started starvation due to the stoppage of the supplies by the Muslims. The siege lasted for seven months. Though the Goths were determined to defend themselves, there were no supplies or reinforcements coming from the outside. Seeing no chink of hope, the brave Duke Sacarus decided to talk to the Muslims. Duke Sacarus sent a delegation to the Muslims to negotiate a deal.

On June 28, 713, the Christian delegation visited the Muslims camp. They saw a heavily built man with long white hairs and beard. The negotiations started but did not reach any conclusion. They agreed to resume the talks. When they came back for negotiation, they found the man with black hairs and beard. They were not aware of the Muslims' tradition of dying their hair. They were surprised to see that, and instead of talking, they went back. They told Duke Sacarus and the people gathered around him that "we are fighting with the prophets who can change their appearance at will, who can transform themselves as they wanted. Their king was old enough who now became young. We think we should give him whatever he demands".[65]

Duke Sacarus decided that further resistance was futile and that the solution to the problem was a negotiated deal which was approved by the Goths. After long discussions, a final treaty was signed by Musa for the Muslims and Duke Sacarus for the Goths. The gates of Merida were opened and the Muslims entered as a conqueror. All the citizens lived in peace as they lived before but under the authority of the Muslims and would maintain good behavior. The Muslims would take the possessions of those who fled the city or those who had fallen in the battle and the treasures of the churches. Merida was captured in late July 713, and with this success, the Muslims had captured the southern half of the Iberian Peninsula. The Muslims allowed the Christians to live peacefully and consolidated the power with the help of Jews. Musa now planned to meet with Tariq at Toledo.

After Musa's departure, a large number of Christians from Beja and Niebla arrived at Sevilla with concealed arms not noticed by the Muslims. They started provoking the locals against the Muslims, but the locals were reluctant to cooperate with them as they did not want to disturb the peace of Sevilla. But the locals became the victim of the miscreants' activities when the Muslims took the reaction to destroy the rebellion. The miscreants attacked the Muslims' guards by surprise and killed many of them and some managed to escape to report to Musa at Merida. Musa became furious and decided to teach miscreants a lesson that they would remember forever.

The Muslims' forces were divided between Musa and his son Abdul Aziz. Musa organized a detachment of a strong cavalry under the command of his son Abdul Aziz and instructed him to go to Sevilla and recapture it and teach a lesson to the rebels. When Abdul Aziz reached near the city, the rebels of Sevilla wanted to fight with the Muslims outside the city. The noble locals advised the rebels to negotiate with the Muslims instead of fighting. The local nobles who were not part of the rebellion wanted to meet the Muslims to show their innocence but were not allowed by the rebels to do so. Battle was now unavoidable.

Abdul Aziz crushed the rebellion and recaptured Sevilla. This time the Muslims showed no mercy which resulted in the suffering of the innocent people not involved in the rebellion. A large number of Spaniards were killed. Abdul Aziz was satisfied that he had taught a lesson to the miscreants. Abdul Aziz informed Musa about his success in the recapture of Sevilla. Musa ordered Abdul Aziz to leave a detachment in Sevilla and march with the bulk of his army to subdue the southwestern part of Spain and bring the region under the Muslims' rule.

Abdul Aziz left Sevilla and one after another captured Niebla, Ocsonoba (now Santa Maria de Faro), Mertola, and Beja. Leaving a small garrison at each place, Abdul Aziz returned to Sevilla and made this city as his headquarters. In February 713, the western region of Spain and Algarve in present-day Portugal was under the Muslims' rule. The Muslims under Tariq had already taken Jaen, Elvira, and Malaga. However, the southeast of Spain was still unconquered. Musa ordered Abdul Aziz to conquer the southeast part of Spain led by Count Theodomir, the governor of the province of Aurariola with its capital at Orihuela.

In March 713, the Muslims left Sevilla. When the Muslims reached near Elvira (Granada), they met the Gothic forces led by Theodomir. Theodomir wanted to fight the Muslims not in the open fields but in the narrow gorges and passes where he wanted to stop the Muslims' advance and inflict upon them heavy damages.

Theodomir fought the Muslims from pass to pass, hilltop to hilltop, and always stayed out of the reach of Abdul Aziz's cavalry. The Muslims could not get hold of him but followed him and pushed him back to the fort of Orihuela. Theodomir knew it well that it was not possible for him to fight the Muslims, so his strategy was to engage them without fighting so that a prolonged pursuit by the Muslims would frustrate them and they would call off the campaign and go back. Here he was mistaken. The procrastination of battle did not help Theodomir as Abdul Aziz was determined to fight and capture the southeast of Spain.

The Muslim forces led by Abdul Aziz marched towards Orihuela, and on their way they passed by the site of Murcia which did not exist at that time, it was built later by the Muslims in 831 and made it the capital of the province. The Muslim forces reached the River Segura and moved along its bank. On the right bank of Segura in the southwest of Orihuela, Theodomir decided to fight the Muslims which fulfilled the desire of Abdul Aziz. The battle was fought a few miles in the southwest of Orihuela. The site was chosen by Theodomir for a set piece battle. In the last week of March 713, a fierce battle took place for hours and a bulk of Gothic army was cut into pieces by the Muslims. Theodomir was lucky to save himself, bolted with a handful of soldiers, and crossed the river and reached the fortified town of Orihuela. The town was easy to defend and difficult to conquer.

In the meantime, an emissary from Theodomir visited the Muslims camp and delivered his message to Abdul Aziz for a peaceful surrender on respected terms. The terms included: the safety of all citizens must be guaranteed; no harm should be done to anyone; and no property destroyed or plundered. If these terms are not accepted then the defense of the town would continue. Abdul Aziz accepted the terms. The emissary was treated with respect. The treaty was prepared and signed. The moment the treaty was signed, the emissary declared that he himself was Count Theodomir. Abdul Aziz treated Theodomir with respect and traditional Arab hospitality. Both the generals sat and ate together. Theodomir returned to his castle.

Next morning, the gates of Orihuela were opened and Theodomir came out to greet the conqueror Abdul Aziz who was accompanied by his chiefs and a group of mounted warriors. When Abdul Aziz and his retinue entered the city, they were surprised to see that there were all women and children and hardly any soldiers inside. Abdul Aziz surprisingly asked Theodomir who was lined up at the parapets. Theodomir told Abdul Aziz that he lost all the capable warriors and equipment in the battle and was left with no warrior to fight. As far as the men at the parapets were concerned, they were not men. They were the women. He had asked them to untie their hair and bind them under their chin to look like beard and gave them one pole in their hand to stand at the parapets. This trick would send a message to the Muslims that the city was defended by a big Gothic force.

The Muslims would have cancelled the agreement due to cheating by Theodomir, but they honored it. The agreement was signed on April 5, 713, by Abdul Aziz and Theodomir. Conde has produced the agreement as:

Written Contract of Peace between Abdelaziz Ben Musa Noseir (Nasyeer), and Tadmir Ben Gobdos, King of the Land of Tadmir. In the name of God, the Clement and Merciful. Abdelaziz and Tadmir make this Treaty of Peace – may God confirm and protect it. Tadmir shall retain the command over his own people, but over no other people among those of his faith. There shall be no war between his subjects and the Arabs, nor shall the children or women of his people be led captive. They shall not be disturbed in the exercise of their religion: their churches shall not be burnt, nor shall any services be demanded from them, or obligations laid on them, – those expressed in this treaty alone excepted. This convention shall extend its conditions alike over the seven cities called Auriola, Valentila, Lecant, Mula, Bocsara, Ota and Lorca. Theodomir shall not receive our enemies, nor fail in fidelity to us, and he shall not conceal whatever hostile purposes he may know to exist against us. His nobles and himself shall pay the tribute of a Dinar or Aureo each year, with four measures of wheat, and four of barley, and mead, vinegar, honey, and oil, each four measures. All the vassals of Tadmir, and every man subject to tax, shall pay the half of these imposts.[66]

After the conquest of Orihuela, Abdul Aziz sent his army along the Levant coast and conquered cities after cities, including Alicante. At each conquered city, a small detachment of soldiers was left as a garrison to maintain control. While Abdul Aziz was engaged in the southeast of Spain, Musa sent another unit of his army from Merida, which captured Lisbon, now the capital of Portugal, on the west coast and Cadiz in the south. By mid-summer, the conquests in the southwest, the south, and the southeast of Spain were complete. After subduing Sevilla's rebellion, Abdul Aziz conquered Coimbra and Santarem territories to the north of Lisbon, which are now a part of Portugal.

By the end of July 713, Musa headed toward Toledo to meet with Tariq. In August 713, both the Muslim generals met at the town of Almaraz in the district of Talavera in the west of Toledo.[67] At Toledo, Musa settled in the palace as the ruler of Spain. He then demanded the state's share of the spoils that Tariq had collected. Then Musa asked Mughith to hand over the prized catch of the prince of Cordoba, which he refused. Mughith said he would present himself this prize to Caliph Al-Waleed. Musa then asked his guards to take the prince away from Mughith and then got him killed.[68] Mughith turned to Musa and Tariq, according to Gayangos, and said that "I served you both with zeal, and yet you behaved ungratefully to me. The East and the West shall henceforth see me your bitterest enemy".[69]

Musa also asked for the treasures of the kings that had fallen in the hands of Tariq at Toledo and the Table of Solomon that Tariq found at Almeida after the fall of the Gothic capital. There had been different versions of the Table of Solomon. According to one source the table was brought from Jerusalem by Ashban,[70] the first king of Spain who built Sevilla. The other sources say that though the table was originally in Jerusalem, it moved to Egypt. When Amr bin Al-Aas invaded Egypt, the priests moved it to Alexandria just before the fall of Babylon and Memphis, and when Amr marched towards Alexandria, they moved it to Tripoli, then to Carthage, and finally to Toledo.[71] The ostensibly true version was given by Ibn Hayyan, who claimed that the table found by Tariq at Toledo, though attributed to Solomon, was never belonged to the prophet. According to this version, it was customary in the times of the ancient kings to bequeath wealth and property to the churches before dying. From the money thus collected, the tables were made of pure gold and silver for the priests. With the help of bequeathed wealth, the table was wrought at Toledo and after that it was adorned with gold, silver, diamond, and other precious stones by each of the successive kings. When the Muslims entered Toledo, it was found on the altar of the principal church.[72]

At Toledo, Musa asked for the celebrated table. Tariq deliberately produced it with one leg missing for reasons best known to him. Musa inquired about the fourth leg, and Tariq responded that he did not know. Then Musa asked Tariq why did he continue the campaigns and disobeyed his orders of not doing that. Tariq said he had done all that in the best interests of Islam and his commander. Under orders of Musa, Tariq was incarcerated. Tariq did not complain and accepted the punishment in service of Islam. Had Tariq uttered a word to his fellow Berbers, the situation would have been different. But Tariq did not do that either.

Mughith protested to Musa about his behavior toward the conqueror of Spain and counted Tariq's victories for Islam but all that fell on deaf ears. Musa now decided to send a delegation to Caliph Al-Waleed in Damascus under a venerable Tabi, Ali bin Rabah. Mughith also asked Musa that he too be included in the delegation. Musa knew that Mughith was very close to Caliph Al-Waleed, so he could not resist. Mughith became a part of the delegation led by Rabah. When Tariq heard that Mughith was also a part of the delegation, he saw a chink of hope. Tariq sent a message to Mughith, his erstwhile subordinate, to present his case to the caliph. Tariq asked Mughith to tell the caliph that it was Tariq who had conquered Spain for Islam and Musa had now imprisoned him and was planning to execute him. To make sure that Tariq was not hurt during his absence, Mughith asked Musa to not be in haste to damage Tariq. "The Commander of the Faithful has come to know about him and I fear for you from his anger",[73] writes Akram. This was a big warning for Musa, and he would now think twice before executing Tariq. The purpose of the delegation was to inform the caliph about Musa's accomplishment in Spain by bringing it under the Muslims' rule.

At Damascus, Mughith told the caliph that Spain was conquered by Tariq and not by Musa. Musa felt a twinge of jealousy about Tariq's victories in Spain and had incarcerated him and was now contemplating to execute him. Musa wanted to take credit of Tariq's victories in Spain. Mughith eloquently and convincingly presented Tariq's case to the caliph. The caliph wrote a strong letter to Musa and warned him from hurting Tariq and restored Tariq to his previous position as Commander. The caliph wrote to Musa that "he must not render useless one of the best swords of Islam",[74] writes Conde. Caliph Al-Waleed also threatened Musa: "If you whip him, I shall whip you. If you kill him, I shall kill your son",[75] writes Akram. On receipt of the letter from Damascus, the orders of the caliph were obeyed immediately. Tariq was released and reinstated. The troops and Tariq were happy that justice prevailed. After this, both the generals reconciled and acted in unison until their fates were decided at Damascus a year later and soon after the death of Caliph Al-Waleed.

Now both the generals were working together for the same objective. Musa was to develop the strategy and Tariq was to implement it. Tariq led a fast movement cavalry division well equipped with arms and food provisions both for men and for horses transported by a mule train. Musa's first objective was what the Muslims called the Upper Frontier, which was the Spanish province of Zaragoza on the River Ebro. Zaragoza was a center of communications and its capture would facilitate further campaigns. To accomplish the objective of Zaragoza, Tariq left Toledo with his cavalry and reached Guadalajara which he captured without any resistance. Now Tariq advanced toward Zaragoza. Zaragoza was an ancient town that existed about hundreds of years before the start of the Christian era. It was then called Salduba. In 24 BC, as a result of the war between the Romans and the Spaniards, the Romans made it their garrison. The Romans called it Caesaraugusts or Caesares Augusta, and the Muslims spelled it Sargusta, writes Akram. The Muslims also called it Madinat-ul-Baiza, the White City.

Tariq arrived at Zaragoza and found the gates closed, and the city was in a mood of defense. Tariq sent a messenger with the offer of three words: Islam, the jizya, or the sword. Bishop Bencio advised the people to evacuate the city with their possessions they can carry, but his suggestion was not supported by the vox populi. Finally, the inhabitants of the city accepted Tariq's offer of peace and agreed to pay the jizya and opened the gates. The Muslims entered the city and occupied it in the summer of 714. Now Musa sent different detachments to subdue the surrounding areas which willingly surrendered without any resistance. The people lived in peace and enjoyed the freedom of practicing their own religion and their churches were safe. The Muslims only took the state's property and treasure and the wealth of the churches. The Muslims believed that the churches were the place of God for worship only and not to be as a storage of gold, silver, and precious stones and other valuable items. The Muslims took all the treasures of the churches. This was a normal practice adopted by the Muslims throughout the conquered Spain.

Musa appointed Hansh bin Abdullah, a venerable Tabi, as the governor of Zaragoza. Hansh built the first mosque in Spain. First it was a simple structure, and later it was adorned by succeeding generations. Tariq advanced for further conquests and conquered cities after cities of the northeast which included Huesca, Lerida, and Barcelona. There was no opposition to Tariq. Musa followed Tariq and reconfirmed his peace agreements and collected the spoils of the war, including the treasures of the state and churches.

After the conquest of Barcelona, Tariq advanced southward and captured Tarragona, Valencia, Jativa, and Denia. Tariq now reached close to Alicante which was taken a year before by Abdul Aziz. Tariq made a peace deal at each conquered city and left a garrison behind to maintain the control of the Muslims' administration. While Tariq was busy in Barcelona, another column was sent by Musa northward which conquered Gerona. Tariq returned to reunite with the main army, and by this time the whole of the east coast of Spain was under the Muslims' rule.

After establishing control on Barcelona and the east coast, Musa turned his attention to the north, which is now France. His next target was Narbonne, an important city of the Visigothic kingdom. The Goths resisted the invaders but finally were defeated by the Muslims. The Muslims collected an enormous amount of booty. According to Akram, in addition to the capture of the wealth of the state and churches, the Muslims also possessed a pond filled with diamonds, rubies, and emeralds,[76] and seven statuettes of horsemen in silver. Of this enormous booty, Tariq alleged that Musa did not send to Damascus the one-fifth share of the state in its entirety. Narbonne was the farthest point Musa went, and from Narbonne he returned back because he had found a monument in the old ruins which was inscribed in Arabic, "O sons of Ismaïl, hither you will arrive, hence you must return, for if you go beyond this stone you will return to your country to make war upon one another and consume your forces by dissensions and civil war",[77] writes Gayangos. Musa was petrified and returned.

Musa returned to Zaragoza laded with spoils, and when he started unpacking, he received a letter from the caliph ordering him to return to Damascus. Mughith brought this letter from Damascus. The orders were clear: leave the command of the army in Spain and return to Damascus along with Tariq. Mughith was responsible for the recall of Musa by the caliph. Mughith also knew what was going to happen to these two generals and the conquerors of Spain.

In 714, the Muslims conquered Aragon, Leon, and Castile. The Muslims spread like a tsunami across Iberia. The Muslims, in August 714, completed the conquest of Hispania known as al-Andalus running from the Atlantic and the Mediterranean to the Ebro River in the northeast, the Duero River in the northwest, Narbonne in France, and Central Portugal. Visigoth Hispania vanished. According to Akram, Prophet Muhammad, Peace Be Upon Him, had said: "I have been promised the east of the earth and the west; and whatever has been promised to me will be mastered by my followers".[78] Now the Muslims had mastered Spain, also known as al-Andalus where the east meets the west.

In September 714, both Musa and Tariq accompanied by Mughith and the caliph's second messenger Abu Nasr sailed from Sevilla for Damascus,[79] writes Lewis. Musa appointed his son Abdul Aziz as the Amir of Al Andalus with its capital at Sevilla with a deputy or wazir named Habib bin Abi Ubaida, a grandson of venerable Uqba bin Nafe, who was engaged in the conquest of Maghreb before coming to Spain. Musa ordered Noman bin Abdullah to control the northeastern frontier along the southern foothills of the Pyrnees and to report to

Abdul Aziz, the governor of Spain. According to Akram, the 4,000-mile-long journey back home was to take five months. The caravan laden with a huge amount of booty was accompanied by 1,100 captives, including 400 royal princes and princesses.[80] The spoils also included gold and silver coins, precious stones like pearls, rubies, topazes, and emeralds, and the Table of Solomon. Musa landed at Ceuta and then reached Tangier, where he appointed his son Abdul Malik as governor of the Maghreb with its capital at Tangier. After this Musa arrived at Qayrawan, where he had earlier spent about 12 years as governor of Africa. At Qayrawan Musa appointed his eldest son Abdullah as governor of Africa. Now Africa, Maghreb, and Spain were ruled by Musa's sons. From Qayrawan, Musa arrived at Fustat, the capital of Egypt, on December 7, 714. After spending a few days at Fustat, Musa started his journey toward Damascus via northern Egypt and Palestine. Up to this point of journey, Musa was very content and happy about bringing trophies from the west.

When Musa, Tariq, and Mughith reached Tabariyya on the west bank of the Sea of Galilee, Musa received a disturbing news. Caliph Al-Waleed was on the deathbed. The next heir was his brother Sulayman. Sulayman did not want that the trophies and the treasures that the conquerors were bringing from Spain should go to Caliph Al-Waleed which would ultimately go to his sons. Sulayman wanted to receive those trophies and treasures by himself. At Tabariyya, Musa received a letter from Prince Sulayman, brother of Caliph Al-Walid, asking them that they should tarry their arrival as Caliph Al-Walid was on the deathbed and that they should come after his death. Musa did not obey Sulayman's order and continued his advance toward Damascus. When Sulayman's messenger conveyed the reply of Musa, the prince became furious and said: "By Allah, once I get him, I shall crucify him!",[81] writes Akram. Both Tariq and Mughith left Tabariyya ahead of Musa to meet with the ailing caliph during his life. The caliph received both Mughith, his childhood friend, and Tariq, a valuable sword of Islam, with great respect.

Tariq explained to the caliph about his role in Spain and the victories of the Muslims over the infidels and the services rendered by him and the warriors of Islam. Tariq briefed the caliph about the enormous collection of spoils of war and about the Table of Solomon, how he got it, and how it was taken by Musa from him and claimed it as his accomplishment. However, Tariq did not mention the fourth leg of the Table of Solomon that he had removed and put it in his baggage. Tariq asked the caliph that he could get the testimony from the Muslim warriors, or "even of our enemies the Christians I might safely enquire if they have ever found me cowardly, cruel or covetous",[82] writes Conde. The caliph was pleased and highly appreciated his acts of valiant deeds as a courageous general, his superb conduct and performance in the conquest of Spain, and lauded his services to Islam.

Mughith also debriefed the caliph about his activities and confirmed what Tariq had already said. In addition to confirming the story of the Table of Solomon as narrated by Tariq, Mughith also brought up the issue of the prince of Cordoba known as The Barbarian who was the biggest prized catch of the Muslims. Mughith explained to the caliph how he had captured the prince of Cordoba and how he was snatched away from him by Musa and how he killed the prince in his presence. In addition, Mughith also gave the details of embezzlement in the spoils of war committed by Musa. As an example, according to Akram and Gayangos, Mughith said that "He had appropriated a diamond of such great value that the kings have not possessed the likes of it since the conquest of Persia".[83]

After debriefing Caliph Al Waleed, both Tariq and Mughith went to see Prince Sulayman who would be the next caliph after the death of Al-Waleed. Both the generals repeated the same statements that they had made before Caliph Al-Waleed and Prince Sulayman believed in every word of what they said. Sulayman became furious on hearing that Musa had rejected his call of delaying his arrival until the death of Al-Waleed. Sulayman became impatient and was anxious to get hold of Musa as quickly as possible to lacerate him.

Now Musa, laden with spoils and treasures from Spain, was marching towards Damascus with an expectation of a heroic welcome by the people and an honorable reception by Caliph Al-Waleed. Musa claimed that the conquest of Spain was his own and that the Table of Solomon he had found. Musa arrived at Damascus on January 16, 715[84]. Caliph Al-Waleed was alive to receive the commander-in-chief, though he was not well enough. Musa appeared before the caliph and presented his gifts of spoils including gold and silver and those things were never seen before in that part of the world and the Table of Solomon. The caliph was not well enough and just gave him a formal audience and he did not take any action against Musa about the charges leveled against him by Tariq and Mughith. After a few weeks, Caliph al-Walid died on February 23, 715, and Prince Sulayman bin Malik became the new and seventh Umayyad caliph.

Caliph al-Waleed's reign (705–715) was successful in expanding Islamic rule by conquering Central Asia, Bukhara, Samarkand, Khwarezm, Ferghana, Tashkent, Khorasan, Makran, and Sind in modern-day Pakistan and Spain. Al-Walid's governor of Iraq, Hujjaj bin Yusuf, played a key role in these conquests. Under Hujjaj bin Yusuf, Muhammad bin Qasim conquered Sind in Pakistan and the governor of Khorasan Qutaiba bin Muslim conquered Samarkand and Ferghana. Al-Waleed had completed the al Aqsa Mosque in Jerusalem, a few yards from the Dome of Rock, which was started by his father Abd al Malik bin Marwan. He also built the Great Mosque of Damascus, also known as Umayyad Mosque, at the site of the church of St. John the Baptist.

The seventh Umayyad caliph was a very greedy person who wanted to covet Musa and Tariq's conquered empire and the spoils and treasures brought from Spain. Fueled by the comments of Tariq and Mughith about Musa, and his denial of obeying Sulayman's order of delaying his arrival until the death of Caliph Al-Waleed made the new caliph furious and hungry for humiliating Musa. Musa was the greatest general of his time. Another person named Isa bin Abdullah At-Taweel who was in charge of the spoils in Spain had reported that "Musa had not sent to Damascus the entire one-fifth of the spoils which was the share of the state but had kept part of it with himself",[85] writes Akram. With this evidence before him, Sulayman was now ready to grill Musa.

Sulayman now became the judge for the trial of Musa and asked him about the fourth leg of the Table of Solomon. Musa answered that he found it as it was without the fourth leg and he got the fourth leg made for it as it stands now. Then Tariq entered the proceeding, who immediately "pulled out the missing leg, which was exactly the same as the three original legs of the table", writes Akram. He presented it to the caliph.[86] Musa was stunned to see this leg and was speechless. Sulayman yelled at Musa and did not proceed further with other charges and declared Musa guilty. Musa tried to defend himself by counting the victories in Africa and Spain, but that fell on deaf ears. Sulayman said, according to Akram, "By Allah, I shall destroy your works and debase you in rank". Musa said that "these matters are in the hands of Allah and not in yours. To Him I return for help against you".[87]

The first punishment awarded to 74-year-old Musa was that he was made to stand under the burning sun on a hot day. He suffered from asthma. Musa did not ask for mercy and stood under the burning sun as long as he could and then fell unconscious to the ground and then was taken away. Musa was removed from all military and civil offices, and all of his possessions were confiscated. Sulayman then ordered that an army officer should escort him to Africa and leave him there in exile,[88] writes Akram. This punishment was suspended at the intervention of Ayub, the son of Caliph Sulayman. Sulayman now imposed a fine of two hundred thousand dinars (gold pieces) on Musa. Musa had one hundred thousand dinars which were taken away. Caliph Sulayman then handed Musa over to one of his friends, Yazeed bin Al-Muhallib, to keep a watch over him and try to recover the balance of one hundred thousand dinars. Yazeed collected the remaining money of the fine from Musa's tribe of Lakhm and persuaded the caliph to allow Musa to live in peace.

After Musa left Spain, the Christian rebels started raising their heads, and it was a big task for Governor Abdul Aziz to maintain peace in the peninsula. Abdul Aziz not only subdued the rebellion but conquered additional territories like Evora, Santarem, and Coimbra, which were not conquered by Musa. Abdul Aziz got married to the daughter of the former Visigothic ruler Roderic, named Egilona. The married couple lived in Sevilla. Abdul Aziz built a mosque called Mosque of Rufeena,[89] write Lewis and Akram. This was the main mosque of Sevilla where Abdul Aziz led the congregational prayers, five times a day. Egilona became Muslim with a Muslim name Ayela.[90] Egilona gave birth to a child named Asim. Egilona had become the matriarch of the royal family and urged Amir Abdul Aziz to adopt the royal etiquettes that she had learnt from her father, King Roderic. According to these etiquettes, any person who is granted an audience by the Amir would bow before him. Abdul Aziz told her that this is not permitted in Islam. In Islam we bow only to Almighty Allah. She insisted that the people must pay respect to their ruler as the Gothic people did to Roderic.

In order to satisfy her, Abdul Aziz made a small entry door in his residence and everybody had to bend the head to enter the room to see Amir Abdul Aziz. This gave the impression that the people are bowing to Governor Abdul Aziz and now Egilona sitting at a place from where she could see this happening. Egilona now became satisfied that the people are showing respect and submission to their ruler. She then asked why he did not wear the crown. Abdul Aziz again said this is not permissible in Islam either. She suggested she had one crown adorned with gold and precious diamonds, which he could wear in the privacy at home. People would not see that. Abdul Aziz wore that crown in privacy with her at home.

As far as marrying Christian women was concerned it was prohibited by the second caliph Umar in the case of an Arab soldier Hudayfah bin Al-Yamam, who, after the conquest of Iraq, had married a Christian woman who did not convert to Islam. When the second caliph Umar heard this, he asked Hudayfah to divorce her. Hudayfah refused to do so on the plea that it was a legitimate marriage with the woman of the book. Umar told him it is true that the marriage with the people of book is legitimate but the Christian women possess such characteristics that they would prevail on his own women. Hudayfah immediately divorced her.

Abdul Aziz remained true to the Muslim cause and loyal to Umayyad caliph in spite of an unfair treatment meted out to his father Musa. After Musa's punishment, Caliph Sulayman now wanted to get hold of his son and the governor of Spain, Abdul Aziz. Caliph Sulayman felt a twinge of envy for the power of Musa's sons in Africa, Maghreb, and Spain, and he wanted to grab that power. Caliph Sulayman received reports that Abdul Aziz criticized the punishment awarded to his father. Governor Abdul Aziz never thought of rebelling against Umayyad caliph in Damascus. But Caliph Sulayman considered even the criticism or even disagreement equivalent to disloyalty and rebellion. Caliph Sulayman in connivance with five Muslim soldiers in Spain decided to eliminate Abdul Aziz. The conspirators were Habeeb bin Abi Ubaida who was Abdul Aziz's deputy or Wazir, and Ziad bin Nabigha who had also married a Gothic princess. The five conspirators cropped up and leveled the charges against Governor Abdul Aziz. The first charge was that Governor Abdul Aziz had his people bowed down before him which is forbidden in Islam. The second charge was the rumor that Governor Abdul Aziz had become a Christian and started wearing the crown on his head. These stories were created to have a casus belli for the murder of Governor Abdul Aziz. Governor Abdul Aziz was assassinated in the first rakat of the morning prayer at the Mosque of Rufeena by Habeeb, Ziad bin Nabigha and Ziad bin Uzra with swords. The assassins immediately finished their job and cut the head of Abdul Aziz which they took along and fled. This happened in March 716.[91] The cutoff head was sent to Caliph Sulayman in Damascus.

Now Sulayman called Musa to come and see the head of his beloved son. Sulayman wanted to finish whatever spirit was left in Musa. As Musa arrived, he saw the cutoff head of his son. Musa looked at the head of his son and remained composed. Caliph smirked and said, "do you know him?" Musa calmly said, "yes, he is a martyr and may Allah curse the one who has killed him". After the elimination of Abdul Aziz, Caliph Sulayman appointed Muhammad bin Yazeed as the governor of Africa who replaced Abullah, son of Musa, who was also tortured and killed. Later, Sulayman ordered Yazeed to arrest, torture, and kill all the remaining male members of Musa's family and all their possessions be confiscated. Yazeed also implemented this order. The head of Abdullah was sent to Damascus and that too was shown to Musa.[92] Later the caliph changed his heart about the great general Musa and approved pension for him along with provisions needed for the maintenance of his household.[93] Musa lived a life of 79 years. During the period, Musa and Tariq conquered Spain; at the same time Muhammad bin Qasim conquered Sind in Pakistan and Qutaiba bin Muslim conquered Samarkand and much of Central Asia.

The main credit of the conquest of Spain goes to General Tariq bin Ziyad. Tariq played a similar role in the Muslim conquests as was played by Khalid bin Al-Waleed and Uqba bin Nafe. Caliph Sulayman had heard about the reputation of Tariq and decided to appoint him as the Governor of Spain. Before doing so, Sulayman sought an opinion from Mughith who made negative remarks about Tariq and Tariq did not get the job. Tariq returned to Spain and spent the rest of his life here. Mughith also returned to Spain and bought a palace in Cordoba known as the Palace of Mughith and spent the rest of his life honorably in Spain.

After the return of Musa and Tariq to Damascus, about 100,000 Butr and Baranis Berbers and the Arabs from Yemen, Jordan, and Southern Palestine arrived al-Andalus. They were carrying along tribal hostilities which affected the Muslim unity in al-Andalus. The northern and southern Arabs (Qays and Yemeni) had long-standing blood feud. These factional differences led to internal conflicts which weakened the empire of al-Andalus. After the assassination of Abdul Aziz, the soldiers chose Musa's grandnephew, Ayub ibn Habib al-Lakhmi, who had earned distinction in the war in Spain. Ayub was a great warrior and was well respected by the soldiers. In 717, Ayub shifted the capital from Sevilla to Cordoba. He founded a town of Calatayud (quarter of the Jew) in the northern region, where Muslims and Jews lived together and cooperated with each other. At Calatayud he built a castle known as the Castle of Ayub (Qalat Ayub). Ayub ruled for only six months as he was replaced by a new governor, Al-Hurr bin Abdur Rahman As-Saqafi, who traveled to Cordoba with 400 horsemen. Al-Hurr removed Ayub from his office and took over as the governor of Spain and a new era started in Spain.

Pelayo, nephew of the former king Roderic, survived and escaped from the Battle of Guadalete river that was fought between Tariq and Roderic's forces in July 711. Pelayo with the support of local people got elected as the prince of Cangas de Onis and later moved to the city of Oviedo. Pelayo raised an army of local people and made preparations for a war with the Muslims. Al-Samh ibn Malik al-Khawlani (718–21), after getting instructions from Damascus raised an army of dhimmis (protected people). The army of Berbers supported by Syrian and Yemeni fighters entered Septimania and captured Narbonne. The Muslims converted the churches into mosques. Following the policy of Abdul Aziz, al-Samh granted religious freedom to the people of Narbonne. After Narbonne, al-Samh captured Carcassonne, 80 kilometers east of Toulouse in southwestern France, and the Muslim army returned to al-Andalus with treasures and women. A portion of the Muslim army was left at Narbonne as a permanent garrison. Narbonne became the capital of the Muslim Septimania.

After Narbonne the Muslim army marched toward Toulouse, the capital of Aquitaine in southern France along the Pyrenees mountains bordering Spain. Duke Odo of Aquitaine was confronted with a complex situation of either surrendering to the Muslims or being annexed by the Franks. Odo did not want to lose his territory. He decided to fight. In 721, Odo of Aquitaine fought for his territory, not for his faith, and destroyed half of the Muslims' army led by Al-Samh. Odo was the first Christian leader in the east of the Pyrenees in Europe who stopped the Muslims' advance beyond Pyrenees. The Muslim forces returned to Narbonne. This was the first defeat of the Muslims in al-Andalus. Later Caliph Hisham, who ruled for 19 years from 724 through 743, ordered his new governor-general of Cordoba, Abdul Rahman bin Abdullah al-Ghafiqi, to wage a holy war over the mountains. The nomadic Arab people called Saracens, who were led by Amir Ambasa ibn Suhaym al-Kalbi, recaptured Carcassonne that was lost in the defeat of Toulouse, and took Nimes in Southern France.[94] Ambasa's forces marched along the river past Lyon to Autun, the capital of Burgundy which was 180 miles in the southeast of Paris, and captured it. Autun, because of its historical importance, was the honor of Roman Gaul.

Odo discovered that when the Muslims were not fighting with the Christians, they were fighting among themselves. Thus, whenever the Muslims' central government at Cordoba became weak, the Muslim governors of the distant provinces at the edges of al-Andalus along Pyrenees, mostly Berbers, tried to seek their independence from the center by resisting the Cordoba's authority. Odo wanted to exploit this situation and wanted to build an alliance of the Christians and Cordoba opposed Muslims.[95] Odo found out that the Berber Amir of Cerdanya was critical of Cordoba's central authority. Cerdanya was located at the southwest of Gaul which could make it a buffer zone between Cordoba and Aquitaine. Odo started working on Cerdanya's Amir. As a part of his plan, Odo, to strengthen the relationships, offered his daughter named Lampegie to Uthman bin Abi Nessa, known to Christian as Munuza, the Amir of Cerdanya.

In the fall of 731, al-Ghafiqi, with an army of 15,000 soldiers, raided the Berber Amir of Cerdanya, Munuza. Munuza fled to the mountains. Finally, Munuza was defeated, and his head was sent to Damascus along with his Christian wife, Lampegie. Lampegie became a part of the harem. Cerdanya was restored to al-Andalus. After Cerdanya, southwestern Gaul was the next target of al-Ghafiqi. Al-Ghafiqi's warriors drove the Aquitanian to the banks of Garonne River near Bordeaux, in the northwest of Toulouse in southwestern France where they were slaughtered. Odo fled for his life.

After Aquitaine, Poitiers, the oldest town of Gallo Roman in south-central France, was the next target. On hearing the news of the Muslim invaders, Charles Martel ordered his army of 10,000 cavalry and infantry to move into Aquitaine where Odo was waiting for Charles at Tours with his force of 2,000–3,000 fighters. Odo reaffirmed his loyalty to Charles. The Muslims' army led by al-Ghafiqi was marching on the Roman Highway toward Tours. Al-Ghafiqi had planned to camp at Tours for the winter. Charles and Odo's forces reached Basilica of St. Martin, where they promised to die for Christ. In the middle of October 732, the armies marched in the south of Tours which was a flat land where wheat and grapes were grown. The Christian forces were equipped with spears, arrows, and swords. On the other hand, the Muslim forces were developed in light of Caliph Umar's reforms. The Muslims' cavalry and infantry were organized into groups led by an officer called qi'ad and arranged in a crescent formation to trap the enemy forces.

The Muslim forces crushed any force that crossed their path on the Roman highway. Franks faced al-Ghafiqi's army along the bank of the Creuse River, a 264-kilometer-long tributary of the Vienne River in western France. Al-Ghafiqi crossed the right bank of the Vienne River, where he camped. Charles crossed the Vienne downstream and attacked al-Ghafiqi from the rear. When al-Ghafiqi saw that the strength of the Christian forces was increasing, he pledged to Allah that in his path the Muslim forces would fight the infidels once for all. In light of the practices of the Holy Prophet, al-Ghafiqi ordered his forces to attack the enemy after the noon prayers. The Muslims attacked the enemy's front. Odo played a clever move by attacking the camp of the Muslims where families and children were living. A group of Muslims rushed to the camp to save the families and children, and this created a gap in the Muslim ranks. Frank and Gallo Roman attacked the Muslims. Charles had hidden his forces for the right time. And, now was the right time to aggressively attack the Muslim forces. Seeing the gap in Muslim ranks, Charles attacked the Muslims' center. Al-Ghafiqi bravely responded to Charles attack until he was struck by an arrow and embraced martyrdom. After the death of al-Ghafiqi, the Muslim forces were demoralized. Now the victory smiled on the Franks, in spite of the fact that some Berbers continued fighting bravely till sunset. At night, the Muslims collected their bodies for burial. The Muslim forces had to retreat. The place of battle was located near the village Moussais-la-Bataille, which was located between Tours and Poitiers. The Christians considered it as one of the greatest victories in the history of Europe that saved Christianity. For Muslims, it was a minor setback and not the end of the campaign in Europe.

In 734, after the setback near Poitiers, Caliph Hashim-I (724-43) ordered the new governor-general of Cordoba, Uqba bin al-Hujjaj al-Saluli, to resume the march against the infidels. Uqba asked Yusuf, the governor of Narbonne, to quickly move out of Septimania on the expedition. Yusuf was successful in getting the support of local Christian collaborators led by Maurontus, duke of Marseille, who thought the Franks are more dangerous than the Muslims to their freedom and decided to side with the Muslims. Yusuf recaptured Carcassonne and Nimes in southern France. Yusuf advanced up the Rhone Valley and collected a lot of booty at Burgundy. Yusuf's advance was considered a threat to the Romans' important city of Arles on the Rhone River in the Provence region of southern France. Uqba himself invaded Aquitaine and advanced through Burgundy into Dauphine and captured Valence. In the summer of 737, Charles along with his illegitimate brother Duke Childebrand took the forces of Austrasians into the Rhone Valley to stop Yusuf. Charles and Childebrand cut off the land and water supply routes to Narbonne. Narbonne not only survived the Franks' siege but compelled Charles and Childebrand to retreat to the north and Narbonne remained a stronghold of the Muslims for the next 20 years.

On hearing that a large Muslim army was on its way, Charles Martel sent messengers to Pavia, located in the south of Milan in Italy, requesting support of Lombard forces to confront the Muslims. The Lombards were the Germanic people who ruled most of the Italian peninsula. Uqba left Ebro in the fall of 739 and captured Lyon and advanced to Dijon after destroying Burgundy. Yusuf along with Christian collaborator Mauronts advanced to Rhone into the Alpine province of Dauphine and then quickly moved into Italian Piedmont which bordered France and Switzerland. The king of Italian Lombard, Luitprand, gathered his force from the Alps to join Charles forces in Dauphine where they were deployed to stop and compel Yusuf to stay behind the Pyrenees.

The governor-general had problems controlling the Berbers, and without Berbers it was difficult to maintain control in al-Andalus. Berbers complained that they were not being treated in the light of the injunctions of the holy Prophet that all Arab and non-Arab believers are equal. Berbers thought that they were considered by Damascus as second-grade citizens and that they were being deprived of their rightful share in the spoils. Arab settlers in al-Andalus, called baladiyyun, possessed a central important valley of the Guadalquivir including the cities of Cadiz, Sevilla, and Cordoba while Berbers got far distant provinces in the ridges of al-Andalus. This distinction between baladiyyun and Berbers resulted in an alliance of the Berbers and the Christians against the governor-general of Cordoba that weakened the Umayyad's control in al-Andalus.

In the autumn of 741, Berbers on both sides of the strait in Afriqia and al-Andalus rejected the authority of Damascus. This came as a bombshell for Umayyad's administration. Now Uqba was replaced by a new governor-general named Abdul Malik bin Qatan al-Fihri. The Berbers' revolt took place in Afriqia and Morocco as well as in al-Andalus. Due to decline in revenue, Damascus imposed kharaj, which was a tax on land, paid by Muslims and non-Muslims alike. In addition, a tax of 2.5% was imposed on all movable goods in the empire. The increase in taxes further accentuated the resentment. The Berbers' advance towards Cordoba was crushed by al-Fihri forces supported by the reinforcement that came from Damascus in 742 led by General Balj bin Bishr bin Qushayari. The ambitious Balj captured and hanged al-Fihri and became the governor-general of

Cordoba. Balj was confronted by the sons of al-Fihri; although Balj was successful in this fight, he was wounded and died after two days.

At the end of 743, Caliph Hisham-I died. During his sway, his empire stretched from the Indian Ocean to the Mediterranean, but at places, there were setbacks as well. In Afriqia, Berbers expelled the Arabs and took control of Maghreb. Hindus rebelled in Sind, Pakistan. Iraq was preparing for rebellion. Because of his administrative skills he did his best to keep the empire united. Hisham was succeeded by al-Waleed-II and thereafter by Yazid-III. After the death of Yazid III, Ibrahim became the caliph which Marwan-II did not like. Without Berbers, Damascus became weak. The Amir of Armenia and Azerbaijan, Marwan bin Muhammad bin Marwan, also known as Marwan-II (744–50), led his troops into Syria, Ibrahim surrendered to Marwan-II. Marwan-II declared himself as the caliph. At the same time, trouble started in Iraq, Iranian Khurasan, and Uzbekistan. This was a big challenge for the new caliph.

Khurasan is a place that is stretched from eastern Iran and beyond the Oxus River where different ethnic groups like Shi'ite, Kharijites, Turkic, Kurdish and Scythian people lived. In 747, an Iranian general, Abu Musa, after getting support at Merv, left for Iraq and captured its capital in 749. Abu Musa supported the cause of Abbas, the uncle of holy Prophet. Abu'l-Abbas, a descendent of Abbas, was chosen as a spiritual leader and caliph in Kufa Mosque. Abu'l-Abbas (749–53) took the title of al-Saffa (the blood shedder). Soon after becoming the caliph, Abu al-Abbas issued the first order of slaughtering of the Umayyads. Abu'l-Abbas defeated Marwan-II of Umayyad at the Battle of Zeb in Iraq on January 25, 750. Marwan fled Damascus and reached Egypt, where he was spotted by the Abbasid and killed on August 6, 750. This was the end of Umayyad and the start of the Abbasid dynasty. The Abbasid general Abdullah bin al-Abbas wreaked havoc in one month's siege of Damascus by skinning off the Umayyad families in the Great Mosque built by Al-Waleed. Under orders of Abdullah the tombs were opened and the bodies were exhumed, disgraced, burned, and tossed in the air with the exception of Umar-II (717–20). The hand and foot of an Umayyad's noble named Aban bin Mu'awiya were cut off, and he was paraded across Syria shouting, "This is Aban bin Mu'awiya, the best horseman of the Bannu Umayya",[96] writes Lewis. Umayyad's property was either burnt or confiscated by the state.

After the death of al-Saffa in 754, his brother Abu Jaffar Abdullah bin Muhammad al-Mansur (754–75) became the caliph and shifted the capital from Damascus to Kufa, where he built a building of Madinat-al Islam (City of Peace). Al-Mansur did not pay any attention to the distant al-Andalus. Abbasid dynasty was a family autocracy. Abbasid eliminated all members of the Umayyad with the exception of a 19-year-old young boy, Abdul Rahman bin Mu'awiya bin Hisham, who escaped and fled to al-Andalus.

Abdul Rahman was at his palace in Rusafa, northeast of Damascus, which was destroyed by Abbasid. On seeing the black banners of Abbasid, Abdul Rahman planned to flee. Abdul Rahman asked his sisters to take care of themselves and took his younger brother and his servant Badr and fled. They were chased by the Abbasids' killers. Abdul Rahman, his brother, and servant Badr reached a nearby river and behind them were the killers. Abdul Rahman and his servant plunged into the river, while his brother who did not know swimming and was reluctant to jump into the river was caught up by the killers and got killed. Abdul Rahman and Badr managed to cross the river and took refuge in an Umayyad's loyalist house in Palestine. From Palestine Abdul Rahman went to Egypt. As Rahman's mother Ra'ha was from a Berber tribe Natza, Rahman made contacts in the Maghreb. He settled in the village Nakur in Morocco under the protection of his Berber uncles.

At the age of 25 years, Abdul Rahman decided to cross the Strait of Gibraltar to reach out to al-Andalus. Before embarking on this adventure, he sent his servant Badr to Yusuf bin Abdul Rahman al-Fihri, governor-general of Narbonne, to apprise him about his claim to the Emirate of al-Andalus. Al-Fihri rejected Rahman's claim. Al-Fihri informed the public that Abdul Rahman's presence in al-Andalus would destroy all of them. However, according to Lewis, "Badr had much better luck with the Yemeni at Almunecar[97] who were happy to see troubles visited on Yusuf".

On August 14, 755, Abdul Rahman with a thousand of Berber cavalry reached Almunecar in the Granada province of Spain. From here he advanced toward Sidonia, where the Yemeni horsemen joined him. By the spring of 756, the province of Ja'en accepted allegiance to Abdul Rahman. Yusuf, supported by Abbasid caliph, became fretted knowing the increase in Rahman's support, played a ruse, and offered Rahman a lot of wealth and the hand of his daughter, if he dropped the idea of becoming the Amir of al-Andalus. Rahman knew that under Yusuf's protection, either a poison or a dagger would be his fate.

Abdul Rahman's forces took Yusuf's forces by surprise and defeated and pushed him across the Roman Bridge. Abdul Rahman entered Cordoba victoriously and Yusuf surrendered to him. Abdul Rahman proclaimed himself as the Amir of al-Andalus in the Friday Mosque. This brought Umayyad's dynasty, that was destroyed in Syria, back in power in al-Andalus. The takeover of al-Andalus by an Umayyad prince, Abdul Rahman, fretted Abbasid caliph al-Mansur. Now the Umayyad ruler would no longer be under the influence of Abbasid ruler. In order to avoid the treachery of Yemeni, Berber, and Syrian tribes, Rahman sought support of all baladiyyun and muwalladun (new Muslims). Moreover, the Umayyads, who were able to survive Abassid's onslaught, reached al-Andalus for safety. Abdul Rahman built a non-tribal regime. Yusuf re-emerged with a force and was defeated and killed in 759. In 763, the infuriated Abbasid caliph Al-Mansur sent an agent with black insignia to al-Andalus, but that attempt was foiled by Abdul Rahman at Carmona in the east of Sevilla. In 764, Amir Abdul Rahman captured Toledo from Yusuf's tribe and their Berber supporters.

Now peace and stability were restored in Al-Andalus. Amir Abdul Rahman introduced a new social contract under which rights and privileges were ensured to all ethnic groups according to their legal codes. Visigoths got their rights and privileges under their Visigothic law, the Lex Visigothorum; Jews enjoyed the same under their rabbinic law. Amir Abdul Rahman intoned these rights and privileges at the Friday Mosque. Christians, Jews, and Muslims collaborated and co-existed. Proselytizing was not allowed. Jewish population in al-Andalus dominated Cordoba, Merida, Ecija, Jaen, Toledo, and Cuenca. Jews provided administrative support to Abdul Rahman in running the government. Rahman transferred some of the Jewish population from their dominated areas to the Christian localities of Murcia, Pamplona, Guadalajara, Salamanca, and Zaragoza to reduce Christians' numbers. Rahman carefully selected his governors and qadis (judges) who were well accepted by the problematic upper region with its capital at Zaragoza, the middle region at Toledo, and the lower region of Extremadura and Portugal governed from Merida.

In order to develop the economy of al-Andalus, Rahman strengthened the irrigation system that was developed by the Romans including huge vertical water wheels called noria that picked up water in scoops and deposited it in gravity-fed channels and "one still to be seen in Cordoba",[98] writes Hopkins. There were some donkey-powered wheels that emptied water from their endless chain of buckets into the scoops of a second horizontal wheel. The Arabs' improved irrigation system in Al-Andalus, containing thousands of waterwheels, noria, and qanat (karez), which were much appreciated and admired by the people. Mining around Rio Tinto in the southwest and manufacturing of luxury items, including gorgeous textiles, metalware, high-quality ceramics including lust wares such as ceramic decorative pottery and Cordoba's leather, were carried out. Rahman introduced world-class wool merina and olives from across the Mediterranean. Rahman introduced many agricultural plants and crops such as palm trees from Syria, lemons, limes, grapefruits, almonds, apricot, saffron, and mulberry trees for silk production from Rusafa. Rice and sugarcane varieties were brought from the then Indian subcontinent. Cordoba and Sevilla became rich economic centers. Trade thrived even with Baghdad's inimical Abbasid regime. State administered the price control, and the loans were interest free. Muslims, Jews, and Catholic Visigoths were engaged in trade and earned profits. Cordoba was the hub of all economic activities. According to Hopkins, Eastern influences were brought into Europe through a Baghdadi poet named Ziryab,[99] who introduced modern haircuts, colors of winter and summer clothing, and meal schedules. All of these and many Eastern traditions were adopted by Europe. Arabic writing had a great impact on the Spaniards.

Abbasid regime in Baghdad supported sedition activities in Zaragoza, Barcelona, and Girona encouraging them to seek autonomy from the Umayyad regime at Cordoba. Rahman handled the sedition activities with the help of his three sons: Hisham governed Merida, Sulayman ruled Toledo, and his youngest and favorite son Abdullah assisted in governing Cordoba. Baghdad was bent on eliminating Umayyad's rule in al-Andalus, no matter even if the empire goes to the Christians. In 778, Baghdad allied with the Franks' forces led by Charlemagne and Duke Bernhard which marched toward Zaragoza. However,

Abdul Rahman, the Falcon of Quraysh, become very powerful as he had gained and firmed his control over two-thirds of Iberia. Raman's forces compelled Charlemagne and Bernhard's forces to retreat on the Roman road toward the pass via the western Pyrenees. Charlemagne ended his campaign of al-Andalus without capturing a single Muslim city.

In 785, Abdul Rahman started the construction of the Friday Mosque of Cordoba. Al-Aqsa Mosque at Jerusalem and the Great Umayyad Mosque at Damascus were also built by Rahman's ancestor, Caliph Al-Waleed. At Friday Mosque's pulpit, Rahman intoned about moral and civic matters. Rahman brought and maintained stability in al-Andalus. Abdul Rahman-I died peacefully in October 788. After Rahman's death his son Hisham succeeded him. Hisham continued the construction of the Cordoba Friday Mosque and completed it three years after the death of his father. Hisham built Friday Mosques at Sevilla, Malaga, and Granada. Hisham built public gardens and established food markets and regulated the market prices of food commodities.

When Hisham became the ruler of al-Andalus, rebellions raised their heads. To handle the rebellions, Hisham started mobilizing the nation for a jihad against the Franks. In the winter of 792, Hisham intoned jihad in the Friday Mosque's pulpit. "In the spring of 793, two large armies commanded by two of Mughith al-Rumi's descendants advanced simultaneously on the Catholic kingdoms of Asturias in the north and Naverra in the northeast", writes Lewis. The first group fell upon Asturias, and the second one departed for Septimania and Languedoc.[100] The king of Asturias, Alfonso-II, got Christians settled beyond the Duero. In 799, Charlemagne's son Louis occupied Pamplona. Louis' forces besieged the port city of Barcelona. Hisham died in 796, and his son Al-Hakam-I was not able to break the Louis' siege. However, in 801, famine and plague compelled the forces of Louis to withdraw and retreat. Al-Hakam ruled from 796 through 822. Al-Hakam had successfully handled all kinds of rebellions. However, in 805, some religious leaders plotted to replace al-Hakam by his cousin for unjust taxes. The plot failed, and 75 conspirators were executed. Another attempt was made by the jurists and the baladiyyun who were the followers of Imam Malik bin Anas of Medina, who was the founder of one of the four schools of Islamic jurisprudence. This revolt was led by Yahya bin Yahya al-Laythi, and the group overwhelmed the shurta, the city police force, and attacked the palace. Al-Hakam escaped capture but remained steadfast and controlled the head of the special guard. Fifteen thousand rebels were expelled from al-Andalus, most of them settled at Fez in Morocco. However, Yahya was condoned and was allowed to return to Cordoba from Toledo. Amir's greatest defeat in 801 was the loss of Barcelona to Louis. He died in 822 and nominated his son Abdul Rahman-II as his successor.

When Abdul Rahman-II became the Amir, Christian Europe was in chaos. Charlemagne jointly ruled with his brother Carloman for 46 years from 768 until his death in June 814. Charlemagne had eight daughters and one son named Louis. Charlemagne did not allow any of his eight daughters to marry just to avoid any claimant of his empire. When Louis took the title of his father, his first edict debarred his sisters from the palace at Aachen. After Louis' death his empire was divided among his three sons as a result of the Treaty of Verdun of 843.

In 844, Scandinavian Vikings raided Guadalquivir and plundered Sevilla. Rahman-II intercepted the Scandinavian pirates and defeated them. Those of the pirates who survived converted to Islam. Rahman-II built a wall around Sevilla. In al-Andalus, 40% of the Christians became Muslim and this alarmed the Christian community. Abdul Rahman-II died in 852 and was succeeded by Muhammad-I (852–86). A small group of the Christian fundamentalists led by Isaac who had committed blasphemy were awarded the death sentence in 852. In another blasphemy in 859, 13 more were executed. Muhammad-I died in 886 and was succeeded by al-Mundhir, who ruled from 886 until his death in 888.

After the death of al-Mundhir in 888, his younger brother Abdullah became the Amir and ruled from 888 until his death in 912. During his sway, the economic conditions were not good and rebellions were on the rise which led to anarchy. One major rebellion was from Abdul Rahman bin Marwan al-Jalliq of Merida who disconnected himself from Sevilla and proclaimed an independent state at Badajoz. The second rebellion concerned Umar bin Hafsun who led the resistance movement in Malaga province during the 890s. When Abdullah died in 912, he was succeeded by his 21-year-old grandson, Abdul Rahman-III.

Rahman-III ruled from 912 to 929 as the Emir and from 929 to 961 as the caliph. Twenty-one-year-old Abdul Rahman-III consolidated the Muslims' state and took quick action and subdued the 50-year-old separation movement in the mountains of Malaga and got complete control over the entire emirate. Rahman-III was blue-eyed with red hair, and he used to dye his hair black for political purposes. Rahman-III was famous for his humbleness, largesse, and love for justice.

Rahman-III's rule was the apogee of the Umayyad dynasty. His external enemies were Franks and Norwegian Viking pirates who carved out a region named Normandy on the coastline of northern France, where the D-Day landing took place. The Abbasid became weak, and their allies started divorcing them. In 909, one of the Abbasid groups, led by Tunisian leader Imam Ubaydullah, who claimed to be a direct descendant of Fatima, the daughter of the Holy Prophet, Peace Be Upon Him, proclaimed its independence as the first Shia regime known as Fatimid dynasty in Egypt. This was a concern for Rahman-III. Having no threat from the Abbasid in Baghdad and in order to do away with both the Fatimid dynasty in Egypt and Umayyad authority in Damascus, "Abdul Rahman in 929 proclaimed al-Andalus an independent Caliphate",[101] writes Hopkins. Abdul Rahman-III built a palace for his family three miles out of Cordoba called al-Rusafa with the city name of Madinat-al Zahra. This palace now is a state-run hotel in Spain.

In 929, Rahman-III destroyed the Bobastro castle in Malaga province and defeated the rebellion Hafsun. Rahman-III established a high-paid professional army of Berbers, Africans, and Slavs. His military successes depended on the Berbers and Northern European mercenaries who later became responsible for the downfall of Al-Andalus. An exemplary cooperation of coexistence between Jews and Muslims prevailed. The Christians used Arab language, food, and dress. Cordoba now reached its apogee. It grew to inhabit 100,000 people and was greater than London and Paris and was half the size of Baghdad. However, due to the slave trade, there were a large number of slaves in Cordoba, including Moorish and fair-haired slaves from Scandinavia and the northeast called Slavs. There was a well-established support system of stud-farms, army, and "a munitions factory turning out, apparently, 20,000 arrows a month",[102] writes Hopkins. In 961, Abdul Rahman-III fell a victim to paralysis and died.

After Rahman-III's death, al-Hakam-II succeeded him. Al Hakam II was a literary person and had established a library with a collection of 40,000 books and encouraged the studies of astronomy and medicine. "State revenues amounted to an extraordinary 6,245,000[103] dinars annually: 5,480,000 dinars from the kharaj and 765,000 dinars from duties and indirect taxes", writes Lewis. This did not include the state's one-fifth share of the spoils because no record was maintained for this activity. Al-Hakam-II died in October 976. During his period of sway from 961 through 976, he gave a stable government that ushered a thriving economy through exports leaving the port of Almeria on the Mediterranean which included olive oil, figs, leather goods, raisins, almonds, and timber. Seventy percent of the total population of six million of al-Andalus was Muslim. Of the total Muslim population, 90,000 lived in Cordoba and 28,000 lived in Zaragoza. The frontiers of the empire were safe. During his life, Al-Hakam-II had chosen his 12-year-old son Hisham-II to succeed him. Now the decline of Umayyad al-Andalus started.

Hisham was too young to rule al-Andalus. Al-Hakam's brother Al-Mughira was an alternative choice to help Hisham until he was grown up. Hearing the rumors of Al-Mughira coming into power, a chancellor (hijab) named Jafar bin Uthman bin al-Mushafi thought that in the presence of Al-Mughira he would have no role in power. Jafar then conspired to kill Al-Mughira to pave a way to usurp power and rule with Hisham as a puppet caliph. Jafar found a 30-year-old killer named Muhamad bin Abi Amir who had fought with Tariq bin Ziyad at the Battle of Guadalete. Amir killed Al-Mughira in late October 976. The killer was promoted to comptroller general of finance for the African army in Morocco. Hisham-II was announced as the caliph, while the real power rested with the usurper Jafar and the killer Amir. Amir was a fighter and loved military campaigns. Catholic states' incursions on the border provided Amir an opportunity to get involved in war. Amir advanced with an army toward Leon and returned successful with a heavy load of spoils from Salamanca in western Spain. The usurper chancellor Jafar awarded Amir the title of chief of shurta – the police force.

Amir, being the head of the police force, became a dictator. He purged all Umayyad's loyalists from the elite army officers and filled the infantry and cavalry units with the Sanhaja and Zanata Berbers. Amir was a great plotter. He sought access to caliphate's general Ghalib bin Abdul Rahman who was the military commander in the north based at military headquarters at Medinaceli. Through his crafty and flattery behavior he managed to get married to the daughter of the general Ghalib. Now Amir returned to Hisham-II and convinced him that the removal of Chancellor Jafar would be in the best interests of everyone. Chancellor Jafar was removed and incarcerated to die. Now on his cards was his father-in-law, General Ghalib, the next target.

General Ghalib was supported by the Christian allies including King Sancho-II of Navarra's son and the count of Castile, Garcia Fernandez. In July 981, Amir led his forces of Berbers and met his father-in-law at Medinaceli. The heir of the Navarrese throne died and General Ghalib surrendered to his son-in-law. General Ghalib disappeared. Amir returned as victorious, and Caliph Hisham-II awarded him with the title of al-Mansur, meaning victorious. Amir was now a de facto ruler and he remained in this position for 22 years. Amir al-Mansur built another palace, Madinat-al Zahira, on the other side of Cordoba, and this was bigger than the previous one. Amir also ordered that his name be recited in the Friday prayers after the name of Caliph Hisham-II. Amir subdued the kingdoms of Leon, Castile, Aragon, Navarra, and Catalunya. In 981, Barcelona was retaken after 180 years of Christian rule.

Amir created a rift between Sancho Garcia of Castile and his father that resulted in a revolt in 997. Confused and desperate Count Garcia Fernandez lost his army and his life to Amir. Amir was aided by a Christian contingent who were paid in silk and gold. Amir destroyed the whole of Galicia, sacked, burnt, and seized the bells of the shrine of Santiago and brought them back to Cordoba Great Mosque and used them as oil lamps. According to Lewis, "Only the bones of St. James[104] remained unmolested". Next year, he raided northern Portugal along the Duero and captured Zamora and Leon. Leon was totally destroyed by Amir in 998.

From their disunity, the Catholic states learnt a lesson and now got themselves united to confront Amir. The consolidated forces of Christian states met Amir at the battle of Pena de Cervera. On the other hand, additional forces from North Africa joined Amir's forces at Medinaceli. Joint forces of Sancho Garcia of Castile, King Alfonso V of Leon, and Garcia Sanchez-II of Navarra faced Amir and were defeated by him. This was a great victory for Amir. Amir returned from the campaign in Castile's La Rioja (home of Spain's best famous wines) to Medinaceli, where he died in 1002.

After Al-Mansur's death, his son Abdul Malik al-Muzaffar bin al-Mansur succeeded him as hajib (prime minister) and followed his policies of higher taxes to support his Berber army. It was alleged that Abdul Malik fell a victim to fratricide as the cause of his death was doubted by his cutting of an apple with a poisoned knife. Hisham-II appointed Malik's younger brother Abdul Rahman al-Sanchol as the new hajib. The new hajib, by taking the advantage of weakness of Hisham-II, asked him to designate him as heir to the Umayyad throne. On acceding to Sanchol's request, it looked like the Umayyad caliph Hisham-II had signed his own death warrant by ending 240 years of Umayyad's hegemony in al-Andalus.

Soon after becoming hajib, Sanchol led his army for the Duero. On February 15, 1009, Sanchol entered Castile. Umayyads did not like Hisham-II's decision under coercion to nominate Sanchol as heir to Umayyad's throne. The furious people stormed out of Cordoba toward Madinat-al Zahra, overpowered the guards, and entered the palace. The mob coerced Hisham-II to abdicate the caliphate in favor of a young Umayyad Muhammad bin Hashim bin Abdul Jabbar, the grandson of Abd al Rahman-III. Muhammad proclaimed himself the new caliph with the name of Muhammad-II al-Mahidi. His first order was the complete destruction of Madinat-al Zahira that was built by al-Mansur. When Sanchol heard this, he returned and saw a large army which had blocked the entry to the city. When Berbers saw this situation, they left Sanchol at the mercy of the Muhammad-II army. Muhammad's army slaughtered Sanchol and thus ended Amirids' role in al-Andalus.

Both Umayyad supporters and the Cordovan citizens despised Berbers and asked the caliph if they are willing to support him if Berbers are expelled from Cordoba. Muhammad-II ordered the Berbers to leave the city in June 1009. The Berbers came back to their quarters in Calatrava. The furious Berbers saw themselves isolated and without any king to fight for. In retaliation, the Berbers started looking for a replacement for Muhammad-II. Now Sulayman, a cousin of Muhammad-II, appears as a claimant for the caliphate. Sulayman asked the Berbers if he could be their caliph if they supported him. This is what Berbers wanted. Berbers pledged allegiance to Sulayman. Both cousins reached out to the Christians for support. The Medinaceli army and the Catalonians allied with Muhammad-II, and Berbers and Castilians sided with Sulayman. Berbers destroyed Muhammad-II's army outside of Cordoba in the winter of 1009. Sulayman celebrated his victory and Muhammad-II retreated to Toledo, where he started gathering a big army with the help of Catalans.

In 1010, Muhammad-II defeated Sulayman and captured the capital city of Cordoba and again installed himself as caliph at Madinat-al Zahra. But soon, hunger and plague erupted in the city. At that time, Sulayman and Berbers sieged the city. Muhammad-II offered a lot of money to Sulayman to break the siege which he refused saying that he needed something else and that was the caliphate. The starved Cordovans lost their patience and killed Mahammad-II and the gates of Cordoba got opened for Sulayman and Berbers. Berbers entered, wreaked havoc, and plundered the city. After the destruction of the grand buildings of Cordoba, the Berbers executed Hisham-II in 1013.

Another Berber Wali from Ceuta led his North African army toward Cordoba to take revenge for the assassination of Hisham-II. Sulayman was defeated and publicly executed in July 1016. Immediately, Sulayman's executor was executed. After the assassination of Sulayman, Abdul Rahman-IV became the new caliph, who ruled from 1016 through 1018. Thereafter Abdul Rahman V ruled until

1024 followed by Muhammad-III (1024–25) and the last caliph of Umayyad, Hisham-II ruled from 1027 to 1031 and that was the end of the Umayyad dynasty in al-Andalus.

Ferdinand-I, king of Castile and Leon, attacked the Badajoz's ta'fa in Portugal, captured Coimbra, and expelled the Muslims. By 1060, after the fall of Umayyad, Sevilla had become the strongest state run by an Arab clan of Banu Abbad which had annexed the territories in the lower Guadalquivir Valley. The Amir of Sevilla wanted to conquer Toledo. In 1064, the Christians under the Pope's standard besieged the Muslim-controlled Barbastro for 40 days. The people of Barbastro surrendered because the water supply stopped. Six thousand Muslims were slaughtered under the order of Pope Alexander, and 12,000 women were captured and enslaved under the command of the Aragonese Count, Armengol-IV of Urgel. When the news of the slaughtering of 6,000 Muslims spread like fire, the ta'fas asked al-Muqtadir for a jihad. In 1065, the Amir of Zaragoza, al-Muqtadir, Chief of the Banu Hud dynasty, arrived with a sufficient army and retook Barbastro from Pope Alexander's crusaders.

In 1065, Ferdinand died and left his empire to three sons and two daughters. During his 29 years of sway, Ferdinand-I gained control over all of Spain and the Muslim kingdoms of Toledo, Sevilla, and Badajoz were reduced to tributary status. Ferdinand distributed his empire among his sons and Alfonso-VI got Leon. Alfonso had reunited the empire that Ferdinand had divided among his descendants. During 1071–72, Alfonso and Sancho acted together and eliminated their third brother Garcia of Galicia. Now threatened by his elder brother Sancho, Alfonso fled and took asylum in Toledo. The enemies of Alfonso accused him of incest with his sister Urraca. Their sister, Urraca, pushed Sancho back from the Duero River. Alfonso got his brother Sancho killed in 1072 and became the king of Leon and Castile. The Muslim ruler of Toledo, Yahya-al-Ma'mun (1043–75) now asked Alfonso to pay the debt of asylum granted to him by Toledo. The debt was paid by providing the Castilian army in support of Toledo to attack Cordoba. The Toledans entered Cordoba and stayed for one year when the Amir al-Ma'mun died. Al-Ma'mun was succeeded by Yahya bin Ismail al-Qadir.

Sevilla's army marched toward Cordoba as its reoccupation was considered to be the first step toward conquering Toledo. The people of Toledo were not satisfied with the new ruler al-Qadir in that he lacked the capability of ensuring the independence of Toledo. Al-Qadir not only lost Cordoba in 1075 but in 1078 the Sevillian took Valencia from Toledo. The people expelled al-Qadir. The Badajoz army entered Toledo in the fall of 1078 and captured the alcazar. Both Sevilla and Castile remained unconcerned about Badajoz's presence in Toledo. Now the competition began between Sevilla's ruler Muhammad bin Abbad al-Mu'tamid and Alfonso. Alfonso defeated the Muslims near the old Roman town of Coira in the mountains of Extremadura. The Muslims surrendered their claim to Toledo. Alfonso brought back al-Qadir to power in Toledo who paid the cost of his bringing back to power. Al-Qadir paid the protection money (paria) to Alfonso.

In May 1085, Alfonso captured the Muslims controlled Toledo. Now, Alfonso proclaimed himself as the king of two religions: Islam and Christianity. Alfonso allowed the Muslims to worship in their mosques without any restrictions. He announced that any Muslim who wants to leave his empire can do so with his belongings, women, and children. Those who want to stay in Toledo can do so by paying a tax equivalent to jizya. There was no change in the status of Jews. When Alfonso-VI saw the mosque, he felt good about it. His governor named Sisnando Davidiz wanted to let the mosque stay as it was. However, Alfonso's queen, a Frenchwoman, compelled Alfonso to convert the mosque into a church. The new archbishop appropriated the Muslims' Friday Mosque and converted it into a church and erected the altars and converted the minaret into a belfry.

After the fall of Toledo, the Amir of Sevilla, al-Mu'tamid, had approached Sanhaja Berber of North Africa and made an alliance with Yusuf bin Tashufin of the Murabitun, the Almoravids of North Africa with their capital at Morocco. Tashufin was a leader of an Islamic fundamentalist sect from Mauritania, who believed in Islam as intoned by the holy Prophet without any deviations whatsoever. Tashufin disembarked with 400 Almoravid cavalry and infantry on July 30, 1086. Tashufin in the Friday Mosque of Sevilla appealed to the believers of Al-Andalus to rise up for a jihad against the infidels. Valencia remained loyal to Alfonso. Murcia and Almeria remained silent. Zaragoza was already engaged against Alfonso for its independence, therefore supported the jihad.

Soon the Arabs, Berbers, and Muwalladun of al-Andalus joined the jihad. Tashufin left Sevilla. The Muslim Berber ruler of Badajoz, al-Mutawakkil, welcomed the Almoravids and joined them. Alfonso, after leaving a small unit of his army at Zaragoza, advanced to confront the Almoravids. The Almoravids were three times greater than the numbers of Alfonso. The two armies met at a place called Zallaqa near Badajoz. Before fighting, Tashufin sent a message of three words to Alfonso: Islam, the jizya, or the sword. Apparently, Alfonso chose the sword and got ready for the battle.

Alfonso first attacked while the Muslims were praying, and this pushed the Muslims center. After the prayer, the Muslims announced loudly "Allah O' Akbar", and immediately attacked. On October 23, 1086, the Muslims crushed the Spanish Catholic army. The Castilians were slaughtered, and Alfonso himself was wounded and retreated with a one-third of leftover army to Toledo. Alfonso-VI, king of Leon, was defeated by the Muslim ruler of Sevilla, Mu'tamid, with the help of Tashufin, the Almoravid Amir of North Africa. Almoravids stopped Alfonso's advance and the Muslims' Al-Andalus spread far in the north up to Zaragoza. Alfonso-VI appealed to the Christians for assistance against the Muslims, but that assistance never reached the kingdom of Leon.

After Zallaqa, Tashufin went to North Africa in 1090 and returned in 1094 with a fatwa from Muhammad-al-Tartushi, a teacher in Alexandria, that legitimized the overthrow of ta'ifa kingdoms and kings as they were not doing any service to Islam. Almoravids attacked Sevilla which fought back for its independence, but soon it surrendered and al-Mutamid incarcerated. Abdullah of Granada surrendered followed by Almeria. Tashufin took al-Mu'tamid and Abdullah along as prisoners and went back to Morocco. However, Almoravids never retook Toledo. Tashufin left behind a sufficient army under the command of a viceroy who was ordered by him to wipe out the ta'ifas and introduce proper Islam in al-Andalus. Al-Mu'tamid died in captivity in Morocco. Almoravids pushed the Christians across the peninsula and captured parts of Portugal, Huesca, and Cuenca in the northeast of Spain.

According to Hopkins, Rodrigo Diaz de Vivar of Burgos, known as El Cid, a brave warrior,[105] took the city of Valencia in 1094 by defeating the Almoravid army for the first time. El Cid died in 1099. In 1102, the Almoravids took it back in spite of Alfonso's help to El Cid's wife Jimena. Valencia remained under the control of the Muslims for another 130 years. Alfonso was defeated many times during the period 1086 to 1109 by the Muslim rulers. According to Lewis, Alfonso-VI "outlived his only son and heir Sancho by fourteen months", who died in the battle of Ucles[106] against Almovarids. Alfonso-VI died in 1109.

In 1118, Aragonese took Zaragoza. By this defeat the Almoravids were shaken. In 1147, another Berber tribe led by Masmuda bin Tumart called Almohads rebelled against Almovarid and killed their king Ishaq bin Ali in Morocco. Conquered North Africa and Egypt and established Almohad Caliphate that ruled in Morocco and Al-Andalus. Almohads crossed Algerciras in 1147 and after defeating their rivals established their empire at Sevilla. The third caliph of Almohad, Abu Yusuf Ya'qub al-Mansur, was just like Abdul Rahman in constructing grand buildings. Abu Yusuf built a 320-foot-high minaret at the Friday Mosque of Sevilla, and this minaret was the world's tallest tower then. Today it is known as Giralda.

Under the Almohads, the philosophy attained its apogee. According to Hopkins, the most notable among them were a Jewish scholar Maimonides[107] (Musa bin Maymun) born and raised in Cordoba, Ibn Tufayl, known as Abubacer, a court physician to Almohads in Sevilla and his successor Ibn-Rushd, known as Averroes, the most admired of all philosophers of Hispania. Maimonides' contribution was in the field of medicines and the Jewish law. It was Ibn Rushd who reinterpreted Aristotle for the Arabs and the Europeans and removed the growth of Neoplatonism based on the principles of an ancient Greek philosopher Plotinus and revealed the unknown and hidden intentions of Plato.

In 1195, Abu Yusuf defeated King Alfonso-VIII of Castile at the Battle of Alarcos near the Guadiana River. The defeated King Alfonso fled begging for life. The victory of Alarcos was the last victory of the Muslims in al-Andalus, and Abu Yusuf died after four years of this victory. Almohad's rule continued in al-Andalus until 1212, when the Muslim ruler Mohammad al-Nasir, son of the victor of Alarcos, was defeated at the Battle of Las Navas de Tolosa[108] by an alliance of Christian princes of Castile, Aragon, Navarre, and Portugal. This battle changed Spanish history, and it also resulted at the beginning of the fall of al-Andalus and the Reconquest of Spain. After this defeat, Cordoba fell to the Christians in 1236,[109] Valencia in 1238, Murcia in 1243, Jaen in 1246, and Sevilla in 1248.[110] Granada was left and the Muslim ruler of Granada became a vassal of Fernando-III. Fernando died in 1254 and "his tomb bore the inscription, King of the Three Religions", writes Hopkins.

After the fall of Cordoba and Sevilla, while Granada was ruled by the Muslims as a tributary state, Spain started recovering its territories from the Muslims' hold. However, Spain was not a united country; it was ruled by the local crowns and kings. "Isabella was crowned queen of the Castile in Segovia on 13 December, 1474",[111] writes Kamen. Both Isabella of Castile and her husband Ferdinand of Aragon worked in unison to protect their interests and security against the internal unrest and external threats from the Muslim emirate of Granada (meaning pomegranate in Spanish) led by Muhammad bin Yusuf bin Nasr. The palace complex was called Alhambra. Alhambra in Arabic means Al-Hamra, the Red One. Mudejar (Muslims living under the Christians' rule) peasants lived far off drier areas near the Ebro River which they used for irrigation. On the other hand, the Christian peasants lived in the mountain areas where they got sufficient rain for their agriculture. The long distance between the Muslim and Christian population diminished the threat of conflict to some extent.

The Muslim kingdom of Granada stretching 200 miles from the east to the west and just 70 miles from the north to the south was ruled by the Nasrid dynasty for 200 years in spite of the Christians' hostility. The inhabitants of Nasrid Granada were a warlike people. Granada produced famous ceramic and textile products. In 1476, Isabella sent a demand to the Muslim ruler of Granada for the renewal of the tributes. Isabella received a baleful response from the Muslim ruler of Granada, which said, "we no longer mint gold, only steel",[112] writes Kamen. Now the Spanish crafted a strategy to launch military campaigns against the Muslims of Granada and beyond the peninsula on the coast of Africa.

Granada of half million people was ruled by a Muslim Amir Abu'l Hassan as a tributary state of Castile. In December 1481, the Muslims captured the frontier town of Zahara, this provided the casus belli for an attack by the Christians. In February 1482, the Christian forces captured Alhamra. Division among Muslims between Mulay Hassan, his brother al-Zagal, and Hassan's young son Boabdil made the Christians' task easy.[113] Ferdinand wanted to exploit this division in Nasrid camp to his advantage by taking the Muslim territories piece by piece. Ferdinand and Isabella officially declared a crusade against the Muslims that lasted for ten years. In 1483, Abu'l Hassan's son Boabdil turned against his father and assured the Christians, while in their captivity, that he would work as Ferdinand's vassal without any problem. In 1485, the emir was dethroned by his brother al-Zagal. Al-Zagal was dethroned in 1487 by Boabdil. Boabdil resisted the Christians' pressure for the surrender of Granada until 1489.[114]

Now Ferdinand had expected Boabdil to surrender Granada which he refused. Ferdinand collected troops from all of Europe which also included volunteers from Swiss, Britain, Italy, Germany, France, and the rest of the peninsula. Catalan and Italian vessels monitored the sea. Artillery was managed by German and Italian. It was the biggest-ever European crusade against the

Muslims. Such a big force sieged the city to compel Boabdil to hand over the city. The money for the crusade was provided by Castile, Aragon, and Pope using the Genoese banks in Sevilla. The Christians sieged the city. No outside Muslim assistance came to Boabdil. Boabdil agreed to a peaceful settlement of Granada, "the last stronghold of the Islamic powers that had been in Iberia for eight hundred years", writes Sale. On January 2, 1492, Boabdil handed over the keys of the Alhambra[115] to the Christian Monarchs. The fall of Granada to the Christians ended the Muslims' rule of al-Andalus.

The aftermath of the fall of Granada was horrible for the Muslims and the Jews. On March 30, 1492, about 120,000–150,000[116] Jews were expelled from Spain through an imperial fiat. The Jews were not allowed to take along their precious possessions like gold, silver, jewels, or currency which were left behind as the property of the crown. Long before in 1391 the Jews were not only considered as aliens but were massacred in their ghettos in Sevilla, Toledo, Valencia, and other cities. To cover the cost of the European crusade, the minorities of Jews and Mudejars were subjected to contribute. Cisneros, archbishop of Toledo, wanted the drastic action of mass baptism which was supported by Isabella. The Christians offered the Muslims and Jews two choices of baptism or expulsion. Many Muslims emigrated to Africa and those who could not drank the poison of conversion to Christianity to save their lives and properties. The Muslims were forced to change their culture by which they could not: carry arms, speak Arabic, wear Arabic dresses and jewelry, or slaughter animals and practice circumcision. It was the end of the jihad and the Muslim Al-Andalus and the end of Islam in the peninsula. In January 1500, Cisneros reported to Isabella that all citizens in Castile were Christians and none was present who was not a Christian. All the mosques in Castile were converted into churches. Thus, a civilization emerged that was intolerant to another civilization.

Notes

1 Lewis, "God's Crucible, Islam and the Making of Europe, 570–1215", p. 112.
2 Ibid., p. 131.
3 Ibid., p. 9.
4 Akram, "The Muslim Conquest of Spain", p. 121.
5 Lewis, "God's Crucible, Islam and the Making of Europe, 570–1215", p. 315.
6 Ibid., p. 340.
7 Akram, "The Muslim Conquest of Spain", p. 121.
8 Ibid., p. 122.
9 Lewis, "God's Crucible, Islam and the Making of Europe, 570–1215", p. 11.
10 Thompson, "The Goths in Spain", p. 39.
11 Ibid., pp. 35–36.
12 Ibid., p. 37.
13 Ibid., p. 26.
14 Lewis, "God's Crucible, Islam and the Making of Europe, 570–1215", p. 115.
15 Akram, "The Muslim Conquest of Spain", p. 124.
16 Thompson, "The Goths in Spain", p. 111.
17 Akram, "The Muslim Conquest of Spain", p. 124.

52 The Muslims' Rule in Spain

18 Ibid., p.125; Thompson, "The Goths in Spain", p. 165.
19 Thompson, p. 178.
20 Ibid., p. 53.
21 Dozy, "A History of the Moslems in Spain", p. 227; Akram, p. 125.
22 Akram, p. 126; Thompson, p. 179.
23 Akram, p. 126.
24 Thompson, p. 186.
25 Ibid., p. 206.
26 Ibid., p. 236.
27 Ibid., p. 246.
28 Ibid., p. 248.
29 Ibid., p. 249; Akram, p. 35.
30 Gayangos, Vol. 1, pp. 262–263; Akram, p. 38.
31 Akram., p.2 gives the complete name as Tariq bin Ziyad bin Abdullah bin Walgho bin Warfajum bin Nabarghasin bin Walnaz bin Yarufat bin Nafzav.
32 Gayangos. p. 256.
33 Hopkins, p. 3.
34 Lewis, p. 119.
35 Gayangos, p. 267.
36 Akram, p. 48.
37 Ibid.
38 Conde, "The History of the Dominion of the Arabs in Spain", p. 55; Akram, p. 49.
39 Akram, p. 49.
40 Conde, p. 55, Vol. I; Akram, p. 50; Gayangos: Vol. 1, p. 268.
41 Conde, p. 55; Akram, p. 52.
42 Akram, p. 52.
43 Gayangos, p. 270.
44 Conde, p. 55; Akram, p. 56.
45 Gayangos, p. 274, Akram., p. 57; Conde, p. 54.
46 Gayangos, p. 274, Akram., p. 62.
47 Akram, p. 63.
48 Ibid., p. 64.
49 Ibid., p. 65.
50 Lewis, p. 122; Gayangos, p. 271.
51 Gayangos, p. 272; Akram, p. 72.
52 Akram, p. 72.
53 Ibid., p. 73.
54 Ibid, p. 75.
55 Gayangos, Vol. 1, appx. D, p. 48, Akram, p. 76.
56 Akram, p. 82.
57 Ibid., p. 103.
58 Ibid., p. 104.
59 Gayangos, Vol.1, pp. 282–283; Conde, p. 65; Akram, p. 115.
60 Gayangos, Vol.2, p. 15; Akram p. 190.
61 Akram, p. 133.
62 Ibid.
63 Ibid., p. 135.
64 Ibid., p. 136.
65 Akram, p. 149.
66 Conde, pp. 75–76, Vol. I, Akram, pp. 160–161.
67 Akram, p. 164.
68 Gayangos, Vol.1, p. 293; Akram, p. 192.
69 Gayangos, Vol. II, p. 17.
70 Akram, p. 165.
71 Ibid., p. 165.

72 Gayagos, Vol. I, pp. 286–287; Akram, p. 167.
73 Akram, p. 169.
74 Conde, p. 77.
75 Akram, p. 169.
76 Ibid., p. 177.
77 Gayangos, Vol. I, p. 289.
78 Akram, pp. 236–237.
79 Lewis, p. 148; Akram, pp. 186–187.
80 Gayangos, Vol.1, appx. D, p. 50; Conde, p. 81; Akram, p. 189.
81 Akram., p. 194.
82 Conde, Vol. 1, p. 82; Akram, p. 196.
83 Gayangos, Vol. 1, p. 293; Akram, p. 196.
84 Akram, p. 197.
85 Ibid., p. 199.
86 Gayangos, Vol. 1, pp. 293–294; Akram, pp. 199–200.
87 Akram, p. 200.
88 Ibid., p. 201.
89 Lewis, pp. 153–154; Akram, p. 208.
90 Akram, p. 208.
91 Ibid., p. 212.
92 Ibid., p. 213.
93 Ibid., p. 216.
94 Lewis, "God's Crucible, Islam and the Making of Europe, 570–1215", p. 159.
95 Ibid., p. 162.
96 Ibid., p. 194.
97 Ibid., p. 197.
98 Hopkins, "Spanish Journeys, A Portrait of Spain", p. 19.
99 Ibid., p.19.
100 Lewis, p. 308.
101 Hopkins, p. 20.
102 Ibid., p. 23.
103 Lewis, p. 332.
104 ibid., p. 340.
105 Hopkins, pp. 51, 70.
106 Lewis, p. 365.
107 Hopkins, p. 73.
108 Ibid., p. 75; Lewis, p. 252.
109 Lewis, p. 379.
110 Hopkins, p. 75.
111 Kamen, "Spain, 1469–1714, A Society of Conflict", p. 1.
112 Ibid., p. 2.
113 Hopkins, p. 118.
114 Kamen, p. 14.
115 Sale, "Christopher Columbus and the Conquest of Paradise", p. 10, Alhambra was the beautiful fourteenth-century ocher citadel of the Moors.
116 Ibid., p. 13.

Bibliography

Akram, A.I., *The Muslim Conquest of Spain*, Army Education Press, Rawalpindi, Pakistan, 2001.

Conde, J.A., History of the Dominion of the Arabs in Spain, Vol. I published in 1820, translated by Mrs. Jonathan Foster from the Spanish into English and published (undated) by Henry G. Bohn, York Street, Covent Garden, London, UK, 1820.

Dozy, Reinhart, *A History of the Moslems in Spain, first published in 1861 and translated by Francis Griffin Stokes*, Chatto & Windus, London, UK, 1913.

Gayangos, Pascual De, The History of the Mohammedan Dynasties in Spain, reprinted in 1964 by Johnson Reprint Corporation, 111 Fifth Avenue, New York, USA, 1840.

Hopkins, Adam, *Spanish Journeys, A Portrait of Spain, Published in Penguin Books*, 27 Wrights Lane, London, UK, 1993.

Kamen, Henry, *SPAIN, 1469–1714, A Society of Conflict*, Fourth Edition, Routledge, 2 Park Square, Milton Park, Abingdon, Oxon, UK, 2014.

Lewis, David Levering, *God's Crucible, Islam and the Making of Europe, 570–1215*, W.W. Norton and Company, 500 Fifth Avenue, New York, USA, 2008.

Sale, Kirkpatrick, *Christopher Columbus and the Conquest of Paradise*, Tauris Parke, London, UK, 2006.

Thomson, E.A., *The Goths in Spain*, Oxford University Press, London, UK, 1969.

2
RISE AND FALL OF SPAIN AS AN IMPERIAL POWER

After the fall of Granada on January 2, 1492, the monarchs announced their ambition to extend the frontiers of their empire. To accomplish the ambition of world power, the financial resources were required which were not available in the poverty and debt-ridden backward Spanish economy in the late fifteenth century. Annual payment of debt at the interest rate of 10% put a heavy burden on the treasury. Some money was provided by the crown of Aragon, but the bulk of resources came from Castile. Castile's 90% revenue came from 10% sales tax, the alcabala. But this money was not sufficient for expedition. Other sources included custom duties collected by taxing the farmer as there was no official tax collection agency. Another source of income was local Hermandad or brotherhood, a council of a village having a population of more than 50 inhabitants who nominated their representatives to the federal parliament called junta. Hermandad collected taxes, maintained law and order through their own resources, and provided militia to the crown for war of Granada, as there was no official army then. Hermandad also contributed to the crown 17.8 million Maravedis (coins) in 1478–79.

The crown found a source of income from the wool. Spain had a very good pastoral industry. Mesta, the Spanish nomad sheep herdsmen association, had 2.8 million flocks of sheep which roamed throughout the country. In addition, there were some sedentary flocks of sheep in the country as well. The wool quality of merino sheep was introduced by the Muslims. Castile soon became the main exporter of merino sheep wool to Flanders, France, and England, and this boosted the economy.

The Castilian merchants had settled in the ports of Normandy and Brittany, and the Castilian ships facilitated the wool trade. The Castilian city of Burgos controlled the export of wool trade. In 1494, a trading body called Consulado was created to facilitate the trade which enjoyed the monopoly power. The

DOI: 10.4324/9781003377719-3

crown had granted privileges to Mesta and Consulado to boost the wool trade. Although the crown did not announce privileges for the agriculture sector, it was helped by the nature. The population had increased, which resulted in an increase in demand for land. Any type of waste, pastures, and common land was brought under agricultural food production to meet the needs of the increasing population. Wheat was the main food crop. In case of good harvest in one region, the surplus wheat was sent to deficit regions of the empire. However, wheat delivery to the Muslim regions was not allowed. In 1500, the export of wheat was authorized by paying export taxes. In 1505, under an imperial fiat, free trade of grain was authorized throughout the empire. Bad harvests were experienced during 1502–7 which resulted in a shortfall of wheat. In December 1502, in order to discourage profiteering and hoarding of grain, the crown promulgated the price control system called tasa,[1] writes Kamen. In 1508, the harvest was very good, and it was called the green year.

Christopher Columbus, the son of a poor Genoese wool-comber, was a tall young man of middle age. He had a dream and was fully immersed in an idea of discovery of the new world from Europe to India. In 1484, Columbus with his real name of Cristobal Colon approached the king of Portugal and presented his proposal of a sea voyage to India in the east. King John referred his proposal for a review to a Jewish mathematician named Moses and the Rabbi Joseph Vecinho. According to Jayne, the proposal was rejected by the reviewers.[2] After the rejection of his proposal, Columbus left Portugal in search of other sources of funding.

Columbus had read and heard from the Portuguese sailors at Lisbon about the stories of the richness of the islands, such as gold, silver, and other precious stones, all over the world. He believed in those stories and became ambitious to undertake the venture. Columbus approached England, Italy, and France and presented his business plan of traveling westward to reach the eastern land including Cathay now called China. All of the three governments did not show any interest in his proposal. Now Columbus turned to the crowns of newly united Spain, King Ferdinand and Queen Isabella. His business plan prognosticated sufficient resources in the form of gold, silver, and other commodities like sugar, tobacco, and slavery, and that these resources would not only make Spain rich and the world power but it would also help it in getting the freedom of Jerusalem from the Turks. Finally, in 1492, Columbus got financial assistance from a Jewish financier who worked for the crowns Ferdinand and Queen Isabella. According to the Memorandum of Understanding, in case of success in his plan, he would be bestowed upon the title of Admiral of the Ocean and would also be given the administrative control of the new territories that he would discover.

On August 2, 1492, according to Sale, 45-year-old Columbus sailed from Palos near Cadiz on his first expedition with three small ships named *Pinta*, *Santa Clara* also called *Nina*, and *La Gallega* also called *Marigalante*[3] and ninety crews, including two representatives of the royal court that sponsored the voyage, an alguazil (marshal) of the fleet, a secretary, an interpreter, and a surgeon. The

Pinta was commanded by Martin Alonso Pinzon of Palos, who was an experienced mariner, and led the other two ships: *Santa Clara*, which was commanded by Vicente Yanez Pinzon, the younger brother of Martin Alonso Pinzon; and *Gallega*, which was the flagship of the fleet and was commanded by Columbus himself. All the three ships were equipped with the supplies for one full year. Other four experienced sailors included one Portuguese and three Italians. All the sailors were criminals and were serving in the jail. They were granted remission by the king to register for the voyage of Columbus. The owners of the ship were also on board as in charge of the administration. All the pilots who navigated the ships were from Palos.

The support staff included carpenters, caulkers, stewards, and ship boys. However, there were no missionaries or priest, or no holy father on board, in spite of the fact that one of the missions of the voyage was to baptize the inhabitants of the discovered territories. As Columbus was expected to deal with the kings and the princes of the territories, he carried a letter of credence from King Ferdinand and Queen Isabella with a blank space for the name of the addressee to be filled in at the occasion. But there was no diplomat, ambassador, or minister or any person on board with the experience of diplomacy. There were no soldiers on board who could deal with the armed conflicts with the princes or the pirates. There were no armaments on board with the exception of some crossbows and arquebuses and a small canon mounted belowdecks on the flagship. The fleet took the route of the Canary Islands of the Spanish Empire in the Atlantic Ocean. The distance from Palos to the Canary Islands was 700 miles. Columbus' intention was to reach Cathay and its outlying islands such as Cipango (Japan) or call it Asia, or India. Columbus was influenced by the travels of Marco Polo that the people of the east would welcome the Europeans.

The main mission of the voyage was to "discover and acquire". To record the characteristics of the land, people, and nature of the new discoveries, there were not on board any of the technical persons to study geological, biological, and anthropological matters. Columbus picked up and loaded a specie which he thought was an aloe, turned out to be an agave which had no medicinal utility. Similarly, there was not any goldsmith or metallurgist on board to identify and determine the nature of precious metals like gold, silver, or precious stones. One of the crew was listed as silversmith. The metal that Columbus thought was a gold turned out to be iron pyrite.

On September 6, Columbus left the harbor of Gomera, which is one of the Canary Islands, and after traveling 3,000 miles in the ocean, on October 12, 1492, made his first landing on an islet of the Lucaya in the former Watlings islands and renamed it as San Salvador islands in the Atlantic Ocean. This islet was also called Guanahani, near the Bahamas freeport located in the north of Cuba and the southeast of Florida, USA. Columbus thought that he had reached the islands that Marco Polo had mentioned in the east in the Sea of China, one of them being Cipango which Columbus confused with Cibao, a mountain in St. Domingo. Columbus in his letters to King Ferdinand and Queen Isabella, called the territories he had discovered as the Indies which were mentioned by Marco Polo in his book, the *Travel*, that was later translated by Nigel Cliff in English, and were not far away from the Ganges and the territories that were conquered by Alexander. He might have thought that he had reached the kingdom of Great Khubilai Khan to see the richness of Cathay. On October 21, Columbus decided to go to the city of Quinsay and present the Letter of Credence to the Great Khubilai Khan from the monarchs of Spain.

After a week, Columbus realized that he was neither on the land of the Great Khan nor on the land of India. Columbus had, in fact, discovered the New World. Because of Columbus' mistake, the newly discovered countries in the Caribbean got the name of Indies and to distinguish them from the East Indies, they were called the West Indies. West Indies were not as rich as were the East Indies. The pretty large lizard called the Ivana or Iguana[4] was the main part of the animal food of the West Indies, writes Smith. The vegetable foods of the people were corn, yam, potatoes, and bananas. Cotton was produced on the islands which was not much valued by the Europeans. However, the cotton of the East Indies was much liked by the Europeans. Columbus was not concerned with the land but gold and was looking for the land that had gold. The main purpose of Columbus' expedition was trade, conquest, colonialization, and exploitation which was based on the need to provide relief to the kingdom. According to Sale, there were 12 important islands that were considered for landing which included: San Salvador (formerly Watlings), Grand Turk, Caicos, Cat, Mayaguana, Crooked, Conception, Eleuthera, Egg, Plana Cay, Rum Cay, and Samana Cay.[5]

Columbus after taking the possession of the islands and to show Spanish ownership named the first colony of the empire as San Salvador, the second as Santa Maria de la Conception, and the third and fourth were renamed as Ferdinand and Isabella, respectively. These colonies were small islands. The two large and fertile islands were colonized as Juana after the name of Prince Juan, and la Ysla Espanola, the "Spanish Island". All the people of the islands were neither black nor white, but looked like the color of Canary Islanders. All the men and women were naked. They were poor and had no knowledge of anything. They had no religion. They bore no arms. Columbus smirked them as inferior due to their backwardness. They lived in the huts with circular walls of cane poles with conical roof made of tree branches and palm leaves. They wore bracelets and necklaces of coral, shells, bones, and stones, and cotton belts, and used shell utensils. They produced yuca (cassava), sweet potatoes, and various squashes and beans. Columbus thought that they were the ideal candidates to be taken as slaves and then baptized. The foundation for American slavery was laid down for the first time.

Now, Columbus, along with the local people called Tainos, which he had picked up from San Salvador, proceeded further to Cuba and Hispaniola islands in the Caribbean Group. Columbus was desperate for gold. There was no gold mine on the islands of Conception, Ferdinand, Isabella, and Juana. Tainos captives on the board were telling him about gold through signs as there was no common communication language. Columbus' frustration increased, and he ordered to depart for a long journey to the southeast. Columbus was just looking for gold and nothing else. Columbus continued traveling along the north coast of Cuba. Columbus set up a harbor which he named Puerto Santo, now called Puerto Baracoa, about a hundred miles from the east of the island. This was the first step toward the European colonialism in the Caribbean through conquest, baptism, settlements, fortresses, exploitation, and international trade. This was his sixth island known as Espanola. Martin Alonso Pinzon deserted Columbus and took the *Pinta* off to the east, while Columbus himself was heading toward the north of Cuba.

On December 18, 1492, a local 21-year-old boy, came on board with some pieces of gold. Seeing this, Columbus expressed that he is close to the source of gold. His ship *Santa Maria* hit the coral reef and was destroyed, and Columbus considered this as nature's intervention in that it provided him with an opportunity to stay at this place and establish a colony. Columbus declared that this is the best place for the Spanish settlement. Damaged *Santa Maria*'s timber was used in the construction of the fortress with the help of Tainos, and this was the first building of the Spanish colony. Columbus named this colony La Navidad, now Haiti. The king of that land Guacanagari promised Columbus an abundant amount of gold. Now Columbus received the news that the *Pinta* is on its way. This news prompted Columbus to get ready for his return journey to Castile as he had now *Pinta* to compensate for the loss of *Santa Maria* and that he found the gold nuggets in Espanola that he was looking for. Columbus had set up the harbor close to the gold mines. Columbus found a river called Rio del Oro which was full of gold. Now Penzon joined Columbus, who did not complain about his desertion. Penzon later visited the people to find the gold fields and found a great amount of gold and many mines, and Columbus appreciated him.

In January 1493, Columbus started his return journey with two ships: *Nina* and *Pinta*. On his return journey two strong storms separated *Nina* and *Pinta*. Columbus reached Palos on March 15, 1493, with gold and other treasures from the three islands. Columbus presented the report of his first expedition of discovery of the Caribbean to the crowns of Castile and Aragon, which was later published. On receiving the report at Barcelona, the monarchs were pleased and granted an audience to Columbus in mid-April for additional information and future plans. The important things that Columbus captured included some fillets, bracelets, and other ornaments of gold and some bales of cotton. Columbus explained the richness of the territories which would be a part of the Spanish Empire and the mass conversion of the inhabitants to Christianity and the use of living capital for Spanish economic development. Columbus proposed that half of gold and silver that should be discovered should belong to the crown, and this proposal was accepted by the council of Castile. The monarchs sought the sanction of the discovery by the pope. The pope finally issued a papal bull allowing the Spanish monarchs to have ownership of all land that has been discovered and that to be discovered in the islands, in the Ocean Sea, and in the region of Indies. The Spanish monarchs appreciated Columbus' services and made him the viceroy and the governor of the conquered land.

On May 23, 1493, King Ferdinand and Queen Isabella authorized the second voyage of Columbus with the grant of authority to him over the islands conquered and to be conquered. The second voyage was the beginning of the status of the empire. Columbus now became a very powerful person. In September 1493, Columbus started his second expedition from Cadiz with 17 vessels well equipped and provisioned for six months' round trip, 1,200 crews, 1,500 colonists, and 12 missionary priests, 2 Indian captive interpreters, a few craftsmen, farmers, miners, and still no women in the expedition. This time he had the plan of establishing settlements in the discovered territories of the Caribbean. At the Salt River on the island, Columbus called it Santa Cruz; the fleet was caught in skirmishes with the natives where about 18 natives were killed and their bodies were tossed into the ocean. The Spanish believed in the theory of violence to subdue the people and make them obedient. The policy of violence was pursued by Columbus during the course of his second voyage. Two captive interpreters on board became worried about the reaction of the Caribbean. The Spanish went ashore in Guadeloupe and looted and destroyed everything they found. The Spanish captured several dozen Caribs and transported them in February 1494 to Cadiz to be sold as slaves. In February 1495, an additional 1,600 Tainos were captured, chained, and brought to the ship. Five hundred of them were sent to Spain. The remainder were distributed to the Spaniards for their services. Some of the Caribs at the settlement of Isabella were driven out to the mountains and across the river.

Columbus returned during his second voyage to La Navidad, the first Spanish colony, which was conquered during his first voyage. He found it as deserted, and neither the fortress nor the buildings were there, and the deformed dead bodies of the 40 Spaniards were lying on the ground. Even one of the forty-man garrison did not survive. This might have been the reaction by the Caribs to avenge the insult meted out to their women by the Spaniards as each Spaniard had five women at his pleasure service. After spending ten days at La Navidad, Columbus abandoned this place and left it on December 8, as it was no more a healthy place to live in. After this Columbus moved to the next colony named La Isabella, now in the Dominican Republic.

La Isabella was a very poor harbor as anchoring of the big ships was only possible at a distance of half a mile offshore. No fresh water was available, and the only source of water was the river which was a mile away. Columbus ordered the construction of the canal to bring the water to Isabella. The soil was not good for the seeds brought in from Europe for the crops of wheat, chickpeas, beans, onion, and lettuce. There were no rains. At this port, Columbus offloaded his 17 ships, 1,500 crew members, two dozen horses, and a large number of cows, pigs, and chickens. Isabella was picked up as the capital of the Spanish colonies. Columbus built a big fortress, a big palace for his residence, and constructed a church for which the furniture was sent by Queen Isabella from Spain.

During this voyage, Columbus discovered Jamaica the first place to the southern coast of Cuba. On June 12, 1494, three ships of Columbus were on the westernmost end of Cuba. In Cuba and Jamaica, the crew did not find any treasury, and whatever the small amount of treasury was found that came from Hispaniola (Haiti and Dominican Republic). Columbus was now worried about the justification of his expensive second voyage. Columbus had taken the oath from the crew men not to speak about the failure of the second voyage. Moreover, Columbus was also worried of not being in the Orient and wrongfully considering Cuba the mainland of Asia.

In September 1494, Columbus sailed through the eastern end of Hispaniola or Espanola and reached an island called Amona between Espanola and San Juan. Columbus became sick and returned to La Isabella on September 29 where he remained ill for five months. At Isabella, Columbus' disease was diagnosed by Dr. Chanca as "gout"[6] with swollen legs and feet, writes Sale. At Isabella most of the crew became sick by certain diseases and dietary deficiency. The food that was available consisted of: cassava bread, sweet potatoes, corn, peppers, peanuts, fish of all kinds, papayas, pineapples, plums, and pears which the Spaniards would hardly eat. During the course of Columbus' illness, the colony was governed by his brother Diego. The Spaniards mishandled the natives who despised them. The Spaniards killed the natives by unleashing dogs who tore their bodies and then captured, chained, and dragged them in the streets.

All colonialism efforts were targeted toward the pillage of the territories under their control through extraction of forced tributes. Columbus followed this practice and ordered that any person above 14 years of age was required to provide a small amount of gold like a size of thimble, or ring, every three months. Gold was not easily available; it required hard labor to pan gold through the gold bearing streams of the river. In those areas, where there was no gold, natives were asked to supply 25 pounds of spun cotton. Those who complied with the order were given a token of compliance that they wore around their necks. And those who did not comply were punished by cutting off their hands and letting the blood flow until they died,[7] writes Sale. On the other hand, the living capital was made slave and the slavery became the major source of tribute to extract wealth from the land. This system was later used in Mexico, Peru, and La Florida. The slavery was not just the practice of Columbus, but it was authorized, under an imperial fiat of April 12, 1495, to be traded officially. The crown allowed Columbus to sell Caribbean slaves in Spain. The Spaniards treated the mass killing of the Caribbean men, women, and children as a sport. The population of the Indies was reduced considerably, and the prosperous territories of the Caribbean were turned into waste land by the Spaniards.

In 1496, the first Spanish city Santo Domingo was founded on the south shore of the island of Hispaniola between the Caribbean Sea and the Atlantic Ocean which is now the capital of the Dominican Republic. After settlement,

Columbus now turned his attention to one of his objectives and that was to find gold. The inhabitants of the Hispaniola found a little bit of gold in the rivulets and torrents which they used as ornaments. Santo Domingo had gold mines which could be a source of wealth to the kingdom of Spain. He sent two captains with 40 armed men and two native interpreters who were acquainted with the area known as Abao to go out and hunt for gold, as plenty of gold was expected in the rivers. The Spaniards captured some gold from the natives which they brought to Columbus and said that's all they could find. Most of gold that could be found was in the beds of the rivers. Although the Spaniards could not find gold mines, according to Sale, they were able to collect 104,000[8] grams of gold worth 30,000 ducats from the natives in St. Domingo and other places that they could send back to Spain. Albeit this amount was not worth the investment made by the crowns, it did provide an opportunity for future prospects of wealth.

Columbus added some cinnamon, pepper, parrots, and Caribbean captives. The crew of the second voyage were hopeful to find gold and then get back, now became frustrated which led to mutiny. Santo Domingo replaced La Isabella as the capital of the Spanish colonies. But there was not much success as life in the Caribbean climate was harsh. Later St. Domingo became a French colony which was established by the pirates and freebooters, who neither sought any protection from the French government nor acknowledged its authority. When the pirates became citizen, then they acknowledged the French authority,[9] writes Smith. The colony was managed by the French company as the subject of the French government; it thrived and became one of the most important sugar colonies of the Caribbean countries. On the other parts of Hispaniola, the Spanish maintained their control.

Columbus returned home in June 1496. Columbus' baggage on two ships included 30 Caribbean prisoners from Isabella, including the Carib leader Caonabo in shackles and 225 Spaniards who were lucky to get an opportunity to escape from Hispaniola to get back home. On his way back, Columbus picked up two additional Caribbean slaves from Guadeloupe. After three months of voyage, Columbus reached Cadiz. Caonabo died aboard. On arrival, Columbus dressed himself in a gray habit, maybe, to reflect the abject poverty of his colony. King Ferdinand and Queen Isabella were not happy about the news of little wealth and no conversion of the Caribbean to Christianity. In late July 1496, Columbus departed to join the court in Burgos with Carib slaves, gold nuggets, and other spoils from the Caribbean.

By mid-1497, the crowns approved Columbus' third trip with a very small fleet. On May 30, 1498, the third voyage of Columbus started. Columbus along with three ships landed on the island of Trinidad on August 1, 1498. Trinidad with the capital city of Port of Spain in the southeast of the West Indies became a Spanish colony. In 1498, Columbus reported that the land possessed everything, bread and meat, with the exception of wine and clothing which were not available. Each Spanish had two Caribbean persons in service and women were beautiful. By 1500, 1,000 white people lived in peace with the local

Caribbean. After Trinidad, on August 5, Columbus discovered a place now called Venezuela in South America. On August 31, 1498, Columbus reached the harbor of Santo Domingo which was founded and named by Columbus' brother Bartolomeu. Santo Domingo was chosen as the site of the capital of the Spanish colonies and a new city of the New World that was built on the west bank of the Ozama River. Columbus was hated by the Spaniards and the Caribbean. By this time, Columbus became rich with a wealth of four million maravedis and did not care about the security of the island. Due to the unrest of Hispaniola, the crowns replaced Columbus by Francisco de Bobadilla. In 1499, the deposits of gold were found in a 250-mile-long gold-bearing veins along the north of the Cordillera Central, 50 miles in the south of abandoned Isabella and 80 miles in the northwest of Santo Domingo. The average gold output was about one ton a year.

On August 23, 1500, Commander Bobadilla arrived at Santo Domingo. On his arrival Bobadilla saw seven bodies of the Spaniards hanging from the gallows. Bobadilla was surprised to see the rebellion situation on the ground where the Spaniards were being slaughtered. Bobadilla entered the Governor's House, incarcerated Diego, and summoned the other brothers of Columbus. Columbus and his brothers were tried for the atrocities that were inflicted on the Spaniards. At the conclusion of the hearing, Bobadilla chained Columbus and his two brothers who were taken to the ship ready for the sail to Cadiz for trial in Spain. When the three brothers were being taken to the ship, the crowds were shouting at them as the King of the Mosquitoes. Bobadilla liberated the island from the clutches of King Pharaoh.

From Cadiz, Columbus still in chain was taken by a jailer to Las Cuevas in Sevilla, where he remained as a prisoner for five weeks. On December 12, 1500, King Ferdinand and Queen Isabella ordered his release. On December 17, the crowns granted him an audience at the court in Granada. The crowns were sympathetic to Columbus who had discovered a new continent with its great riches that would make Spain wealthy, and that now they had received the reports of discovery of gold in the Cordillera,[10] writes Sale. King Ferdinand and Queen Isabella, after hearing the Columbus petition, reconfirmed him the title of the Admiral of Ocean Sea. In September 1501, the crowns appointed a new Governor of Hispaniola named Nicholas de Ovando.

Columbus proposed his Fourth Voyage in February 1502, which the crowns approved with the condition that he would not enter the Hispaniola but would sail to the new world. On May 9, 1502, Columbus on his Fourth Voyage sailed from Cadiz with small sailing ships and 143 men. Columbus sailed 6,000 nautical miles and discovered nothing. All the four ships were destroyed. Captain and crew remained stranded in Jamaica for one year. Now Columbus reached Central America off modern Honduras and thereafter the coast of Veragua (now Panama). The fourth trip of Columbus failed completely and that was the end of his Fourth Voyage and his career. Columbus died in 1506 and is buried in Sevilla.

The grant of the land by the Spanish crowns to the elite who would help in defense of the borders is called repartimientos. However, in Spanish colonies in Americas, instead of land, the forced labor was granted to the Spanish colonists as repartimientos. Each encomiendero, the Spanish official who was the recipient of the repartimientos or grants, could exact tribute from the West Indians in gold, in kind, or in labor and was required to protect the bonded labor. The recipient in Americas was not allotted the land; he just held control over the West Indians' lands.

About three million West Indians perished in Hispaniola during the period 1494 through 1508,[11] due to warfare, forced labor, and epidemic diseases. To fill the gap of forced labor, the colonists now hunted for labor by raiding the neighboring islands and, during the period 1509–12, were able to catch 40,000 people of the Bahamas islands between Florida and Cuba. Now the Spaniards settled in the various islands; Puerto Rico in 1508 and Cuba in 1511. The colonists found the wealth in the form of gold extracted and panned from the streams of the mountains of Hispaniola and shipped more than 30 tons of gold to Spain from the West Indies by 1520,[12] writes Kamen.

In 1509, the colonists reached the Cartagena port on the northern coast of Columbia. This port was used for major trading activities between Spain and its overseas colonies. Through this port, Peruvian silver was shipped to Spain. Spanish conqueror Rodrigo de Bastides established the first settlements in Columbia at Cartagena and Santa Marta on the Santa Marta Bay of the Caribbean Sea. The Spanish explorer Vasco Nunez de Balboa discovered the city of Panama in 1519 which led to further expeditions in Peru and Mexico.

Spanish conqueror Hernán Cortés was completely ignorant of Aztec in the mainland of Mexico. In July 1519, Cortés with 550 Spaniards, well equipped with long swords and impenetrable armors, landed on the beaches of modern-day Vera Cruz on the eastern coast of the Aztec Empire. The Aztecs were surprised to see the aliens. The Aztecs did not know what to do about them. The natives carried wooden swords and flint spears which were no match to the Spanish equipment. The Aztec Empire was much smaller than the present-day Mexico, but it had ruled 371 different tribes and people,[13] writes Harari. The aliens came in giant ships which the Aztecs had never seen before. Cortes told the natives, a naked lie, that they were there on a peace mission from the king of Spain and asked them to take him and his entourage to the king, Montezuma-II. This was not true as the king of Spain had never heard about Cortes and Aztec, and this was Cortes' private expedition. Cortes now marched toward the capital of Aztec, the metropolis of Tenochtitlan. The Aztecs led Cortes to the Emperor Montezuma. During the course of the meeting, the emperor's guard was killed and the emperor was captured, made a prisoner, and kept in the palace. Cortes asked the natives to join him to get rid of the Aztec ruler. The naïve Aztecs were unaware of the Spanish genocide in the Caribbean. The Aztecs provided a local army of 10,000, and Cortes captured Tenochtitlan city. Now more and more Spanish soldiers and settlers from Cuba and Spain started arriving in Mexico.

After the defeat of the Aztec Empire, Mexico was brought under Spanish control in 1521. The Aztecs noticed that the invaders were very hungry for gold. The Aztecs asked the Spaniards why they are so enthusiastic about the gold; Cortés replied that they were suffering from a heart disease that could only be cured by the yellow metal, gold. The Aztec Empire consisted of three states: Mexico-Tenochtitlan, Texcoco, and Tlacopan. After ten years of Cortes' conquest of Mexico, Francisco Pizarro along with 168 men arrived on the shore of the Inca Empire which included the territory of Peru. Here again, Pizarro repeated the modus operandi of Cortes in Mexico. According to Kamen, Pizarro sought an interview with the ruler of Inca, Atahualpa, and kidnapped him. With the support of the natives, Pizarro conquered the Inca Empire in 1532.[14] The Caribbean gold and Peru's silver and exotica were the additional foreign resources which came to Spain, and by 1520, Spain was on the threshold of becoming a world empire.

After the death of Ferdinand in 1516, Charles V, son of Princess Juana of Spain and Philips, was proclaimed the ruler of Castile and Aragon. Both Ferdinand and Isabella are buried in Granada. In addition to al-Andalus, Charles had control of north Europe such as Italy, Germany, and the Netherlands and had an enmity with France. One of his advisors, named Mercurino Gattinara, flattered Charles to think of universal kingship. Gattinara wrote to Charles: "Sire since God has conferred on you the immense grace of raising you above all the kings and princes in Christendom, – you are on the path to a universal monarchy, you will unite Christendom under one yoke",[15] writes Kamen. Charles did not show any enthusiasm in this regard. However, he announced his commitment to anti-Muslim activities. Charles had the king of France as his captive and in January 1526 signed a treaty with his captive Francis I, who ceded Burgundy to Charles in return for his release. Later, Francis I reneged on the treaty because of its unrealistic terms. The hostility between Charles and France persisted.

Before 1525, there was no Spanish naval presence in the Mediterranean. The same year, Charles was advised by his Genoese admiral to build up the naval strength to discover different sea routes. Consequently, a limited Spanish naval appearance in the Mediterranean occurred. In 1539, Spain had four naval squadrons consisting of ten Spanish galleys; Doria led 20 Genoese ships in 1539; 9 ships of the Naples (Italy) in 1568, and 12 ships of Sicily (Italy). Because of resource limitation, the government preferred to own a small number of galleys and signed contracts with the private sector to contribute additional ships to the armada. The two men in the private sector who contributed were Andrea Doria of Genoa and Alvaro de Bazan of Spain.

Charles pursued an anti-Islamic policy. In 1529, Muslim ruler of North Africa, Khayr al-Din Barbarossa, not only seized, from the Spanish, the fortress of Penon of Algiers but also destroyed their fleet of eight ships off Ibiza. Charles, in 1535, with the help of Andrea Doria of Italy raided and captured Tunis and appointed Muley Hassan as his vassal. Barbarossa fled to Istanbul. In October 1541, Charles tried to capture the city of Algiers but failed. The Muslims took

Tripoli in 1551, Penon de Velez in 1554, and the port city Bougie on the Gulf of Bejaia in Algeria in 1555. The Spanish presence eroded in North Africa.

Charles had a military presence in Italy, Germany, France, the Netherlands, and Switzerland which proved to be very expensive. The expenses of maintaining the forces in Northern Europe were far greater than the tax receipts of the region. Peoples of Northern Europe were reluctant to pay taxes to cover the cost of the defense forces. The economic conditions of Spain were not good either. Castile was under debt. The only potential source of revenue was the Caribbean. The budget deficit of Northern Europe compelled Charles to take his hands off Northern Europe and just concentrate his energies on Spain.

Before the conquest of the Spaniards, there was no cattle either in Mexico or in Peru. There was no plow, and they did not know about the use of iron. There was no coined money and no established system of commerce, and the barter trade was practiced. A wooden spade was their agricultural implement. Sharp stones were used as knives and hatchets for cutting, and fish bones and hard animal sinew were used as needles for sewing purposes. The Europeans introduced cattle, plow, and use of iron. Initially, the natives were destroyed and the Spanish colonies became less populous but were progressing as compared to those of the other European countries. The city of Lima had a population of 50,000, Quito was of the same size, and the city of Mexico had a hundred thousand inhabitants which were greater than the cities of Boston, New York, and Philadelphia of the then British colonies. The Spanish colonies of Mexico and Peru made considerable progress.

Spain's four main sources of revenue were Castile, Aragon, the church, and the Americas. Charles' revenue receipts were at the most 500,000 ducats (golden coins). Church, though, exempt from taxes, was required to contribute to the state in the form of donations. However, the clergies were heavily taxed as compared to the ordinary people. The clergies, in addition to paying normal taxes such as the tercias reales, subsidio, and cruzada, were obligated to make additional grants or donations to the state. The tercias reales were paid to the crown at the rate of two-ninth of the income that came to the church in tithes like the Muslims' system of kharaj on the production of commodities and productive land. The subsidio (or subsidy) was the portion of the church income that was given to the state by the pope. This share was later fixed at an annual rate of 420,000 ducats. The cruzada, a papal bull of crusade, was preached at the church and was payable by all faithful, clergies, and laymen. The annual average contribution of cruzada was 121,000 ducats during the period 1523 through 1554. Thus, church was the major source of State revenues.

The taxes were mostly indirect such as the sales tax called alcabala which was imposed at the rate of 10% of the value of the commodity. The sales tax along with tercias reales accounted for three-fourth of the Castile revenues of 1.25 million ducats. The external sources of revenues were the Caribbean islands which included the precious metals of gold and silver. Gold was panned in the streams of the mountains of Hispaniola which is an island in the West Indies located between Cuba and Puerto Rico, also known as Antilles, and comprises the states of Haiti and the Dominican Republic. Haiti was later ceded to France by the Spaniards in 1697. The second important metal was silver, which was mined at the mines of Bolivia, also known as Potosi in 1545, and Zacatecas and Guanajuato mines of Mexico in 1548. In 1532, the explorer Francisco Pizarro raided the Peruvian empire of Inca in South America and captured the emperor and gold. The crown Charles also confiscated 3.5 million ducats worth of gold that came from the Caribbean to the private individuals in Spain. The crown was also getting revenues from the colonies by imposing a 20% tax on the mineral production called quinto or royal fifth. According to Hamilton cited in Kamen,[16] during the period from 1503 to 1600, 153,500 kilograms of gold and 7.4 million kilograms of silver were brought from the Caribbean to Spain. According to Sale, from 1503 to 1660, Spain brought about 200 tons of gold and 18,600 tons of silver from the New World worth $1.25 billion in gold-standard American dollars.[17] In addition to bullion, the crown received royal fifth (Quinto) as excise duty on bullion production and the other colonial taxes and custom duties imposed in 1543.[18] According to Harari, the gold and silver that came from Mexico and the Caribbean to Europe were used to buy silk and porcelain from China[19] and spices from the East, and this triggered the growth of the economies of both Europe and the East Asia.

Even after having the huge influx of bullion and other taxes from the colonies, the crown was still running into deficit because of the increasing demand for expenditures and the inheritance of the public debt left by Ferdinand and Isabella. In order to balance his budget, Charles had to borrow, and for this purpose he established an investment unit called Juros for the repayment of the debt. The burden of debt was not on the Spaniards, but it was shifted onto the colonies through additional taxes. In 1522, the debt service consumed 30% of the revenues which rose to 68% in 1556. The interest rate that the crown paid in 1520 was 17.6%, which rose to 48.8% in 1550.

The influx of bullion in Spain was envied by the Europeans. The Europeans tried to get the bullion out of Spain. Spain was just exporting the raw materials and did not develop the infrastructure to process the raw materials into finished goods. The Europeans bought the raw materials from Spain at very low prices and after processing them into manufactured goods, exported them to Spain at higher prices to capture golden coins. The pig iron exported by Spain to France came back as metal products such as aluminum, brass, and other steel products. These finished foreign products were highly expensive in Spain. And some gold was exported illegally under the guise of exports from Spain. The gold was hidden under the commercial commodities which were being exported from Spain. According to Venetian ambassador Soranzo,[20] in 1556, 5.5 million gold crowns annually entered France illegally. Through legal trade, the wealth of the West Indies was rerouted from Spain to other European countries. In addition to outflow of bullion through trade, the crown Charles also exported bullion in payment to German bankers, and to the Netherlands for the materials they had supplied to Spain. The Cortes of Castile had filed at least 12 petitions to block the outflow of bullion from Spain, but these efforts failed.

The Europeans flooded the Spanish market with the manufactured goods at higher prices to meet the demand created by the influx of bullion. This resulted in hyperinflation. During the first half of the sixteenth century, in the Castilian economy, the prices of wheat, oil, and wine had increased by 109%, 197%, and 655% respectively. The hyperinflation adversely affected the living standards of all the nobles and the laymen. The hardly hit were the people with fixed incomes, and the beneficiaries were those who were engaged in trading activities. During the period 1530–55 land rents increased by 86% and house rents increased by 80%. The wages in Spain did not emulate the inflation.

In October 1555, Charles abdicated the imperial power in favor of his son and heir Philip II. In January 1556, Philip at the age of 22 years was proclaimed the king in Valladolid. Vasco da Gama from Portugal was influenced by an Italian explorer's, Marco Polo, travel of Asia. In 1498, Vasco da Gama embarked on his voyage of Asia. In 1553, the Portuguese established a permanent trading base at Macao at the southern coast of China. Knowing about the Portuguese's presence in Asia, Philip became interested in the region. Philip sent a mission to Asia from the Pacific coast of New Spain under the command of Basque Migual Lopez de Legazpi. The mission landed on the coast of China and in 1571 established their base at Manila, and they called the various islands as the Philippines which became a Spanish colony. The Spanish had a minimal role while the territory was managed by Filipino and Chinese. The big ship *Manila galleon* left Manila with goods, spices, and textiles for the port of Acapulco in Mexico. The first *galleon* sailed in 1565 and the last in 1815. The Philippines got independence from Spain on June 12, 1898.

Philip's empire included Spain, South America, the Netherlands, half of Italy, England through marriage with Queen Mary of England, and the eastern region of France known as Franche-Comte along with the rest of the Burgundy lands which were ceded to Spain at the time when Charles became the Spanish king in 1516, the Philippine Islands, and a string of bases along the coasts of Africa and Asia. The North and the South American and Asians' ships loaded with the treasures anchored at the ports of Sevilla and Cadiz. Spain was the most powerful country of Europe. Franche-Comté was ceded to France in 1678[21] under the treaty of Nijmegen. Philip had problems with France. Peace was negotiated and restored with France in April 1559 on the condition that Philip would marry the daughter of Henry II of France, Elizabeth of Valois. Philip also married the Portuguese princess Maria in 1543 who died two years later giving birth to Don Carlos in 1555. In 1570, Philip married his niece Anna of Austria who was 22 years younger than him. In November 1558, Queen Mary of England died and Philip had to forgo his rights of England according to the treaty of marriage.

Philip inherited all the Hispanic kingdoms, the Low Countries, Sicily and Naples, and the whole Latin America with the exception of Brazil. Philip was wary of Turks' expansion in the 1560s. However, Philip failed to stop the Turkish advance in the Mediterranean. Spain wanted to be a self-appointed international police force. After this, Philip dealt with William of Orange in the Low Countries. Most of the forays were unsuccessful such as the Armada that was sent against the British in 1588. These military operations led to heavy expenditures that compelled Philip to declare bankruptcy in 1575. Now he did not have to pay the soldiers. Due to lack of payments, a large number of mutinies took place which were crushed, and Antwerp, the northern city of Europe, was destroyed and 8,000 men were killed.

In the middle of the sixteenth century, the arrival of Caribbean bullion in Spain provided a boost to the economic growth. The bullion was shipped through international creditors. In 1581, Philip, through military force, annexed Portugal and made a claim to the vacant throne and spent much of his time in Lisbon. Borrowing increased, and again in 1596, Philip refused to pay the debt. At the same time, the population increased by 24%, which created a demand for food and services. Now more money was in circulation in the economy. In order to feed the increased population, more land was brought under cultivation in the 1550s. During the period 1560–1580, the production of wheat, wine, and rye increased by 26%, 51%, and 54% respectively. The increase in agricultural production was due to increase in acreage and not due to increase in its productivity.

The Caribbean money was invested in the textile sector which resulted in the increase of wool production. The major wool manufacturing centers in Castile were Segovia, Toledo, and Cuenca. After meeting the domestic demand, the surplus wool was exported. By 1580, Segovia had 600 looms and produced about 13,000 pieces of cloth. Silk production was started at Granada by Moriscos community who were Muslims and were compelled by the church and the crown to accept baptism or face death after the practice of Islam was prohibited in Spain in the early sixteenth century. The agricultural boom was affected by an epidemic which wreaked havoc in the country. Overall, one-fifth of the population perished in the epidemic.

The main beneficiaries of the wool and textile business were the middle-class merchants and financiers of Castile who were linked to international wool trade. The businesses were operated from two trade centers of Medina del Campo in the province of Valladolid and Burgos in northern Spain. These two centers were linked to other trading centers of Sevilla, Toledo, and Segovia in the northwest of Madrid in central Spain. The famous Spanish capitalists and businessmen who earned good fortune in this trade included Maluenda, Bernuy and Curiel of Burgos, and Simon Ruiz of Medina del Campo, writes Kamen.[22] The Spanish economy was thriving, and the main outlets for Burgos' supplies were Flanders, Italy, and France. Flanders alone consumed 60% of Spain's total output. The Netherlands supplied Spain with wheat, naval supplies, and textiles, and this was the reason for Spain to have control on the Netherlands. Antwerp and Genoa were the two main ports that were used by the Spanish and the Europeans for international trade.

The Caribbean wealth started pouring into Spain in the sixteenth century. Castile, just a small trading center, became the world's biggest commercial center. The ships entered Sevilla carrying tobacco, hides, dyes, sugar, and precious metals, and, for the first time, Spain became a part of the world market. The ships from all over the world exchanged commodities with Sevilla and earned profits through globalization of the world trade. The international trading centers included: St. Lawrence (Ontario, Quebec), the Rio de La Plato (Argentina, Uruguay), Brazil, Nagasaki (Japan), Macao (China), Manila (the Philippines), port of Acapulco in Guerrero state of Mexico on the Pacific coast, Gallao in Peru, Havana in Cuba, Antwerp in Belgium, and Genoa in Italy. African slaves went to Mexico, Mexico's silver went to China, and China's silk went to Spain. In 1594, the wealth that reached Sevilla was 10 million ducats, of which 6 million ducats were charged to debt service payments and only 4 million ducats were left with the treasury.[23] Most of the actors involved in the international trade were non-Spaniards. All the Caribbean trade was handled by the bureaucracy that was housed in a building called the Casa de Contratacion close to the foot of Giralda tower. Later in the seventeenth century, according to Hopkins, when the Guadalquivir was silting up, the monopoly of the Caribbean trade shifted to Cadiz.[24] A monumental building of a tobacco factory left by the Muslims is now a part of Sevilla University. Another inheritance from the Muslims was the alcazar, a palace enjoyed by the people and the king of Castile, Pedro I, did contribute to it. Under Pedro's orders, the Granadans inscribed in Arabic script on the Christian king's façade the famous "Nasrid Ghaliba" – "la ghalib illa allah" – God alone is conqueror, writes Hopkins.[25]

The expansion of trade with the Caribbean required credit facilities which were not available in Spain. Consequently, in 1566, the export of silver from the peninsula was outsourced to foreign financiers, a step which the Spanish people later regretted. The foreign financiers understood the weakness of Spain and then decided that instead of investing in Spain, it would be more appropriate to invest in the Caribbean where silver was being extracted for export purposes. Spain, instead of becoming a rich country through the discovery of wealth of the Caribbean, was now being dictated by international capitalists. Spain was now having a current account deficit with the Europeans due to import of manufactured goods. The international capitalists now thrived and possessed expensive properties, and bulk of the kingdom was in their hands. Sevilla, through its trading links with the Caribbean, had become the hub of international trade. Sevilla's population increased from 35,000 in 1480 to 120,000 in 1553. With a thriving trade with the Caribbean during the period 1562 through 1609, the number of vessels on the Caribbean route increased by 176% and the volume of tonnage increased by 238%. The supply of silver mined at Bolivia and Zacatecas in Mexico reaching Sevilla tripled during the period 1560 through the 1590s. The thriving business at Sevilla was controlled by the international capitalists, including Italian and French, who made heavy investments. Now Spain's job and money went to foreign capitalists, and the locals in Sevilla, in 1626, protested to the Spanish government for failing to protect the sons of the soil and acting as a foster mother for making the foreigners rich.

During the period 1550 through 1566, Spain was wary of continued Turkish expansion. Through marriage with Elizabeth of Valois, Philip was able to maintain good relations with France. In 1565, Elizabeth and the duke of Alba pressed Catherine de Medici, mother of the king and a de facto ruler, to stop allying with the Turks. In 1560, Spanish had led an expedition to recapture Tripoli. This expedition, led by the duke of Medinaceli and Admiral Gian Andrea Doria, was intercepted by the Turkish on the island of Djerba who got 28 Spanish galleys sunk and 10,000 troops captured. However, on October 7, 1571, Spain as the lead of fleet of 200 galleys of Holy League supported by Spain, Venice, the pope, and Italy confronted the Turkish fleet and defeated them in the naval battle of Lepanto. The war cost Spain 5 million ducats which were paid through loans from Genoese bankers.

The Europeans envied the Spanish trading activities overseas and were interested to plunge into an opportunity for the wealth of overseas. In the 1540s French vessels appeared in the Caribbean, followed by a host of other vessels that were swarming in the Atlantic and the Caribbean to capture the fruits of the trade. The French who tried to capture the Spanish colony of Florida were all killed by the Spaniards. The British vessels led by Admiral John Hawkins and Francis Drake raided the Spaniards in 1585 on the coasts of Santo Domingo, Cartagena, and St. Augustus. They also raided the Pacific coast. In 1586, Philip sent Roman military engineer Gian Battista Antonelli to the Caribbean to build defensive forts for protection of the Spanish territories. In 1587, the British captain captured the Spanish *Manila galleon*. Now the European interference was rapidly increasing in the territories held by Spain.

In 1568, British made a channel that stopped the north route for the Spanish. When Alba's ships were seized, it forced Philip to use land routes via France for transportation of bullion to the Netherlands. The French civil war made that route unsafe as well. After 1578, the Spanish government sent money by road to Barcelona for onward transmission by sea to Genoa and Germany. This became now the main route through which the Caribbean silver was transported to Europe. In 1576, Philip wrote that the quickest way to transmit money was by bills of exchange. The new credit system was operated with the help of German bankers and financiers and later Genoese and Portuguese financiers.

As soon as Spain plunged into a conflict of the Netherlands, it was compelled to upgrade its military strength to become a world power. New recruitment system was introduced with an average annual intake of 9,000 men during the period of 1567–74. Philip got 300 new galleys built at a cost of 3.5 million ducats. Philip's force was four times greater than his father, Charles V's. Now the acquisition of Portugal and the assurance of safe sea route to the Netherlands became the sine qua non for future campaigns. In 1570, a fleet of eight ships under the command of Pedro Menendez de Aviles was launched for the protection of the Caribbean trade route. Now Spain emerged as an Atlantic power, and in 1587, it had 106 ships in the Atlantic. In 1594, the Spanish force was known as an armada of the Ocean Sea. Philip now more focused on Atlantic than the Mediterranean. An army of 40,000 was dispatched to fight in Italy and Low Countries (coastal region of the northwestern region of Europe consisting of Belgium, the Netherlands, and Luxembourg) bordering Germany to the east and France to the south. The fortifications on the Levant coast (eastern Mediterranean, Middle East, Egypt, Turkey, Syria, and Cyprus), and the expansion of military strength increased the defense expenditure fivefold during the period 1577–1611. The state could not bear the burden of an alarmingly increased defense expenditure, and the men did not get paid for four years. Without getting paid, the men deserted and left the African forts to join the Moors in Penon de Velez on the coast of Morocco in Northern Africa.

The young king of Portugal, Sebastian, in 1578 ventured to launch a crusade against Africa. His forces were cut in pieces at the battle of Alcazarquivir, and he himself was killed. Philip, who was the son of Isabella of Portugal, expressed his claim to the throne. In the meantime, other claimants also emerged on the scene: duchess of Braganza and Antonio, prior of Crato. Philip's intention was to reunite Portugal and Spain. Philip prepared a plan of invasion of Portugal to bring it into the Spanish fold. In June 1580, Philip assembled an army of 47,000 from Germany and Italy and placed it under the command of Alba. This force was supplemented by a Spanish-Italian fleet of 60 galleys under the command of Marquis of Santa Cruz. The fleet left Cadiz. In the meantime, Antonio was proclaimed the king by the people of Portugal and expected assistance from England and France. Before the foreign assistance could reach Portugal, Spain captured Setubal and Lisbon. Antonio fled and later died in 1595.

To restore peace, a three-year treaty of peace was negotiated with the Turks in January 1581. The Spaniards settled in the Philippines, and the rebellion in Inca in Peru also faded. Now Spain was on the apogee of world power through capture of Portugal and the expansion of the Spanish authority in India, Indonesia, and China, writes Kamen.[26] In 1581, the Portuguese acknowledged Philip as the king under difficult circumstances as they still despised him. The Portuguese did not want foreign rulers. Philip reunited Spain and Portugal and gave complete autonomy to Portugal. The control of Portugal opened ways for Spanish fleet to use Lisbon port for the Caribbean. Most of Portugal's income came from the Asian and the Atlantic trade through Brazil.

England's Drake discovered California (1577–80) and started conflict with Spain on the western coast. Now Philip focused his attention on making Spain as an imperial power by safeguarding the routes of bullion trade from the Indies, controlling the Netherlands' rebels in the northern provinces and England's ambitions. Because of Spanish conflict with England's Drake, Philip secretly worked an agreement with Mary Queen of Scots to make sure that she got proclaimed as Queen of England. Philip also signed a secret agreement with Guises in northern France and Catholic League and granted them subsidies in return for their support for the Catholic cause in the Netherlands.

Through this agreement France would refrain from any intervention in the Netherlands.

In May 1585, Spain seized British ships at Spanish ports. In August 1585, Elizabeth declared war against Spain and sent a force of 6,000 men under Earl Leicester in support of the Dutch. A fleet of 25 ships under the command of Drake started attacking Vigo adjoining the Atlantic Ocean in the northwest Spain and then moved further to the West Indies and reached Santo Domingo in Dominion Republic and Cartagena in Colombia. Philip now ordered an armada for invasion of England. The purpose of the armada was to protect the Indies and the conquest of the Netherlands. As far as the proclamation of Mary of Scots as Queen was concerned, it did not happen because the secret agreement between Philip and Mary became open and she was executed.

The main problem of Philip in managing his empire was the lack of quick communication to reach out the distances of his vast empire. This has been reflected in the fact that Philip knew three months after Santo Domingo was captured by the British commander Drake. A quick communication system was needed to be able to make decisions about the transfer of money and deployment of forces, when and where. In the absence of a communication system, the Spanish government depended on Italian and Genoese soldiers, bankers, and Flemish traders who dipped into the opportunity of the Caribbean wealth of the Spanish Empire and made huge profits.

In February 1588, Admiral Santa Cruz died and was succeeded by the duke of Medina-Sidonia in the province of Cadiz. A fleet of 130 ships left Coruna in July 1588 with 7,000 seamen and 17,000 soldiers and headed toward the Netherlands to pick up the additional force of the Flanders. British warships divided in groups that were led by Lord Howard of Effingham, Francis Drake, John Hawkins, and Martin Frobisher. Spaniards could not pick up Flanders, and the British also could not get intended French support. The Spanish armada was defeated with the loss of 70 ships and 15,000 men on board. After the defeat of the Spanish armada, Philip sent another fleet in 1596 to the port of Brest in France, and another fleet in 1597 was sent to seize the port of Falmouth in Jamaica, but both of the fleets were destroyed by a storm.

In 1593, Henry of Navarre renounced his heresy and became Catholic. In 1595, Henry declared a war against Spain. In 1596, Henry made an alliance with England and France. In June 1596, earl of Essex, Antonio Perez, led a surprise attack on the port city of Cadiz, sacked it, and held it for 17 days. The failure of armadas in 1596 and 1597 compelled Philip to reevaluate his finances. In November 1596, Philip had to reschedule the state debts. In May 1598, the financial difficulties compelled Philip to seek peace with France under the Treaty of Vervins, a city in northern France, and to grant autonomy to the Netherlands under Albert. Albert was a cardinal, and Philip waived his oath as a cardinal to allow him to marry Philip's daughter Isabella.

The expansion of the imperial power was not because of Spain's military strength but was prompted by the bullion of the Caribbean which not only enriched the state of Spain but all those settlers, traders, and bankers who were engaged. The Spanish bullion was diverted to other beneficiaries which included Portugal, Flanders, England, Genoa in northwestern Italy, and Germany through payments for armament. Genoese bankers who provided finances controlled the economy of Spain during the period 1557–1627.

Spain rose to be a world power under Philip II without any large army. Spain's troops were just a contingent of the collaborating forces. Small detachments were deployed at different locations to safeguard the African forts. This shows that the empire that Philip II got did not come through conquests but through inheritance. Even in the Caribbean, the territories were not conquered by the Spanish conquistadors, but came under the Spanish control through the help of local collaborators. The naval campaigns to the Caribbean were not launched by the crown but by private entrepreneurs. There were no royal ships on the Atlantic route in the early sixteenth century.

Spain did not have a big army, and its army was about one-fourth of the total strength of the collaborators. Spain's most of the forces were deployed overseas, and not much was left for internal security of the country. On detecting the Spanish internal weakness, Drake attacked the Spanish port of Vigo in 1585 and Cadiz in 1587 and inflicted upon Spain heavy losses of 20 million ducats. The contribution to the Spanish naval strength in the Mediterranean was dominated by the Italians. Almost all of the Spanish campaigns in Djerba, Malta, Lepanto, and Tunis were led by the Italians. In the Atlantic, the Portuguese were an important part of the armada. In addition, auxiliary contingents were drawn from Germany and Italy. Alba had commanded 67,000 troops in the Netherlands in 1572, of which 57,000 were non-Spaniards.

Philip knew his bounds and never thought of becoming a world power because of limited resources. His troops were constantly engaged in wars in parts of the Europe, but these wars were not for the conquests or annexation. The people at home did not like the government's involvement in the Netherlands' conflict or acquisition of Portugal. The secret of the expansion of Philip's empire was not through aggression but through collaboration. There were no conquests of the Americas as their affairs were run by the native collaborators. Although Spain was a small part of the campaigns of the empire's expansion, the major role was played by the non-Spaniards which included the Portuguese navy, German financiers and armament engineers, Italian bridge builders, Belgian technicians, and Chinese traders. The motive of all participants was a profitable business associated with the expansion of the Spanish Empire.

However, the cost of these collaborators was finally picked up by Spain which tumbled its economy. The financing contracts with the financiers increased from 21 in 1556 to 50 in 1567. Only one Invincible Armada cost ten million ducats. Lots of resources were eaten up by the Netherlands' conflict which further led to the involvement of England and France that knocked down the Spanish economy. The Flanders army increased from 13,000 in 1570 to 67,000 in 1572. In 1587, the military strength increased to 100,000 men. Between 1567 and

1586, the Flanders received at an average of 1.5 million ducats per annum. The total military expenditure by the end of the sixteenth century rose to 80 million ducats.

To fill the resource gap, inter alia, the church increased its contribution to the state by granting the excusado based on the income from the church property in each administrative district. In addition, a war tax was imposed by the church through a papal bull of crusade known as cruzada. The excusado and cruzada were paid by the church to the state, despite the fact, that the church enjoyed the tax exemptions. The defeat of Armada in 1588 increased the fiscal difficulties. Philip now imposed additional taxes on four food items which included meat, oil, vinegar, and wine. The wealth coming from the mines of Potosi in Bolivia and Zacatecas and Guanajuate in Mexico was a big support to the Spanish Empire. This wealth came as the royal fifth (quinto) imposed as excise duty on the production of bullion and other taxes from the Caribbean islands such as the alcabala (sales tax), custom duties, and cruzada. According to Kamen, the total revenue receipts during Philip's sway amounted to over 64.5 million ducats.[27] In addition, the state seized large quantities of the bullion imported or smuggled into Spain by the private sector. The bullion represented one-fifth of the state's resources, and most importantly it was internationally negotiable.

The continued increase in the resource gap compelled Philip to take additional fiscal measures. The additional measures included sale of community lands, sales tax on sale of property in the towns and cities, and sales of nobility and sales of offices. But the sale of nobility was not the only source to become a noble. The sale of office was very successful in Spain and the Americas where oligarchies wanted to maintain their political power and influence. Philip also asked clergy and nobles for gifts, donations, and loans to the state. The total annual income increased from 3 million ducats in 1559 to 10.5 million ducats in 1598. During the corresponding period the tax burden on taxpayers increased to 430% while wages increased by 80%. Despite the resource generation efforts, Philip could not raise enough money to cover the fiscal deficit. Consequently, Philip was compelled to declare bankruptcies in 1557, 1560, 1576, and 1596. In April 1574 the state's debt was 74 million ducats against an income of only 5.6 million ducats. The loans mostly came from Genoese financiers, and in September 1575, Philip stopped the payment of debt. The stoppage of debt payment to the Genoese created an opportunity for the local financiers to come forward to grab the opportunity of investment. The Spanish financiers who captured the opportunity were Simon Ruiz of Medina del Campo and Juan de Maluenda of Burgos, writes Kamen.[28] But the sack of Antwerp by the Spanish mutineers forced Philip to go back to international financiers because that was the only way to rescue the economy. In December 1577, Philip through an imperial fiat converted the debt into long-term annuities (juros).

In November 1596, Philip approached the Portuguese financiers for financing. The Genoese financiers immediately reacted and reduced the interest rate to the lowest level of 10% and earned another financial arrangement that created a juro of 7 million ducats. The empire was in debt trap as more and more of its income was pledged to the payment of annuities. In 1598 debt reached the level of 85 million ducats and the annual debt interest payment was more than 4.6 million ducats.

Now the question was how the debt-ridden Spain was able to maintain control over a vast empire stretched from Europe to the Americas, to the Philippines in Asia. The answer to this question was to be found in the four basic principles of the empire's policy. First, the crown never managed to occupy the entire empire but kept control on a small segment of the empire. Second, because of the communication problems due to distance and time, the decision-making power was given in the hands of the native people who lived there. Control of the townships and chief centers of the Americas was given to the settler oligarchies. Philip sold the office to the oligarchies. Much of the power in the Americas rested with Creole elite. Third, Spain had no military power to defend its territories of the Americas. No regular forces were deployed in the Americas. The Americas' local militia was the only regular force for defense. There was no Spanish naval power in the region which led to the British raids by Drake in the 1580s. After the British attacks, the Spaniards under the engineer Antonelle began to fortify the ports and the Spanish ships started patrolling in the Caribbean and the pacific coasts. It was an expensive exercise and was soon discontinued. Now the Caribbean territories became an easy prey for the British. Fourth, the trade system that was monopolized by the Spaniards started slipping into the hands of the foreigners. The wealth started changing the hands from the Spaniards to the foreigners, including the Flemings, the English, and the French.

Philip II died on September 13, 1598, at the age of 71 years. After the death of Philip II, his son Philip III succeeded him at the age of 20 years. In 1599, the copper coins were minted under Philip III. By 1601 the major source of crown's income was the taxes on food items of meat, oil, vinegar, and wine, called millones. Unlike his father, Philip III delegated the decision-making powers to the bureaucracy. Philip III allowed the Cortes to approve the taxes and expenditure thereof. In 1608, under an imperial fiat the main cities and town were authorized to collect taxes. In the northern provinces the tax collection authority was given to the local oligarchies formed into assemblies. In 1616, Castile contributed 73% of the imperial cost, Portugal 10%, the Netherlands 9%, Naples 5%, and Aragon 1%. Philip III died in March 1621 at the age of 43 and was succeeded by his 16-year-old son Philip IV.

Olivares, an aggressive Prime Minister under Philip IV, advised the crown to be a king of a united Spain. In this connection, Olivares prepared a proposal called "Union of Arms" which called for raising an army of 140,000 men to be contributed by each component of the empire. According to the proposal, Castile and the Americas together would raise 44,000, Catalonia 16,000, Milan 8,000. In January and March 1626, the Cortes of Aragon and Valencia defied the proposal respectively. Finally, both the Cortes of Aragon and Valencia voted a tax revenue of 72,000 ducats a year for fifteen years with a caveat of not sending the troops outside Spain. This amount was just sufficient for a small number of troops. The Cortes of Catalonia at Barcelona on 28 March refused to give any money or men. In May 1626, the government stopped minting the copper coins which had led to inflation. In August 1626, the Spanish silver fleet in the sea route that linked the territories of the Caribbean and the Atlantic was seized off the Cuban coast by the Dutch admiral Piet Heyn. The lack of financing crippled the empire which led to the germination of crisis in Portugal, Catalonia, and Castile.

The war declared by France in 1635[29] shocked the Spaniards, writes Kamen. In 1636 the French besieged the Basque fortress of Fuenterrabia in Catalonia. The Catalan troops did not show up for defense. Disaster started. In 1637 the Portuguese revolted against the taxes in Evora and other cities and towns. In April 1640, the civil war started and the peasants of Catalonia attacked the troops of Philip IV and transferred the title of count of Barcelona from Philip IV to Louis XIII of France and placed themselves under the control of France. The revolts of Portugal and Catalonia in 1640 became the spearhead of the Spanish collapse.

Portugal had maintained control over its own affairs and over the Spanish bases in Africa, Brazil, and Asia. The Portuguese penetrated the Spanish economic interests in Peru, New Spain, and Asia. The Portuguese also developed their links with the Spanish merchants in Manila. The Portuguese financiers along with Genoese and German bankers made the empire dependent on them for financing of the royal army in northern Europe and navy in the Atlantic. Despite the Portuguese role in the world trade, its economy remained poor and the Portuguese blamed Spain for their underdevelopment. Portugal had its control over Brazil. When one of the states of Brazil, Bahia, was captured by the Dutch, Spain helped Portugal to recover that state from the Dutch. The relationships between Spain and Portugal were damaged by the policies of Olivares, under which the Portuguese defense forces were damaged against the French and at the same time compelled them to forgo their interests in Asia and Brazil in favor of the crown. Portugal was losing its Asian spice trade to the Dutch. The Portuguese held protest in Lisbon in December 1640 when they divorced their partnership with Spain and proclaimed the duke of Braganza Joao IV as their king.

The Italians also wanted to get rid of Spain. The Italians, supported by the French, rebelled in Naples and Sicily in July 1647. A fish vendor named Tommaso Aniello provoked the masses in the cities and towns of Naples against the unjust taxes, and soon his movement got momentum. Aniello, expecting the support from the French, declared in October 1647 a republic, independent of Spain. But the French duke of Guise did not honor his commitment, and by April 1648 the Spaniards retook the control. Another revolt in the city of Palermo in Sicily took place in 1647. In 1649, a volcano erupted in the southwestern Italy, which was considered a good omen by a Sicilian friar for expulsion and elimination of the Spaniards. King Philip IV died on September 17, 1665, and left Spain in grave crisis where the treasury was empty.

After the death of Philip IV, his four-year-old son Charles II succeeded him, and the empire was ruled by a five-member regent team until the prince reached the age of 14 years. In December 1677, Philip IV's illegitimate son and a general in his army, Don Juan Jose (1629–79), rose against the regent team and marched through Catalonia and Aragon with 15,000 troops heading toward Madrid, where he offered his services to the king on January 23, 1677. This was considered the first military coup in Spain. Juan ruled for a period of two and a half years, from January 1677 through September 1679.

In early 1679, Charles II married Marie Louise of Orleans, a niece of Louise XIV of France. The queen died in an accident in February 1689. The king then married Mariana, daughter of a German prince. The flaccid, indolent, and impotent Charles did not produce an heir either by Marie or by Mariana. To continue the male line of kingship, an heir was needed. The French and the Germans were now competing for this opportunity. Finally, in June 1700, Charles II and his advisors decided to have a grandson of France as the king with the caveat of not merging the Spanish monarchy with the French monarchy. On October 3, Charles II signed a testament in this regard and died on November 1, 1700, after ruling for a period of 35 years, and this period was the nadir in the history of the Spanish Empire.

The decline of the Spanish Empire continued. There was no Spanish navy in the sea. There was no land force to protect the ports. The well-established fortresses were demolished. The Spanish hegemony over Europe had vanished. All the peace treaties were unfavorable to Spain and favorable to France. The series of peace treaties of Westphalia signed between May and October 1648 ended the 30 years' religious wars, fought between the Protestants and the Catholics. Under the peace treaty, the 80-year-old war between Spain and the Dutch Republic ended with the recognition and independence of the latter. The peace treaty of Pyrenees ended the war between France and Spain, and this treaty was signed in the presence of King Louis XIV of France and Philip IV of Spain. France got Sundgau on the eastern edge of France and cut off the Spanish access to the Netherlands from Austria.

Now in Asia, the Philippines was less known as the Spanish colony but was more famous for an international trade center run by the Chinese and the Japanese. The British, the French, and the Dutch had occupied about half of the Spain's possessions in the Caribbean. The British colonialization in the Spanish territories of the Caribbean was led by George Donne. By the middle of the seventeenth century, the British[30] had captured the Spanish territories and established their settlements in the islands of St. Kitts, Barbados, Nevis, Antigua, Montserrat, and Jamaica. However, a small part of Kitts was captured by the French. The islands of Kitts and Nevis produced tobacco, ginger, and indigo dye and sugarcane. The windmills were installed in Nevis which were used to extract the juice from the sugarcane. In the later part of the seventeenth century, the Spanish recognized the British colonies in the Caribbean on the promise that there would be no pirate attacks on the Spanish interests.

During the seventeenth century, the French captured and colonialized the territories of Martinique, Guadeloupe, and Santo Domingo.[31] During the period 1630 through 1640, the Dutch captured and colonialized St. Eustace and Curacao. The Dutch also took St. Thomas in 1672. The entry of the British, the French, and the Dutch in the Caribbean led to a change in its landscape. The Atlantic trade in slaves was controlled by the Dutch. The invasions of the British and the French of the Caribbean territories compelled the onetime great Spanish Empire to limit to a small part of the Caribbean such as St. Augustine and Pensacola. The Spanish control became weak as there was no defense of the ports.

The French cardinal Mazarin suggested to Spain to hand over the Spanish Netherlands (the Flanders) to France in exchange for the Catalonian provinces which had become a part of France under the treaty of Pyrenees. This suggestion shocked the Dutch, who smelled the expansion designs of France and strongly opposed it. For their survival, the Dutch wanted to maintain the control of the Flanders as a barrier to the French expansion move. In order to win Spain, the Dutch provided naval supports to Spain both in the Atlantic and in the Mediterranean. The Dutch expanded their trade in the Mediterranean and carried the Spanish wool to Northern Europe, and, also provided money to Spain to finance the Caribbean slave trade.

In 1670, Spain allowed the Dutch to garrison their army in the fortresses on the border between Spain, the Netherlands, and France. The Flanders' troops were placed under the prince of Orange, who led the joint Dutch-Spanish forces against France. Similarly, the Spanish navy was placed under the Dutch admiral De Ruyter. Dutch made a lot of investment in Spain. All the foreigners were in favor of having the Caribbean territories under the control of Spain because in this scenario it was easy for them to exploit the wealth of the territories to their benefits.

Portugal, on one hand, through its military campaigns, was eroding the Spanish territories in the western world and on the other hand was benefiting from the Spanish trade. The French exports to Castile, Valencia, and Aragon tremendously increased. The Spanish trade was controlled by the British, Dutch, and French traders who captured most of the Spanish silver that came from the Spanish colonies. Ninety-five percent of the goods traded with the Caribbean were non-Spanish.

The 30 years of military campaigns had impacted the Spanish economy despite the fact that the Portuguese wars had ended in 1668. Harvest failures during 1676 through 1679 resulted in famine and food prices increased, followed by the floods and drought during the period 1680 through 1683, and the locust attack in Catalonia wreaked a disaster which led to the peasants' revolt. The worst was not over yet when a plague erupted in Cartagena, from 1676 through 1682,[32] and reached Spain. During the period 1683–5, half a million people perished due to the outbreak of typhus and other disasters.

Due to increase in birth rate, Spain attained the population level of the sixteenth century. Spain remained an economic backwater. The copper coin was devalued by 50% in 1652, 150% in 1664, and 275% in 1680. Now the consumers needed more coins to buy the same amount of goods. The government reduced the devaluation of copper by 75% in 1680 and by another 75% in 1686. During this period, the manufacturers made good profits. Foreign and local industrialists were granted tax holidays for establishing new industries. During the period 1670 through 1700 the average import of bullion increased to 8 million pesos per year. But most of bullion either did not enter or did not stay with Spain but went to foreign traders of France, England, and the Netherlands. The discovery of new land by Spain in fact benefited the foreign countries who made investments in trading activities.

The impact of four voyages of Christopher Columbus on Spain and the rest of Europe was tremendous in that it had not only discovered the new world, but it had also transformed the new continent by killing the millions of natives and their culture through imposition of the European culture and traditions via the settlement of the millions of the Europeans and making the territories their colonies and then extended this pattern throughout the world. The economic impact was even bigger than the Europeans' expectations. It provided an opportunity to Spain first and then to the rest of Europe to go beyond their borders to dominate and plunder the richness of the Caribbean islands in the form of plants, timber, food, gold, silver, other precious metals, stones, and slaves' trade. The pillage of the Caribbean richness helped Spain and the rest of the Europeans to establish themselves as powerful nations through the development of affluent economies. Later, these powerful nations extended the model of the pillage of Caribbean richness to Asia, Africa, and the Middle East and became their imperial masters for centuries. Peru remained a part of the Spanish Empire until it became an independent country in 1821. In 1898, the last remnants of the Spanish possessions, Cuba, Puerto Rico, and the Philippines, fell to the United States.[33]

Notes

1 Kamen, "Spain, 1469–1714, A Society of Conflict", p. 47.
2 Jayne, p. 30.
3 Sale, "Christopher Columbus and the Conquest of Paradise", p. 8. *Pinta* derived from the Pinto family who owned the ship, meaning "painted one"; *Santa Clara* but called *Nina* after her owner Juan Nino of nearby Monguer, meaning "little girl"; *La Gallega*, meaning she was built in Galicia but her nickname was Marigalante meaning "Dirty Mary" officially known as Santa Maria.
4 Smith, "The Wealth of Nation", p. 604.
5 Sale, "Christopher Columbus and the Conquest of Paradise", p. 66.
6 Ibid., p. 150.
7 Ibid., p. 155.
8 Ibid., p. 144.
9 Smith, "The Wealth of Nations", p. 616.
10 Sale, p. 185.
11 Kamen, "Spain, 1469–1714, A Society of Conflict", p. 52.
12 Ibid., p. 53.
13 Harari, "Sapiens, A Brief History of Humankind", pp. 213, 325–330.

14 Kamen, p. 86.
15 Ibid., p. 64.
16 Ibid., p. 95.
17 Sale, p. 259.
18 Kamen, "Spain, 1469–1714, A Society of Conflict", p. 83.
19 Harari, "Sapiens, A Brief History of Humankind", p. 206.
20 Kamen, p. 97.
21 Ibid., pp. 273–274.
22 Ibid., p. 114.
23 Ibid., p. 147.
24 Hopkins, "Spanish Journeys, A Portrait of Spain", p. 83.
25 Ibid., p. 86.
26 Kamen, "Spain, 1469–1714, A Society of Conflict", p. 120.
27 Ibid., p. 155.
28 Ibid., p. 156.
29 Ibid., p. 189.
30 Ibid., p. 266.
31 Ibid., p. 266.
32 Ibid., p. 268.
33 Ibid., p. 283.

Bibliography

Harari, Yuval Noah, *Sapiens: A Brief History of Humankind*, Vintage Books, 20 Vauxhall Bridge Road, London, UK, 2011.

Hopkins, Adam, *Spanish Journeys, A Portrait of Spain*, Published in Penguin Books, 27 Wrights Lane, London, UK, 1993.

Jayne, K.G., *Vasco Da Gama and his Successors (1460–1580)*, Methuen & Co. Ltd., 36 Essex Street, W.C. London, UK, 1910.

Kamen, Henry, *SPAIN, 1469–1714, A Society of Conflict*, Fourth Edition, Routledge, 2 Park Square, Milton Park, Abingdon, Oxon, UK, 2014.

Sale, Kirkpatrick, *Christopher Columbus and the Conquest of Paradise*, Tauris Parke, London, UK, 2006.

Smith, Adam, *The Wealth of Nations (Modern Library Edition)*, Random House, Inc., New York, USA, 1994.

3
THE PORTUGUESE DISCOVERIES AND COLONIALIZATION

In 1038, the autonomy of Portugal as a province was recognized by Fernando the Great of the Navarrese dynasty. In the last years of the eleventh century,[1] the county of Portugal was created by Burgundian Henry by detaching it from the kingdom of Leon, writes Livermore. The territories of modern-day Portugal and Castile were a part of the kingdom of Leon. Portugal was a tributary state of the kingdom of Leon which later became a part of Castile. The king of Leon, Alfonso-VI, had granted the county of Portugal to Henry, a Burgundian, who had successfully defended the territory against the Muslims' invasion during the eleventh and the early twelfth centuries. After the death of Queen Constanza, Alfonso-VI married a Muslim girl named Zaida, the daughter of the Muslim amir of Sevilla. From Zaida, Alfonso-VI had a son named Sancho. After the death of Count Henry, his son named Afonso Henriques proclaimed himself as the prince of Portugal in 1128 after defeating the forces of his mother Teresa at the battle of São Mamede near Guimarãis. Teresa was captured and expelled from Portugal. Leon recognized Portugal as an independent country in 1143 under the treaty of Zamora. Afonso stretched his territories beyond the Tagus River, captured Lisbon and Santarém in 1147, with the help of Northern Europe, annexed Beja in 1162[2] and Evora in 1166.[3] On May 23, 1179, Afonso became the king of Portugal[4] recognized by Pope Alexander III. Afonso died on December 6, 1185, after a sway of 57 years and was succeeded by Sancho I. The Burgundy dynasty continued swaying Portugal until the death of Fernando on October 22, 1383, writes Livermore.[5] On April 6, 1385, John of Avis became the king. King John defeated the Castile's forces at the battle of Aljubarrota which assured the independence of Portugal from Castile. This was not possible without the Anglo-Portuguese alliance[6] under the Treaty of Windsor of May 9, 1386.

Later in the middle of 1415, King John decided to attack the North African port of Ceuta. To conceal the armament, a devious stratagem was developed

DOI: 10.4324/9781003377719-4

through which a fake war on the Duke of Holland was announced so that the Berbers of Ceuta were not alerted. Queen Philippa died of plague, and after her death, the fleet left the Tagus River on July 25, 1415,[7] accompanied by John and two princes, Pedro and Henry the Navigator. Ceuta, the African Gibraltar, was captured by the Berber Muslims and became the Portuguese's first colony and garrison. The conquest of Ceuta opened the way for the Portuguese to gain control over the oceans, expand trade and economic activities and maintain hegemony overseas through colonialization. The motive of Prince Henry's maritime exploration was, inter alia, religious. Prince Henry was concerned more with the success of the Cross and the halt of Islam than any other business or territorial concerns.

Prince Henry had very famous navigators, including Antonio da Nola of Genoa and Venetian Cadamosto. According to Livermore, the motives[8] of Henry the Navigator were to: (1) explore the African coast beyond the Canaries and a cape called Bojador; (2) find whether or not there were Christian peoples in Africa with whom it might be possible to trade; (3) find how far the territories of the Moors distended and to know their power; (4) to see if it was possible to find a Christian kingdom who may help us in the war; and (5) extend the holy faith of Jesus Christ and bring into it all souls that wished to find salvation. All of these motives encompassed the aspects of discovery, economic, military, political, and religion, which were in the mind of Prince Henry. The dominant thing in Henry's mind was the destruction of Islam in Africa. The pilgrimage route to Palestine was important from the reconquest point of view. The ships were developed in Lisbon for crusade purposes.

During the fourteenth and fifteenth centuries, the Venetians' trade in spices and other eastern goods with Egypt was very profitable when sold to the European countries. The Venetians purchased spices at low prices from Egypt under the Mamluks and distributed them among the European countries at higher prices making considerable profits as these commodities were not available in Europe. The Mamluks were the enemies of the Turks and the Venetians also despised the Turks and thus the interests of the Egyptians and Venetians coincided which led to the establishment of business relations and the Venetians got the monopoly of trade. The huge profits by the Venetians were envied by the Portuguese. During the fifteenth century, the Portuguese were looking for a way, either through sea or through land, to the countries from where the Moors had brought the ivory and gold into Al-Andalus. The Portuguese had been watching with great enthusiasm the utility of Venetians' trade.

In those days the trade routes between India and Europe were in the control of the Muslims. One of these routes was up to the Persian Gulf to Basra and then via land to Aleppo in Syria and the ports of Levant. Another route was from Kandahar and Central Asia to Constantinople, Turkey. But the main direct route was by sea to Aden and also to the port of Alexandria, Egypt, writes Dunbar.[9] Aden Gulf links the Red Sea, the Arabian Sea, and the Indian Ocean and had been an ancient trade center. The Europeans depended on the Muslims who monopolized the trade in the east. The Mamluk Sultans of Egypt received an enormous amount of revenue through custom duties. This trade also benefited Venice and the south German cities who were acting as the distributing channels.

During the fifteenth century, the Portuguese discovered the islands of Canaries (1424), Madeira (1420), and Azores (1432), the archipelago in the North Atlantic Ocean and the Cape de Verd islands, off the northwest coast of Africa. Cape de Verd islands discovered by Cadamosto in 1456 with its capital at Praia remained Portugal's colony ruled by the first king Afonso until its independence in 1975. The Guinea region of the coast of West Africa, where ivory, gold, and black pepper were traded, was contested by the Castalian armada of 35 ships and the Portuguese ships. The battle of Guinea was the first colonial battle in the water off Elmina in the south coast of Ghana to gain exclusive control over the lucrative trade of ivory, gold, black peppers, and slaves. The Portuguese prevailed over the Castilians. Almina became the Portuguese headquarters in the West Africa colony which was used for further occupation of the territories in West Africa and capture of commercial opportunities. The main interest of the Portuguese was to discover, collect, and ship gold to Lisbon. After Portugal, the Dutch, the French, and the British also plunged into the valley of opportunities of trade in gold, ivory, and slaves in Africa.

Prince Henry asked King Duarte to attack Morocco. King Duarte first resisted and then procrastinated. The queen convinced King Duarte, and finally the arrangements were made and the expedition started in August 1437. The Muslims cut off the Portuguese from their ships, and Prince Fernando with his men was captured. This was a big setback for the Portuguese. Negotiations for the release of Prince Fernando started. The Muslims took the position that the release of Prince Fernando would only be possible in exchange for Ceuta. Prince Henry accepted the demand of the Muslims to surrender Ceuta in exchange for his brother prince Fernando. When the news arrived in Portugal, King Duarte decided that the town of Ceuta could not be given back to the Muslims without the approval of the pope. Prince Henry returned to Portugal and suggested that the money should be used in exchange for the release of Fernando or another attack on Tangier should be organized. The possibility of attack was ruled out due to the fact that Fernando was now moved to the city of Fez in Morocco. Fernando languished in Fez and died there in June 1445. King Duarte became a victim of the plague and died in Tomar on September 9, 1438. Afonso V became the king. After the disaster of Tangier in 1437, no offensive was carried out against Morocco.

Prince Henry died in 1460, and King Afonso V had to carry on that role. In 1471, problems arose in the Merinid dynasty in Fez. Afonso V saw in it an opportunity. Afonso V arranged a big expedition of 30,000 men for Africa. He captured the town of Arzila and to his surprise, Tangier was vacated by the Muslims and Portugal got a stronghold on the North African coast. The weak Fez ruler recognized the Portuguese possession down to the River Lukkus. Afonso V took the title of King of Portugal and beyond the sea in Africa. The Portuguese passed through the delta of Niger and reached Cape Catherine and then traveled across the entire Gulf of Guinea. Afonso abdicated his power in 1481 in favor of John II.

Now John II decided to establish a Christian empire on the mainland of West Africa. Under John's order, Diogo d' Azambuja discovered and established a fortified factory in 1482 at Sao Jorge da Mina, "St George of the Mine", which was the central part of the precious ores of the Gold Coast. Black men with frizzled hair came on board and traded ivory for cloth. At the same time Diogo Cao discovered the Zaire River that watered the kingdom of Congo. He continued his voyage as far as Cape St. Mary (Cape Cross). There he erected another padrão and returned to Lisbon in April 1484. He again returned to Congo and presented gifts to the king and asked him to abandon idolatry and embrace the true religion. Missionaries were introduced, and churches were built. Cao from Congo reached Cape Cross. After the discovery of Congo, his ships returned home before August 1487. Cao died at sea off Cape Cross in 1486.

After the death of King John II, Manuel I, cousin and brother-in-law of John II, became the king of Portugal on October 25, 1495. In December 1496, King Manuel issued an order of expulsion of all the Jews and the Moors who were reluctant to baptize. While Portuguese discoveries had spread abroad, Lisbon became the resort of international adventurers from all parts of Europe, especially from Italy, Flanders, and England. A diverse crowd of businessmen dealing in slaves, goldsmiths, spice merchants, and shipbuilders gathered at the waterside when the royal ships were arriving. To all of them Lisbon provided an opportunity of fortune and fame. King Manuel was interested in the expeditions abroad in search of wealth and the spread of Christianity. Based on the early expeditions by Cao, King Manuel wanted the exploration of the east. The king offered this opportunity to Vasco's elder brother, Paulo da Gama, who expressed his inability due to ill health.

Vasco da Gama, born around 1460 in the town of Sines on the Alentejo coast of Portugal, was chosen for the Indian voyage at the age of 36 years. Early in the summer of 1497, King Manuel called him at Montemor-o-Novo near Evora where he took the oath of fealty and was given the standard with the Cross of the Order of Christ. After the oath, Vasco da Gama returned to Lisbon to take command of four ships which were already anchored in the Tagus River. Two sister ships of 100 or 120 tons, the *Sao Raphael* and *Sao Gabriel*, were built by Bartolomeu Dias, especially for this voyage.

Vasco da Gama chose *Sao Gabriel* as his flagship, while *Sao Raphael* was captained by his brother Paulo da Gama. Diogo Dias, a brother of Bartholomeu, served as a clerk. The total number of men aboard was about 170; some of them were convicts who were taken along to perform any dirty job needed. The chief captain was Pedro de Alemquer who had already steered Bartolomeu's flagship. Gama, Dias, and other technical advisors finalized the arrangements for storage of supplies for three years; technical equipment and training of the crews, books including the *Book of Marco Polo*, and the voyage reports of the Portuguese explorers who had been sent to Asia, maps, and charts. The daily rations of Vasco da Gama's 170 crews in the voyage of 1497–99 comprised 1-1/2 pounds of biscuit, 1 pound of beef or half a pound of pork, 2-1/2 pints of water, 1-1/4 pints of wine, and smaller quantities of oil and vinegar. On fast days, half a pound of rice, dried stock fish, or cheese was served out instead of meat; and the victuals were to last three years, also included flour, lentils, sardines, plums, almonds, garlic, mustard, salt, sugar, and honey, writes Jayne.[10] A lavish expedition. Before departure, Gama lectured his crews to get the skills of carpenters, rope-makers, blacksmiths, caulkers, and plank-makers, and he gave them a stipend of two cruzados a month beyond their monthly payment of five cruzados. Gama bought them the tools which they took along.

After completion of the arrangements, the royal standard was hoisted on top of the *Sao Gabriel* ship led by Vasco da Gama and the captain's red pennant fluttered above its crow's-nest. The four ships, commanded by Vasco da Gama and accompanied by Bartolomeu Diaz, left the Restelo, Lisbon,[11] on July 8, 1497. Gama took his own ship *São Gabriel*, his brother Paulo led *São Rafael*, Nicolau Coelho commanded *Bérrio*, and the fourth was a supply ship carrying victuals and crews mostly convicts. They arrived at the Cape of Good Hope on July 27, 1497, and Dias accompanied the fleet up to this point. Dias was not the first one to discover the Cape of Good Hope in 1488 as it was earlier discovered by an Arab navigator, Ahmad Ibn Majid, in 1450 while sailing westward and to the west coast of Africa, writes Ghazanfar.[12] Gama left the Cape of Good Hope on August 3, 1497. Cape is a point where Benguela, the cold water of the eastern part of the South Atlantic Ocean, meets Agulhas, the warm water of the Indian Ocean. This meeting point is within the 1.5-kilometer range of the Cape of Good Hope. The Portuguese also crossed this point to reach out the Far East for trade. This point is simply called Cape.

After spending 96 days in the South Atlantic, the fleet, on November 7, 1497, anchored at Angra de Santa Helena Bay in South Africa, some 30 leagues short of Cape. The fleet had sailed for 4,500 miles without sight of the land. At Helena Bay, Gama obtained additional victuals to make up for the consumption. On seeing the Portuguese, the natives attacked them with stones and arrows and a fish-spear struck Gama in the leg. Gama was wounded. Vasco da Gama resumed his voyage on November 16. A few days later on November 25, they found and anchored at the Angra de Sao Braz-the Bahia dos Vaqueiros of Dias (Dias' Bay of the Cowheads), the Mossel Bay in South Africa. Here Gama was welcomed. He traded some red caps and small round bells for ivory armlets and bought a black ox for food. On December 8, Gama sailed again and by December 16 passed the Rio de Infante, now Great Fish River. Later, Gama reached the shore, where he was received by the Bantu people living between Central and South Africa. The Bantu people provided Gama a sufficient amount of water.

On January 16, 1498, Gama continued his voyage and reached Cape Corrents in Mozambique. On January 24, 1498, Gama anchored in the mouth of the Kiliman or Quilimane River and called it the Rio dos Bons Signaes or River of the Good Tokens because here he had observed some signs of civilization.

Gama spent 32 days from January 24 to February 24 replenishing his supplies, cleaning the ships, and doing some repair work. On March 2, Gama with three ships, as the fourth ship of supplies had already been destroyed, arrived at the actual port of Mozambique. Here Gama saw the vessels of the Arabs laden with gold, silver, cloves, pepper, ginger, and quantities of rubies, pearls, and other precious gems.

On March 13, the fleet left Mozambique and on April 13, arrived at Malindi, Mombasa, now Kenya. The ruler of Malindi gave a pilot to Gama who could guide him to Calicut in India. On April 24, the fleet sailed again under the guidance of a Gujarati pilot named Cana, steering in the east-north-east across the Arabian Sea to reach Calicut on the Malabar Coast of India. Here, Gama found that the sultans of the regions were making enormous profits from the trade in gold, ivory, and slaves. Malindi and Portugal entered into a peace agreement.

On Friday, May 18, the guest pilot ordered to move toward the east and watch for the land. On May 21, after a journey of ten months and two weeks from Tagus, the fleet anchored off Calicut in Kerala on the southwestern coast of India. The sea route between the East and the West had been discovered. Gama ordered one of the convicts, Joao Nunes, a Jew, to go on shore and get information. He reached the house of two Moors from Oran. They asked him sapid questions, "The devil take you! What has brought you hither?" writes Jayne.[13] Joao was surprised with this greeting and answered their question that he came with a Portuguese armada, looking for the Christians and the spices. Calicut was called the "city of spices" where Gama was received by the local rajas and thus inaugurated the sea route to Asia, writes Sale,[14] and linked Europe to Asia by creating access to the Indian spice routes that thrived the economy of Portugal. Portugal became the richest country in Europe, in terms of money. Before this, Portugal was behind Spain. The main spices that reached European markets were pepper and cinnamon. Portugal maintained a monopoly in trade with Asia for several decades which was protected by the armed forces which had set up fortified coastal bases. Calicut, a free port, was a big trading center ruled by a Hindu ruler, where traders brought goods from different foreign countries. The Hindu ruler, Samuri, decided to receive the foreigners with respect. Due to bad weather caused by excessive rains, Gama was not willing to leave the ships inside the harbor. Samuri sent one of his pilots to guide them to a safe berth near Pandarani Kollam, 15 miles in the north. He also granted an audience to foreigners. Gama landed with his 13 companions and went to Calicut. On the way he was taken to a building thought to be a church with a small image which they thought as a figure of the Virgin Mary. The Portuguese knelt in prayer while the Hindus prostrated. The person who administered the so-called church sprinkled holy water on the guests and gave them some dust to sprinkle on their forehead. The Portuguese did not know what type of the dust was. It was a mixture of dust and cow-dung.

At Calicut, Kerala, Gama and his men were escorted by the natives to the royal palace. After listening to Gama's details of the honorable King Manuel, Samuri welcomed the ambassador. Next day, King Manuel's gifts were to be presented to Samuri. The gifts presented to Samuri were not appropriate for him as these included ordinary things like wash-basins and casks of oil. Samuri and his attendants smirked at seeing the gifts and asked them to just give them gold or nothing. Gama tried to save his embarrassment by saying that these gifts are from him and not from the king. On June 2, Gama started his journey back to Pandarani. The Portuguese unloaded some of their stuff to be sold in the market, and the Muslim traders ridiculed them. Finally, Samuri helped them in selling their stuff. From the last week of June through the middle of August, the fleet remained off Pandarani. Gama now sent Diogo Dias with some gifts to Samuri to inform him that they were leaving for Portugal and ask him for a consignment of spices for King Manuel.

Samuri then informed them that before leaving, the Portuguese must pay the custom duties on the goods that landed here. This amounted to 600 xerafins, equivalent to 600 rupees. The goods were in the warehouse of Calicut. The Portuguese guards in the warehouse will be kept as captives until the duty was paid. Gama retaliated by making the Hindus as captives who had come to his ships. Gama wanted to exchange one Hindu captive for one Portuguese captive. Gama received a letter from Samuri to King Manuel. The letter, according to Jayne, said that "Vasco da Gama, a gentleman of your household came to my country, whereat I was much pleased. My country is rich in cinnamon, cloves, ginger, pepper and precious stones. That which I ask of you in exchange is gold, silver, corals and scarlet cloth".[15]

Now the hostages were exchanged one for one, and still a few Hindus were left with Gama. In order to develop good relations with Samuri, Gama released all the captive Hindus. A part of the Portuguese goods was restored while the rest was kept as payment of custom duties. Gama was happy that he had discovered India with its spices and precious stones. On August 29, the Portuguese sailed homeward. The weather over the Arabian Sea was not good, and the voyage was delayed. During this stopover, a scurvy disease erupted that took the life of 30 men. Only six or seven sailors per vessel left. On January 7, the fleet again anchored at Malindi. By now many of the crews died. Due to a lack of attendants, the *Sao Raphael* was abandoned and burnt near Mozambique. Two ships, *Sao Gabriel* and *Berrio*, survived and reached Good Hope on March 20, 1499. Now the group split. Nicolau Coelho took *Berrio* and reached Lisbon on July 10, 1499. Gama using his flagship steered for the Azores, and his brother Paulo da Gama died on the island of Terceira. Gama reached Lisbon on September 18, 1499. The first voyage of Vasco da Game was over, and it took 2 years and 2 months, and only 50 of 170 crews survived. Gama's ship was loaded with pepper, cloves, cinnamon, and precious stones. Now Portugal was the only country which was the master of the sea route from Europe to India. Gama did what Christopher Columbus could not do, and he was the first one to explore India, while Marco Polo ended his voyage at the state of Kublai Khan in China. With the discovery of the new lands in the east by Gama, King Manuel sought the pope's confirmation of his authority over the new lands.

After the return of Vasco da Gama from his first voyage of discovery of the sea route to India, King Manuel now thought about how Portugal could make the best use of this advantageous opportunity. King Manuel now wrote to Ferdinand and Isabella that the Christians in this region are weak in faith due to a lack of understanding of Christianity. "By strengthening the Christians in the region, we can divert the benefits of trade currently enjoyed by the Muslims towards Europe. Our policy is now based on the principles of friendship with the Christians and war with the Muslims in the region."

In March 1500, Pedro Alvares Cabral left Lisbon with 13 strongly armed ships. The crew on board included gunners, Franciscan friars, and merchants who will do trading in the name of the King. Cabral was accompanied by Bartolomeu Dias, who had to establish a factory in Sofala. Nicolau Coelho, Bortolomeu's brother Diogo, Duarte Pacheco Pereira, and a total of 1,200 men were on board.[16] The victuals for 18 months were also on board. On April 22, 1500, the fleet of Pedro reached South America and discovered a new land which they called Terra da Santa Cruz or Vera Cruz, which later became Brazil. They captured it for the kingdom of Portugal, and this was the first and beginning of Portuguese colonialization in South America and Asia. In Brazil, neither gold nor silver mines were found, and a little revenue occurred for the crown. At that time Portugal was a dominion of Spain and the Dutch attacked Brazil and got possession of seven out of its fourteen provinces. The Portuguese with the connivance of Spain drove the Dutch out of Brazil. The colony had more than 600,000 people either Portuguese or their descendants and a mixed race between the Portuguese and the Brazilians. Brazil was the biggest colony in South America which remained under Portuguese rule from the sixteenth to nineteenth centuries until it became an independent Brazilian republic in 1889.

After Brazil, Pedro Cabral sailed again to reunite with his scattered armada. Only six ships reached Sofala, Mozambique in the month of July, and on September 13, 1500, the ships anchored off Calicut. Samuri gave Cabral an audience and allowed him to establish the first-ever factory in India. But the Muslim traders, competitors of the Portuguese, immediately protested, resulting in a riot and the Muslims attacked the factory and killed all those present in the factory. Cabral retaliated, destroyed, and burnt the city. Pedro Cabral sailed to the nearer Malabar port of Cochin, where the Hindu raja allowed the establishment of a second factory. Now Cochin in Kerala state on the West Indian coast became the headquarters of the Portuguese in India. After Cochin, Pedro Cabral visited Cananor (Kannur) district in Kerala state at the invitation of the Hindu rani and got a big consignment of pepper for the homeward journey. Cabral left India in January 1501 and took along ambassadors of the kings of Cochin and Cananor and left a group of the Portuguese to run the factory. Diplomatic relations were now well established between the kingdoms of Portugal and India. Cabral arrived in Lisbon on July 31, 1501. The traffic of spices was diverted from the old routes and carried by the Portuguese around the Cape to Europe. Pepper consignment turned out to be a profitable venture after covering the cost of sea transportation. The Eastern trade changed the economic life of Cadiz, Corunna, Lisbon, Antwerp, Dieppe, and Bristol.

After Pedro Cabral's return, a large fleet of 15 ships was put under the command of Vasco da Gama, followed by another fleet of five ships led by his cousin. Gama sailed from Tagus on February 10, 1502.[17] Pedro Cabral had left behind a Portuguese squadron led by Sancho de Toar to cruise in the water along the coast of East Africa in search of a trade prospect. The commander Sancho had already visited Sofala in Mozambique and met and established good relations with Amir Isuf. Gama touched the same port in Mozambique and then turned to the north to Kilwa in Tanzania. The Amir Ibrahim of Tanzania, who was neither willing to convert to Christianity nor willing to compromise on his share in the Sofala gold trade on the dictation of a stranger, was despised by the Portuguese. Vasco da Gama threatened the defying Amir Ibrahim that he would burn the town if he does not become a vassal of King Manuel and pay the tribute. Ibrahim finally accepted the authority of the foreigner and offered a rich man named Muhammad Ankoni as security for the tribute. Muhammad paid 2,000 mithkals or gold coins (£1041), which Gama accepted. On Gama's departure, Samuri invaded Cochin and drove out its ruler who was a vassal of the Portuguese king and the Portuguese working in the factories took refuge on the island of Valpi from where they were later rescued by Francisco Albuquerque in 1503, writes Livermore.[18] The ruler of the Cochin was restored as a vassal of King Manuel. Duarte Pacheo with 160 Portuguese defended Cochin against any threat from Samuri. Duarte Pacheo also defended the factory at Quilon against the Muslims' attacks. In September, a fleet of 13 ships led by the commander Lopo Soares arrived. At the time of the return of the fleet, five ships with 500 men stayed behind to safeguard the Portuguese factories.

On October 1, 1502, according to Jayne, Gama overtook a dhow named *Meri*,[19] near the Malabar Coast in southwest India between Karnataka and Kerala states, which was carrying 380 Muslim pilgrims from Mecca. The pilgrims included men, women, and children along with their wealth. The Muslims of *Meri* resisted. The despicable behemoth pirate and murderer Gama fired at the *Meri* which started burning. The women carrying their babies complained which went unheard. The Portuguese plundered 12,000 ducats and goods worth another 10,000 ducats. The ship and all the people on board were burnt. That was the first prize of the pirate and murderer Gama.

After burning the ship and people and the plunder of wealth, Gama moved forward and anchored off Calicut on October 30. Now Samuri sent messages to Gama for the establishment of good relations, but Gama rejected his offer. Gama asked Samuri to ban the presence of Muslims in Calicut. To show his seriousness, Gama captured the vessels at the harbor of Cananor; killed the Muslim traders; cut off their heads, hands, and feet; and tossed them in a boat which was pushed ashore with a written message in Arabic. Calicut was bombarded and then Gama moved to Cochin, Cananor, and other ports for loading spices. After spreading blood and ashes in India, Gama sailed back home and arrived in

Lisbon on September 1, 1503. Unfortunately, Europe did not regret the blood of the Muslims and ashes of the *Meri*. Gama left behind four ships in India to guard the factories in Cochin and Cananor and keep an eye on the Strait of Bab el-Mandeb to intercept the Muslims' vessels carrying merchants and pilgrims. After his second voyage, Gama retired from public service.

Under King Manuel, from 1506 to 1514, a chain of fortresses was built in Morocco which included: Santa Cruz on Cape Guer near Agadir built by a merchant named Jollo Lopes de Sequeora in 1506, later taken by the crown; the Royal Castle at Mogador built by Diogo de Azambuja in 1506; Safi occupied in 1508; Azemmour taken in 1518; and Mazagan (al-Jadida) founded in 1514. The Portuguese never forgot the crusade against Islam. The Portuguese wanted to establish their empire in Morocco in which they not only failed but even lost their possessions of Agadir, Safi, and Azemmour.

In 1505, D. Francisco de Almeida became the first viceroy of India who sailed from Lisbon in March 1505 and ordered the law wherever the flag of Portugal fluttered. Almeida presented a strategy paper to King Manuel containing the principles about the form of government and commercial interests. The objective was sea power. The policy included no annexation of the territories and the building of no more fortresses than needed for the protection of the Portuguese factories. Since 1505 the viceroy or the governor had been the highest legislative and executive authority in Portuguese India. The term of office was three years.

Almeida had absolute powers in Portuguese India. He had brought 22 ships carrying 2,500 men, including 1,500 soldiers contracted for three years of service in Portuguese India. He built a fort at Kilwa and burnt Bombasa. In India he crowned the ruler of Cochin with a gold crown and built a fort in the city. Without Almeida's license, no Eastern ship was to anchor. This move destroyed the Muslim trade. The Muslims diverted their trade in spices to Malacca and Sunda Islands by sailing through Ceylon or Maldives directly to the Persian Gulf and the Red Sea. To cut off this route of the Muslims' trade, the Portuguese reached Ceylon.

The sole mission of the Viceroyalty of India was to secure for King Manuel the monopoly of the Indian and East African products to Europe. In the Indian waters, the trade was exclusively carried out by the Muslim Arabs, the Persians, the Turks, and the Egyptians. In line with King Manuel's policy of war with the Muslims, Almeida's plan was to eliminate the Muslims from the seas and replace them with Portuguese traders and divert the Indian trade route to the Cape. To have control over the land, alliances were to be made with the local Hindu rajas, who would supply the consignments and guard the factories in return for the Portuguese' naval protection. King Manuel's policy of friendship with the Christians and the war with the Muslims was in effect. Almeida found a counselor in the form of a big pirate named Timoja who commanded single-masted small ships. Timoja used to pirate the Muslim traders for raja of Honawar (a tributary to Vijayanagar).

Timoja had advised the viceroy to reconcile with the Hindu empire of Vijayanagar which was stretched throughout the Indian peninsula in the south of the rivers of Krishna and Tungabhadra. When the Muslims captured northern India, Vijayanagar was the only force to fight for Hinduism. It had a large fighting force possessed numerous resources. When the Portuguese were settling in India, Vijayanagar confronted the Muslims and captured their forces, which otherwise would have driven the Portuguese to the sea. Almeida thought the cooperation of Vijayanagar was vital for the Portuguese to drive out the Muslims.

In order to control the Red Sea, Tristao da Cunha, with a fleet of 15 ships, after exploring the coast of Madagascar and the mainland of East Africa, seized Socotra islands on the major shipping route. After the capture of Socotra, Cunha went straight to India and Affonso De Albuquerque took a different route. Albuquerque destroyed the cities of the Oman coast. Those cities which resisted were captured and plundered. On September 25, 1507, six Portuguese ships appeared off Hormuz in the Persian Gulf. There were about 200 ships at the harbor. Albuquerque demanded tribute, and after three days of negotiations, Albuquerque attacked the ships and bombarded the city until the regent agreed to pay a tribute of 15,000 gold xerafins a year and would also contribute to the construction of the Portuguese fort. The Portuguese crews took part in the construction of the fort and were fed up with the hot weather. Secretly, three Portuguese ships disappeared overnight and Albuquerque was compelled to return to India.

With the presence of the Portuguese, Egypt, and Turkey were not willing to lose their Indian trade. The Mamluk sultan of Egypt challenged the Portuguese. In 1508, an Egyptian fleet commanded by Mir Hussain left Suez for India. The Portuguese called Mir Hussain as the Admiral of the Grand Soldan of Cairo and Babylonia, writes Jayne.[20] Mir Hussain defeated a small Portuguese ship off Chaul, which does not exist now, and the viceroy's only son D. Lourenco de Almeida was killed in the fight. Lourenco's ship was captured by the Muslims. However, the escorting Portuguese ships escaped and reported the incident to the viceroy. By the time Almeida collected 19 ships with 1,600 men, the Egyptian fleet entered the Indian Ocean and reached Diu and made it its base and was reinforced by Samuri of Calicut. On February 2, 1509, a severe naval battle took place off Diu. The Muslim warriors gave their best but their ships sunk due to heavy artillery firing, and by the end of the day the Portuguese prevailed and maintained their hegemony in the Indian Ocean.

Now Almeida's term as Viceroy was over and his successor Affonso de Albuquerque was ready in Cochin to take charge from him. But the Portuguese in India conspired against Albuquerque and asked Almeida not to give him the charge of viceroy. Later in November 1509, a fleet from Lisbon led by Marshal Fernando do Coutinho, a representative of King Manuel, arrived. The Marshal of Portugal installed Albuquerque in the office of the viceroy and Almeida sailed for Lisbon on December 1, 1509. On his way back, Almeida was killed along with 60 Portuguese by the natives at Table Bay, then known as the Agoada de Saldanha.

Albuquerque's motives of the conquests of Goa, Malacca, Aden, and Hormuz in the region were clear. Albuquerque wanted to occupy Goa as a naval base and a colony; Malacca for its importance as a hub of maritime trade between the Far and the Middle East; Aden, a port city in Yemen; and Hormuz Strait in the Persian Gulf for an opportunity to enter the Red Sea and the Persian Gulf. The conquest of Goa was a step in the direction of the establishment of a Portuguese empire in the east. The occupation of Malacca, Aden, and Hormuz was to result in a commercial dominance and naval supremacy of Portugal in the Indian Ocean and the Arabian Sea and a complete monopoly of the Cape route to Europe. The Portuguese endeavored to manage the exclusive trade with India by claiming the sole right of sailing in Indian waters on the plea of being the first to explore the naval route to India. No other European nation claimed the exclusive right of sailing in the Indian Ocean.

Goa was the first to be captured. The capture of Goa was a beginning point for the Portuguese for transformation of their expedition from having control of the sea to the territorial empire in the east. Goa was a Hindu seaport which, according to Stephens, the Muslim king of Deccan, Muhammad Shah II,[21] had conquered in 1470. After Calicut, Goa was the main seaport for them in Western India. After the death of Muhammad Shah II, Goa fell to the kingdom of Bijapur, ruled by King Yusuf Adil Shah, son of Ottoman sultan Murad II. When Murad died in 1451, his elder son struggled for the throne which compelled Adil Shah to escape to Persia. When Shah was 18 years old, he sailed to India and started his life as a warrior slave and culminated to the king of Bijapur in 1489. Under Shah's sway, Goa prospered. The Goa seaport was built on the island of Tisvadi. Its territory was separated from the main land by two rivers, namely, the Mandavi in the north and Zuari in the south. Both rivers fall into the Arabian Sea. In its east is the Maharashtra state and in the south is Karnataka state.

In early 1510, Albuquerque sailed from Cochin for Hormuz, and at Honawar he was joined by Timoja, who informed him that Adil Shah left Goa by leaving the 4,000[22] Turks and the Persians soldiers under the command of Rasul Khan, who had created havoc and now it was the time to capture Goa. In the middle of February, the Portuguese entered the Mandavi River and then stormed the fortress of Panjim, which is located at the entrance of the harbor. The Hindus remained quiet, and the Muslims were not prepared for a surprise attack by the Portuguese. The Muslims, not finding themselves in a position to defend Goa, peacefully surrendered. The noble citizens met Albuquerque and handed over the keys of Goa. Albuquerque moved to the palace of Adil Shah, and the Hindus considered him their savior. Albuquerque appointed Dom Antonio de Noronha to control the city. This was the first capture of Goa by Albuquerque, but his victory was short-lived as Adil Shah came back on May 17 and compelled Albuquerque to surrender Goa, which he did on May 23, 1510.

The Portuguese fleet marooned for three months at the harbor of Goa due to bad weather. When the weather was good, the Portuguese fleet left Goa on August 15, 1510. Soon Albuquerque saw four squadrons of ships which had just arrived from Portugal under the command of Diogo Mendes de Vasconcellos and this made him happy. Albuquerque now left for Honáwar, where he met Timoja, who was ready with his local galleys. Timoja advised Albuquerque that after the departure of the Portuguese fleet, Yusuf Adil Shah left Goa for Bijapur and the main Muslim army had gone to deal with the insurgents in the neighborhood of Goa. Timoja urged Albuquerque for a second attack on Goa.

The Portuguese fleet of 14 vessels arrived from Portugal. Some were the merchants who were supposed to load spices for the king. The remainder two squadrons were destined for Malacca and the Red Sea which were forcefully taken by Albuquerque in spite of the protests by their commanders. Now Albuquerque had 28 ships and 1,700 Portuguese soldiers, and at Honawar he was joined by Timoja's troops. Albuquerque, on November 24, 1510, arrived in Goa. The island of Tisvadi was garrisoned by 8,000 Persian and Ottoman fighters under Rasul Khan. The Portuguese attacked the city of Goa in three columns, and each of them was successful. The Turks lost 2,000 men and the Portuguese lost 50 men and 150 were wounded. The Portuguese plundered and destroyed the city and killed every Muslim available in the city. Albuquerque did not interfere with the Hindus' culture with the exception of banning of Hindu Sati funeral practice.[23] Albuquerque built a fort and the names of the Portuguese warriors, who fought and took Goa, were inscribed on the wall. Albuquerque appointed Malhár Rao, brother of the raja of Honáwar, as the governor of Goa. The governor agreed to pay an annual tribute of £30,000. Albuquerque left 400 soldiers under the command of Rodigro Rebello with sufficient artillery and ammunition for the defense of the fort.

After securing Goa, Albuquerque on April 20, 1511, sailed with 17 ships for Malacca. On July 1, Albuquerque anchored off Malacca and demanded of the sultan to release the Portuguese prisoners held by him. The prisoners were Siqueira's men left behind. Most of the population was Malaya Muslims while other ethnic groups such as the Chinese, the Javanese, the Gujaratis, the Bengalis, the Burmans from Pegu and Chittagong, the Ceylon cinnamon-dealers, and the Japanese from the Riu-Kiu islands were living there. The port of Malacca was the center of the trade where the ships came from different countries with immense volume and varieties of goods. The sultan refused the surrender of Ruy de Araujo and other prisoners without a peace deal. Albuquerque rejected the sultan's point of view. Albuquerque sent boats to fire at the house, and consequently Araujo and his soldiers were released. Albuquerque now asked for a grant of the land to build a factory. The sultan did not want the hold of the Portuguese in his capital, so he procrastinated on the plea of negotiations. Now Albuquerque wanted to act.

Albuquerque had only 600 Portuguese troops with a small number of local slaves, and the sultan of Malacca had well-equipped 30,000 fighters, including some artillery. On July 25, 1511, the Portuguese attacked the only bridge for some hours until the Malaccans were compelled to retreat. Now Albuquerque secured the cooperation of the Chinese traders to negotiate with Utemuta Raja of the Javanese settlers to be part of the struggle against the sultan of Malacca. The Javanese warriors joined the forces of Albuquerque. After nine nights of bombardment and street fighting, Malacca fell and the sultan of Malacca fled and was pursued into the interior by an army of 400 Portuguese and 600 Javanese. Albuquerque immediately started building up a fort and a factory. He expelled all Malaccan Muslims and appointed Hindu conspirator Ninachetty headman of the Hindus. A Portuguese captain took Sultan's palace. After making administrative arrangements, Albuquerque returned to India and reached Cochin in February 1512.

After securing Goa and Malacca, on 18 February 1513, Albuquerque sailed for Aden with 1,700 Portuguese and 1,000 natives of Malabar in 24 ships. Aden was an important strategic port city in that it allowed entrance to the Red Sea. Albuquerque wanted to capture this city in order to have control over the Red Sea and then strike at the Mamluks of Egypt. When the Portuguese reached near the city, Mir Amrjan, the governor of Aden did not show any tendency to surrender the city. On March 26, Albuquerque decided to attack the city. The Portuguese took the boats laden with ladders. Albuquerque's nephew D. Garcia de Noronha was beckoned to the gate on the right and the two other attacking parties led by Joao Fidalgo and Albuquerque tried at different points of the wall. Noronha's men set the scaling-ladders on the right gate. A soldier named Garcia de Sousa was the first to set the foot on the parapets and shouted, "Victory, Victory, Portugal, Portugal". Joao Fidalgo's men also made to the top of the wall. Albuquerque's men also rushed to join them. Albuquerque ordered that the ladders be supported with halberds. The ladders could not carry the weight of the mounted people and collapsed. This device turned out to be a fatal one as those who fell were wounded.

The Portuguese soldiers were repulsed, and even the retreat became risky. Many jumped from the wall and broke their bones, and others slid down a rope ladder. Garcia de Sousa and his men were left alone in a turret where no reinforcement was possible. Garcia de Sousa told his men, "safe yourself. I want to see my end here". Garcia de Sousa was hit by an arrow that pierced through his brain, and that was his end. The Portuguese dropped back in a state of confusion to their boats, writes Jayne.[24] Considering the threats of the Portuguese, the Egyptian Mamluks also tried to capture Aden but failed. Albuquerque tried to capture Aden a second time, but again failed. For Portuguese Aden remained impregnable and the desire to reach Jedda remained unfulfilled. On July 15, the Portuguese ships returned toward India; 500 Portuguese and all local natives died. From September 1513 to February 1515, Albuquerque remained in India and paid attention to the management of various forts and factories on the Malabar Coast. Finally, Aden fell in 1538 to Sulayman Pasha of the Ottoman Empire. Ottoman rulers thought that the control of Aden was strategically important to control the advance of the Europeans toward the holy cities of Mecca and Medina rather than considering it just as an entrepôt for trade.

After the failed attempts at capturing Aden, Albuquerque now focused on the capture of Hormuz. On February 21, 1515, he sailed with 27 ships and 3,000 men which included 1,500 Portuguese and 600 Malabar archers. Hormuz provided entrance to the Persian Gulf. Abd-ur-Razzak, an envoy from Shah Rukh to the sultan of Vijayanagar, informed that the distant states of China, Pegu (Bago), and Siam sent their wares to Hormuz for trading. The Egyptian and the Persians were busy in trading activities in fur from Moscow, silk from Baghdad, and horses in the market.

In March 1515, Albuquerque reached Hormuz. Rais Nur-ud-Din, a powerful wazir (minister) of King Saif-ud-Din, killed the king by poisoning him and installed the king's 18-year-old brother Turan Shah. Nur-ud-Din was a de facto ruler of Hormuz. When Nur-ud-Din got old, he invited his nephew Rais Ahmad to be part of the government. Rais Ahmad deposed his uncle and imprisoned him. Rais Ahmad had the full support of Ismail Shah of Persia. At the arrival of Albuquerque, Ismail Shah's ambassador Ibrahim Beg was in Hormuz. To secure the support of the Persian king, Rais Ahmad accepted Ismail's "cap and prayer", meaning the Persian suzerainty and the Shia creed.

Albuquerque found Hormuz fortified. King Turan Shah and Rais Nur-ud-Din did not oppose Albuquerque and thought that he could be their ally against the usurper Rais Ahmad. They were of the view that the Portuguese were only interested in trade and tribute and not the occupation of Hormuz. On April 1, King Turan Shah allowed Albuquerque to land his forces and take possession of Hormuz. The Portuguese flag fluttered over the island. King Turan Shah informed Albuquerque that Rais Ahmad had prepared a plan for his murder. Albuquerque sought an audience with the king and the ministers, and there he had Rais Ahmad killed by his soldiers. Turan Shah was terrified that he might be killed. Albuquerque moved forward and congratulated the terrified king on the death of a traitor. King Turan Shah was freed from the yoke of Rais Ahmad and became a Portuguese vassal.

With the murder of Rais Ahmad, the grip of the Portuguese over Hormuz became strong. On May 3, 1515, Albuquerque inaugurated the construction of a Portuguese fort. Many died of fever in hot weather, and Albuquerque himself suffered dysentery. He was now tired and weak. On November 8, he bid farewell to his comrades and sailed for Goa. In the Arabian Sea his ship overtook a small ship carrying freight from India. When the dispatches were opened, Albuquerque learnt that he was to be superseded by Lopo Soares de Albergaria. When Albuquerque's ship arrived in Goa, people were surprised to learn that Albuquerque was dead. The body was placed on a bier covered with a black velvet cloth. His body was carried to the church of Nossa Senhora de Serra in Goa which was founded by Albuquerque himself and was buried there. Albuquerque had built forts of Goa, Calicut, Malacca, and Hormuz and reconstructed the fort of Cananor and Cochin. Shipbuilding industries were started in Portuguese

India, and diplomatic relations were established with Ceylon, Bengal, Burma, Siam, and a number of islands.

King Manuel was saddened by Albuquerque's death and said he would never permit the transfer of his bones from Goa, India, to Portugal. Later John III also followed the same policy. However, in 1566, his bones were transferred from Goa to Portugal with the permission of Queen Catherine. Finally, Albuquerque was buried in the Chapel of Our Lady of Grace at Lisbon. According to Stephens, Albuquerque's desire of seizure of the body of the Holy Prophet from Medina[25] to be used as a ransom for the restoration of Jerusalem remained unfulfilled. King Manuel had earned fortunes by trade and established governments in the occupied territories. He was lucky that in his period, Gama had reached India, Cabral discovered Brazil, Almeida secured command of the Indian seas, and Albuquerque founded an empire in Asia. He used the wealth of the overseas Portuguese empire to secure the hegemony of Europe.

After the death of King Manuel in 1521, his son John III succeeded him as the king of Portugal. In February 1524, in appreciation of Gama's services in the east, King John III appointed him the governor with the title of Viceroy of India. Gama was the second governor who had the privileges of the viceroy. The first viceroy was Francisco de Almeida. Gama left Lisbon in April and arrived in India in September 1524. Gama took the charge from the retiring governor, D. Duarte de Menezes, in Cochin. Gama now suffered from abscesses on the back of his neck, and he was unable to move his head. Gama realized that death was approaching him. Consequently, Gama delegated his authority to Affonso Mexia and Lopo Vaz de Sampayi until a new governor was appointed by the king. After this Gama made his will and prayed that his bones be taken back to Portugal. Gama died on the eve of Christmas in 1524. Gama was laid in his grave wrapped up in silk cloth along with his possessions such as the Knights of Christ, sword in his belt, gilt spurs on his riding boots, and a dark biretta on his head, writes Jayne.[26] Gama ruled Portuguese India for three months.

The Portuguese now reached Guangzhou, also called Canton, an inland port city in the South of Central China and the capital of Guangdong Province. The Portuguese met the emperor who allotted a house to Thome Pires and gave license to Fernao and his men to trade. The ships anchored with a big cargo. Fernao wisely handled the hosts. In August 1519, Fernao's brother Simao arrived and started building a fort and setting up gallows. He also kidnapped the children of the Chinese traders, including boys and girls, and kept them on board as security for debt. Simao tried to escape, but the Portuguese fleet was blocked at Tamao. The emperor was dead, and all the foreigners were ordered to leave the country. The Portuguese refused to do so. At last, most of them fled, some were killed, and some were captured and made prisoners. Thereafter it was ordered that any foreign ship that enters the Chinese ports should be captured and confiscated. Now the Chinese called the Portuguese the men of the devil. Thome was not treated like other ambassadors. In 1524 he died in captivity. All his retinue met the same fate.

Now D. Garcia de Noronha, nephew of Albuquerque, was to sail to India as the viceroy-elect. The viceroy openly declared that he had come to make money, and he even did not hesitate to pocket the salaries of the soldiers who were compelled to get involved in bribery for their living. The Portuguese officers got involved in illegal private trading activities. In 1540, the king of Portugal issued deplorable orders of destruction of all Hindu temples in the territory of Goa. The interference in the religion of Hindus led to hostility by the locals against the Portuguese. Before the completion of his tenure, Garcia de Noronha became ill and died on April 3, 1540, and was succeeded by D. Estevão da Gama, the second son of Vasco da Gama, as the governor of Portuguese India.

In September 1545, Castro became the governor of Portuguese India and remained in this position until June 1548. The Portuguese did not allow any ship to visit any of the ports of Gujarat without paying custom duties at their own fortresses, where if the Portuguese officials, wanted to buy any part of the cargo, they could do so by fixing the price of their choice. The Sultan of Gujarat was not happy. In March 1546, the captain of Diu, D. João Mascarenhas, thought that war now was inevitable. Mascarenhas' apprehension was supported by confirmed identification of the two traitors, namely, Ruy Freire, a Portuguese, and a mulatto named Francisco Rodrigues who had dug a passage to the powder-magazine where they were to explode at the behest of their sponsors.

The island of Diu is in the south of the Kathiawar Peninsula, measuring two miles from the north to the south and seven miles from the east to the west. The city was in the westernmost part, and the Portuguese selected the opposite site for their fortress. On its three sides was the sea and fourth side the land which was linked by the three Portuguese bastions. Mascarenhas' strength was 200 warriors against the 10,000 Gujaratis, the Turks, the Egyptians, and other mercenaries led by Sifr Aga, an Italian deserter. On April 20, Sifr positioned his siege train, and for the next four months the defenders were isolated. Bombardment continued day and night. The walls started breaking down, and then the wives and children came to repair the walls. One of the bastions was blown, and both Diogo de Reynoso and D. Fernão were dead. Seventy Portuguese had been killed or wounded by the explosion. All people of the garrison were disabled.

On August 29, a flotilla of 40 small ships led by the commanders D. Alvaro de Castro and D. Francisco de Menezes arrived as a fresh Portuguese reinforcement. On September 1, 20 Portuguese marched toward the 20,000 Muslims entrenched outside the fort. The moment the Portuguese stepped out of the fort they were fired upon, killing Menezes and many other Portuguese. Castro ordered his men to retreat. Ramadhan started on October 10, and the Muslims fasted and prayed for victory.

On November 6, 1546, Castro appeared off Diu with 12 galleons and some small ships. Castro's men, within three days, managed to enter the fort without being noticed by the Muslims. Castro had only 3,500 men to fight. On November 11, Castro attacked Gujarat's Rumi Khan's position and killed him, and his men fled. Castro broke the siege and earned a victory for Portugal. Castro was the savior of Diu. Castro came back to Goa. Castro received a message from Portugal that he was granted the title of Viceroy with three years of extension beyond June 5, 1548. Castro was sick, became flaccid, and ruled for 14 days and died in the arms of priest Xavier on June 6, 1548.

Jesuit Francis Xavier arrived in Goa, the capital of Portuguese India, on May 6, 1542. Goa was the seat of the viceroy and the military and naval headquarters. The mission of Xavier was to baptize the Hindus in the Portuguese territories. The plan was to first target poor people and innocent young minds. Xavier wanted to do this in an organized system of conversion. On January 25, 1543, Xavier founded a college at Goa for the instruction of Christianity to young innocent boys from every part of India, writes Jayne.[27] The college was dedicated to St. Paul. The young boys were to be trained as priests or catechists to serve Christianity. The graduated priests would be the pioneers of Christian teaching among the Hindus. In 1540, all the temples and mosques were destroyed under the order of the Portuguese king, and the properties were confiscated and allotted to the church. Through the courtesy of the viceroy, funds were arranged for the running of the college. Xavier advised the Portuguese soldiers to marry the local women instead of keeping them as concubines. In this way their children will become Portuguese and Christians.

In India, people used to worship idols. Priest Xavier wanted to break the tradition of idolatry. For this purpose, Xavier raised and trained a corps of children who were engaged in the campaign against idolatry. Wherever the people worshiped the idols, Xavier took the force of children who not only humiliated the worshipers but also treated the idols with contempt by spitting on them, hitting, and breaking them into pieces and walking over them. Xavier also asked the young students to preach to their parents and guardians. Elder converts were still confused about the new faith. Xavier left in each Christian village qualified native Christian teachers who were to teach the principles of Christianity and to baptize the newborn infants and to register marriages. The catechists were paid by the church.

Xavier traveled through India, Malacca, the Malaya Archipelago, and Japan preaching, catechizing, and baptizing. In Malacca and Malaya the Muslims did not want to listen to an infidel preacher and asked him to get lost. In Japan, Xavier outrightly condemned Buddhism which was rejected by the Japanese and the king of Japan issued a fiat prohibiting all of his vassals from embracing Christianity that carried death penalty. Xavier had success in forcefully proselytizing the Hindus into Christianity. During the period of ten years (1542–52), according to Jayne, Xavier converted 700,000[28] natives until his death on December 3, 1552.

Camoes, who had lived and was incarcerated in India, returned to Portugal in April 1570 and now was ready to publish his epic of the Golden Age of Portugal. Finally, "The Lusiads" was printed in 1572. The poems were about maritime adventures in the east. For over 300 years, the influence of "The Lusiads" upon the Portuguese was compared with the influence of the Bible in England.

The subject of the poem was the first voyage of India wherein the heroic deeds of the Portuguese heroes, including Vasco da Gama, Affonso Henriques, Albuquerque, Castro, and the great men of the sixteenth century, were beautifully presented. King Sebastian awarded Camoes with a meager award of 10 pounds for three years.

King Sebastian was overwhelmed with the idea of a crusade against Morocco which was under the control of the Ottoman Empire. King Sebastian discussed this idea with King Philip II of Spain, who refused to be a part of the crusade. However, Philip II did agree to provide some volunteers. Philip II said if Sebastian should win, "we shall have a good son-in-law; if he should lose, a good kingdom", writes Jayne.[29] The advice of all the Portuguese leaders against the crusade went unheard. Even D. Joao Mascarenhas, the hero of Diu, asked King Sebastian to drop the idea of a crusade. On this the king set up a medical board to investigate the problem. "Do advancing years diminish courage"? King Sebastian asked Mascarenhas his age and he replied, "I have twenty-five years of your service- and eighty for advising you not to invade Africa".[30]

In 1574, King Sebastian visited Tangier in North Africa, where he enjoyed hunting. In 1576, Mulai Ahmad, a claimant to the throne of Morocco, visited King Sebastian and sought his help in his ascension to the throne and promised that he would be a faithful vassal of the Portuguese king. Sebastian had dreamed of taking Fez, and the entire Morocco and Mulai Ahmad had provided him with that opportunity. The irony is that the king dreamed of the conquest of Morocco while his own kingdom was bankrupt of men and money and the Portuguese armies were engaged in India. King Sebastian, sure of victory, announced that he would fry the ears of the sultan of Morocco and would eat them with oil and vinegar. The resources for the war came through extortion of the New Christians.

On June 24, 1578, King Sebastian sailed from Lisbon with a force of 18,000 men which was composed of untrained young men and worn-out veterans and some foreigners. Sebastian stopped at Lagos and Cadiz. On arrival at Tangier, instead of fighting, Sebastian got engaged in hunting. Then he transported his troops to Arzila. The waste of too much time by Sebastian helped the reigning Sultan Mulai Abd al-Malik in making preparation for a fight with the Portuguese. The sultan arranged a force that was numerically superior to Sebastian's. The Muslim army of the sultan crushed the Portuguese force, and only 50 Portuguese managed to the ships. Now the dream of King Manuel's Iberian union and King Philip II's prediction of a good kingdom became true. King Sebastian died in the battle in Morocco. The body was buried at El-Kasr, reinterred at Ceuta, and, in 1582, removed by Philip II to the Convento dos Jeronymos.[31]

Portugal as a nation has lost the opulent self-reliance that had distinguished it from the rest of Europe during the period of discoveries and conquests of South America, Africa, and Asia. To recover its status needed a miracle. Now the Europeans started settling in the south of London, and the freemen of the old time were becoming fewer. The nation had diminished in size due to war, accidents of the sea due to bad weather, diseases of cholera, malaria, dysentery, famine, and bankrupt economy. It was very difficult for such a small nation to maintain garrisons in the colonies that had stretched from Brazil to Amboyna in Moluccas, Indonesia, from Africa to India, and to guard the trade route in the Atlantic and the Indian Oceans.

Portugal successfully won its fortune overseas, and it had been the pioneer of trade in Africa and India. Lisbon was the port for the ships bringing wealth and richness of Africa and Asia, and Portugal enjoyed a complete monopoly in trade. Most of the spices from the East to the European markets were delivered from Lisbon. Later, European rivals like the Dutch had broken the Portuguese monopoly. The profits of the voyages came to Portugal in bullion, heaps of gold and silver. The wealth that came was lost in investment in the wars. No economic policy could save Portugal from bankruptcy. The main volume of the Indian trade was diverted to other places like the great world-mart of Antwerp, which had a harbor close to the European markets and was the headquarters of the European finance center. Now merchants from all nations came to Antwerp. The irony was that now the Portuguese traders from Lisbon were visiting Antwerp.

The English entered the Indian waters by the end of 1612 with the two ships of the English East India Company, the 600-ton *Red Dragon* and a pinnace, the *Osiander*, commanded by Thomas Best with a crew of about 250 men. The destination was Surat. The English advantage was that Governor Makarrab Khan had fallen and the new governor was friendly with the English. The English had not settled in Surat as yet when they heard that a big Portuguese force was being gathered at Goa to drive the English away from the coast. Commander Best was ready for the offense and defense. Best had gathered his men and addressed them that though the Portuguese were far superior to them they should not fear them as they were cowards. He exhorted the English to maintain the valor the English are famous for, and trust in God and not fear death, writes Wright.[32]

Thomas Best initiated the fight. On the first day, the *Dragon*'s long boat was damaged. Next day, Best aggressively attacked the enemy. On November 30, 1612, the Portuguese ships floated off which were attacked by the *Dragon* assisted by the Osiander. The whole day fighting continued without any result until night fell. The Portuguese now got fresh supplies and challenged the English ships but failed to impress their enemy. Finally, the Portuguese gave up and let Best enter Surat unmolested. The new governor had issued a "firman" (an edict) from Agra on January 11, 1613, under which the English were granted the right to trade at Surat. Now the English were able to establish their strong foothold on the soil of India in January 1613. The Mughal government, in the form of concessions, gave the English as much as they could. After the conquest of Surat, Best sailed for England within a week. Best left behind at Surat a few factors under Thomas Aldworth.

After the departure of the English fleet, the Portuguese captured the *Guzerat* ship in the south of Tapti and carried it to Goa. This was done to intimidate the Mughal ruler in retaliation for the concessions given to the English.

The Mughal ruler was incensed and declared war against the Portuguese and ordered the seizure of all subjects of the Portuguese. The Mughal ruler also sent Makarrab Khan to seize the settlement of the Portuguese at Damaun on the western Indian coast in the south of Surat. In the middle of October 1614, the long and eagerly awaited English fleet commanded by Nicholas Downton and consisting of four vessels, *New Year's Gift*, *Hector*, *Merchants' Hope*, and *Salmon*, returned off Surat. Makarrab Khan asked the English to help them against the Portuguese as this war with them was a consequence of the concessions granted to the English. Downton was reluctant to take risk; he was just interested in the trade. Because of the reluctance of Downton, Makarrab Khan termed the English as an ally of the Portuguese. On the other hand, when the Portuguese knew about Downton's fleet, they called it the fleet of the enemy and asked them to leave the Indian waters. Downton rejected an insolent demand by the Portuguese.

On January 14, 1615, the Portuguese fleet under the command of Don Jeronimo appeared off the port, but it remained anchored at Swally. The fleet was big in that it included six large galleons, two smaller ships, and sixty small ships called frigates. After a few days the Portuguese ships attacked the *Merchants' Hope* and prevailed on it. While the *Merchants' Hope* was on the verge of being captured, Downton arrived with his ships to rescue it. A severe battle took place in which 300 to 400 Portuguese were killed and the water reddened with the blood of the victims. The English loss was limited to the *Merchants' Hope*. Jeronimo did not accept the results. He tried a couple of nights but failed. Jeronimo was now convinced that it was not possible to overcome the English fleet. Jeronimo sailed for the south and left the territory for Downton as a prize of victory. Surat was now English's realm. In 1615, Downton arrived at Bantam, where he became sick and died.

The Portuguese trading posts on the Eastern lands were lost to the Dutch. The Portuguese had been trying hard to defend their hold of Goa and to protect their interests in the Persian Gulf. When the Portuguese heard that the English are intruding in the Persian Gulf, then in 1619, five ships led by Ruy Freire de Andrade were dispatched from Lisbon to the Persian Gulf.[33] The information of the departure of the fleet was sent to India by the English Company. Based on this information the English at Surat sent a powerful force into the Gulf to protect their trading interests.

In Persia, the Portuguese ambassador adopted an insolent attitude toward Shah Abbas and demanded the restoration of Gombroon (now Bandar Abbas) and other territories that were occupied by Persia as they were part of Hormuz over which the Portuguese had control. The Portuguese ambassador also demanded of Shah for the exclusion of all Europeans from the Persian ports. Shah Abbas was incensed, scorned the letter of demand from the Portuguese ambassador, tore it, and said not only that but also the Portuguese would be expelled from their factory at Hormuz. To humiliate the ambassador further, Shah, through an imperial edict called "firman", granted the sole trading rights in silk to the English.

The Portuguese Discoveries and Colonialization 103

In November 1620, two ships, the *London* and the *Roebuck*, led by the English commander Shilling arrived at Swally in Surat of the Indian Gujarat. Surat was captured by the British from the Portuguese in 1612 and they established their factory there. Before Shilling, two ships, *Hart* and *Eagle*, had been dispatched to the Persian Gulf. When Shilling heard the news of Shah's expulsion of the Portuguese from Hormuz and granting of the silk trade rights to the English, he immediately decided to move from Swally to the Persian Gulf by following *Hart* and *Eagle*. Shilling reunited with the fleet which was now ready to take the control of the trade in silk at Bandar-i-Jask in Hormuz.

In the middle of December 1620, the Portuguese fleet was encountered off Bandar-i-Jask. After a few days an attempt was made to burn Andrade's ships but without any success. On December 28, the engagement started. The major burden of the fight fell on *Hart* and *Eagle*, while the other two ships, the *London* and the *Roebuck*, were kept in waiting at a distance. The two ships damaged the Portuguese ships and made them run. The four English ships then followed the Portuguese, and when their ammunition fell short, they returned to Jask. With the flight of the Portuguese fleet, the way for trade in the Persian Gulf was opened for the English. In this fight the English lost their brilliant commander Shilling, who was given a funeral at Jask. Thereafter the English fleet returned to Surat. The Portuguese in retaliation for the Persian hostility destroyed the coast and burnt all the Persian ships that they confronted on the way. The Persians now got control of Hormuz. The Portuguese trading activities in Hormuz ended like elsewhere.

The Portuguese carried out trade in Africa and India without an exclusive Company, and they did it for more than a century. Their settlements at Congo, Angola, and Benguela on the coast of Africa and at Goa in India bore resemblance to the American colonies. After a century of Portugal's commercial monopoly in Asia its naval hegemony in the warm water on the Cape route was challenged by other European countries. The Dutch entered as the Dutch East India Company from 1605 through 1825 and traded textiles for spices. England landed in 1612 and established a trading post in 1664. France entered the colonial game in 1698, followed by Denmark. The Danish entered as the Danish East India Company (1620–1777), the Dano-Norwegian colonies (1777–1814), and the Danish colonies (1814–1869), and they were solely concerned with the trade without the military presence and without affecting the trade of other European countries in the region. Norwegians established their trading posts at Balasore (1625–43 and 1763–1845), Oddeway Torrre (1696–1722), Serampore, now West Bengal (1755–1808, 1818–1845), and established factories and settlements in Tamil Nadu, West Bengal, the Nicobar Islands, now part of India's union territory, and had colonial possessions in India for more than 200 years.

A small nation of Portugal transformed its sea power into an empire through discoveries and conquests. The Portuguese plantations included: Angola, Mozambique, Guinea, Cape Verde Islands and Sao Tome in Africa; Portuguese India, Macau (China) in Asia; Timor in Oceania; and Brazil in South America.

Portugal through the annual influx of treasures from the colonies in the form of gold, ivory, spices, and slaves became the richest nation of Europe. The wealth was squandered on wars instead of investing it into a productive investment which led to the loss of the splendid self-reliance which it had enjoyed during the discoveries and conquests. The trade was diverted from Lisbon to Antwerp. The colonies and the trading exclusive rights were lost to the other European countries. The causes of the fall of the Portuguese Empire in the east Archipelago, Africa, and India, inter alia, included: misgovernance where the Portuguese governors, viceroys, and their friends became rich and the soldiers starved; the engagement of the employees of the company into their illegal personal trading activities; diseases of cholera, malaria killed more people than were killed by the enemies; the Portuguese interference in the religious affairs of the colonies through forced conversion of the Hindus to Christianity, the destruction of the temples and the mosques which created hatred among the natives and they switched their support to the Dutch and the English.

During the seventeenth century, the English, the French, the Dutch, the Danes, and the Swedes who had strong naval power and ports tried to settle in the new world. The Swedish had established their colony of New Jersey. Due to a lack of support from the mother country the colony became weak and was finally taken over by the Dutch colony of New York. In 1674, it became part of the British dominion. The Danish had established their colonies in the small islands of St. Thomas and Santa Cruz which were progressing until the government-owned exclusive company was dissolved. The exclusive company had then the sole right to purchase and sale of the produce of these colonies. The government of an exclusive company of merchants was the worst one in that it hindered the progress of these colonies. Then the king of Denmark dissolved this company, and after that these colonies progressed rapidly. The poor countries of Europe like Sweden and Denmark did not think of risking their small capital in distant and uncertain adventures in the East. Both of these countries had neither sent a single ship to Asia nor had established an exclusive Company to trade with them. Both of these countries bought Asian goods from other European countries at higher prices.

Notes

1 Livermore, "A History of Portugal", p. 44.
2 Ibid., p. 82.
3 Ibid., p. 82.
4 Ibid., p. 87.
5 Ibid., p. 174.
6 Ibid., p. 179.
7 Ibid., p. 184.
8 Ibid., p. 187.
9 Dunbar, "India and the Passing of Empire", p. 57.
10 Jayne, "Vasco Da Gama and His Successors", p. 18.
11 Livermore, p. 229.

12 Ghazanfar, "Vasco da Gama, the Explorer: Motivations and Myths", p. 49.
13 Jayne, p. 52.
14 Sale, pp. 169–170.
15 Jayne, p. 58.
16 Livermore, pp. 230–231.
17 Jayne, p. 64.
18 Livermore, p. 232.
19 Jayne, p. 65.
20 Ibid., p.74.
21 Stephens, p. 74.
22 Ibid., p. 85.
23 Ibid., p. 160. Sati was a Hindu funeral practice in which the widow is burnt alive with her dead husband.
24 Jayne, p. 92.
25 Stephens, p. 128.
26 Jayne, p. 128.
27 Ibid., p. 193.
28 Ibid., p. 237.
29 Ibid., p. 282.
30 Ibid., p. 281.
31 ibid., p. 284.
32 Wright, "Early English Adventurers in the East", p. 119.
33 Ibid., p. 246

Bibliography

Dunbar, George Sir, *India and the Passing of Empire*, Ivor Nicholson & Watson Ltd., 26 Manchester Square, London, UK, 1951.

Ghazanfar, S.M., Vasco da Gama, the Explorer: Motivations and Myths, *Journal of Global Initiatives: Policy, Pedagogy, Perspective*, Vol. 11, Number 1, October 2016, pp. 43–58. https://digitalcommons.kennesaw.edu/jgi/vol11/iss1/8

Jayne, K.G., *Vasco Da Gama and his Successors (1460–1580)*, Methuen & Co. Ltd., 36 Essex Street, W.C. London, UK, 1910.

Livermore, H.V., *A History of Portugal*, At the University Press, Cambridge, UK, 1947.

Sale, Kirkpatrick, *Christopher Columbus and the Conquest of Paradise*, Tauris Parke, London, UK, 2006.

Stephens, H. Morse, *Indian Rulers, Albuquerque*, Cosmo Publications, 24-B, Ansari Road, Darya Ganj, New Delhi-110002, India, 2003.

Wright, Arnold, *Early English Adventurers in the East*, Sang-e-Meel Publications, Lahore, Pakistan, 2000.

4
THE CONQUESTS OF THE DUTCH COMPANIES OF EAST INDIA AND THE WEST INDIES

The Spice Islands in the Eastern Archipelago had become the focus of the world in that the richness of these islands had contributed to the local kingdoms which attracted the Europeans. The Portuguese had already entered the Eastern Archipelago and now was the time for the Dutch to contest them. The Dutch took the advantage of the opportunities available. Instead of sending a few ships in the beginning, they sent big fleets one after another, and in a short period of time their vessels penetrated all regions of the Eastern Archipelago. In their early expeditions the Dutch had to confront the Portuguese, already well established in Malacca, who had blocked the advancement of the Dutch adventurers. The Dutch accepted the Portuguese challenge.

Early in the sixteenth century, based on the economic growth, the Dutch shipbuilding industry got a boost and focused on building the long merchant vessels with large capacity for cargo meant for long-distance international trade. The Dutch ships were smaller than the Spanish, the Portuguese, and the English ships. The Spanish, the Portuguese, the French, and the English were the pioneers of entering the world's oceans and the Dutch followed them after a century. In 1590s the Dutch started sailing in the waters to have an access to the commodities of Asia to extend their trade beyond the European's domain. In 1594 and 1595, the Dutch made two attempts, via the Open Polar Sea, to sail to India under the command of Jan Huygen van Linschoten, but both of these attempts failed. In 1596 a third attempt was made under the command of Willem Barents and Jacob van Heemskerck, writes Wendy.[1] They took a 100-ton ship of Willem Barents. The third attempt was to sail to India via the Open Polar Sea on May 10, 1596. They could not find the passage to India. Willem Barents and Van Heemskerck continued searching for an alternative route. The ship was finally captured by the ice at the northeast coast of Nova Zembla in the Arctic Ocean in the north of Russia and was abandoned in 1596. The crews returned to the ship's boats on October 29, 1597.[2]

In 1595 another attempt was made via the Portuguese route of Cape of Good Hope sponsored by a consortium of nine Dutch businessmen united as the Compagnie van Verre (Far Distant Lands Company) with a capital of 290,000 guilders from the different investors, writes Parthesius.[3] According to Wright, the fleet of four ships under the command of Cornelius Houthman[4] completed the voyage in three years and returned laden with Indian spices such as nutmeg and black pepper. The sale of the cargo just covered the entire cost of the expedition without commercial profits.[5] One 260-ton ship *Amsterdam* and 162 out of 249 crews could not make back home. In spite of the lack of commercial profits and losses, this expedition demonstrated that the Dutch could make to India for trade in spices by challenging the exclusiveness of the Portuguese in the Asian trade. The Dutch in this expedition made direct links to the Indonesian islands for the Asian commodities by circumventing the Portuguese entrepôts.

The Dutch sailor Wybrant van Warwijck[6] discovered the island of Mauritius on September 17, 1598, and named it after the name of Dutch Viceroy and prince of Orange. The island of Mauritius proved to be a quick stopover and a post en route for repair and maintenance. It was a good source of wood for shipbuilding and food for the crews. Mauritius had an abundance of fruits such as coconut, turtles, fish, and birds. Ten of thousand trees of all kinds were cut down for the maintenance of the ships and the construction of the warehouses and used for firewood to make charcoal. In the later years, the Dutch planted fruit trees and left animals on the island to ensure future food supplies. The trees and animals were brought from Madagascar and Bantam on the Island of Java.

By 1600, the Dutch trade with the Baltics grew.[7] The Dutch vessels arrived in the Baltics with salt from Portugal and France, fish and construction materials from the Netherlands, French and German wine, and textiles and other exotic goods from England and India. These goods were traded for grain and timber from Poland, hemp and flax from Russia, tar from Finland, and copper and iron from Sweden. The Dutch played a pivotal role in the trade between northern and western Europe. This led to the Dutch primacy in the world trade in the seventeenth century. The timber that came from Norway and the Baltic region was used in the shipbuilding industry which built ships at a low cost, that are easy to sail, and that carry large cargo.

By the year 1601, 14 Dutch fleets including 65 ships sailed to Asia, and one of them was led by Jacob Corneliszoon van Neck who completed the voyage in 15 months and returned with four laden ships that earned a high profit of 400% on their cargo, writes Winchester.[8] By 1601, the Dutch volume of trade had exceeded that of the Portuguese, the Spanish, and the English. The expeditions to India were organized by joint stock companies called Voor-Compagnieen from the different regions of the Netherlands. Lack of coordination by the Voor-Compagnieen resulted in the increase of prices of the spices at the source.

In order to control the trade of Asian commodities by combining all efforts, the Dutch Verenigde Nederlandse Geoctroyeerde Oostindische Compagnie

(United Netherlands Chartered East India Company), called the VOC or the United East India Company, was established as a joint stock company in 1602 after approval by the Dutch Government. The VOC, a limited liability company, was provided with a capital of 6.5 million[9] guilders from 1,143 investors, and the shareholders were liable for their investment and there was no guarantee of returns, and they had little influence over the management. The payment for the shares was in installment, due in 1603, 1605, 1606, and 1607, subject to the condition of article 17 that called for that the payment would be made to the shareholders as soon as the profits equivalent to 5% of the initial capital had been made. The capital of its rival, the English East India Company, was £68,373, equivalent to 820,000 guilders, which was subscribed by just 219 subscribers. In 1602 the VOC was given a charter of 21 years which was renewed in 1623 with changes in different clauses. The VOC operated in the Indian Ocean. All Voor-Compagnieen were amalgamated into the VOC or the United East India Company. The organizational structure of the company was divided into six chambers representing the port cities of Amsterdam, Hoorn, Enkhuizen, Rotterdam, Delft, and Middleburg (also known as Zeeland). These chambers then selected the Board of Directors from each Chamber and convened as the Heren XVII (or Gentlemen XVII). The Directors of the Board came from the highest class of shareholders. The Board of Directors met twice or thrice a year. The Board of Directors was represented by eight delegates of the Chamber of Amsterdam, because it provided 57.4% of the total capital, and four delegates from the Chamber of Zeeland and the rest of the Chambers were represented by one delegate each. The 17th delegate would come from Zeeland or the five small chambers to block the dominating decision-making by Amsterdam.

The VOC was given extraordinary autonomy from the Dutch Government and enjoyed a complete monopoly in the east with the powers of appointing governors, raising army, building fortresses, and signing treaties with the rulers of Asia and conducting military operations but was not completely independent of the Dutch government. The Dutch government also sanctioned the distribution of the loot among the crew, and this provided the crew an incentive to attack and capture the foreign ships for lucrative plunder. The VOC made more money from plundering foreign ships than from trade. The Dutch arrived in Indonesia in 1603 with the sole purpose of trade. The VOC conquered Indonesia, which is the world's biggest archipelago with thousands and thousands of islands which were governed by different tribes, kings, and sultans. The VOC armed its ships with cannons and hired mercenaries from Europe, Japan, India, and Indonesia and prepared itself for full-fledged wars with European competitors and the local rulers. Island after island was captured by the VOC. In 1800, the Dutch took the control of Indonesia and made it the Dutch national colony for the next 145 years.

In 1604, the admiral of the VOC fleet, Wybrant van Warwijck, got allotted a stone building in Bantam on the Island of Java, where he had established the

VOC's first headquarters in Asia. Bantam had a long history as an international center of pepper and spice trade and international contacts such as the Chinese traders. The headquarters were staffed with a Mission head with the task of organizing the trade and shipping, the housing of the Dutch families, and preventing the Portuguese. However, the Dutch were surprised to see the presence of the Portuguese merchants in Bantam, but that was not a threat to the Dutch as their power was limited. The Spaniards and the Portuguese had already maintained their control of the market that stretched from the east coast of Africa to the shore of Japan and China.

On May 12, 1605, seven ships of the VOC Chamber of Amsterdam sailed from Texel. After 12 days they were joined by two additional ships that left the Dutch port of Wielingen. These ships sailed to Asia under the command of Admiral Cornelis Matelief de Jonge, who had carried a secret plan of besieging the Portuguese stronghold of Malacca. Two additional ships from the Chamber of Delft left on May 30 and joined the fleet at Malacca on July 14, 1606. The Dutch burnt the four Portuguese ships, on April 30, 1606, and thereafter the bloody battles occurred. The Dutch were supported by the sultan of Johore who had provided hundreds of galleys and provided them with a safe haven in the Johore River, where they could retire their ships after the battle. The Portuguese were supported by an armada of the viceroy of Goa. The Dutch burnt three large Portuguese ships and slaughtered or wounded the Portuguese men. The Portuguese lost 18 ships to the Dutch fire. The Dutch gave up on December 13 without getting control of Malacca. The Dutch lost 600 men and 2 ships in the Strait of Malacca, writes Wendy.[10]

From 1609 onward, the VOC appointed a governor-general as the highest authority in Asia who was to safeguard the interests of the VOC. The important business of the VOC was the trade in spices from the Eastern Archipelago. In 1609, the Amsterdam Exchange Bank was established and the Dutch bankers started accepting the Company's shares as collateral for loans and started advancing credit for the purchase of shares; thus, the capital of the Company was ensured through the collaboration of the joint stock company and the financial sector and remained unchanged throughout VOC's existence. In 1610, the Board of directors announced the payment of the first dividend in the shape of spices rather than cash, as the Company was short of cash. The cash dividends were paid in 1612, 1613, and 1618. In 1612, it was announced that the Company would not be liquidated as planned, therefore, the shareholder cannot get back cash but instead can sell their shares to another investor. The assignment of the first governor-general, Pieter Both (1610–14), followed by Gerard Reynst (1614–15) and Laurens Reael (1616–19), was to get the Dutch monopoly in spices. The governor-generals were allowed to sign the treaty and use the force in defense whenever needed. Through the various treaties made by the admirals, the VOC had the exclusive right to trade in cloves, nutmeg, and mace. In order to safeguard their interests, the Dutch had to get involved in the politics of the Spice Islands and the use of force became an official part of the trade policy. The truce that prevented the war with Spain and Portugal in Europe did not include Asia. Therefore, the confrontation with Spain and Portugal in Asia was permissible. Another European competitor, the English East India Company, had refused to recognize the claims of the VOC in the area.

The Dutch issued warnings to the English commanders who were trying to enter their yard of spice trade, Moluccas. Early in 1613, the English commander named Jourdain reached Moluccas from Bantam; he was warmly received by the natives who were fed up with the Dutch harsh handling of them. Immediately after his arrival in Moluccas, he received a warning from Steven Coteels,[11] the Dutch Resident at Amboina, not to trade with the natives as it would violate the rights of the Dutch. This warning was endorsed by a letter from the governor of Amboina. The English commander defied and sent a reply that the right of trading with the natives of an island was free for all men. He started to trade at Hitoe,[12] and soon he found that the natives were so fearful of the Dutch that the possibility of trade was minimal. He moved to Seram (Ceram), where the Dutch influence was not much as was in Amboina. At Luhu port of Seram island, Jourdain requested the natives for a site to build a factory. The natives informed him that this request could only be granted by the king of Ternate.

Finally, Jourdain sought an audience with the Dutch governor. At the Dutch headquarters he met with Jan Pietersoon Coen,[13] a member of the team of the governor-general of Dutch India. Coen was a person who would never compromise on the Dutch monopolistic right of trade on the islands. Coen was of the opinion that trade without war and war without trade was not possible. Both the gentlemen met with their clashing interests. The session was stormy and remained without any result. Jourdain maintained that trade was as free for the English as it was for the Dutch and that they would not leave because of the Dutch threats. Coen made it clear that whosoever would buy cloves from these countries without their permission, they would not let it go. Next day the English commander, Jourdain, was asked by the Dutch to leave the country or face the consequences. Although the natives were in favor of the English and offered the sites for building factories at Luhu and Cambello, the Dutch had more strength than the English. Luhu on the southwestern coast of Indonesia in the province of Moluccas was famous for the trade in cloves. Jourdain, not feeling in a position to confront the Dutch, decided to leave for Bantam.

After Jourdain's departure, the Dutch dealt the natives with a heavy hand as to why they supported their enemy. When the Dutch landed on Banda, they were attacked by the natives who killed 300 Dutch and compelled them to retreat. This was the time when the natives needed the English's support. Encouraged by the strike, the natives sent an envoy to the British at Bantam to get their support. Jourdain re-equipped *Thomassin*, the *Concord*, and the *Speedwell* along with the ships *Clove* and *Defense* which just arrived from England and dispatched them to Banda in the early days of 1616 under the command of George Ball and Cokayne. The British little squadron arrived at Poolo Ai on March 2, 1616,[14] and found that the Dutch had concentrated a big force at Neira port opposite to

Lonthor in Banda. On March 11, a fleet of nine Dutch ships arrived at Poolo Ai with the determination of driving the English out of the area. Jourdain ordered his men to cut hawsers and go out to confront the Dutch. The move was very risky against the Dutch who were well equipped with the force with their ships. The English commander again reviewed the situation and thought that it would not be worth fighting with the odds much against him. Jourdain then negotiated with the Dutch and withdrew his vessels and left the natives at the mercy of cruel and cutthroat Dutch. Still the natives took courage and hoisted the English flag, but the Dutch came and tore it down and built a strong Fort Revenge to strengthen their hold on the island.

Jourdain, though not successful, did not give up to break up the monopoly of the Dutch on the islands. Jourdain sent another expedition of 300-ton *Defense* and 400-ton *Swan* to the eastward led by Commander Nathaniel Courthope.[15] Nathaniel was instructed to move toward Poolo Roon, an island near Poolo Ai. Nathaniel was tasked to conduct a reconnaissance mission to see if the natives who were currently under the Dutch were willing to defy the Dutch and were ready to pledge their allegiance to the English by surrendering their territories to them. As far as Poolo Ai was concerned, Nathanial was ordered to just capture it and notify the Dutch that this was English territory.

When Nathaniel arrived in Poolo Roon in 1617, he was welcomed by the natives who accepted his request of surrendering their territories to the English. Now the English flag was hoisted and a ceremony was held. After three days of the English announcement, the Dutch commander named Cornelis Dedel, stationed at Neira on Banda islands, arrived off Poolo Roon with his three ships. Cornelis anchored two of his ships near the *Swan* and *Defense* ships of the English, and the third was positioned between the ships and the ocean. Cornelis did not know about the English shore batteries. After discovering this fact, Cornelis withdrew and waited for additional reinforcements from Amboina.

The Dutch sent a pinnace to take the soundings of the small island called Nailaka near the northern shore of Poolo Roon. The English detected it and fired upon it. No damage was done. On the other side, Davis, the captain of *Swan*, was not willing to stay more on this place and wanted to leave. This situation weakened Nathaniel's position. Failing to convince Davis, Nathaniel ordered him to go to Rosengyn and establish a factory over there as was requested by the natives. After completing his task at Rosengyn, Davis started his return voyage to Poolo Roon and on his way his ship *Swan* was attacked and captured by a Dutch ship *Morgenstine* which was commanded by Dedel. The Dutch then sent *Swan* to Neira and demonstrated to the Bandanese their glorifying prize and boasted that the king of England was not to emulate the king of Holland.

When Nathaniel heard the capture of *Swan*, he decided that he would depend on his own resources. He dismantled the *Defense* and took her armaments to Nailaka to build fortified camps for long-term defense against the Dutch. The empty *Defense* was anchored, and some of the traitors in the camp took it and delivered it to the Dutch. Laurence Reaal, the Dutch governor-general, invited the English commander for a talk. Both met. Laurence offered Nathaniel that he would return both the ships, *Swan* and *Defense*, with the men and compensate for the goods taken from the ships and that the English ships with the spices loaded at Poolo Roon could return to England safely. Nathaniel rejected the offer. Laurence Reaal ran amok and threw Nathaniel's hat on the ground and pulled his beard.[16]

In November 1617, Laurence Reaal, from his headquarters at Jakarta then known as Batavia, issued a strong protest against the efforts for destabilizing the monopoly of the Dutch in the trade of spices in the Eastern Archipelago. Batavia, a Dutch colony, was a port where all the ships between Europe and China touched it. Batavia was the trade center of the East Indies where not only the Europeans but also the native Indians, the inhabitants of China, Japan, Tonquin, Malacca, Cochin-China, and island of Celebes were seen engaged in trade. He did not mention directly in his protest the name of Nathaniel or the English. In the early months of 1618, the English sent three ships to the Moluccas in support of Nathaniel to strengthen the base of the English spice trade on the islands. One of the ships, *Solomon*, which was off Banda, was attacked by the Dutch. The English and the Dutch ships got so close that even their commanders were able to talk. The Dutch were able to take control of the English ship which disappointed Nathaniel who said that he would continue fighting rather than yielding as the English commander Cassarian did. He further said that yielding is a great disgrace which he would not take.

In 1619, the good news heartened Nathaniel when he heard that Sir Thomas Dale's fleet[17] had defeated the Dutch. Nathaniel was happy that his patience and steadfastness for the cause of his country had started bearing the fruits. Sir Thomas Dale was sent from India to Bantam for the protection of the English interests against the Dutch. Dale was the first governor of the first British colony of Virginia in America. Dale got experience in the west and not in the east. At Bantam he received secret information about the Dutch movement. His blood boiled and became furious to avenge the Dutch in general and Coen in particular who had ill-treated the English.

Dale captured the Dutch vessel called *Zwarte Leeuw* (Black Lion) and put the crew ashore with the intimation that if he found them again, he would hang every one of them. The Dutch authorities at Jakarta (Batavia), on hearing the seizure of *Zwarte Leeuw*, sent a strong letter of protest. When the letter was given to Dale, he became furious and asked why the letter was written in Dutch, why it was not written in other languages like French or Spanish if the Dutch hated to write in English. He told the messenger that he would take the reply to Coen himself.

As a reaction, the Dutch burnt the English factory at Jakarta, and Dale wanted to do the same thing with the Dutch factory at Bantam, but the natives resisted and Dale reconciled. Now Dale started gathering forces for a full-fledged attack on Jakarta. In December, Dale attacked the Dutch headquarters at Jakarta. The Dutch had the problem of attacks from many sides. On the one side they were being attacked by the English, and on the other side they were expected to be attacked by the Javanese. The Dutch therefore decided to withdraw from the shore to the ship and fight in the sea.

On December 30, the English fleet appeared off Jakarta, and Pietersoon Coen, now the Dutch governor-general, decided to confront them and a small ship was sent to Amboina with the instructions of gathering the entire Dutch forces in the Moluccas to handle the English invasion. When the two fleets got close, Dale demanded the surrender of the Dutch commander. The Dutch response was the negative. Severe fighting took place. Many Dutch men were killed or wounded, the supply of ammunition was running out, and many of their ships were damaged. The Dutch, instead of surrendering, decided to procrastinate the decision.

In the meantime, the Dutch received information that three additional ships had come to the aid of Dale and now the Dutch thought that it was an unequal balance of strength and then decided to leave Jakarta. The Dutch proceeded to the Moluccas, where they depended on their fortified camps for defense. The Dutch were weak, and based on his strength, Dale should have pursued the enemy while retreating, and this was a good opportunity for him. But he missed the golden opportunity which may not smile at the English again. Dale thought it important to capture the Dutch headquarters at Jakarta rather than destruction of the Dutch fleet. According to the terms of surrender, the fortresses, garrisons, and ammunition were surrendered to the English and the other movable property went to the king of Jakarta. But the Dutch had secretly signed an agreement with the local king for the exclusion of the English from the area. Soon after the capture of Jakarta by the English, the locals started showing a hostile attitude. Dale thought that in these circumstances, it would be impossible for the English to keep control of Jakarta because of the threat of attacks from both the Dutch and the natives. Dale decided to leave Jakarta and proceeded on his return journey. Soon after his arrival in India, Dale died.

After the departure of the English, Coen reappeared off Jakarta and retook it on March 12, 1619. In 1619, Jakarta became the international center of shipping in Asia and the connection center between the European and the Asian branch of the VOC. In order to get monopolistic control of the trade in nutmeg and its by-product mace, Coen wanted to have complete control of the Banda Islands. In 1621, Coen sent a military expedition of 2,000 soldiers who occupied the main centers in Banda and replaced the existing population with the Dutch chosen population and thus got the monopoly on nutmeg and mace. Banda Island's traditional community no longer existed. For obtaining monopoly on cloves which were grown on many islands near Amboina in Seram and the North-Moluccas, Coen was successful in signing a treaty with the local ruler of Ternate who had control over the large parts of the area. This treaty ensured that all the shipments of cloves from these areas would solely be done through the VOC. Coen destroyed all trees of nutmeg, cloves, and other crops in the Moluccas. Coen was determined not to allow the illegal production of cloves. The VOC accomplished the goal of monopoly over the trade in cloves. By 1663, only Goa and some smaller settlements in India remained in the possession of Portugal, writes Dunbar.[18] The Dutch had now factories in India and took Ceylon and Portuguese coastal settlements from them. These factories were in fact the collection centers and not the manufacturing factories.

Jan Pietersoon Coen, the Governor General of the Netherlands in India, after consolidating his position in monopolizing the trade in spices at Jakarta, looked for other areas of opportunities of asserting Dutch power. His next victim was the English Commander Jourdain who had effectively implemented the English policy of carving out an independent position in the Moluccas. In April 1619, Jourdain received two ships named the *Sampson* and the *Hound* from India to re-establish an English factory at Patani on the east side of the Malay peninsula. After the arrival of the English at Patani, the English were attacked by the three large Dutch ships. After 11 men of the *Sampson* were killed and 30 became wounded and a number of men of *Hound* were also lost, Jourdain then raised the flag of truce for negotiation. During the course of peace talks, someone from the Dutch side fired at Jourdain and after half an hour he died.

When the sad news reached Poolo Roon, that Dale's fleet had returned to India and the body of the Englishman was abandoned on the island, Nathaniel remained steadfast in his mission. When Nathaniel proceeded on his expedition to Lonthor, the Dutch sleuths gave that information to the authorities at the Dutch headquarters. A boat well equipped and manned was sent at night to intercept the English commander on his return. The fearless Nathaniel was betrayed and entrapped, but he took courage and faced the challenge. He fought like a lion until he lost all of his ammunition and then the shot from the Dutch struck him at his breast; knowing that he will be no more, he jumped into the water and that was his end.

In 1623, Coen completed his assignment and handed over the administration of the Eastern Archipelago to his successor, General Peter De Carpentier. Coen told Carpentier to "maintain carefully the sovereignty and highest jurisdiction" of the Dutch in the Eastern seas "without sharing or suffering the English or any other to encroach thereupon". "Treat them not any more than open enemies". The Dutch policy was aimed at the exclusion of the English from trade in the eastern region and the holding of the Dutch monopoly in the trade. During the year the English scattered through the eastern Archipelago by building their factories and showing their existence based on the resources provided by the Company. The main establishment of the English was at the capital of Amboina which was the center of the spice trade and where the Dutch had maintained their headquarters. In addition, the English had set up the branches of the company at Hitoe and Larica and had established their factories at Cambello and Luhu on the large island of Seram. Carpentier decided to let the private traders play their role in the trade with the exception of spice island, the Coromandel Coast, and the Chinese and Persian silk and indigo. Carpentier further directed that through a price policy and by force at sea, the trade should be directed to Batavia and this would result in closing the other posts. In 1623, according to Parthesius, the

The Conquests of the Dutch Companies 115

Dutch trading posts at Patani, Sangora, in the north of Patani, Siam, Cambodia, and Atchin, were closed,[19] with the exception of Surat, Coromandel, Japan, and Solor. During this period most of the private European traders took initiatives and developed shipping on these routes and sent ships to Jambi, Siam, and Patani to develop trade and bring back much sought-after food supplies of spices to Batavia.

Now Gabriel Towerson took responsibilities of the office of the English company at Batavia. On the other hand, the Dutch governor, Herman Van Speult, was trained by Coen who had appointed him at the time of his departure. He was a stern person. Amboina, located between the Islands of Banda and Moluccas, was the capital of Molucca province, on Leytimor island.[20] It had a strong fortification called Ford Victoria. It was a big castle and inside it the Dutch had their headquarters and garrison. One evening a Japanese sleuth hired by the Dutch wandered around the fortification and asked questions about the number of soldiers inside and the timing of the guard change. Next day he entered the area inside the fortification which was prohibited. In the past, the Japanese had developed very friendly relations with the Englishmen. Suspicion arose among the Dutch and the Japanese were arrested and sent to the torture cell. When the torture became unendurable for the Japanese, he confessed that he was associated with the English and that he acted at the instigation of another Japanese named Cevice Michick who was previously associated with the English and now was on the payroll of the Dutch.

When the Dutch governor, Speult, heard about this conspiracy he was surprised. The prisoner was confined under strict guards. Eleven other Japanese soldiers were brought in and were disarmed. Now the Dutch turned their attention to the English. First of all, Towerson was captured at the English factory and kept as a prisoner there. After this, the Englishmen working in the factories at Hitoe, Larcia, and Cambello were captured, brought in, and placed in confinement. Investigations of the English started in the torture cell. All the Englishmen were dreadfully tortured and compelled to say what the investigators wanted of them.

On February 23, 1623, all of the English prisoners were assembled in a hall of the castle of Amboina to deliver them the condemnation. Governor Speult, accompanied by the members of the Council, chaired the proceedings. The notorious and condemnable investigators named Fiscal and De Bruyne, who had taken part in the unspeakable and horrible investigations, were also present. The hall was surrounded by armed Dutch soldiers. A few natives with their astonished eyes were looking at how one European nation was handling the other European nation. De Bruyne presented the investigation report and his conclusion. Now the court of Speult was to deliver the verdict.

The unfortunate Towerson and his Englishmen with trembling lips, shivering bodies, and fallen pale faces threw themselves at the mercy of the cutthroat enemy and stood to hear the verdict. The verdict that Towerson received was to cut his head and the cutoff head was to be hung on a post as a lesson for others. The remaining Englishmen received the verdict of just decapitation.

The properties of the victims were confiscated. After the announcement of the verdict, with the exception of Towerson, all the prisoners were left in a room in the castle. The Dutch ministers visited them and asked them to give the truth. All of them claimed innocence and asked for forgiveness for the false accusations which was not to be granted.

While the English were passing through their last agony, the good-natured Dutch guard offered them the wine for some peace which they rejected. The English decided to pass the last night of their lives in religious prayers. On the day of execution, all the English prisoners were escorted by armed guards to the ground of execution. Now the executioner started his dirty job. One by one each man came forward and said that he was innocent in the matter for which he was going to die, and cheerfully presented himself for the last action of his execution. After the execution was over, the burial arrangements were made. In deference of the rank, Towerson was buried in a special grave, while the remaining nine dead bodies of the Englishmen were buried in one grave. After their burial, the Englishman, who had testified against his fellow Englishmen falsely, came to the graveyard and cried and acted madly. After two days he died.

When the sad news arrived in Batavia, a small British colony, the president of the factory arranged a protest procession against Speult for wrongfully capturing, torturing, and executing the English and, on top of it, the confiscation of their properties. The act was in violation of the treaty and it disgraced the king of England. Carpentier had peacefully dealt with the protests and felt that the matter was handled in a wrong manner. When the details of the massacre reached England, the king became sad and condemned the shameful and gruesome treatment meted out to his subjects. In 1667, the sole English factory in Batavia was closed due to the Dutch action.

In the early seventeenth century, the Dutch built a 1000-ton warship called *Hollandse Tuin of the Amsterdam Admiralty*[21] which sailed to Brazil in a flotilla of five ships commanded by Paulus van Caerden in 1603. The large ships came from Holland as the transportation of small ships from Holland was expensive. Now, the Dutch had their shipyards in Asia at Jakarta and Cochin for the repairment of the ships. In 1632, the Company decided to set a standard 12.5% dividend that was twice the rate of borrowing of money by the company. Consequently, the entire net profit was distributed to the shareholders. By 1650, the total dividend payments were eight times the original investment showing a rate of return of 27%. In 1651, small ships of 120–200 tons were built at Dutch shipyards in Japan and Siam. These ships were not for long distance but were used for intra-Asiatic trade.

The Dutch ships had instructions from the VOC to attack the Spanish and the Portuguese ships wherever they were found in the water. On June 4, 1623, a Dutch fleet of 11 vessels under the command of Admiral Jacques L'Heremite and Vice Admiral Huygen Schapendam, voyaging near Sierra Leone, spotted and captured a Spanish sugar-prince and renamed it *Windhond*. The slow-sailing *Windhond*, along with the two barques all loaded with sugar, was sent to Holland in June 1623. The *Windhond* was escorted by the one Dutch warship from the Amsterdam Admiralty, *Overijssel*, which had sighted the fleet on June 12 in Safia, modern-day Morocco, in the south of Cape Cantin.[22]

On November 6, 1641, the English East India Company bought the 260-ton ship from John and Thomas and renamed it *Blessing*. On 19 February, the British sent *Blessing* to Bantam. The three Dutch ships on March 25, 1653, attacked the *Blessing* and captured it in the Persian waters during the First Anglo-Dutch War of 1653 and the Dutch renamed it *Avondster*. *Avondster* was sent to Batavia with the VOC flag on it. Thereafter, *Avondster* remained in the service of the VOC until it sank on July 2, 1659, while anchoring near the Black Fort in the harbor of Galle, Sri Lanka.

In the early seventeenth century, the VOC had stretched its trading activities in Asia in the regions of Java, Sumatra, the Arabian Sea, the Bay of Bengal, the Strait of Malacca, the Spice Islands of Banda Sea, and the Far East and the South China sea.[23] The VOC trading activities in the Java region of the Eastern Islands were centered around its headquarters at Batavia and included other places in and around the Java Sea such as Bantam in Northwest Java. Bantam is a port town close to the Sunda Strait through which the trading vessels carrying pepper pass between Java and Sumatra. At Bantam the English had established their trading post in 1603. The Dutch and the Portuguese fought for the control of Bantam. The Dutch established their trading factory in Batavia in 1611, and they were in a position to control it. The trading points in the Java north coast included Japara and Grissee ports and Sukadana, Banjarmasin, and Martapura ports located in the south Kalimantan.

The Strait of Malacca was strategically very important in that it connects the Far East and the Indonesian Archipelago on one side and the Indian Ocean on the other. The Sunda Strait was already under Dutch control. The control of both the Straits of Malacca and Sunda was the target of the VOC. The Dutch made an alliance with the Sultan of Johore, who was driven out of Malacca by the Portuguese. After 1640, when Malacca was taken over by the Portuguese, the Dutch tried to establish an international trade center to monopolize the trade of pewter, but this effort was prevented by the local producers of pewter.

The main Dutch entrepôts in the Bay of Bengal included: Hooghly in West Bengal; the ports of Colombo and Galle in Sri Lanka, the ports of Pegu in southern Myanmar and Martaban or Mottama in the Gulf of Martaban in Myanmar; the Andaman Islands in the Bay of Bengal between India to the west and Myanmar to the north and the east; on the Coromandel Coast the ports included Machilipatnam port in Andhra Pradesh on the coast of the Bay of Bengal, Nagapattinam, and Pulicat. Pulicat was a seaport in Tamil Nadu on the Coromandel Coast of south India, which was the headquarters of the Dutch where the Dutch built a fort called Geldria in 1608, as a defense against the local kings and the Portuguese and then monopolized the trade in nutmeg, cloves, cinnamon, pepper, tea, silk, and the Chinese porcelain.

Textiles from India occupied a pivotal place in the barter trade in Asia. The Portuguese established posts around India. However, the Portuguese were not strong along the Coromandel Coast. In 1605, the Dutch established their first factory in Masulipatnam. The VOC Governor established his residence at Pulicat on the south coast, and this place remained the Dutch headquarters until 1690. The Dutch were in constant conflict with the Portuguese in the region. The local rulers moved the Dutch from Pulicat to Geldria. The town and fort of Nagapattinam were captured by the Portuguese in 1658. The area was destroyed by a tsunami in 1680, and the Dutch built a new fort. The military action led by the Dutch commander expelled the Portuguese from Ceylon and reestablished its strong position on the coast of Coromandel.

Another important textile center was Bengal. The Mughal rulers of Bengal provided trade concessions to European companies. The Dutch established their position at Chinsurah near Hooghly. In addition to textiles, the other commodities included silk, opium, sugar, and saltpeter (potassium nitrate), a raw material used in the production of gunpowder. After 1620, the VOC reached Myanmar and the exports from this region were rice and slaves. In the 1630s, the Dutch established a garrison in Ceylon. In 1640, the Dutch captured the port city of Galle in Sri Lanka from the Portuguese. During the 1640s and 1650s, the Dutch captured the coastal area from the Portuguese. Ceylon played an important role in trade. For trade in silk and spices, the VOC established a post at Gamron (Bandar-e-Abbas) in 1623. The presence of English in Persia was a threat to the Dutch.

The Dutch trading points on the Arabian Sea ranged from Maldives in the southeast, the west coast of India to Persia and Arabia in the west. The specific ports included: Surat port on the Gulf of Cambay, Goa port, Cochin port on the southwest coast of India, Bandar-e-Abbas and Basra ports in Persia, Mocha port in the Arabian Peninsula, and Maldives. In 1620, the Dutch built a big naval force in the Arabian Sea to counter the threats from the Portuguese and the English. In the west, the Dutch established a post at Mocha in the Arabian Peninsula. Coffee became an important trade item in this region. The Dutch could not expel the Portuguese from the region but kept them engaged. Now the Dutch focused on the west coast of India. In 1656, the Dutch after a prolonged siege captured Colombo from the Portuguese, which was their strong base after Goa. The Dutch feared that the Portuguese could use the Malabar Coast as a base to recapture Ceylon. Pepper was the key product of this region. The Dutch made many attempts to gain control of the Malabar Coast but failed, and finally in 1663, they were able to bring the coast under their control. The pepper of India reduced the Dutch dependence on the pepper producers of Indonesia and Malaysia.

The VOC trading points in Sumatra include the whole of the island with the exception of the Strait of Malacca. The main entrepôts of the VOC were Banda Aceh in the north, Tiku in the West Sumatra, Jambi on the east coast of Central Sumatra, Bengkulu in the west coast of Sumatra, and Palembang port in the South Sumatra. The ports of Phuket or Udjong Salang, Malacca, and Singapore in the Strait of Malacca in the South China Sea served the trading activities of the VOC.

VOC's trading spice islands in Indonesia included the regions of Ambon and Seram, Banda, and the Moluccas. The route started from East Java and Bali, the Lesser Sunda Islands to the south-east of Kalimantan and Sulawesi including east of Banda around the Arafura Sea. The principal trading points were Makassar port in Sulawesi (Celebes), the Ambon islands, the Banda Islands, the Kupang port in Timor Island, and the Moluccas.

The VOC's entrepôts in the Far East included: the ports of Firando and Nagasaki in Japan, Fort Zeelandia in Taiwan, Pescadores Islands in the Taiwan Strait, Macao on China's southern coast, Manila in the Philippines, Ayutthaya and Pattani in Thailand, Phnom Penh in Cambodia, Sarawak in Malaysia. Taiwan and Japan were the main centers for the Dutch trading company, while China and the Philippines were the secondary points. The Chinese market was important for the VOC since its inception. The VOC expected that the silk trade with Japan alone would be sufficient to finance the whole VOC trade in Asia. Many nations had been conducting trade with China. The Portuguese transported the commodities from Macao to the European markets via Molucca and Goa. The Spanish used the Chinese junks to transport their cargo to the Philippines for onward transportation to Mexico and then finally to Spain. The Chinese directly traded with Indonesia and Malaysia. The Portuguese, the Spanish, and the Japanese traders were working through the coasts of Malacca via Siam, Vietnam to Japan. The Dutch were interested in direct trade with China, but the Portuguese were successful in preventing them. The Dutch then thought that the best way to get Chinese merchandise was to capture the Portuguese and Spanish ships carrying Chinese products. The Dutch made money by pirating the Chinese junks which were on their way to the Philippines. These captured products facilitated, for the Dutch, access to the Japanese markets but did not let Japan trade directly with China.

In order to obtain complete control over the Chinese market, Coen wanted to repeat the same course of action that he had adopted on Banda and sent an armed fleet to the Far East. In 1622, his raid on Macao failed. In 1624, a large Chinese fleet surrounded the Dutch stronghold on the Pescadores and compelled them to move toward Taiwan; from there the Dutch continued their attempts on China market. In 1632 the Dutch made their last attempt and that too failed. Finally, China expelled them from Taiwan in 1662. However, the Dutch were allowed limited trading activities off Nagasaki. Japanese gold, silver, and copper were important products for the Europeans, and the Dutch had an advantage over the competitors. Japanese precious metals were exchanged for silk and luxury items and were used to purchase textiles from India. The Dutch had no control over the prices of the commodities in the Japanese market. The VOC ships made 11,700 voyages between 520 destinations in 35 areas of Asia.[24] During the period 1700 through 1760, the tonnage of the VOC's shipping sailing back around Cape was about three times of the English shipping.

At the same time when the VOC was engaged in the east, the Dutch had established the government-owned exclusive Company in the west known as the Dutch West Indies Company that was to operate in the Atlantic Ocean for trade in the west. The main target was trading activities around the Hudson River. For this purpose, the Dutch built a settlement called the Nova Belgia, or the New Netherlands, or New Amsterdam, on an island at the mouth of the Hudson River. The Dutch colonized Suriname, which later became a part of the kingdom of the Netherlands. According to Smith, the colony of Nova Belgia[25] now divided into two states of New York and New Jersey remained under the Dutch government. The colony of Nova Belgia prospered due to the abundant and cheap land of good quality. The Dutch company enjoyed a complete monopoly and allowed the Dutch ships to trade to Suriname on payment of 2.5% of the value of their cargo to obtain a license, and the Company reserved the rights of the slave trade from Africa to America. The relaxation of the Company's privileges led to the development of the colony. The Caribbean islands of Curacoa and Eustatia were owned by the Dutch West Indies Company and were free ports for all the nations, and this was the source of development of the barren islands. Their colonies in the West progressed well compared to the other colonies of the Europeans. The Dutch colony of Nova Belgia was resisted by the local Indians and later was attacked by the British, who, after defeating the Dutch, finally occupied it in 1664 and renamed it New York. The Dutch had built a wall for the defense of the colony and the remains of the wall are now paved as the Wall Street of New York. The expensive continental wars compelled the Dutch to vacate the space for the British and French competitors in the west.

Notes

1 Wendy, "The Batavia Shipwreck", p. 256.
2 Ibid.
3 Parthesius, "Dutch Ships in Tropical Waters", p. 33.
4 Wright, p. 33.
5 Parthesius, p. 34.
6 Wendy, p. 361.
7 Ibid., p. 397.
8 Winchester, "Krakatoa, the Day the World Exploded", p. 19.
9 Parthesius, p. 35.
10 Wendy, p. 273.
11 Wright, p. 182.
12 Ibid., p. 183.
13 Ibid., p. 183.
14 Ibid., p. 187.
15 Ibid., p. 189.
16 Ibid., p. 194.
17 Ibid., p. 199.
18 Dunbar, p. 62.
19 Parthesius, p. 40.
20 Wright, p. 213.
21 Wendy, p. 331.
22 Ibid., p. 358.
23 Parthesius, pp. 19–26.
24 Ibid., p. 9.
25 Smith, p. 615.

Bibliography

Dunbar, George Sir, *India and the passing of Empire*, Ivor Nicholson & Watson Ltd., 26 Manchester Square, London, UK, 1951.

Parthesius, Robert, *Dutch Ships in Tropical Waters: The Development of the Dutch East India Company (VOC) Shipping Network in Asia 1595–1660*, Amsterdam University Press, Amsterdam, Holland, 2010.

Smith, Adam, *The Wealth of Nations (Modern Library Edition)*, Random House, Inc., New York, USA, 1994.

Van Duivenvoorde, Wendy, The Batavia Shipwreck: An Archaeological Study of an early Seventeenth-Century Dutch East Indiaman, A Ph. D dissertation submitted to the Office of Graduate Studies of Texas A&M University, College Station, Texas, USA, 2008.

Winchester, Simon, *Krakatoa, The Day the World Exploded, August 27, 1883, New York*, Harper Collins Publishers Inc., New York, USA, 2005.

Wright, Arnold, *Early English Adventurers in the East*, Sang-e-Meel Publications, Lahore, Pakistan, 2000.

5
THE CONQUESTS OF THE FRENCH COMPANY OF THE INDIES

Influenced by the Dutch experience of large commercial enterprises on foreign lands, Colbert, a minister of Louis XIV, decided that France should also play its role in international trade through the establishment of a powerful government-owned Company with exclusive monopolies. Colbert's proposal of establishing the Compagnie des Indes Orientales was approved by the king. The king's declaration of establishing the French East India Company, to carry out international trade in the East Indies and to direct the expansion of France across the seas, was given at Vincennes in August 1664 and was registered in Parliament on September 1. Americas and the Indies were the targets of Colbert's expeditions. The initial capital of the Company was £600,000, writes Dunbar.[1] Nine out of twenty-one directors came from outside Paris. Colbert wanted to organize the Company on the pattern of the Dutch VOC with five regional chambers established at Lyon, Rouen, Le Havre, Nantes, and Bordeaux. Each regional chamber enjoyed fiscal, commercial, and operational autonomy and was required to nominate one to three of its members to the central chamber in Paris. The central chamber in Paris played a dominant role by appointing its 12 directors to the board of 21 directors.

The task that was given to Colbert and his main focus was North America and the Indies. The French Company of the West's areas in North America stretched from Hudson's Bay to Florida, and it was called Canada or New France. It had sovereign and territorial rights, monopoly of trade and settlements. It did not care for the English colonies of New England and Virginia. All kinds of resources were provided for the systematic development of Canada. The role of the French in Canada was as explorers, colonizers, and competitors with the English settlers in America. In 1665, Colbert's company reached Montreal and established its upper station of the French in Canada, writes Woodward.[2] Jesuit missions reached Lake Ontario and from there to Lake Superior and then

DOI: 10.4324/9781003377719-6

penetrated to the north and the south of St. Lawrence. In 1632, the Treaty of St. Germain recognized the French's possession of the basin of St. Lawrence and the district of Acadia which covered Nova Scotia and New Brunswick. These settlements did not pose any threat to New England. In 1697, a French naval captain named D'Iberville led the expedition, built a fort, and laid the foundation of the Louisiana colony.

Just like the Dutch, the French, in 1717, also established a Mississippi Company with the task of colonizing the Mississippi valley and establishing the city of New Orleans. The Company had the support of King Louis XV, and to raise the capital, it sold shares on the Paris Stock Exchange. According to Harari, the Company's director, John Law,[3] was also the governor of the central bank of France and was entrusted with the additional financial powers equivalent to the finance minister.

Later, in 1717, the Company found that there were no treasures in the Mississippi valley waiting for them. But still the Company exaggerated the juicy fortune story of Mississippi to attract the French elite investors, and as a result of this device the prices of the Company's shares skyrocketed. The initial price of a share was 500 livres, and on August 1, 1719, it was traded at 2,750 livres. Livre was a French currency in use until 1794. By December, the price of a share crossed the mark of 10,000 livres. The people in Paris who wanted to become rich overnight sold their assets to buy the shares of the Mississippi Company. Soon the people realized that these prices are artificial, unrealistic, and unsustainable and started selling the shares while the prices were at the peak, and this created panic.

As the sale of shares increased, the prices of the shares plummeted, and John Law introduced the central bank's intervention to stabilize the prices but in vain. John Law, as governor of the central bank, printed more money to buy additional shares of the company. Now the whole of the French financial system was inside the bubble. The prices of the share fell from 10,000 livres to 1,000 livres and then collapsed. The big investors sold their stock in time, while the small investors lost everything. The Mississippi bubble crashed the entire financial system of France which lost the trust of the investors and the French king Louis XV could not get credit, and this led to the fall of the overseas French empire into the hands of the British. The king raised money at a higher interest rate which increased his debt service liability which had risen to 50% of the annual budget. With the fall of the overseas French empire, the British overseas empire was expanding rapidly through the private joint stock companies listed on the London Stock Exchange. In the early seventeenth century, the first British settlements in North America were established by joint stock companies such as the London Company, the Plymouth Company, the Dorchester Company, and the Massachusetts Company, writes Harari.[4]

The colonialization of the 13 states, which became the United States in 1776, was complete. Now further expansion of the British Empire was at work. By 1773, both France and Spain together resisted the commercial and expansion interests of the British. The loss of Gibraltar and Minorca disturbed Spain. The British colony Georgia pressed hard on Florida which was a part of the Spanish dominion. The right of search which Spain enjoyed in her own waters was extended to the high seas. The traders from Boston and the West Indies complained that their ships had been searched, seized, and carried to Havannah or Cartagena, and the officers and crews were imprisoned, and cargoes plundered. The English people were irritated with Spain who offended their interests. In 1739, the English demanded the abandonment of the right of search and the admission of the British claim of Georgia.

A war broke between Spain and England, and France stood behind Spain because it was hoping to get back its colony of Acadia from the British. In 1744, France joined Spain in war. The naval war was carried out in the Mediterranean. In 1747, the British defeated both powers. In 1746, the British captured Louisburg, the French fortress in Cape Breton Island, Nova Scotia, now New Brunswick in Canada. At the same time the French took Madras in India. Both England and France struggled in America during the period 1740 through 1760. In 1739, the French from Louisiana, in search of the Pacific, penetrated the mountains of Colorado, the region of Dakota, and the easternmost range of the Rocky Mountain. In 1752, the French reached Saskatchewan, some hundred miles in the west of Manitoba. The occupation alone determined the possession of the territory in the absence of boundaries.

The French made an important alliance with the Indian tribes of the west to circumvent the expansion of the British. The French's policy was to link the colonies of Canada and Louisiana through the fortified posts. Louisburg fortress in the northeast guarded the mouth of St. Lawrence against the naval attack and threatened the English possession of Acadia. In the west, a fort at Crown Point upon the Lake Champlain was built in 1731 which closed the access from New York to St. Lawrence through which the English might have cut off Montreal and the lakes from access to the sea. The French Fort Frontenac, on the north shore of Ontario, guarded the outlet of the Lake; Fort Niagara secured the communications from Erie to Ontario and barred the English from their Iroquois connections across the lakes. Posts on Miami and Wabash led on to Louisiana, where at the entrance of the southern colony, Fort Chartres blocked the waterway of Mississippi to New Orleans. The occupation of the basin of Ohio was still needed to block the traders of Virginia and Pennsylvania. These were the defenses that the French had prepared against the British. The distance between Frontenac to New Orleans was about 1,500 miles. The French travelers navigating along the lakes to the great river and the Gulf of Mexico claimed their right to occupation.

The British defense front on the extreme right was Acadia taken from the French, not well governed, and was a source of weakness rather than strength. Maine and New England were protected by dense forests and covered the watershed of St. Lawrence which went through the counties of Penobscot and Kennebec of Maine State and Connecticut which were vulnerable to Indians' attacks. New York was defended against the French through an alliance with the Iroquois, a confederacy of six North American people, namely, Mohawk, Oneida, Seneca, Onondaga, Cayuga, and Tuscarora, who held the forests of the Upper Hudson. Fort Oswego on Lake Ontario was the extreme outpost, which provided an access to the lakes and was envied by the French. To the south, Pennsylvania and Virginia were far from the French's reach.

On New England's border and along the Upper Hudson, the Indians were a source of trouble. Unprovoked, surprised, and sudden attacks by the Indians from the forests occurred and disappeared instantly. The French had a longing for the recovery of Acadia. In 1744, the French attacked but failed to regain Acadia which stayed with the British. Next Louisburg, in Cape Breton, a strong naval station, stood for a fight. It was built in 1716 to replace Port Royal which fell in 1710 to the colonial and British forces. Shirley, the governor of Massachusetts, struck and Louisburg fell in 1744 after a siege of three months. This was the most strategically important post which the New Englanders got. However, the New Englanders were disappointed when Louisburg was given back to the French in 1748 in exchange for Madras in India.

In 1740, the English traders moved across the Alleghenies into the Ohio basin and in 1748 found villages of Logstown and Pickawillany, and some of them reached Mississippi. Mississippi was first reached by the French named Marquette in 1673 while travelling from Wisconsin by Lake Michigan and passing the junction of Missouri and at the mouth of Arkansas and then turned northward. Later, under the orders of the French Commander, La Salle completed the discovery of Mississippi to its mouth in the Gulf of Mexico in 1682. In 1668, La Salle also discovered the Lakes Erie, Huron, and Superior. In 1749, the French expedition was sent to take possession of Ohio and consider it within the limits of their Louisiana colony. But the Indians expelled the French and sided with the English traders. In 1751, the Ohio Company was formed by George II with the rights of over half a million acres of land. To secure this advance post, a fort was built where Pittsburg now stands. In 1753, Governor Dinwiddie of Virginia sent a young and smart major, George Washington, to stop the French advancement in Ohio. In April 1754, the French expelled the English from the Ohio outpost and a war broke out.

The French colony of Canada was under the French Company managed by the French Government. The colony did not progress under the control of the Company. The Company was dissolved after the Mississippi scheme of John Law. In February 1755, in response to Dinwiddie's request, the British sent Braddock, who arrived in Virginia with two British regiments to expel the French from Ohio. The British attacked Montreal and Quebec from the west, the south, and the east. In 1760, Montreal fell to the British. Braddock attacked Fort Duquesne, but due to a lack of supplies, he failed and the Indians of Ohio joined the winning side. The Indians made forays against Virginia and Pennsylvania. In 1756, the French repelled the British attack on Niagara. The French commander general Louis Joseph de Montcalm took Oswego and moved southward along the

Lake Champlain and built an impregnable fort at Ticonderoga and was hoping to capture the valley of Hudson, a big threat to the English colonies.

The French strengthened their positions on the lakes and Ohio when the Indians joined the winning side. The French took the advanced post of the British army at Fort William Henry. In June 1757, Pitt took the charge at home and the American conflict became a national war and new preparations were made. In 1758, Pitt's men crossed through the Alleghenies in July and took Fort Duquesne. Louisburg fell to the British commanders Amherst and Wolfe. In September, Fort Frontenac was captured and Oswego recovered. With Ontario in the British hands, Fort Niagara and the whole of Louisiana were delinked from St. Lawrence and now the way was clear for the British attack on Canada.

Now the British were making preparation for a major attack on the heart of Canada. After the capture of Louisburg, the fortress of Quebec was ready for the British catch, and the French navies were now vulnerable. The British fleet of 9,000 troops under the command of General Wolfe captured Quebec on September 14, 1759, by defeating the French general Montcalm and won Canada on September 18, 1759. Montreal surrendered unconditionally to Amherst on September 8. Under the terms of surrender, all the French officers, troops, sailors, and civil officials were sent to France in British vessels, and Canada came under the British rule.

In 1675[5] the headquarters of the French East India Company was built at Pondicherry, about 100 miles in the south of Fort St. George. At the headquarters there were only 450 French troops. Similarly, the English East India Company at Madras had only 200 men led by an inefficient commander. In Bengal, the French held Chandernagore under Joseph Dupleix just like the English held Calcutta and Mahé port on the west coast. The French Company also held Ile de France and the Ile de Bourbon (Mauritius and Réunion) and claimed rights in Madagascar. Moreover, the three British presidencies of Madras, Bombay, and Calcutta were hundreds of miles apart and were independent of each other. In 1741, 50,000 Marathas invaded Carnatic and made the Muslim governor Chanda Sahib prisoner. During the siege, the Marathas wrote to Pierre Benoit Dumas, the French governor-general of Pondicherry demanding the surrender of Chanda Sahib's family. Dumas wrote back, "the family is under the protection of King of France. Each of the French on the soil of India would die for their protection".

While competing in North America, at the same time, the French and the British got engaged in the east in India where they were involved in local politics. France was interested to make India a part of the French empire. In 1741, Joseph Francois Dupleix, governor-general of the French Company of the Indies, arrived in Pondicherry. In 1742, Dupleix became the governor of southern India and his general de Bussy controlled Deccan.[6] Albeit Dupleix was very enthusiastic to establish France as the suzerain power of an Indian Empire of vassal princes. He was confident of establishing the French Empire by expelling the British from the east. Dupleix and his admiral La Bourdonnais were determined to restrict the interests of the British in India. Bourdonnais was cognizant of the fact that sea supremacy was the key factor in this game. Through his crafty behavior, Dupleix was the first foreigner to have an access to the court of Delhi and became a part of the political system of India. However, he forgot to realize that the key to success remained with the strength of the naval power that was to secure the sea transportation which was the sine qua non upon which the French could establish its supremacy in India. Due to a lack of strong naval powers in the Asian waters, Dupleix was doomed to fail.

In 1744, war broke in Europe between France and Great Britain. In 1745, a British fleet arrived off Pondicherry. In September 1746, Bourdonnais arrived in Pondicherry with 2,000 troops and attacked and captured Madras and Fort St. George and a ransom of £400,000[7] was agreed upon without consulting Dupleix, writes Woodward. Anwaruddin, the nawab of Arcot, protested the interference by the French and demanded Dupleix to surrender Madras. The nawab attempted to get it back but was defeated in 1747. The French ground victories were challenged by the nature and a hurricane destroyed the French fleet. In January 1748, the English first commander-in-chief of the Company in India, Major Stringer Lawrence, landed at Fort St. David. In July Admiral Boscawen arrived at Fort St. David with a very strong fleet and 1,000 troops of criminals released from jail. Boscawen superseded Lawrence. The British sieged Pondicherry but failed and it stayed with the French. According to the treaty of Aix-la-Chapelle,[8] the British got Madras in exchange for Louisburg which the English in North America had taken from the French. In 1749, in Carnatic, Chanda Sahib with the help of the French defeated and killed Nawab Anwaruddin. Dupleix installed Mozaffar Jung as the nizam of Hyderabad, who was protected by the French. In Deccan and Carnatic, French authority was established under the control of the French governor-general. The French involvement in the local disputes provided a casus belli for the British to get involved.

Dupleix controlled Pondicherry, and his deputy Bussy controlled Hyderabad. A 26-year-old British merchant, Robert Clive, who worked under Lawrence, attacked Arcot with an army of 200 British and 300 Indian soldiers and entered the fortress. Chanda Sahib sent an army of 10,000 Indian soldiers with a detachment of French troops under Reza Sahib to recover his capital. Clive sought help from the Marathas, who agreed to join him with 6,000 horsemen. On November 14, Reza's attack was repulsed and he abandoned the siege. In June 1752, Chanda Sahib's army along with the French forces was defeated. Clive captured Arcot, and Chanda Sahib was killed in 1753. The French government dismissed Dupleix for his hostile policies toward the English East India Company. Dupleix returned to France in October 1754 and, after ten years, died in 1764.

In 1758, the French commander Comte de Lally arrived in India with a fleet and a force of 1,000 troops. Lally's officer, Conflans, was defeated and Masulipatnam fell in April 1759. Understanding the ground realities, the nizam changed his partnership from the French to the English, ceded Masulipatnam to them and dismissed the French Corps. This sealed the exit of the French from the Indian subcontinent. The French general Lally was defeated by Sir Eyre Coote at the battle of Wandiwash in 1760 and lost Pondicherry in January

1761. Mahé was captured in February. Chandernagore fell to Clive. The English East India Company annexed Madras. The French power in India disappeared. On his return, Lally was executed. In India the French did not possess a square yard of territory. Within two years every French island in the West Indies, with the exception of San Domingo, fell.[9] Goree and Senegal were captured, and France lost all the opportunities for the slave trade in West Africa. According to the Treaty of Paris in February 1763, France surrendered all of its territories in North America lying in the east of Mississippi, except the city of New Orleans. In the West Indies, the British restored St. Lucia, Martinique, and Guadeloupe to France and kept the islands of Tobago, St. Vincent, and Dominica. In India, France got her territories back as trading posts. Spain lost Florida and kept Cuba. India and America now belonged to the British.

The French again attempted their entry into the subcontinent after 20 years. In 1775, Haider Ali, the ruler of Mysore, sought an alliance with the French against the British. When Haider Ali attacked Carnatic in July 1780, the French just supplied military equipment as they did not receive reinforcement from France. During the Second Anglo-Mysore War, the French army of 2,500 men under the command of Duchemin arrived in India. The goal of the French army was to recapture the French possessions and to assist Haider Ali against the British. Marathas and Nizam had aligned with the British. On February 9, 1783, the peace treaty was signed at Versailles between the French and the British. After this news the French refused to fight against the British which annoyed Tipu Sultan. Due to the French betrayal and devoid of their support, Tipu finally agreed to an armistice, which he signed at Mangalore on August 2, 1783. In the Third Mysore War, the French also remained neutral. France again failed to bring India under its empire.

Notes

1 Dunbar, p. 68.
2 Woodward, "A Short History of the Expansion of the British Empire", p. 163.
3 Harari, "Sapiens, A Brief History of Humankind", p. 360.
4 Ibid., p. 363.
5 Woodward, p. 196.
6 Dunbar, p. 72.
7 Woodward, p. 199.
8 Dunbar, p. 75.
9 Woodward, p. 206.

Bibliography

Dunbar, George Sir, *India and the passing of Empire*, Ivor Nicholson & Watson Ltd., 26 Manchester Square, London, UK, 1951.
Harari, Yuval Noah, *Sapiens: A Brief History of Humankind*, Vintage Books, 20 Vauxhall Bridge Road, London, UK, 2011.
Woodward, William Harrison, *A Short History of the Expansion of the British Empire, 1500–1902*, Second Edition, Cambridge University Press, London, UK, 1902.

6
THE BRITISH COLONIES IN THE AMERICAS, AFRICA, AND AUSTRALASIA

On June 24, 1497, Giovanni Cabotto, sailing for King Henry VII of England and using the English name John Cabot, sighted the coast of northern New England and established contacts between Northern Europe and North America. After more than a century later, the British established settlements in Virginia and Plymouth, writes Sale.[1] John Hawkins of Plymouth learnt that the acquisition of human capital was good in Hispaniola (Haiti) and the most of it could be obtained on the coast of Guinea. Hawkins became the first merchant to start English procurement of human resources from Africa. African trade in human capital has been an important part of the Spanish trading system. In October 1562, Hawkins sailed with three ships of 120, 100, and 40 tons with 100 men on board, writes Woodward.[2] Hawkins arrived in Sierra Leone, where he captured 300 natives. With this catch, Hawkins moved to San Domingo to challenge the Spanish monopoly of the Indies. Hawkins returned to England after a voyage of one year with his merchandise of hides, sugar, ginger, and pearls. A year later, Hawkins started his second voyage by crossing to Jamaica, San Domingo, and Cuba and returned via Florida with gold, silver, pearls, and other precious stones. In the third voyage in 1567, he captured about 500 natives and the trade with Dominica was opened. Now the Spanish got alerted, and it became difficult for Hawkins to attack Cartagena. William Hawkins returned to England via the Gulf of Mexico.

John Hawkins' 21-year-old cousin, Francis Drake, expressed his willingness to risk his life in the waters of the West Indies as an intrepid sailor. Hawkins gave Drake his 50-ton barque named *Judith* for the expedition. Spain and Portugal made their fortunes through their plantations in North, South, and Central America; the West Indies; and the east. Drake challenged the Spanish power in the seas and wanted to engage them in the Spanish Indies. From 1568 until his death in 1596, Drake remained engaged in irregular naval wars with the

DOI: 10.4324/9781003377719-7

Spaniards. Drake sailed for his first voyage to the West Indies in May 1572. In August 1573, Drake returned to Plymouth from his first voyage with the profitable spoils of the Spanish treasures that he had plundered in the Spanish Indies.

In November 1577, Drake embarked on a secret mission from Plymouth on a 100-ton *Pelican* named *Golden Hind* which was equipped with 18 cannons along with 150 armed men. His departure was kept secret in England, and only the queen and the Secretary of State Earl of Leicester, Walsingham, were privy to Drake's mission. One of the goals of Drake was to enter the Pacific Sea which was under the exclusive control of the Spaniards and which was protected through their possessions of the coast line from Mexico to Chile, writes Woodward.[3] From the Cape de Verde islands, Drake arrived on the Brazilian coast and saw the land near Rio Grande do Sul. On August 24, Drake landed on the island and took possession as the English territory for the queen. One of his three vessels sunk in the waters. The second ship got separated, and Drake was left with the one vessel in the Pacific. Drake discovered the island of Tierra del Fuego. On December 5, 1578, Drake came across the Spanish port and took the Spanish trading vessel as a prize and searched the warehouse and found gold, silver, and fresh provisions. After the plunder of the Spanish treasure, Drake moved northward. After plundering the treasure ships on the way, Drake arrived in Costa Rica and, after that, California. In the middle of June 1579, Drake anchored in a bay to the north of San Francisco. Drake was welcomed by the Indians of northern California who promised to protect him as they were fed up with the Spaniards. Drake took possession of the territory and named it New Albion (California). Drake wanted to return via Spice Islands and the Indian Ocean.

On July 26, 1579, Drake started his Pacific voyage. He arrived at Pelew Islands, then the Philippines, and Ternate in the Spice Islands which were the territories of the Portuguese Empire. Drake negotiated and signed the treaty of alliance with the Sultan of Spice Islands (Ternate) which was important for the British government as it had opened the gate for the British to trade in the east and to secure a share of the wealth of the east. After crossing Java, Drake took the southern route to the Cape passage. Nothing was heard about him until he returned to Plymouth on September 26, 1580. Drake reached the East Indies by travelling to the West which Columbus could not do. The voyage was successful in that it undermined the Spanish power by capturing its treasures and created an opportunity for the British for the establishment of plantations and trading links.

As the population of England grew faster than the manufacturing sector, there was a need for additional land for production and employment which led to the motive of necessity and utility for the establishment of the colonies across the borders in the west and the east. According to Adam Smith, the establishment of the European colonies in America and the West Indies was not based on the motive of necessity, albeit they were based on the expected utility.[4] The motives of necessity and utility were supplemented by the motive of the religion to introduce and strengthen Christianity by baptizing the poor people of the colonies. The earl of Southampton and Sir F. Gorges, the governor of the port of

Plymouth, sought a charter of the Virginia Company from James-I, which was granted in April 1606,[5] for the establishment of the colonies in North America.

In December 1606, three British small ships started their first voyage by sailing down the Thames River to the New World along the North American coast what the British called Virginia, named after the Virgin Queen. The mission of the first voyage was to find mines for gold, copper, and silver; find the sea passage to Asia; and establish a colony that would act as the first outpost for future expansion in America, writes Sale.[6] Twenty years earlier, Sir Walter Raleigh had sponsored the first English voyage to Virginia, a land that he wanted to see to be populated by the English. Sir Walter Raleigh was now imprisoned in the Towers of London on charges of having blasphemous opinions and treasons on account of being an agent of Spain. He was convicted in 1604 and awarded the death sentence.[7]

The fleet of three ships was captained by a 46-year-old mariner and navigator, Christopher Newport,[8] and carried about 150 men and boys who were the potential settlers which included a dozen laborers, four carpenters, a couple of masons, a blacksmith, a barber, two surgeons, and no farmers. The potential settlers did not include women which was the most important factor in a successful settlement. The mission of this fleet was not only to establish a colony but to replace the dwindling Spanish Empire in North America and further British expansion. Interestingly, the fleet was not sponsored by the king but was managed by a private company known as Virginia Company listed on the London Stock market which expected fortunes from overseas. The famous expert of the British colonialism Richard Hakluyt gave tips to the fleet before its departure. The tips[9] included: how to search for minerals, not to offend the naturals, and how and where to plant, writes Sale. To correct the deficiencies of administration of the previous companies, an elaborate constitution for the Virginian Company was provided which included two councils, one at home and one at the colony. The Royal Council of Virginia based in London included 14 members nominated by the Crown. Its first function was to elect from the original 140 settlers a Resident Council to elect their own President.[10] The Resident Council was to run its administration by developing its local rules and regulations subject to the approval of the Crown and home council. In 1609, a new charter was granted whereby the Company would be represented by a council of the Directors vested with entire control, who would nominate a governor in the colony. Lord Delaware was sent out as governor, and Sir Thomas Smith became the chief executive at home. The governor had the authority to impose martial law to ensure the rule of law.

Christopher Newport was a member of the piracy business run by London merchants which was fetching up to £200,000 per year.[11] Christopher Newport had sailed with the prince of pirates Sir Francis Drake who raided Cadiz and pulled King Philips' beard in 1587 and captured the Portuguese carrack *Madre de Dios* with half million pounds' worth of treasure in 1592 which was then the biggest loot. Drake lost his right arm during raids on the Spanish ships and ports in the Caribbean. The lucrative business of piracy fueled the urge for capital generation through exploring additional resources and thus providing the capital, naval experience, and ships to the British government for building the British Empire overseas.

The three ships of the Virginia Company secretly left on the night of December 19–20, 1606. The sailing was kept secret to avoid any conflict with Spain that had claims to the lands of Northern America. But the secret sailing of three ships remained no secret when the Virginia Company published in London a poem in honor of the sailing crews. The fleet confronted the bad weather in the Channel, and the horrible storms compelled it to anchor along the English coast for about a month. In February, the fleet turned its direction southward toward Canaries. On March 24, 1607, the fleet reached Dominica and then turned north along the Florida coast. On April 26, the fleet reached the mouth of the Chesapeake Bay, now in the US states of Maryland and Virginia, the largest harbor on the Atlantic coast, which the British thought the place for their settlement.

In 1607, the British established their first colony on the bank of the James River in the Chesapeake area and on May 13, 1607, named it Jamestown, now in Virginia, in honor of the monarch. The location of the Jamestown colony was near modern Williamsburg, Virginia, and they called it New England. With this, the period of colonialization started. The Spanish had no regular garrison post at St. Augustine, Maryland. The British concept of a colony was quite different from that of the Spanish, in that the British settlers here would be permanent not just to pillage the richness and go back. The British had come to stay and make a life here as an independent country under the British Empire. The British had a need and capacity for colonialization, exploitation, and expansion just like the Spanish Empire had done in the west. The relationships between the British and the Spanish were maintained through the wedding of Isabella's daughter Catherine to British prince Arthur in 1501.

The purpose of the invasion of North America was to discover and conquer the new territories and then to convert the possessions into European economic benefits. The exploitation of the New World began with gold and silver. The transfer of bullion from the Americas to European counties triggered their economic development. The wealth accumulation by commercial and industrial sectors in Europe became an instrument of capitalist exploitation. The American bullion inflow into Spain financed its military-related procurement which was further used to expand imperial power overseas. In addition to gold and silver, other commodities such as fish were another source of profitable trade. On average, by 1578, 400 European ships made round trips to the Americas which included 150 French, 100 Spanish, 50 English, 50 Portuguese, and 30 Basque and which were loaded with fish.

After the establishment of the first British colony at Jamestown, Virginia, during the next four years, other European countries jumped in the process of colonialization; the French established a small colony at Quebec, the Dutch explored a water passage where the Hudson River meets the Atlantic Ocean, and the Spanish in Mexico moved across the Rio Grande and established a post at Santa Fe. During the next 30 years, the Spaniards established 29 additional colonies in North America and the Caribbean, a dozen more in Mexico, and a garrison at St Augustine. The French established trading posts along the St. Lawrence River such as France-Roy and Quebec. The Dutch established colonies on the Hudson and Delaware such as Fort Orange (the New Netherlands) in modern-day New York. These establishments were just the entrepôts. In 1664, the British won New York from the Dutch in a war. The Spanish settlements in the southwest such as Isabella, Santo Domingo, were the military posts and the mining centers engaged in digging gold and silver and baptizing the local natives. The British colonies in New England (Northeastern region of the United States including Vermont, Maine, New Hampshire, Massachusetts, Rhode Island, and Connecticut), Maryland, Virginia, and Plymouth were permanent settlements and engaged in occupation and agricultural activities. The colonies in the Caribbean were for trade or piracy purposes. For the British, Jamestown was the base camp for further expansion and occupation.

Though the modus operandi for the conquests by the British and the Spanish was different, their intentions were the same in terms of imperialism such as the settlement of the European people in the colonies, gaining political power to maintain their hegemony, military control of the big territories and the inhabitants, exploitation, and extraction of resources from the colonies to send back home. Newport along the river found a town called Powhatan in eastern Virginia populated by the people called Powhatans. The Indian population of the Chesapeake area was decimated and dispersed.

When Christopher Newport returned to London, he presented to the Virginia Company a big stock of gold-bearing stones which proved useless. Next time when he returned to Jamestown in 1608, he took along two goldsmiths, two refiners, and a jeweler and 115 settlers. After his second trip, Newport took some samples of gold back to London. The people of Jamestown were tortured, extracted, and executed. The corn was bartered or plundered from the fields of the Powhatans. The population of the settlers dwindled due to diseases as Virginia was a marshland, an ideal breeding ground for malaria. The settlers were not settled and they were accusing each other and there was chaos in the colony. The colony was abandoned on June 7, 1610, and the settlers returned to England. The London investors of the Virginia Company decided to refinance the Virginia colony by sending experienced soldiers like Thomas West and De La Warr as the new rulers of Virginia tasked to subdue the natives and make the Virginia colony more profitable. Warr sailed through the James River and reached Jamestown on June 10, 1610, and read out his orders for military rule. The colony was ruled by cruel and barbarous cut-throat officials of the Virginia Company. It was like a military attack on a foreign land.

Upon landing of Warr, the Anglo-Powhatan War was started. The Powhatans were ordered to accept King James and pay tribute in the form of corn. Warr's first raid was on a village of Kecoughtan, where the dissidents were killed, the village was burnt, and the cornfields were destroyed. Upon return of Warr, his successor Sir Thomas Dale, in May 1611, continued the brutal activities. Ultimately, the Powhatans pursued peace. The British got victory in the first Anglo-Powhatan War, and thereafter the natives were never able to rebel against the British. Bermuda was annexed to the Crown in 1612, and in 1614 the Company was strong enough to destroy the French settlements on the coasts of Maine and Nova Scotia which were part of the territories under the charter of the Company.

Virginia and Bermuda were the major producers of tobacco, and in 1623 both of these countries were granted a monopoly of the English market. Virginia's variety of tobacco was very harsh, and this was replaced by the one brought in from the West Indies around 1611 or 1612. The first shipment of Virginia tobacco was sent to London in 1613 or 1614. The shipment of tobacco increased from 2,300 pounds in 1616 to 60,000 pounds in 1620, leading to a fall in its price from 40 shillings a pound in 1614 to 3.5 shillings a pound in 1619.[12] In order to maintain their livelihood in the event of falling prices, the farmers stretched out into Powhatan country and brought more area under the tobacco crop. The cropping activity was very laborious, and the British brought 20 African slaves for farming activities for a certain period of time. After the completion of the service, the slaves were set free with a grant of land for farming as independent farmers. Thousands of English men and women were brought to Jamestown on these terms. The African slaves were traded. Terms and conditions for the laborers were harder than in England, and the wages of labor were very low.

The Virginia Company was not making money for its investors and was even in debt of about £9,000 after 12 years. Now to rebuild the new hopes for the investors of the Company, the Company focused on land under its new Charter of 1619. Now Sir Edwin Sandys was appointed Company's new treasurer. According to the Charter, 100 acres were given to the settlers who had settled before 1616 and were still there in the colony, plus an additional 100 acres for every share they might hold in the Company; 50 acres were granted to any contracted servant after completion of his contract. London investors of the Company were given rights to land according to their shares, plus 50 acres for every tenant that they would sponsor, and all the officers of the company who would serve in Virginia would be given an appropriate estate. The governor would get 3,000 acres, treasury would get 1,500 acres, and 100 acres would go to other ministers. On average, 560 acres were granted to the English who settled in Virginia. In 1608, the local natives were of the view that the white strangers in Powhatan had come to take their land from them.[13] Eastern forests were depleted by the lumber industry as there were 50 sawmills only in Massachusetts by 1675. The New Englanders cut down 260 million cords of wood. In Virginia, by the end of the seventeenth century, the forests on half a million acres were cleared to clear the land for tobacco production. The species of white oak, black walnut, and white cedar were eliminated. This disrupted the environmental system which was done just by a few hundred thousand of English settlers in North America.

The British wanted to coronate the tribal chief Wahunseneka to make him a vassal of King James, and for this purpose Newport asked him to kneel before them which he refused. This was a message to the white strangers that the tribal chief of the American Indian would neither kneel, nor pledge allegiance to King James, nor would change his culture. Newport now thought that there was no option other than a war. In March 1622, the natives under the command of Opechankano,[14] who succeeded Wahunseneka, rebelled and attacked the colonists at Jamestown and as far as 100 miles on each side of the James River, and thus the Second Anglo-Powhatan War began. About 400 people were killed in this war, where the total number of English settlers was about 1,240. In order to repulse the rebellion, the Virginia Company sent harsh orders which led to genocide to eliminate the natives from the land. Under the Company's orders, Governor George Yeardley was sent with orders to kill on sight all Indians of any age, or sex, burn fields and villages, and destroy all infrastructure, including canoes and weirs. The English settlers, on the pretext of making a peace treaty with Powhatan villagers, invited them and then killed them all when they assembled for the occasion. The British captain William Tucker visited a village near the Potomac to negotiate a peace treaty. When the villagers assembled, and, after signing the peace treaty, Tucker asked them to drink the poisoned wine which they did and 200 American Indians died. Consequently, all land in Virginia was confiscated by eliminating the natives, and this land was used for a profitable tobacco enterprise. This not only ended the resistance but ended the Powhatan society. Of the total population of 40,000, only 5,000 were left in the Chesapeake Bay. The English invasion succeeded, and the American Indians were barred from their lands. By 1685, the Powhatans became extinct and Virginia became the property of the crown by establishing the right of the British on the American lands.

The British continued ruling the territories of America, until the British general Lord Cornwallis surrendered to George Washington at Yorktown, Virginia. The American 13 states were supported by the French navy which broke the blockade of the English ships and brought them arms and soldiers from Europe. The United States announced the Declaration of Independence on July 4, 1776, and formed the Union. The Continental Congress declared that the 13 American colonies were no longer the subject of the British Crown. The 13 British colonies established by the British during the seventeenth and eighteenth centuries were part of the British's possessions in the New World including Canada and the Caribbean. West Florida was given to Spain. The 13 British colonies in America included New Hampshire, Massachusetts, Rhode Island, New York, New Jersey, Connecticut, Delaware, Pennsylvania, Maryland, Virginia, North Carolina, South Carolina, and Georgia (see Figure 6.1). In 1784, a college of New York called itself Columbia[15] was established in the memory of Christopher Columbus in spite of the fact that America was not discovered by Columbus. In 1787, Yale tutor Timothy Dwight's song "Columbia" became so famous with the

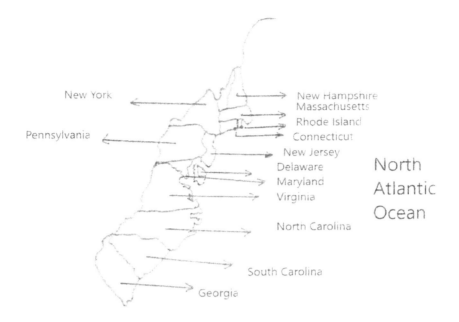

FIGURE 6.1 British American colonies

Revolutionary troops that it was regarded as an unofficial national anthem for decades. In 1791, the leaders of the government decided to build a national capital on the banks of the Potomac River to be called the "Territory of Columbia". In 1792, a ship named *Columbia* captained by Robert Grant discovered a massive river feeding into the Pacific called the Columbia River.

In the nineteenth century, Columbia became a symbol of the United States. Public started this name using for various activities such as the Columbian Institute for the Promotion of Arts and Sciences in Washington, DC, which later became the Smithsonian Institution and many states named their capital and towns as Columbia. The leaders of the Union were thinking of naming the country the United States of Columbia. But in 1819, when the Spanish colony of Nueva Granada announced its independence from Spain by declaring it as Columbia, the leaders of the Union dropped the idea of Columbia and declared it as the United States of America. Construction of the White House began in Washington District of Columbia under the guidance of James Hoban which became the official seat of the union in 1800. Vermont was admitted to the union as the 14th state, followed by Kentucky as the 15th state. About two-thirds of the population of the natives of North America was in Massachusetts.

The British colonies in North America thrived because of two factors, namely, plenty of good quality land but not as good as that of the Spanish and Portuguese colonies, and the liberty to manage their own affairs. The political environment and the institutions contributed to the improvement through the cultivation of the land. Pennsylvania was the only state where the right of primogeniture was not in practice and the land was distributed equally among all the children of the family, writes Smith.[16] In three other states of New England, the elder son got double the share. In the rest of the English colonies the right of primogeniture was prevalent under which the right of succession belonged to the eldest son. In the Spanish and Portuguese colonies, the right of succession was based on Majorazzo, under which all the estates go to one individual. In the French colonies, succession was favored by young children.

In the British colonies in North America, the civil administration expenses were moderate and so were the taxes. There were no tithes for the clergy who were supported by the voluntary contributions by the people. In the Spanish and Portuguese colonies taxes were imposed to support the mother governments. France never imposed taxes for the mother country's support, and whatever taxes were imposed, those were spent within the colonies. The British and other European nations monopolized the trade of their colonies by prohibiting them from trading with foreign countries. The trade of the colonies was exclusively carried out by the Company of the mother country which was confined to the specific ports and ships of the mother country. The poor colonies were marooned to sell cheap and buy dear, and the pillage of the colonies by the Companies of their mother countries kept them underdeveloped. The trade of the enumerated commodities not produced in the mother country at all or produced in a small quantity was confined to the mother country alone which included sugar, tobacco, cotton, wool, indigo, ginger, and other spices. The non-enumerated commodities, produced in small quantities in the mother country, were allowed to be traded with other nations included grain, timber, cattle, fish, and rum. The British allowed free trade among its colonies in North America and the West Indies. The surplus of the British colonies of America and the West Indies that came to England was exported to European countries like France and the Netherlands. Virginia and Maryland used to send 96,000 hogsheads of tobacco to England annually; England's own consumption was just 14,000 hogsheads, and the remainder of 82,000 hogsheads was exported by the British to the other European countries.[17]

The benefits that the British received from the colonies of North America were the pride of the British nation as a great country and the conqueror of the foreign lands which was capable of establishing its colonies. The other advantage was the prosperity of the British citizens through the possession of the goods from the American colonies which were neither produced nor available in Great Britain. The benefits that emerged from the exclusive trade of the enumerated goods were not available to other European countries. England further sold the enumerated commodities from the American colonies to other European countries at a higher price resulting in an abnormal profit which became the source of happiness and enjoyment for the British citizen. For example, the tobacco of Maryland and Virginia, which the English manufacturers purchased in abundant quantities at low prices due to monopolization of the colonial trade, was not available to France and other European countries. Had the European countries been allowed to purchase tobacco from Maryland and Virginia, the farmers of Maryland and Virginia would have got a higher price and the price in the European market would have been low as compared to the price when purchased exclusively from England. The British citizens enjoyed the pleasure of using American goods for the purposes of convenience, enjoyment, and ornament. All the countries that had established their colonies in North America such as Spain, Portugal, France, and England gained through trade. The wealth of the British, through exclusive trade with the colonies, increased rapidly, while the wealth of the colonies did not increase proportionately. With the exception of the trade benefits and the British colony in India, the American colonies neither provided any military services for the protection of their mother country nor provided revenues to England. The taxes that were imposed on the American colonies were only used for the operation of the civil administration. However, this was not the case for other European colonists such as Spain, Portugal, and the Dutch who received both military services and revenues from their colonies. France received only military services without revenues from its colonies.

After the fall of Montreal in September 1760, the administration of Canada switched from the French to the British hands and General Amherst became the military governor of Canada until peace was restored. In 1763, 65,000 people of Catholic and French origin were settled around St. Lawrence. The territory westward of the river Ottawa was given to the Indians. The colony of Quebec was established as a separate government. Nova Scotia, the old province of French Acadia, got its new capital Halifax founded in 1749. In 1755, the French settlers refused to take the oath of allegiance to the British. The administration of Canada remained under semi-military rule until 1774. The British government desired to treat Canada just like the other English colonies.

The Catholic Church in Canada was not just a religious but a political power, and it was anti-English. The Canadians had no experience of self-government. The use of the French language was universal. Judges were appointed who neither knew the French nor the prevailing French law. The Executive officers sold their posts on cash to their deputies who did not have any qualification to run the business. However, Canada got two good administrators named Murray and Carleton, who were not only honest but were very capable of running a good government.

Under the Quebec Act of 1774, Roman Catholicism as the religion of the colony and the church clergy were allowed to hold, receive, and enjoy their accustomed dues and rights, with respect to such persons only as shall profess the said religion, writes Woodward.[18] In civil matters, French law remained in force; criminal charges were to be decided by the English code. A nominated Council was to govern the colony, and the sovereignty of England was accepted by everyone. In 1778, a large number of settlers came to Nova Scotia from the Middle and the Southern states, and a land in Upper Canada was taken to form a new province called Ontario. By 1806, Canada and Nova Scotia received more than 80 000 immigrants. With the arrival of new immigrants, the district of New Brunswick became a separate colony in 1784.

Now the colony was no more a homogeneous nationality. By the Canada Act of 1791, Upper Canada, Ontario was separated from Lower Canada, Quebec. Each province was governed by an elected council. However, the constitution was that of the British. The executive was independent and enjoyed the power at the will of the governor. The constitution of 1791 aimed at colonial autonomy. The French and British settlers enjoyed equality. Upper Canada was able to protect protestant worship, and Lower Canada stayed with the French language and its own civil and religious institutions. Quebec accepted settlers from the United States and from the UK and was more populous of the two provinces. The British thus recognized that Canada consisted of two nations, and the constitution was so devised to meet their distinctive needs.

In 1812, the United States attacked Canada with the motive of humiliating the British. The major attack was on Upper Canada where the old loyalists strongly resisted. The war ended in 1814, leaving behind resentful feelings which are still alive. After the war, Canada grew economically and became the outlet for the British population. Economic development projects of engineering and public works such as the Ottawa canal and the industrial centers were established in Manitoba along with economic and educational reforms.

In 1837, an unrest broke out based on partly racial and partly constitutional concerns. With the increase of the English population, Lower Canada held its racial privileges. The French-populated Quebec raised the question of nationality which caused friction between the English officials and the Assembly. In Upper Canada, the land granted to the support of the Anglican church was the concern. In both provinces the measures of self-governance granted by the Constitution of 1791 were inadequate. The rapid growth of the United States under the Republican institutions created a sense of dissatisfaction among the Upper Canadians.

In 1837, a movement in favor of independence was started by a Scotchman named Mackenzie,[19] and in Lower Canada a revolt was led by Papineau. The British sent Lord Durham as High Commissioner to the colony who identified and reported two basic sources of discontentment, which were racial feelings and constitutional grievances. He advised the political union of the two provinces with one Legislature, an executive Ministry responsible for the affairs of the union, elected bodies for local affairs, and a railway connecting Halifax with Quebec. Consequently, a Reunion Act of 1840 was passed. It was the success of Canada that through its struggle a form of self-government emerged. Now, Canada was able to work for itself. Consequently, the British North America Act of 1867 was passed by which Ontario, Quebec, New Brunswick, and Nova Scotia were formed into one Dominion. To this federation, Prince Rupert's land and Manitoba joined in 1870, British Columbia in 1871, and all other territories of British North America in 1880, with the exception of Newfoundland. When

Canada started formulating the principles of the self-government, Australia and South America also pursued the same path. Under the treaties of 1818 and 1846 the boundary of Canada was accepted from the Lake Superior to the Pacific.

The Gold discoveries of 1858 led to the establishment of British Columbia as a separate colony to which Vancouver Island was added in 1866. In 1869, the landed rights of the proprietors were purchased by the Federal government. In 1870, an agitation movement was led by the French Canadian Louis Riel which was suppressed by Si Garnet Wolseley. In the same year British Colombia joined the federation, and Prince Edward Island joined in 1873. The Indian tribes were protected from extinction. In 1880, the North West Territories emerged as a separate government with its capital at Regina. Newfoundland remained an isolated colony.

The Canadian Dominion successfully implemented the federal constitution for 35 years. The local interests of the different regions were completely protected. The internal freedom of Canada was complete, and the relations with the mother country England were very cordial. The negotiations and agreements with the foreign states were conducted by the Imperial government acting in the name of the Crown. The issues that directly affected the Dominion were addressed through joint consultation of the colonial authorities and London.

In 1770, Captain Cook proclaimed British ownership of the eastern coastline called New South Wales. In 1783, the British government sent an expedition to New South Wales to convert Cook's proclamation into the actual occupation. In May 1787, the first expedition for the colonialization of Australia was led by Captain Phillip as governor of 750 convicts who were later joined by their families and became settlers. In January 1788, Botany Bay was reached and the colonialization of Australia began. Now Governor Phillip left the first landed place and reached a more suitable place called Port Jackson, and the site was named Sydney. England acquired Australia. The British government asked Governor Phillip to govern the territory of New South Wales including the eastern coast of Australia from Cape York in the north to the extreme point of Tasmania in the south. The effective settlement took place on the shore of Sydney Cove and Norfolk and Lord Howe Islands occupied by Phillip in 1788. The convicts settled on Sydney Cove occupied rich agricultural lands, 15 and 20 miles from Port Jackson, and within three years produced their own supplies. Prisoners on expiry of their sentence were allotted land. Sheep and cattle were produced. Three important industries of Australia, pastoral, agricultural, and mining were firmly established. In 1898, the Constitution was developed by the colonies that was sent to England and by the Act of the Imperial Parliament became law in 1900. All Australian colonies, including Tasmania, were part of the federation. On January 1, 1901, the first Federal Parliament was opened by the Prince of Wales. By the Act of 1900, the federating units of Australia gave certain power to the Federal Government. The Cabinet was responsible to the Parliament, the Governor General represented the Crown, the Upper House or Senate elected by the several states, and a Veto of the Crown on legislation was recognized.

On the other hand, New Zealand had been independent of Australia and the Maoris of New Zealand were vigorous warriors. They were organized in communities and were engaged in agriculture and navigation. In 1839, New Zealand was annexed by the governor of New South Wales. Captain Hobson was appointed to take charge of the new colony. The aborigines of New Zealand played a key role in the development of New Zealand. The Treaty of Waitangi of 1840 stipulated two things: first, the acceptance of the sovereignty and protection of the Queen by the Maoris; second, the guarantee of the rights of ownership of the natives in their lands by the governor. The treaty of Waitangi admitted the title of the land to the Maoris and thus recognized their status within the subject population of the empire. New Zealand was separated from New South Wales and established its own capital at Wellington in 1865.

The New Zealand Company, a joint stock company with large capital, was very powerful to amend the policy of the Imperial governors. The company had acquired large areas of land from the local chiefs in violation of the Waitangi treaty. The company was dissolved in 1851. The new constitution in line with local conditions was developed and introduced in 1852. The constitution provided for a responsible government. Parliament included the Governor, an Upper Chamber nominated by the Governor, and a House of Representatives. Elective provincial councils for local government were set up. The House of Representatives was represented by four members of Maoris.

Now a general anti-European movement started rising. The struggle that started with the land encroachments culminated in a struggle for an independence. War broke out in 1860, and the security of the English in the north became vulnerable. In 1861, Sir George Grey was recalled from the Cape for the second time. The war spread, and the guerrilla tactics of the Maoris were posing trouble for the British. In 1862, the governor facilitated the transfer of native affairs to the local government. In 1871, the natives were defeated and the islands remained in peace. The Maoris had supported the British in the South African War and the English were keen to solve their problems. With the solution of the problems of the Maoris, New Zealand marched on the road to progress. In 1870, New Zealand was looked upon as a second home for the English. New Zealand enjoyed Dominion status within the British Empire.

In 1652, the Dutch East India Company established a permanent port at the Cape of Good Hope for the Indian fleets, just like the French were trying in Madagascar and the British in St. Helena. In 1652, three Dutch vessels landed in False Bay and a settlement was made.[20] Due to a variety of reasons such as bankruptcy and discontent, the Dutch Company became vulnerable to management. In 1795, France changed Holland into the Batavian Republic. To secure the Cape against the French, the British government decided to occupy it. In 1795, the British captured Cape Town.[21] For seven years Cape Town remained under military influence, and this town was strategically important for the British for their Indian campaign. After some time, it reverted to Holland, but finally the British occupied it by force and possession was confirmed by the Treaty of 1814. The British compensated the Dutch by paying an amount of £6,000,000. By the Act of 1834, slavery was abolished in all British colonies.

In 1842, the British decided to occupy Natal from the Boers. The British troops were sent to Durban which was besieged by the Boers. In 1843, the British proclaimed Natal as its colony. From 1845 through 1856, Natal formed a part of the Cape Colony for administrative purposes. Later it became an independent colony. In 1853, a representative self-government was introduced in Cape that enjoyed the powers exercised by the Parliaments of Canada and Australia.[22] The British finally recognized two additional states, namely, the Transvaal Republic and Orange River State. In 1877, Transvaal was vulnerable to dissolution, and finally it was annexed. In March 1881, the Transvaal State was recognized by the British government as an independent Republic under the suzerainty of the British Crown. Later in February 1884, the clause of suzerainty was withdrawn.

During the period 1884–85, gold was discovered at Witwatersrand. This aspect became a new element in the politics of South Africa. Now the flow of immigrants from Cape Colony, Natal, and Great Britain started. In 1895, the Reform Movement at Johannesburg attempted to impose a forced solution. The invaders surrendered to the Boers on January 1, 1896. In 1889, Mr. Rhodes founded the British South Africa Company which had been granted control of the British Empire beyond Bechuanaland and Transvaal was occupied by the Matabele and Mashona Kaffirs. The Boers resisted the influence of British expansion. In May 1899, due to the failure of a conference between Sir Alfred Milner and the president of Transvaal, the latter declared war in October 1899. Lord Robert took over the command in January 1900. The British forces cleared Natal and occupied Johannesburg and Pretoria in June. The two Boer Republics were annexed to the British Empire. The Boers continued the irregular warfare which spread to Cape Colony. Lord Kitchener forced the Boers to accept defeat, which they did on May 31, 1902, and accepted the annexation to the British Empire and peace was restored.

The capture of the Cape of Good Hope in 1795 was very crucial for the British's interests in India. Ceylon had changed hands from Portugal to the Dutch in 1656, writes Wright,[23] and it was feared by the British that the Dutch might not transfer Ceylon to the French. In 1795, British took Ceylon from the Dutch and controlled it for 150 years.[24] The British's motive was the profitable spice trade. The Ceylonese welcomed the British. The British developed the resources, and tea and coffee became exportable items. In 1798, Ceylon came under the direct control of the Crown by becoming a British colony.[25] In 1798, Napoleon on his way to Egypt captured Malta. The British expelled the French in 1800, and the island joined the British. It was important in that it connected Western Europe with the East. It became the chief station of the British in the Mediterranean. The Maltese had a big share in the legislative and faced not much interference in their institutions.

Early in the eighteenth century, Ile de France or Mauritius remained under Dutch control until they abandoned it in 1710, when the French took it. Bourdonnais had established a naval station which irritated the English East India Company due to its privateers and its location as an advanced base of the French fleet. Wellesley put pressure on it and captured it in 1810. Each of the possessions of Ceylon, Malta, the Cape, and Mauritius gained from the Dutch and the French was important for the military security of India.

Many of the islands in the West Indies had been occupied by French troops, and the British captured Tobago in 1803. St. Lucia, one of the best harbors, was finally taken by the British admiral Jervis in 1803. Trinidad, which was under Spanish control, was attacked in 1797. The French settlers on the island resisted. The island was taken from the Spaniards in 1802. The British were able to get another possession in the South American continent in 1796, and that was Guiana. The French and the Dutch were already there. The British did not impose their institutions. British Guiana was almost a sugar colony (see Figure 6.2).

Until 1798, the settlements at and near Belize were under the protection of the British under a treaty. In 1798, the Spaniards decided to get rid of the intruders, but with the aid of the British, the settlers fought back. Honduras became

FIGURE 6.2 British colonies in Canada, the West Indies, and South America

a British colony in 1798.[26] The West Indies had been British colonies for a long time.

The main centers of British trade in West Africa were Gambia, Sierra Leone, the Gold Coast, Lagos, and the Niger[27] (see Figure 6.3). The first three were connected with the slave trade; the latter two were acquired. When the British competed with the Dutch and Portugal for its share in trade, it built Fort James at the mouth of the river and which became the main center of the British-African trade. Gambia remained under British control, while France controlled Senegal. The British also built a post at the Gold Coast on the north shore of the Gulf of Guinea. The Dutch, the Danes, and the Prussians had also their own forts. These forts were used for trade, and the trade was in human beings. The British forts, including Gambia and Sierra Leone, came under the direct ownership of the British government in 1821. In 1861, Lagos came under British control and became a profitable trade center dealing in palm oil. The British now reached the delta of Niger in 1884. Under the Berlin Conference of 1885, the British got the protectorate of the Lower Niger as well as the protection of its interests in Nyassa-land.

In Central Africa, the Berlin Conference accepted the British's interests in Nyassa-land; however, the Portuguese created a problem by claiming this territory. In 1891, under a treaty, the British sovereignty, over a territory lying north of the Zambesi River bounded on the west and east by the Portuguese territory, and on the north by the Congo Free State and German East Africa, was recognized. The British Central Africa's main products were coffee and tobacco and a great wealth of copper deposits.

FIGURE 6.3 British colonies in Africa

In 1895, the British Government proclaimed the East Africa Protectorate when it took over the territory of the Chartered Company of East Africa to secure British interests in the region. In 1885, when Germany intervened in East African affairs, the British secured its interests partially. By the Convention of 1890, the control of the coast between the rivers Umba and Juba fell to England, and with it that of the islands of Zanzibar and Pemba. The headwaters of Nile and Egypt became a British protectorate. In 1882, the British invaded Egypt and occupied it after losing 57 soldiers in the battle of Tel el Kebir, writes Harari.[28] After Tel el Kebir, the British did not face any resistance and got control of the Nile Valley and Suez Canal and held it for more than six decades. The British occupied Sudan in 1892 (see Figure 6.3).

In 1838, Aden on the coast of Arabia was captured by the British. Perim, a small island at the mouth of the Red Sea, was occupied in 1799 and was annexed in 1857. Both of these points were important in relation to India and therefore were governed by the government of Bombay. The rivalry between the Dutch and the British traders continued in the archipelago eastward of Sumatra. At the end of the eighteenth century, the English East India Company retained the posts in the region and held Penang off the coast of the Malay Peninsula. During the Napoleonic War, Java had fallen to the British, but it was restored when the Dutch ceded Cape to England. The British did not like the monopoly of trade by other nations. The English East India Company had already reached out to China. Sir Stamford Raffles, who controlled Java, captured Singapore in 1819 from a native raja, under instructions from Lord Hastings, the then governor general. After five years, under a treaty with the Dutch, Malacca was exchanged for Sumatra settlements and then the entire peninsula came under British control. In 1837, the British possessions of Penang, Malacca, and Singapore were administered from Singapore. After 1875, the neighboring independent states were gradually brought under British control which was managed by the governor at Singapore. The Malay Peninsula, specifically Singapore, served as the center of the meeting point of all Asiatic races, the Arabs, the Indians, Malay, and the Chinese.

The English East India Company started trade with China as early as 1670 through the port of Canton. To protect the interests of the British traders, Hong Kong islands close to main China and within the reach of port Canton were taken by the British in 1842 and confirmed under the peace treaty of Nanking between England and China. Under this treaty five ports were provided for British trade. In 1842, Hong Kong was opened for free trade by all European nations. The major population of Hong Kong is Chinese. Hong Kong's development was contributed by free trade, its position on the trade route from Japan and Shanghai, and its nearness to Canton, supplemented by British security. Its legislative included two Chinese representatives. British New Guinea was proclaimed a Protectorate in 1884 and was annexed as a Crown Colony in 1888. In 1874, the Fiji Islands were acquired by the governor of New South Wales.

The United States also followed the expansion patterns of Europeans and in 1846 invaded Mexico and captured California, Nevada, Utah, Arizona, New

Mexico, and some territories of Colorado, Kansas, Wyoming, and Oklahoma, and the earlier occupation of Texas was also confirmed under a peace treaty. The United States lost 13,000 soldiers and got 2.3 million square kilometers, writes Harari.[29] The United States now realized that the goal of imperialism was no longer possible through winning the wars. Instead, the United States pursued the policies of soft and hard tracks of achieving economic hegemony for political and military influence. The soft track policy was pursued to destroy the economy of the country concerned through economic sanctions, stoppage of aid by the United States, and international financial institutions like the International Monetary Fund (IMF) and the World Bank. According to Ferguson, the United States used the IMF and the World Bank as its agents to implement its agenda of economic hegemony.[30] The loans advanced by both financial institutions were to be used for the procurement of goods from the United States. The conditionalities were very rigid in the name of structural adjustments aimed at reducing fiscal deficits, broadening the tax base and lowering the tax rates and free market to determine the interest and exchange rates. The cost of the structural adjustments had to be paid by the people of the recipient countries. The American direct aid to the developing countries was also tied to the political and military conditions that were not in the best interests of the recipients of the Africans, Asians, and Latin American countries. The hard track policy was aimed at a regime change through a military coup. According to Chomsky, in 1973, in Chile, the social democratic government of Salvador Allende was overthrown by the Pinochet military coup, resulting in a dictatorship.[31] After the war with Vietnam in 1979, China, an emerging power, did not get engaged in a war like the Europeans and the United States and concentrated more on its economy.

By the middle of the eighteenth century, the islands of Barbados and Jamaica had become the centers of human capital. The human resources of the islands were very strong labor that were used in agricultural production activities. In Barbados, the natives were used to uniform cultivation of one crop such as sugar, cotton, or tobacco. In Jamaica cocoa and indigo were replaced by sugar production. In 1673, the Europeans in Barbados were 22,000 as compared to 45,000 natives. The island was rich. Eighty years later the population of the Europeans decreased to 17,000 and the natives rose to four times this number. The major production was sugar. In Jamaica, the natives were tenfold the white Europeans, and it was the single big purchaser of the African human capital. Both Barbados and Jamaica supported the English influence in the islands. During the wars between the Dutch and the French, the islands exchanged hands and finally became British colonies. Islands like St. Vincent or Dominica came under partial British occupation. The Buccaneers who had fought against Spain in the Western waters in 1700 had their headquarters in the ports of Jamaica and the neighboring islands. They were very powerful and opened the Spanish seas to trade and settlement. They forced their entry followed by the settlers. They had good relations with the British and the French. The Council of Jamaica sent their captain Morgan, who sacked Panama.

Notes

1 Sale, p. 169.
2 Woodward, p. 23.
3 Ibid., p. 34.
4 Smith, p. 601.
5 Woodward, p. 86.
6 Sale, p. 241.
7 Ibid., p. 245.
8 Ibid., p. 243.
9 Ibid.
10 Woodward, p. 88.
11 Sale, p. 243.
12 Ibid., p. 283.
13 Ibid., p. 286.
14 Ibid., p. 292.
15 Ibid., p. 338.
16 Smith, p. 617.
17 Ibid., p. 651.
18 Woodward, p. 251.
19 Ibid., p. 255.
20 Ibid., p. 281.
21 Ibid., p. 283.
22 Ibid., p. 291.
23 Wright, p. 264.
24 Woodward, p. 297.
25 Ibid., p. 298.
26 Ibid., p. 300.
27 Ibid., p. 301.
28 Harari, "21 Lessons for the 21st Century", p. 172; Woodward, p. 308.
29 Harari, p. 172.
30 Ferguson, "The Assent of Money, A Financial History of the World", p. 310.
31 Chomsky, "Consequences of Capitalism, Manufacturing Discontent and Resistance", p. 44.

Bibliography

Chomsky, Noam and Marv Waterstone, *Consequences of Capitalism, Manufacturing Discontent and Resistance*, Hamish Hamilton, Penguin Random House, London, UK, 2021.

Ferguson, Niall, *The Ascent of Money, A Financial History of the World*, Penguin Group, 80 Strand, London, UK, 2009.

Harari, Yuval Noah, *21 Lessons for the 21st Century*, Jonathan Cape, s, 20 Vauxhall Bridge Road, London, UK, 2018.

Sale, Kirkpatrick, *Christopher Columbus and the Conquest of Paradise*, Tauris Parke, London, UK, 2006.

Smith, Adam, *The Wealth of Nations (Modern Library Edition)*, Random House, Inc., New York, USA, 1994.

Woodward, William Harrison, *A Short History of the Expansion of the British Empire, 1500–1902*, Second Edition, Cambridge University Press, London, UK, 1902.

Wright, Arnold, *Early English Adventurers in the East*, Sang-e-Meel Publications, Lahore, Pakistan, 2000.

7
THE ENGLISH EAST INDIA COMPANY

The discovery of America in 1492, the Cape route to India in 1498, and Marco Polo's travel to the east turned out to be a tipping point in the history of Europe for building and expansion of the trading networks in the east. Papal bulls were issued by Alexander-VI in 1493 which allowed the entitlement of territories to Spain that it had discovered. The papal bulls, de facto, became the legal orders in Christianity for the capture of the land of the foreigners. These papal bulls were smirked at, albeit not protested. The British followed the Spanish, the Portuguese, and the Dutch who were the masters in the waters to discover new territories for beneficial trade. This was a great challenge for the British to end the Spanish hegemony in the waters to get access to the trade in the Indies. The African slavery trade had been an important part of the Spanish trading system for over 50 years. Hawkins during his first three voyages captured and brought home about 800 natives from Sierra Leone and other places along with other precious commodities such as gold, silver, pearls, and other jewels. After Hawkins, Francis Drake challenged the Spanish in the waters. On his first voyage, Drake arrived in the West Indies in May 1572 and plundered the Spanish silver carrier and a Portuguese ship laded with gold and silver valued at more than £100,000, the highest return on his investment, which he further invested to finance his three-year global voyage, writes Dalrymple.[1] In August 1573, Drake returned to Plymouth from his first voyage with the profitable spoils of the Spanish treasures. During the second voyage Drake established contacts in the Spice Islands in the east.

However, the Dutch were able to break the spice trade monopoly of Portugal and Spain and earned the monopoly through contracts with the local suppliers who were bound to sell their spices to Dutch company on their conditions. In July 1579, the commander Jacob Corneliszoon van Neck of the Dutch Compagnie Van Verre, the Company of the Distant Land, returned from Indonesia with a

DOI: 10.4324/9781003377719-8

cargo of 800 tons of pepper, 200 tons of cloves, and a great quantity of cinnamon and nutmeg. This cargo resulted in a 400% profit.[2] Taking advantage of a trading monopoly, the Dutch increased the prices of spices sold in Europe from 3s, to 8s, per pound. When their ships came to England, then the London merchants took it as a challenge.

In September 1599, the project of establishing trade relations with the East was approved with an initial capital of £30,000, which was later raised to £72,000, writes Wright,[3] with the price of £120 for ten volatile shares as compared to £550,000 raised by the Dutch East India Company, known as VOC (Vereenigde Oostindische Compagnie). VOC was soon able to offer investors a dividend of 3,600%.[4] Under the leadership of George Earl of Cumberland, the Association of 215 Merchants approached Queen Elizabeth with a formal application. On December 31, 1600,[5] Queen Elizabeth granted the English East India Company its first charter with Lancaster to act as their "Governor and General" of the Company, writes Dunbar. The charter gave them immense powers and custom duties exemptions on their first six voyages and a monopoly for 15 years over the trade to the East. The area of operation was not fixed, and the company was given the authority of governing the semi-sovereign territories to rule and raise armies, mint money, raise fortification, make local laws, wage war, conduct an independent foreign policy, hold courts, award punishment, and plant English settlements. The Company had the authority over anything that was needed for the protection of the Company's interests. The wording of the charter was vague in that it left a chink of opportunity of becoming an Imperial power. The English East India Company was a joint stock company open to all investors. Up till then, the British were purchasing the peppers from the Muslim middlemen at higher prices. England then was an agricultural country.

On February 13, 1601, the British fleet of a 600-ton *Red Dragon* bought at £3,700 from the earl of Cumberland, escorted by four smaller ships – a 300-ton *Hector*, the *Susan* of 240 tons, the *Ascension* of 260 tons, and the little *Guest* of 130 tons – commanded by Sir James Lancaster, sailed from the Thames on its first voyage. Lancaster carried six letters from the queen, with a blank space for the names of the recipients, for presentation to the native rulers. Based on his previous experience, Lancaster took lemon juice for his crew to prevent scurvy and 38 guns for any competition that could arise during his voyage. When the fleet reached the coast of Guinea it spotted a Portuguese vessel and captured it with its possessions including 160 butts of wine and 176 jars of oils with sundry hogsheads and casks of meal.

From Africa, Lancaster moved to the coast of Brazil, where, in July, he dismantled the *Guest* off Cape St. Augustine because of death of crew due to scurvy. On September 9, the fleet reached Table Bay in South Africa. When the fleet reached Madagascar, more than ten men on the *Red Dragon* died. The captain of the *Ascension*, who was going ashore to attend the funeral of the dead, was shot dead by one of the guns fired at the ceremony.

From Madagascar, Lancaster sailed for the Strait of Malacca. On June 5, 1602, the fleet anchored off Acheen, which was one of the big centers of the spice trade. Acheen (Banda Aceh) was located on the northeast coast of Sumatra, where an unending war between the Dutch and native Malaya occurred. The native Malaya did not like the arrangement that was made between the Dutch and Britain nearly a century ago,[6] under which the British gave Sumatra to Dutch in exchange for Singapore. The Dutch had established a permanent factory in the spice-growing region of Acheen. However, Lancaster was welcomed by the two resident Hollanders.

After the third day of the landing of Lancaster, the king sent his men to escort him to the court of the king. On arrival at the court, the king courteously welcomed the guests. The gifts were exchanged between the Englishmen and the king. The letter from the queen was delivered to Acheen's king appreciating the value of the establishment of trade connections and assuring the king that he would be served better than the Spanish and the Portuguese. Then an application was presented to the king for allotment of a site for the establishment of a factory and the protection of those who will stay behind to look after the factory. The king did not make any concessions immediately, but the application was referred to two of his officials for review and consideration. In the meantime, the British were granted permission to trade.

Lancaster thought that profitable trade without favorable terms was impossible. Lancaster was thinking of how to load his ships with cheap spices. In the meantime, a Portuguese ambassador appeared and demanded of the Malaya king a site for the establishment of a factory and a fort at the entrance of the river for their security. This request incensed the king. The king's response, according to Lancaster's narrator, was, "Hath your Master a daughter to give that he is so careful of the preservation of my country? He shall not need to be at so great a charge as the building of a fort, for I have a fit house about two leagues from the city which I will spare him for a factory where his people shall not need to fear enemies, for I will protect them", writes Wright.[7]

The Portuguese ambassador was stunned by the king's sarcasm and started thinking of new plans that would make the British uncomfortable. Lancaster thought that the only solution was a war with the enemy. The war would go through raiding the Portuguese ships in the Straits. This was due to the fact that without the war it was not possible for Lancaster to get spices at cheaper prices. Lancaster sought assistance in this connection from the king. The king had developed a liking for Lancaster and did not see any problem with his scheme. Lancaster was out in the sea looking for a Portuguese galleon. On October 3, he saw one big Portuguese ship. The English fleet got across the Portuguese ship, and when it came within its range the English fleet fired upon it. The *Red Dragon* humbled the 900-ton Portuguese ship laden with all kinds of merchandise and other valuable goods like jewels. This was a big prize for English. Lancaster got filled the holds of all of his four ships with the merchandise.

Lancaster now thought that he got what he had wanted and now decided to return home via Sunda Strait. Lancaster found out that Acheen was not the right place for trade, but the real centers of spice trade were Priaman southward on the eastern coast of Sumatra and Bantam on Java Island which was the headquarters of the Dutch. The English were not able to compete and prevail on better armed, better financed, and more skillful fleets of the Dutch East India Company. Lancaster returned to Acheen to inform the king that he was leaving for home. At the farewell meeting the king gave Lancaster a reply to the queen's letter and then offered a few gifts for the queen and Lancaster. After the meeting, Lancaster was back in the sea and wanted to touch bases at Priaman, where the supply of spices was waiting for him. After Priaman, Lancaster proceeded to Bantam. Bantam port was not a healthy place and his second-in-command John Middleton had died, and this compelled Lancaster to leave the place as soon as possible. After settling the staff at the factory under William Starkey, Lancaster left for England on February 20, 1603.

On September 11, 1603, the British fleet returned and anchored at Downs. Lancaster's voyage was highly prolific in that it had brought with it 1,030,000[8] pounds of pepper on which there was a huge profit. Therewithal, there were other items, which fetched a big amount in returns on investment. Over and above, the more important was the discovery of the passage to the eastern trade, identification and testing of the spice markets, knowledge and customs of the native traders, and the enabling of England as a competitor in the race for commercial hegemony. Another important factor was that Lancaster had returned home with his original four ships and most importantly Lancaster had laid the foundation for the British Indian Empire which existed for a long period of time.

After Lancaster, another expedition was led by Sir Edward Michelborne to discover the countries of China and Japan and to trade with their people. His fleet consisted of a single 240-ton *Tiger* and a pinnace. On December 5, 1604, the *Tiger* sailed from the City of London and on August 21, 1605, reached near Bantam. Now Michelborne started looking for an opportunity for piracy. An Indian ship of 80 tons with miscellaneous cargo was captured and taken to Sillebar, a port in Sumatra. On seeing no other opportunity for piracy, Michelborne reached Bantam and then reached Patani port on the eastern coast of the Malaya peninsula which was a center of trade. Michelborne started freebooting by chasing any native sailing crafts. There was no big success. Finally, Michelborne found a Japanese junk with about 90 Japanese crew on board, mostly soldiers than the sailors and they, like the English, were the freebooters who could pick up anything they could find on the ocean. The Japanese pillaged the coasts of China and Cambodia and were returning to Japan. After discussion, the English were admitted on board.

When the English started emptying the hold of the Japanese junk, the Japanese did not resist and remained calm. While transferring the quantities of the plunder from the junk to the *Tiger*, the Japanese expressed their desire to visit the *Tiger* to see the facilities it had. The request was granted, and the English did not bother to disarm the Japanese. The Japanese visited all parts of the *Tiger*. They also saw the cabin, and all of a sudden fight broke out. In the fight all members of the cabin were killed, with the exception of one. Davis, an important member of Michelborne's crew, was also killed. All of the Japanese crew in the junk were slaughtered by the English with the exception of one who jumped into the sea and then approached the *Tiger* and decided to surrender. The Japanese admitted that their plan was to plunder the *Tiger* and to cut everyone inside the *Tiger*. He was tied up to the ship for execution the next morning. At night the rope broke, and he swam to the shore. Michelborne abandoned the idea of China and returned to England, where he faded into history.

On August 28, 1608, the first English vessel *Hector*, under the command of William Hawkins, anchored off Surat in India, then inhabited by 150 million[9] people. India was a very famous center of manufactured textiles which adversely affected the textile industry of Mexico. The profits of £100 million of this industry went to the Mughal emperor in Agra. During the period 1586 through 1605, European silver flowed into India at the rate of 18 metric tons a year in exchange for commodities. Surat then was under the control of local governor Makarrab Khan, who was appointed by Mughal emperor Jahangir. Hawkins had difficulty in dealing with Makarrab Khan, who took his cargo without any payment. Hawkins left Surat for Agra. On April 16, 1609, Hawkins arrived in Agra after two and a half months of his departure from Surat.[10] Agra was the capital of the Mughal Empire. At Agra Hawkins was well received by Emperor Jahangir (1605–27) and presented a letter to the great Mughal king from James I seeking permission for the English East India Company to trade in India. Jahangir was aware of the arrival of the English mission after it left Surat. Hawkins was now an ambassador to the Great Mughal kingdom. The gift that Hawkins had with him was the cloth which was not of Jahangir's taste, but the Emperor did not mind it and everything went smoothly. When Hawkins presented the letter from King James, it was translated by the Portuguese translator. The great Mughal Emperor graciously informed him that he would grant everything that his Majesty had requested in the letter. Jahangir developed a liking for Hawkins and asked him to be present in the court daily.

Emperor Jahangir offered a proposal to Hawkins for acquiring his services permanently. The Emperor promised to grant a license to the Company to establish a factory at Surat. The king offered Hawkins a personal annual allowance of £3,200 with the command of 400 horses.[11] Hawkins asked the company to place somebody else in his place at Bantam, and he himself took his office in the court of Mughal Emperor Jahangir. The great Mughal Emperor Jahangir gave Hawkins his commission "under his great seal with golden letters".[12] Hawkins immediately sent this to Company's representatives at Surat, William Finch and Thomas Aldsworth, asking them to keep their fingers crossed for the golden opportunity of trade.

The Portuguese had a stronghold in India and thus influenced the Mughal emperor to deny the trading rights to the English in Gujarat. The Portuguese despised England and disdainfully called the king of England the king of fishermen. When Hawkins again asked Emperor Jahangir for a license for the factory at Surat, Jahangir reneged and said that he had finally decided to withhold it. Hawkins was kept away from the king. To avoid further humiliation, Hawkins started preparation for his departure. On his way home in the *Peppercorn* commanded by Nicholas Downton, Hawkins died. The English Company had a strong navy led by Henry Middleton and Captain Best who were capable of handling the larger Portuguese navy. The traffic in the Red Sea was blocked from Surat and Diu by the English navy. The situation resulted in the grant of a factory at Surat to the English, and the English chartered company's representative was well received in Agra to monitor the company's interest at court.

In 1615, the first English ambassador to the Mughal emperor, Sir Thomas Roe, arrived in Ajmer with gifts for Emperor Jahangir. In the beginning, he received resistance from the locals. After a long struggle, Roe was able to get the permission of Emperor Jahangir that confirmed the building of a factory at Surat. The Emperor did not grant any trading privileges to the English as he thought it below his dignity to do so. However, after four years when he left India, the factories at Surat and elsewhere were functioning satisfactorily under the protection of the Indian government. Roe used his spin control strategy to outmaneuver his enemies – the Spanish, the French, and the Portuguese – to get favors from the Emperor.

On his return to London, Roe recommended to the Company's directors that the army was not an option for dealing with the Mughals and thus advised against fortifications. Roe advised that the profitable trade can be sought at sea. In the meantime, the British dispatched Captain Hippon on the *Globe* to start textile trade with the eastward Coromandel Coast and establish a second factory at Masulipatnam port of Mughal's rival of Deccan which was the diamond-rich Sultanate of Golconda.[13] The finest jewel and chintz were available here for procurement. And, a third factory, dealing in trade in saltpeter, the potassium nitrate, which is used in gunpowder, was established in Patna. The trade in textiles, jewels, pepper, and saltpeter was more profitable than the Dutch's trade in spices. The Company made huge profits which attracted investors from all over Europe who were keen to buy the Company's stock. In 1613, the subscriptions of the stock rose to £418,000, and in 1617 it rose to £1.6 million, which boosted the London Stock Exchange and the Company became a rich source of British prosperity. By the 1930s, the British imported £1 million worth of pepper from India which was later exported to Italy and the Middle East through its sister, the Levant Company.

However, the supremacy of the Dutch in the East was a great concern for the English. Across the Bay of Bengal, the islands were under the control of the Dutch. The English tried their best to share the Far East trade among the Dutch and English, but this hope ended with the incident of Amboina in 1623 where the officials of the English company were captured, tortured, and killed on charges of conspiracy against the Dutch. These charges were not proved and all the officials were innocent, but the tyrant Dutch investigators got what they wanted to kill their competitors. The Europeans at home were at peace and in the East were at war.

The barter trade in India was not possible as the local did not like the European goods. Some sort of currency was needed as a medium of exchange. Then English company was authorized to mint money in India just like the Indian currency with the inscription of the Mughal emperor or local rulers. During the reign of Charles II, the superscription of the "King of Great Britain France and Ireland" appeared on the Company's rupees, writes Dunbar.[14]

In 1632, the Mughal king was incensed when he discovered that the Portuguese were engaged in building illegal fortifications and dwellings in Hooghly in Bengal and violated the Mughal rules by proselytizing the Indians to Christianity. The Mughal king ordered to attack on the Portuguese settlements and expel them. The Portuguese were defeated, and the city fell to the Mughals. About 400 Portuguese were captured who were sent to Agra to beg mercy. Those who refused were either given as slaves to the Amirs, according to the Badshahnama,[15] or put in prison where they perished.

The English on the Coromandel Coast of India had established the trading post at Fort St. George in 1639 around which the city of Madras grew.[16] The factory was fortified in the name of Fort St. George. It was the first land held in full sovereignty by the British. The growth of commerce of the company from its base at Surat started in 1641. The European guards helped the Indian watchmen to protect the factory. In 1661, Charles II granted a new charter, which authorized the Company to make war and peace with the non-Christian rulers, to appoint governors with civil and criminal jurisdictions of their territories. The settlements of Surat and Madras and the factories in Bengal were the concessions granted by the Indian governments.

In 1661, Charles II married the Portuguese Infanta, Catherine of Braganza. However, Bombay was the Portuguese sovereign territory, and its sovereignty was transferred by the Portuguese to the English Crown as a part of the dowry of Catherine of Braganza. Catherine was the wife of Charles II and daughter of the king of Portugal. In 1668, Charles II transferred it to the company of the king. In September 1662, when Sir Abraham Shipman with 450 men first arrived to claim Bombay, his mission was blocked; maybe, the Portuguese at Bombay did not get instructions in this regard from their home office. It took the British three years to take possession of Bombay from the Portuguese, which happened in 1665. By this time, Shipman and his 111 officers were dead due to fever and heatstroke. Bombay became the best port of South Asia and Company's naval base in Asia. The British had a small garrison of 300 English soldiers and 500 native militia.

In 1669, Gerald Aungier[17] became the governor of Bombay. He encouraged the merchants and the businessmen to settle in Bombay and introduced a sound local government and judicial system. Aungier established the law courts in the country, and for the first time the British law was administered to the Indians. When Bombay was transferred, the troops of the royal garrison opted for the service with the company. Following the Dutch example, the English also built the military posts on the coastline to protect the trade. In 1681, Sir John Child took over as the director of the Company. Nawab of Bengal Shahista Khan despised the British and complained to Emperor Aurangzeb that these insolent foreigners are engaged in undesirable and foul things.

In 1683, the English raised two companies of 200 Rajputs who served under their own officers, and this was the beginning of the creation of the Indian Army for the Company. The governor of Bombay, Sir John Child, was appointed the commander-in-chief of the Indian Army. In 1686, a British fleet sailed from London for Bengal with 19 warships, 200 cannons, and 600 soldiers. The Mughals had just conquered the two great Deccan states of Bijapur and Golconda and were in high spirits. The British factories at Hooghly, Patna, Kasimbazar, Masulipatnam, and Vizagapatam were seized and destroyed. The British were expelled from Bengal. The captured British soldiers were put in chains and paraded in the streets and were kept fettered in Dhaka Red Fort and Surat castle. The British factory at Surat was closed, and Bombay was sealed off. The English seized some Mughal ships, and this led to the war with Mughal Emperor Aurangzeb. The Company's factors at Surat were prisoned, and in 1690 the English lost the war to Aurangzeb. After paying heavy indemnity, the Company's trading rights were restored by Aurangzeb.

Now a new British sleuth Job Charnock emerged on the scene. The British sleuth decided to build new factories to replace those which were destroyed by the natives. On August 24, 1690, Charnock started establishing a new factory at Hooghly in West Bengal between the villages of Calcutta and Sutanuti near the Armenian trading post, and the Portuguese were across the river. The land was granted to the Company, and the Company acted as the tax collectors for the Indian government. The factory was named after William Orange and, in 1700, became the headquarters of Sir Charles Eyre, the first governor of Fort William in Bengal. Bengal was the richest region in the world. There were 25,000 weavers in Dhaka alone, and there was no match for its textile production of silk. Bengal was the Europeans' single-most supplier of goods in Asia. In the early eighteenth century, both the Dutch and the English East India Companies sent cargoes to Bengal then worth rupees 4.5 million and 85% of the shipment was in silver. The Company was making a profitable business in Bengal. The Company's clerk asked the farmers of Bengal to grow poppy among rice and other grain crops because opium was sold at a higher price making extraordinary profits. The source of revenue of Bengal was the land rent which depended on the quantity and value of the produce. Like the Dutch, the British had also restricted the production of the commodities, of which they enjoyed the monopoly, according to their market demand and supply conditions. The policy of the English East India Company was to buy the native goods as cheap and sell the European goods to the natives as dear. The Company's monopolistic position stunted the growth of the surplus produce of the native country to the level of their demand and supply. Moreover, all the members of the management were engaged in their personal trade under the cover of the Company's monopoly.

The private trade by the employees of the company was very harmful in that it affected the public trade of the company. The employees of the company pursued their interests rigorously against the interests of the company and the country.

In 1693, the Company became so powerful that it started bribing the native parliamentarians for buying favors. The Company spent annually £1,200 through its own shares of the Company, and it became a big lobbying scandal. On parliamentary investigations, the Company admitted to the guilt and the Lord President of the Council and the Governor of the Company were put behind bars.

The regnant Emperor Aurangzeb banned wine and Hashish. In 1679, he reimposed the jizya on non-Muslims. He executed Teg Bahadur, the ninth guru of the Sikhs. He crushed every rebellion that occurred in his empire. In 1680, he fought and conquered the Shia-Muslim states of Bijapur and Golconda. Maratha leader Shivaji Bhonsle rebelled against the Mughals. In 1663, Shivaji raided Mughal headquarters at Pune and killed Shaista Khan, the governor of Deccan and the uncle of Aurangzeb. Aurangzeb dismissed Shivaji and he died in 1680. The Mughals crushed the Maratha's resistance. Aurangzeb's armies captured Sambhaji, the eldest son and the successor of Shivaji, who was brutally killed. His body was thrown to the dogs, and his cutoff head was sent to the cities of Deccan before being hanged at the Delhi Gate. By 1700, the emperor took the Maratha's capital, Satara. During the last period of his rule, the Mughals' victories became slow. The Mughal Empire had stretched from Kabul to Carnatic. Aurangzeb died on February 20, 1707, and was buried at Khuldabad in Deccan.

From Babar to Aurangzeb, the Mughal monarchy of India had become very powerful. After Aurangzeb's death the Mughal Empire began to dissolve in Deccan. Maratha leader Baji Rao later stretched his rule to the larger areas in central and western India. The Mughal succession disputes further weakened the empire. In 1719, four different emperors occupied the throne one after another. The regional Mughal governors started becoming independent. Chin Qilich Khan, Niazm ul-Mulk also known as Asif Jah I, became an independent governor of Deccan and built his power base at Hyderabad. Oudh (Avadh), now Uttar Pradesh, was independently controlled by Nawab Sa'adat Khan and his nephew and son-in-law Safdar Jung with their base at Faizabad in the heart of the Ganges plains. However, Murshid Quli Khan, the governor of Bengal, remained loyal to the young Emperor Muhammad Shah and sent him revenue regularly through the financier Jagat Seths. The governor of Bengal established his new capital at Murshidabad. Marathas were ruling most of central and western India. Peshwa controlled Maharashtra and was the head of the Confederacy. Bhonsle controlled Orissa, Gaekwad controlled Gujrat, Holkar prevailed in central India, and Scindia commanded Rajasthan and north India. The Marathas used the Mughal's procedures and practices.

The officials of the English East India Company thought that the Marwari bankers, Jagat Seths, could be their natural ally as they both have common interests. The Company started enjoying credit facilities from Jagat Seths.

During the period 1718 through 1730, the English East India Company borrowed, on the average, Rs 400,000 annually from the Jagat Seths. Now the English East India Company and the Marwari bankers entered into an alliance of handling the financing of India.

When the British found out the weakness and dwindling control of the Mughal Empire, it saw a chink of opportunity for interference in India. The governor of Carnatic Da'ud Khan despised the insolent British. The Company's official, Niccolao Manucci, announced that the sea beach had been converted into a profitable port and that if Da'ud did not change his behavior, the Company would shift its operation somewhere else. The sufferers would be the local weaver and business community who would lose their flourishing businesses. Da'ud refrained from further criticism of the Company.

After the death of Aurangzeb in 1707, the change occurred for the Company. By 1744, Madras, previously a waste land, had now grown to the level of big cities after Goa and Batavia. In 1710, the English East India Company destroyed 52 villages along the Coromandel Coast, killed innocent people, and destroyed the crops in the field which were ready for harvesting. This was the beginning of the British unprovoked violence in India to terrorize the natives. This act of terrorism was approved by London. In Bengal, Murshid Quli Khan was incensed because of British aggressiveness. He wrote to Delhi that these aliens, when they came first, they submitted humble petitions for the grant of the rights to trade and now they have crossed the red line. The site they got for building the factory was turned into a strong fort with guns mounted on the walls and a ditch dug around the fort. They had started bringing the merchants under their protection and started tax collection which amounted to Rs 100,000.[18] They started pillaging Bengal and making men and women as slaves.

Old Delhi, then Shahjahanabad, was a big city of two million people in 1737, and the emperor still ruled from the Red Fort. Chandni Chowk, or the Chowk of Sa'adullah Khan, was a very crowded area. The rich empire was now ruled by Emperor Mohammad Shah, called Rangila, or Colourful, the Merry-Maker. Mohammad Shah introduced the folkloric music of sitar and tabla into his court. He had left politics to his advisors and himself was enjoying the partridge and elephant fighting and the acts of jugglers in his court. The regional nawabs became independent in decision-making and started usurping the authority and resources in the name of the emperor. The poor emperor then was confined to Salim-garh fort. The Marathas of Deccan, once tributary, challenged the empire by pillaging the natives. On April 8, 1737, the Maratha leader, Baji Rao, raided Agra and Delhi and plundered and burnt the then-suburban villages of Malcha, Tal Katora, Palam, and Mehrauli. The Marathas encamped near Qutub Minar. Qutub Minar was built by the first Muslim ruler of Delhi, Qutub-ud-Din Aibak, as a mark of Muslim victory over the last Hindu ruler. Marathas had an army of 80,000 men as compared to 34,000 men of the Mughal army, writes Dunbar.[19] When the Marathas heard that the Nawab Sa'adat Khan was on his way with his army, the Marathas dispersed. The Marathas had now been collecting rupees one million from the people of Malwa alone, and the funds were now being transferred to the Marathas that led to the drying of the treasury of the Mughals. On January 7, 1738,[20] the Marathas defeated the Nizam near Bhopal. The nizam was forced to give the whole of Malwa to the Marathas and an indemnity equivalent to £500,000.[21]

Now another problem was brewing up for the Mughals. Nadir Shah Afshar, a Turkman from Khorasan who had seized Persia through a military coup in 1732 and later ended the 200-year rule of the Safavids by deposing the Safavid prince, Tahmasp Mirza, and became the Emperor of Persia. In May 1738 he invaded Afghanistan with his army of 80,000 fighters, and Bala Hisar of Kabul surrendered in June. After conquering Jalalabad, Nadir Shah crossed the Khyber Pass and conquered Lahore and then reached Karnal, 100 miles north of Delhi and defeated the one-million-strong Mughal army on February 13, 1739. The Mughal generals Nizam-ul-Mulk and Sa'adat Khan were not on the same page, and it made Nadir's business easy. When Sa'adat advanced to fight Nadir, Nizam stayed behind and in a few minutes Nadir's musket balls crashed Sa'adat's arrows.

After the defeat of the Mughal's army, Nadir Shah wanted to capture the emperor, and he did this by a simple ruse of inviting him to dinner. On March 29, 1739, Nadir Shah entered Delhi where a big massacre took place and 100,000 people were killed because they had resisted the Persians. Women and children were enslaved. The neighborhood of Jamia Masjid Delhi was completely destroyed. The nizam, whose hands were tied with his turban, was brought before Nadir and begged on his knees to Nadir to stop the massacre. Nadir agreed on the condition that Nizam would deliver him one billion rupees.[22] The poor nizam had to plunder his own people to pay the indemnity. Emperor Mohammad Shah was captured. Nadir Shah got the Peacock Throne of Shah Jahan from Mohammad Shah, whose jewels were worth rupees two crore, which later became the symbol of the Persian Empire. Nadir Shah also plundered Koh-i-Noor diamond which was once with Mughal emperor Babur. The other plunder was so huge that Nadir did not impose any tax on the Persians. The Mughal Empire was near its end, and all of its wealth of 348 years, including pearls, precious gems, gold, and silver, was now in the hands of the Persians. Now the Persian Empire was to rise. Nadir was not interested in ruling India. He was only interested in the plunder to get huge amounts to fight his rivals Russia and Ottoman. After 57 days Nadir Shah returned to Persia with a huge amount of plunder carried on 700 elephants, 4,000 camels, and 12,000 horses, including the Peacock Throne, the Kohi-i-Noor, and the great Mughal diamond, Daria-i-Noor, precious stones, gold, and silver which were valued then at £87.5 million.[23] Mohammad Shah Rangila remained on the throne, and the territory that Nadir Shah overran through east of the Indus River was ceded back to him. Now both of his governors, Nizam ul-Mulk and Safdar Jung, stopped sending the tax money to Delhi, The Mughal emperor dipped into a financial crisis. The regional governors became independent. The Mughal Empire shattered into pieces. The British and the French watched the weakening of the empire. Nadir

Shah of Persia had shown the way to the Europeans to grab the opportunity of whatever is left in India after his huge plunder.

Joseph-Francois Dupleix became the new Director General of the Compagnie des Indes who was watching the invasion of Nadir Shah. In 1742, Dupleix moved from the French base in Bengal at Chandernagar to Pondicherry to take over as the Governor of Pondicherry and Director General of the Compagnie des Indes. Dupleix appointed De Volton as his representative to the Mughal court. Dupleix asked De Volton to petition in the Mughal court to make him a nawab with the rank of 5,000 horses and give the French the right to mint the money. The Mughal emperor granted both requests, and this surprised Dupleix that to such an extent the Mughal Empire had depreciated after Nadir Shah's invasion.

Now Dupleix, following the pattern of Nadir Shah, started building up his army for the Company. He hired and trained the local soldiers and raised two regiments of the sepoys. Dupleix appointed Charles-Joseph Patissier and Marquis de Bussy as his military commanders. Dupleix had become rich not through his salary but through his private trading activities. Dupleix informed Governor Morse of the English East India Company in Madras that the French in Pondicherry would not be the first attacker on the British interests. Morse informed Dupleix that he had no authority to make any pact. In February 1745, the British navy attacked and seized several ships in which Dupleix had his trading interests. Dupleix called a naval squadron from the French naval base at Ile de Bourbon and sent one of his members to Madras on a reconnaissance mission.

In September 1745, Dupleix received his reinforcement of 4,000-strong men, including the well-trained several battalions of African slaves. The French, without warning to the British, attacked them from behind. The siege started on September 18. Governor Morse had just 300 men with him who were unable to stand against the big French army. His chief gunner Smith immediately died of a heart attack. On September 20, 1746, Governor Morse surrendered Madras to the French. The Mughal nawab of Carnatic, Anwar-ud-Din, was incensed in that Dupleix attacked Madras without his permission. He was not expecting a trading company to defy his orders. Consequently, the nawab sent his son Mahfuz Khan with an army to punish Dupleix.

On October 24, Mahfuz Khan blocked the passage of 700 French sepoys led by Paradis, at the mouth of the Adyar River. The Mughal army fired rockets, but they did not hit the French and fell in the river. The French retaliated with a volley of musketry which killed many of the native soldiers, and the Mughal army fled and reached Kunattur. The Mughal army lost 300 men, while the French lost just two men. Dupleix now started providing his services as a mercenary to Mughal princes who were competing for succession. Dupleix made more money from this enterprise than he could make from the textile trade. Dupleix now started working on a plan of overthrowing the English East India Company and replacing it by the French Compagnie des Indes.

The English East India Company, after getting the secret information about the French Plan, alerted by forwarding the intelligence information to Roger Drake, the governor of Fort William at Calcutta. The English East India Company felt that now war was imminent. The French could attack either Calcutta or Madras. Now both the French and the British got engaged in intrigues by selling their military services in return for influence, payment, or land grants. In 1749, the English East India Company supported the princes in succession in the Maratha kingdom of Tanjore, and this was the first interference by the company in a regime change. Similar types of interventions were also carried out by Dupleix in Carnatic and Hyderabad after the death of Nizamul Mulk. Dupleix received £77,500 and the highest Mughal rank of Mansab of 7,000 horses in return for support to the succession of the prince. The French were over ambitious to make the Indian princes as vassals of the French Empire. Soon Dupleix realized that without securing sea transportation it would not be possible for the French to fulfill their ambitions. In fact, it was the sea power which the French neglected and the British rightly relied upon it. Both the British and the French trading Companies transformed their role from trade to military force, influence, and control of the territories.

In the eighteenth century there were no threats from the Portuguese or the Dutch companies to the English East India Company. The Danish, Ostend, and Scottish companies had gone bankrupt. The only threat was from the French. Unlike the Dutch and the English companies which were established by private merchants, the French compagnie des Indes Orientales Company had been established by Louis XIV in 1664 on the lines of the French Chamber of Commerce and was under official control. The French Company had the trading monopoly from the Cape of Good Hope to the South Seas, colony of Madagascar, and in 1673, Sher Khan Lodhi of Bijapur surrendered the possession of Pondicherry to the French. In India, the French Company was run by very competent representatives. Due to financial mismanagement, the company ran into debt, and for 40 years it was unable to deliver any dividends. The people stopped investing in the company.

The English company was run by private merchants, and the government had no control over it. The company's management made decisions independent of the government, earned a lot of capital, and was able to advance loans to the treasury. However, the company had grown and possessed vast territories in the east which became unmanageable. At the behest of the Parliament, the British government got involved to improve the Indian administration. The English had two missions: the first was the elimination of the French from India and this happened in Carnatic, and the second and the most important was how to subdue the local rulers of India. The English had maintained small garrisons for the security of the company's settlement and factories, and the level of garrison force was not that big to challenge the Europeans in the sea and on inland.

According to Dunbar[24] at Pondicherry, the French headquarters had 450 French troops as compared to 200 men of the English East India company at Madras led by an old man, Swede, who rose from the ranks. The three English presidencies of Madras, Bombay, and Calcutta were located at a far distance and were not able to reach immediately at the place of help. On the other hand, the Nizam of Hyderabad was quite comfortable with his 80,000 men reaching Carnatic in 1743 to maintain order in his realm. But these numbers did not matter. In 1741, 50,000 Maratha cavalry men raided Carnatic and took Trichinopoly and made the Muslim ruler Chanda Sahib as prisoner. During the siege, the Maratha commander wrote to Dumas, the governor of Pondicherry, in which he had demanded the return of the wife and the family of Chanda Sahib which were taken there for safety. In case of refusal, he would take them perforce and then demand 40 years' arrears of tribute. Dumas wrote back that the wife of Chanda Sahib was in Pondicherry under the protection of the king of France and every French there would die rather than returning the family to him. The Maratha commander evaluated the French strength at Pondicherry and thought that it was too big for them to assault.

Anwar-ud-Din, the nawab of Arcot, and the governor of Carnatic followed the successful policy of Ali Wadi Khan in Bengal to maintain peace in his province. In 1746, Bourdonnais with a fleet of eight ships encountered a British squadron. The British commodore changed the direction and let the 2000 French troops take Madras and Fort St. George. Both places were bombarded and surrendered. Anwar-ud-din protested that instead of sending 10,000 cavalries to enforce his order, they had hoisted the French flag at Madras. Both the armies got engaged, and the French army, which outnumbered the Anwar-ud-din's army, defeated the nawab's army. The French victory had far-reaching impacts on the future shape of the region.

The old Nizam died in 1748, and his state was in civil war. Both the English at Madras and the French at Pondicherry wanted to exploit the situation to their beneficial positions. The French gained confidence through their victory over the nawab of Arcot, and Lawrence reorganized and transformed the English East India Company's forces into an impregnable force on which the local princes had the confidence of victory. A small event triggered enmity among the British and the French. In 1749, the British troops supported the deposed Maratha ruler of Tanjore and got him restored. British got a small settlement on the coast. Though this was a victory for the British, politically it was a dangerous movement in that it provided Dupleix with the casus belli for the engagement of their forces in local conflicts.

The Hyderabad realm was now important in the whole scenario. Asif Jah's elder son stayed with the Mughal court, and his second son Nazir Jang took the control of the government in his hand and he was challenged by Muzaffar Jang, a grandson of old nizam. The situation of Carnatic further fueled the situation as Chanda Sahib was released by the Maratha who was well respected in his province and had a great influence on his people. Chanda Sahib allied with the French, defeated and killed the ruling Nawab Anwar-ud-Din in August 1749, and became the governor of the province.

Now the division of the alliances started emerging. The English East India Company backed Mohammad Ali, son of Anwar-ud-Din, in his claim to the

Carnatic and supported Nazir Jang, the ruler of Hyderabad. Dupleix allied with Chanda Sahib, but he was insecure in Carnatic as he had no control over Deccan. By the end of 1750, Nazir Jang was defeated and killed in the fight and Muzaffar Jang was welcomed at Pondicherry as the nawab of Hyderabad. Chanda Sahib was installed as the nawab of Carnatic. This was a big victory for Dupleix, and he became the governor of all India in the south of Krishna River. However, Dupleix misunderstood the British that they would accept the defeat. Dupleix sent his general de Bussy to Deccan with a strong force of French and Indians to support Muzaffar Jang as the new nizam of Hyderabad.

On the way to the north, de Bussy heard that Muzaffar Jang had been assassinated. Despite this, he continued his march. In connivance with the nobles, he was able to install Salabat Jang, uncle of Muzaffar Jang, and got not only the concessions for the French reconfirmed but got even additional rights. De Bussy stayed in Hyderabad in support of the new nizam. At 350 miles to the south, Dupleix was ruling Pondicherry. The French position was now strong, and now they planned to make Salabat Jang the ruler of Bengal. The English East India Company had hardly any role in Carnatic. Lawrence returned to England. The English Company's position was at a low ebb.

Dupleix, in order to keep control of Deccan, had drawn the strength of his forces in the south. Chanda Sahib was left with one garrison in his provincial capital of Arcot. Twenty-six-year-old Lord Clive, a young merchant at Madras, who had served under Lawrence, decided to attack upon Arcot to compel Chanda Sahib to surrender his provincial capital or to weaken his army by besieging Trichinopoly. The governor of Madras agreed with Clive's plan. Clive marched with 200 Europeans and 300 Indians toward Arcot and sieged the city on September 25, 1751. To recover his capital, Chanda sent 10,000 men along with a French detachment of troops under the command of Reza Sahib. Clive failed and sought help from Maratha chief Morari Rao. With Marathas' help and additional force from Madras, Clive defeated Reza Sahib on November 14. With this victory, the prestige of the English East India Company surged, and this was the turning point of the fall of the strength of the French. In June 1752, Chanda's army along with the French troops was forced to surrender, and Mohammad Alim, son and heir of the nawab of Carnatic, executed his rivals. Dupleix was dismissed by the French.

When the English East India Company explored trade links with Bengal, they discovered Calcutta, in the south of Hooghly. Calcutta grew into a big city and a trading center which provided wealth opportunities for the English East India Company. Calcutta became a base for the English East India Company from where they spread power throughout the subcontinent. The nawab of Bengal, Ali Wardi Khan, came to power in 1740.[25] In 1756, the nawab of Bengal, Ali Wardi Khan, died and was succeeded by his grandson Siraj-ud-daula. The new nawab Siraj-ud-daula had concerns about the European trading companies which took the control of Deccan and Carnatic through their invasion of the states' affairs. This led to the loss of sovereignty of the Indian states. The trading privileges granted to the English company 40 years earlier by the Mughal ruler resulted in a big loss to the revenues of Bengal. Nawab Siraj-ud-daula despised the English Company for the destruction of the Bengal economy.

In 1756, Siraj-ud-daula decided to seize the English East India Company's possession and the wealth of Calcutta and to expel the foreigners from the soil of his province. After taking a small factory at Kasimbazar, Nawab Siraj-ud-daula marched toward Calcutta with a big force. When the Bengal army reached Calcutta, the commander of the garrison of the Europeans and his soldiers defected and joined the nawab's army. Calcutta fell on June 20. The news of the fall of Calcutta reached Madras in mid-August. The governor Pigot and the deputy governor Clive decided to retake Calcutta.

A big British force of 900 European and 1,500 Indian troops sailed from Madras in October. This force was led by Clive with a naval escort led by Admiral Watson. Calcutta was reoccupied in January 1757, and Watson was appointed the governor of Calcutta. Siraj-ud-daula made another attempt to take, but Clive foiled his attempt by a sudden attack at night. Siraj-ud-daula conceded the privileges of the English Company and retired to Murshidabad. Siraj-ud-daula was now convinced of the British military prowess.

In March 1757, Siraj-ud-daula authorized the British Company to attack the French settlement of Chandernagore. It was a strange move as the French were his friends. Siraj-ud-daula changed his mind, but it was too late as Watson had done his job and took the place after the bombardment of the fleet. Because of his policies, Siraj-ud-daula was now despised by his people. He lost the loyalty of his army and the people. Now the big businessmen called Seths turned against him and conspired to replace him with a traitor Mir Jafar, an ex-member of his council. Now Calcutta became the underworld of conspiracies and treachery. This definitely paid dividends to the English East India Company.

Clive with 3,000 European and Indian troops left Calcutta to fight Siraj-ud-daula. The traitor Mir Jafar led 10,000 nawab's forces, and when he got close to the striking range of Clive, Mir Jafar assured cooperation to Clive. On June 23, 1757, the forces met at Plassey. Severe fighting took place, and the situation changed when Siraj-ud-daula's loyal general was killed. Mir Jafar's advice to Siraj-ud-daula was so disastrous that it confirmed the fear of conspiracy and Siraj-ud-daula just abandoned his army in confusion and defeat. Mir Jafar entered Murshidabad and executed Siraj-ud-daula.

Mir Jafar had mortgaged his kingdom to the English East India Company, and the English got a strong military hold on Bengal. The power was divided between the English East India Company and the ruler of Bengal. The Company's objective was to make profits from the trading activities, and one of the objectives of Mir Jafar was to get freedom from the English East India Company. Both the Company and the Fort William Council were unable to give Bengal an efficient government. Consequently, there was lawlessness, misrule, and injustice. The people despised both the ruler of Bengal and the Fort William Council.

The French started a new expedition, and the French forces reached Pondicherry in April 1758. Madras was besieged. Clive informed Pitt about the big French force led by M. Lally marching toward Carnatic. The English forces were supported by Bengal through money and supplies, while the French lacked such type of support. In September 1759 a French fleet led by Admiral d'Ache appeared in the Indian waters which was driven out by the British admiral George Pocock. A month later, the British received fresh reinforcements under Lieutenant Colonel Coote. In January 1760, Lally suffered a crushing defeat at Wandiwash, and in 1761 surrendered Pondicherry and this destroyed the French power in India.

In the Carnatic where Mohmmad Ali was installed as the nawab by the English East India Company, the nawab had to pay the Company for the services rendered to him. The nawab was unable to pay. As a part of the payment, nawab mortgaged parts of his province in 1761 to the Company. Nawab's financial difficulties continued surging due to corruption and mismanagement. The English East India Company annexed the province and introduced administrative reforms. According to the treaty of Paris in 1763, the French recovered some of their possessions. But the future expansion in India rested with the British

Clive became governor after the death of Watson in 1757. In January 1759, Clive advised Pitt to take over the sovereignty of Bengal, the richest province of India, and the law and order could be maintained with the help of just 2,000 Europeans. There will be no resistance as the natives were more worried about their lives and properties. Clive further advised that the British government should take over the control of Bengal, as the Company lacks administrative capability. As Bengal was technically under the authority of the Mughal emperor, and purging his authority would warrant a reaction not only in the British Parliament but also throughout Europe, Clive's proposal was rejected by the British ministry.

After Clive left India in February 1760, the Fort William Council decided to change Mir Jafar, the nawab of Bengal, because of his doubtful attitude. Mir Jafar was replaced by his son-in-law, Mir Kasim, who was a man of integrity and great capabilities. After three years of his rule, the crisis of the Company's trade emerged that led Kasim to war. After the defeat, in 1763, Kasim went to Oudh and took refuge there. Mughal emperor Shah Alam and the nawab of Oudh made an alliance to restore Kasim, but that attempt was foiled by Hector Munro at Buxar.

Now the presidency council once again brought Mir Jafar back and made him the nawab on the council's terms regarding internal trade and capping the strength of his forces. A clause was also included in the agreement which ensured the payment of the compensation of all public and private losses that were incurred due to the war with Kasim. Mir Jafar died and was succeeded by his son Najm-ud-daula. Najm-ud-daula was a ruler hostage to the council who had no independence even in the selection of his chief minister and was reduced to a figurehead.

To become the nawab, one had to shower an enormous amount of money to the council as bribe which was to be arranged by the chief minister. The British officials had become corrupt by accepting presents from the natives. The orders came from England asking not to accept any present and asked Governor Clive to arrest this situation. Clive had now complete authority to do so. Clive had tried his best but without much success. However, when Clive returned to India on May 3, 1765, for his second term, he had corrected the things that were created by his predecessor between the Company, the emperor, and the nawab of Oudh. Clive restored most of Oudh to Shuja-ud-daula on the payment of a large amount in cash, and the districts of Allahabad and Kora were given to Emperor Shah Alam, who, in return, in 1765, granted to the Company the Diwani rights of Bengal, Bihar, and Orissa at a rental of Rs 26 lakhs per year, equivalent to £292,500 at the then exchange rate. Under Diwani, the British company collected the revenue of a province, and after the annual payment of the required amount to the Imperial treasury the balance was kept as office expenses. This was the tipping point for British imperialism in the Indian subcontinent.

In August 1767, Haider Ali of Mysore declared war against the Company. Haider Ali's force of 50,000 men was well trained, disciplined, and equipped with modern arms of French designs. In September 1767, when Haider Ali was engaging the Madras Army near Trinomalee, his son, Tipu Sultan, raided the Company from behind. The Company was defeated, and it appealed for peace. Haider Ali, after signing a treaty, returned home.

The collection of revenue by the British involved corruption through extortion and injustices that led to a decline in the government revenue. The situation had come to a head that compelled the British government for the tax reforms. In 1772, when Warren Hastings became governor at Fort William, he set up an English board of revenue under himself. The nawab of Bengal was reduced to the level of a pensioner and was at the mercy of the Company. The complete financial control now vested with the British. The Company had been reformed by an Act of the Parliament. The initial attempts to arrest corruption in the company were not successful other than the removal of one expert. Consequently, as an alternative, a foreign untrained agency was appointed to collect taxes and the taxes they imposed were over-assessed. Both the Company and the British government were introducing revenue reforms through trial and error.

Clive had laid the foundation of the British dominion in the subcontinent through sea power. Warren Hastings drove it further when the Company was brought under the control of the British government during the governorships of Warren Hastings to Lord Cornwallis. Warren Hastings had been appointed governor by the board of directors of the Company, who enjoyed the full authority to reform the Bengal civil service which he did good to some extent. In 1773, the English East India Company was reformed under an act of the Parliament and Hastings became the first governor-general of three presidencies which were previously independent. The Company was more concerned with its profit than the welfare of the people of Bengal. The disastrous economic policies of the

Company led to the outbreak of famine in the rich Bengal province of India. It began in 1769 and lasted until 1773, in which ten million[26] Bengalis died in the calamity, writes Harari.

Soon after the disclosure of the Company's financial statement, a parliamentary committee of inquiry was set up to investigate the situation. The financial situation was not compatible with the previous records in which the company had declared a dividend of 6% in 1766 which rose to 12.5% in March 1772. On June 8, 1772, a Scottish banker Alexander Fordyce disappeared from his office, leaving a debt of £550,000 which led his bank, Neal, James, Fordyce, and Down, to declare bankruptcy.[27] Next week another bank which invested in Company's stock, Ayr Bank, closed down. This was followed by many Dutch banks that invested in the English East India Company, and almost 30 banks collapsed within three weeks. Financial crisis erupted in Europe, spread globally, resulting in the bankruptcy of Sir George Colebrooke, the chairman of the English East India Company. The Bank of England, which was the main creditor for the Company, was shaken and felt cautious. In the wake of widespread bankruptcies, loss of credit and confidence, David Hume, a Scottish economist and philosopher of Edinburgh, wrote to another Scottish Classical economist, Adam Smith, in June 1772: "Do these Events, any-wise affect your Theory? Or will it occasion the Revisal of any of the Chapters of the Wealth of Nations," writes Dalrymple.[28]

In July 1772, the English East India Company sent bills amounting to £747,195 to London which were in fact a rude awakening about the English East India Company's financial health. During the period of two years between 1771 and 1772, London received bills amounting to £1.5 million from the English East India Company. Questions were raised, but the accountants maintained that the payments must be honored to avoid the damage of the credit of the Company. In the meantime, the famine that erupted in Bengal led to the decline of the revenue. The stocks of overpriced tea remained unsold at the warehouses of London. The value of unsold stock rose from £1 million in 1762 to more than £3 million in 1772. The expenses of the military also increased enormously. The dividend of 12.5% required £1 million a year.

Now the directors of the company informed the Ministry in London that not only the Company would be able to make the annual payment of £400,000 to the treasury but that the Company would go bankrupt unless an immediate loan of £1 million was provided to the company. The company was maintaining an army of 30,000 men who had to be paid. Moreover, the Company's employees indulged in private trading that led to the transfer of resources from the company to the individuals. The Company was running into a deficit of more than six million sterling and was close to bankruptcy. The Company first defaulted on the customs payments and then on its payment of loans to the Bank of England. The stocks of the Company fell to 60 points in one month. Now the Company had to apply for a loan to survive.

On July 15, 1772, the directors of the Company applied to the Bank of England for a loan of £700,000, but the bank was able to provide only £200,000.

The Company had unpaid bills of £1.6 million and obligations of over £9 million. The Company's assets were less than £5 million. In August, the directors of the Company told the government that they would need further £1 million to bail out the company. During the period 1769 through 1772, the Company borrowed £5.5 million from the Bank of England. London informed Warren Hastings in Calcutta that this state of affairs had adversely affected the domestic economy and the public credit and that their only source of credit, the Bank of England, had become cautious. This Company was ruining the mother country.

The survival of the British economy depended on the extracted wealth of India. To discuss the grave financial crisis and the allegations of corruption and malpractices of the Company, the Parliament was called on November 26, 1772. The Company became poor and its employees became rich, and this situation was to be investigated. If the Parliament voted for a loan of £1.4 million, then the Parliament would supervise the performance of the Company. The Parliament had set up a Select Committee led by General John Burgoyne to examine the directors of the Company.

On December 18, 1772, the directors of the company were called to the Parliament for investigation of the allegations of corruption, embezzlement, and bribery. The charges were leveled against the Company's employees, including Clive. The Select Committee in its final report identified the presents worth £2 million were distributed in Bengal during the period 1757 through 1765 and that the great amount of money that was appropriated by Clive and his men should be recovered and deposited to the treasury of the Crown. Clive defended the allegations for two hours. Clive made an emotional speech before the Select Committee which he ended with "leave me my honor, take away my fortune" and walked out of the Chambers with tears in his eyes and jumped into his car. Finally, Clive was cleared of the charges against him by a vote of 155 against 95. Although Clive got a clean chit from the Select Committee, he suffered depression and committed suicide on November 22, 1774, at the age of 49 in his new house in Berkeley Square.[29]

After the defeat of Burgoyne's motion, the prime minister, Lord North, was still determined to bring the English East India Company under his control. He recommended that it was the right of the Parliament to have control of the English East India Company. This meant having the Company's Indian territories along with its 20 million inhabitants under the authority of the State. But again, the prime minister failed because the Company enjoyed the privileges under the charter granted by the Crown. Moreover, 40% of the Parliamentarians who had bought the stocks of the Company opposed this move.

However, the Parliament agreed to a loan of £1.4 million as a quid pro quo for bringing the Company under the Regulating Act, of Lord North's India Bill of June 1773, which was passed on June 19, 1773. Now the Company was bailed out and was under the Parliament scrutiny. Parliament would now appoint a governor-general, who would supervise the three presidencies of Bengal, Madras, and Bombay. The Regulating Act was the beginning of the State's interference in the Company's affairs which led to its final nationalization in 1858. The British government seized the possessions of the company, and Bengal became a British protectorate. The new governor-general was 41-year-old Warren Hastings. The Act also provided for three government-appointed councilors who would oversee the governor-general on behalf of the Parliament. One of these councilors was Philip Francis, who was a son of an Irish Protestant clergyman and was a literary person. Philip and Hastings were not on the same page. Philip wanted to recall Hastings back and take his position as the ruler of Bengal.

Under the Regulating Act, the British penal code was introduced which was not compatible with the local laws. Under this law a native Brahman named Nunocomar was convicted and hanged on the charges of forgery which in India was a simple minor wrongdoing. The Act was modified in 1781 which defined the supremacy of the governor-general and the council and also declared the court to have jurisdiction over the natives of Calcutta. Hindu or Muslim law was administered according to the religion of the defendant in cases of inheritance, contract, and successions.

On October 19, 1774, three councilors of the three presidencies appointed under the Regulating Act, Philip Francis, General Clavering, and Colonel Monson, arrived in Calcutta. They were offended by getting a 17-gun salute instead of a 21-gun salute. To further compound their grievances, Warren Hastings gave them lunch at his residence in an informal attire. General Clavering wrote a complaint to London. By the end of the informal lunch, Warren Hastings had made up his mind to resign. Next day on October 20, the councilors inquired from Hastings as to why the Company's troops were given to Company's ally Shuja-ud-daula of Oudh for use against Rohilla Afghans to stabilize his western border. Francis pointed out that the Company's troops had been leased out as mercenaries and under Shuja's command they had committed atrocities against the Rohilla Afghans.

Hastings took this as an insult and said he cannot live in the air of ill-will and stepped out of the room. He wrote his complaint to London and so did Francis. Francis was of the view that Hastings was the source of trouble in India and that he was involved in corruption in Bengal. The other two councilors took sides with Francis. Before the arrival of Francis, no charge of corruption was leveled against Hastings from any quarter; he was a spotless person then. He was a man of justice and supported the poor and needy. From the date of his appointment in February 1772 until the arrival of Francis, Hastings had brought many reforms in the operation of the Company in Bengal which included: the collection of revenue, provision of investment and trade, the administration of justice and police. He moved the functions of government from Murshidabad to Calcutta which became the capital of Bengal.

Unlike Lord Clive, who was disdainful of the Indians, Hastings gave them respect and strictly ordered the Company's officials not to disrespect and mishandle the Indians. Francis followed Lord Clive's policy and disdainfully termed the Bengalis as ignorant and unimproved. Governor-general Warren Hastings failed to perform as he did not enjoy the confidence of the majority of the members of the council. Francis boasted that "we three are the king", and at the same time the other two kings of Madras and Bombay started defying Hastings. This political conflict and confusion paralyzed the government of Bengal as the authority was invested with the council and Governor-General Hastings was powerless. After five years, when Hastings got control over the council, he was overruled by the men who lacked wisdom and experience. With a powerless governor and the non-performing three independent presidencies, the executive council had to engage with the complex political issues of India. The weakness of the Company was felt by its enemies.

The first challenge was the Marathas who had strong military power in India. On January 7, 1761, the Marathas were defeated at the Third Battle of Panipat by the Afghan army of Ahmad Shah Durrani. The Maratha commanders were killed one after another, first Balavant Rao Mehendale, followed by Govindpant Bundele, and so on. On this fatal day, 28,000 Marathas were cut into pieces, including the young Maratha leaders and the Peshwa's only heir. On January 8, 40,000 Marathas, who had surrendered and put themselves at the mercy of the Afghans, were executed on orders of Durrani. The heartbroken Peshwa Balaji Rao died soon after this event. After ten years of their defeat by Ahmad Shah Durrani, the Marathas regained their strength and were now in control of much of the central and western India.

The second force was the Mysore Sultanate of Haider Ali and his behemoth warrior-son Tipu Sultan. Haider Ali was of Punjabi origin, who rose to the highest rank in the Mysore army and who had introduced many innovations in the Mysore army which were based on his experience with the French troops who had performed in the Carnatic Wars. In the early 1760s, Haider Ali deposed the ruling Wodeyar Hindu Raja of Mysore in a military coup and became the ruler of Mysore. Haider Ali hired the French to train his army, and the French engineers were engaged in building the fortress of Srirangapatnam for defense purposes. Haider Ali and Tipu Sultan built their small navy, comprising two warships, seven smaller vessels, and forty galleons, which was commanded by a European seaman named Stannett. Both the Marathas and Tipu Sultan of Mysore were two fiercest and strong enemies of the Company and were the main hurdles in the way of the British occupation of the peninsula.

During the last quarter of the eighteenth century, the balance of power was between the Marathas, the English East India Company, and Mysore. The source of power was the strength of army. And on top of them was the Mughal emperor who was powerless. After the victory of the English East India Company at Buxar in 1764, the Company got the guardianship of the emperor but lost it to Marathas on the departure of Shah Alam from Allahabad to Delhi, where he came under the protection of Mahadji Rao Scindia. At Delhi, the emperor remained as a prisoner of Marathas. Marathas were leading in the politics of India as their territories were stretched to far-flung areas of the subcontinent. Their new leader Peshwa Madhu Rao succeeded in 1761 at the age of 17 years.

He proved to be a very capable leader who challenged the power of Haider Ali Khan of Mysore. Madhu Rao died in 1772. After his death, hostility developed among the princes, and the Marathas power center was shifted to strong rulers of the states.

The great soldier and the statesman Mahadji Rao Scindia became the chief of the House of Gwalior in 1761. Scindia decided to be in peace with the English East India Company and negotiated a treaty of Salbai in 1782. Hastings described this treaty as a successful peace agreement in the event of a difficult period. Before his death in 1793, Scindia ruled as a deputy wazir of the empire that stretched from Sutlej to Narbada and managed the provinces of Delhi and Agra.

During Haider Ali and his son Tipu Sultan's reign, Mysore had been a flashpoint in southern India. Haider Ali's relations with the English East India Company were not friendly. Haider Ali was of the view that he could have destroyed the English East India Company's possessions on land but he could not have dried up the sea. Haider Ali died in 1782. The strength of the English East India Company was in Bengal, and Calcutta was its capital which enjoyed the security of the Nawab of Oudh. As far the state's welfare was concerned, the first act of the council at Fort William was to overrule Hastings's objective of making Oudh a well-governing state. The nawab of Oudh gave up his two richest districts and also increased the subsidy to the Company for the maintenance of the troops, and this ruined the fiscal position of the state which Hastings later failed to correct.

Nana Farnavis, a stateman of the Maratha Empire, secretly received a French who wanted to make an alliance of Franco-Maratha, a move in Nana's committed opposition to the growth of the Company's power; it was a straw which showed the way the wind was blowing. Consequently, a war between the French and the Company broke in 1778, when the Company took Pondicherry. Haider Ali was a friend of the French. Haider Ali warned the Madras council that the settlement of Mahe was under the protection of Mysore. Mahe port was an easy source of communication between the French and Haider Ali. The presidency troops from Calcutta seized the port in March 1779.

In February 1778, the Bombay Council got involved in the Marathas' internal conflict by signing an agreement with the ousted Maratha leader, Raghunath Rao, offering to bring him back to power in Pune. On November 24, 1778, the Bombay Council without consulting Hastings in Calcutta sent a small force of 2,000 soldiers, a few hundred European cavalry and artillery to be joined by a rebel force of 7,000 from Raghunath. The army left Bombay harbor and advanced toward Pune. The army was led by an old Colonel Egerton with John Carnac as second-in-command. On December 30, 1778, the army with 19,000 bullocks pulling the guns and supplies reached Karle, a location famous for Buddhists' cave monasteries. At this point they had run out of supplies. At Karle, Egerton was surprised to see a force of 50,000 Marathas that had gathered up against the Company. The Marathas forces were led by their leader Mahadji Scindia. Carnac realized that they were not in a good position.

On January 9, the Company forces reached Talegaon, 18 miles from Pune. This place was destroyed, and no supplies were available. Later the British found that the Company's forces had been surrounded by the Marathas and their supply lines were cut off. Egerton became ill, and Raghunath was begging for continuing their march toward Pune. But the Company's officers lost their hope and courage as they were out of any supplies. They threw and burnt everything and started their retreat at midnight. The Marathas attacked the retreating Company's army and killed 350 men. Now the old Egerton had no option but to surrender by signing a humiliating Treaty of Wadgaon. Egerton handed over Raghunath along with several Company's hostages and gave up the Company's territory to the Marathas' leader, Nana Farnavis, who celebrated the victory at Pune.

After the victory of Pune, a year later February 7, 1780, Nana Farnavis wrote to Sultan Haider Ali of Mysore, asking him to forget the internal conflicts and get united against the foreign intruders to get them out of their soil. Haider Ali and Tipu Sultan, who were against the Company, immediately welcomed the initiative of Nana Farnavis. Within a month the nizam of Hyderabad also joined the alliance. In June 1780, the news spread that Haider Ali had gathered a big army around Bangalore.

On July 17, 1780, Haider Ali attacked Carnatic with 100,000 men, including 60,000 cavalry men, along with a French detachment, 35,000 infantry, and 100 guns. On August 25, 1780, the Company forces of 5,000 soldiers left Madras and marched toward Kanchipuram to confront Haider Ali. Another Company's army of 2,800 led by Colonel William Baillie marched toward Kanchipuram to join Munro. Munro, the victor of Buxar and the commander-in-chief of Madras, should have waited for Colonel William Baillie, but instead of doing so, he marched to face Haider. On August 25, Baillie camped on the bank of river Kortalaiyar, in the northwest of Madras. Now Tipu Sultan brought his 11,000 cavalry and placed them between the forces of Baillie and Munro. On September 6, 1780, the first engagement started and Baillie's forces suffered heavy casualties. Haider Ali sent a large force to support his son, Tipu Sultan. On the other hand, Munro refused to move from his fortified Kanchipuram temple and decided to resist the siege. Munro sent 1,000 soldiers with nine camels carrying ammunition in an effort to bring Baillie's forces back to temple. Baillie ignored Munro's advice to get to the temple at night and decided to move off at dawn which was a great tragedy for the company. On his way Baillie was blocked by a fortified village Pollilur which was well equipped with Tipu's troops and artillery. Now Tipu had blocked all the paths to Kanchipuram. Baillie was attacked by Tipu's men, and Baillie was hit in the leg by a cannon ball and was wounded. Soon Baillie was surrounded by Haider Ali's forces. Baillie and deputy David Baird, ordered their men, to lay their arms on the ground. Soon the Baillie's soldiers were attacked and cut into pieces. Out of 86 officers, 36 officers were killed and 34 were wounded and taken prisoners. Only 16 soldiers captured were not injured. Baillie lost his leg and was wounded on his back and head. Baird received two cuts in the head. Only 200 were taken prisoners, and the rest of the 3,800 were slaughtered. Baillie was brought before Haider, who asked him to sit at his feet. Munro failed in helping and rescuing Baillie and returned to Madras with whatever army was left. The Battle of Pollilur was a serious blow to the British. Of the total of 7,000 prisoners that Tipu kept in his fortress of Srirangapatnam, 300 were circumcised and converted to Islam. The news of the disaster of Pollilur arrived in Calcutta on September 20, 1780. Hastings was perturbed. However, Haider did not pursue the demoralized British army but continued damaging the supply line of the British.

Hastings sent Sir Eyre Coote with a European detachment and a strong column of Indian troops to drive Haider Ali's forces out of Carnatic, but Coot failed. At the same time, Tipu collected the richness of villas of St. Thomas and San Thome Mount, when Haider Ali was attacking Madras, Vellore, and Arcot by setting the villages on fire and destroying the British food supplies. The animosity between Hastings and Francis reached the pinnacle of failure that paralyzed the administration of the Company.

On August 15, 1780, Francis challenged Hastings to a duel.[30] Both the duelists, accompanied by their second-in-commands, met at the former summer house of Mir Jafar on the western edge of Belvedere at 5:30 AM. Before the duel, Hastings wrote a letter to his wife Marian which was to be delivered later. Both Francis and Hastings were suggested to stand at a distance of 14 paces. Each chose his own time to fire. There was no wind. Both did not know how to operate pistols. Francis never fired before in his life, and Hastings did it just one time. The pistols were loaded by their second-in-command.

The brave and gentleman Hastings offered Francis to fire first. Francis triggered his pistol which misfired. Again, Francis's second-in-command fresh-loaded the pistol and gave him back. Again, Francis triggered but the pistol did not fire. Now Hastings fired at Francis, and Francis's pistol went off at the same time. Nobody knows who was the first, but it was the Hastings fire that hit Francis who fell down saying, "I am dead". Francis was hit in the limbs and he could not stand. Both Francis and Hastings joined hands and Hastings expressed his regrets. Francis was taken to Hastings' physician Dr. Campbell in Belvedere. The physician found that the wound was not dangerous and the bullet was extracted. After this, Hastings sent Mr. Markham to Chief Justice Sir Elijah Impey, to inform him what had happened and he was ready to surrender to take the justice its course. But because of a minor injury there was no need to arrest Hastings.

The year 1782 was a bad year for the Company in that Braithwaite's forces were completely defeated by Tipu Sultan near Tanjore, where Tipu Sultan seized all the guns and took the entire detachment as prisoners. However, the treaty of Salbai provided some relief to the Company which was ratified by Nana Farnavis in the following February. The immediate effect of the treaty signed between Scindia and Hastings was to break the alliance of the Marathas and Mysore. It resulted in a peace between the Marathas and the Company for the next 20 years.

In 1783, Tipu Sultan succeeded Haider Ali and continued fighting with success. The loss of the Marathas was balanced with the French troops led by Bussy, and the alliance was militarily strong enough to face the British troops led by Coote's successor. When the French and the English returned to peace, France was no longer available to Tipu Sultan as an ally, and this was a big setback to Tipu Sultan. With the loss of the French as an ally, Tipu's resources exhausted. His capital was at risk as the Marathas were threatening to attack him. The governor of Madras made peace with him. A treaty was signed in Mangalore in 1784 that all the territories that were conquered would be restored to Tipu, and Hastings reluctantly ratified it.

In 1785, Hastings gave up his office. Hastings did his best in carrying the interests of his country, but he had many problems. The biggest one was the lack of money to perform his business. Hastings tried to raise money following the practices of Tudor sovereigns of England by imposing the capital levy on wealth and benevolence. The adaptation of the European practice in the foreign country was not possible. This was a serious problem that became the cause of his indictment later during his impeachment.

According to Dalrymple, on February 13, 1788, the impeachment[31] proceedings started against Hastings in Westminster Hall by the 170 members of the House of Lords, 200 members of the House of Commons, and judges and lawyers on both sides. The queen took her place in the royal box along with her son and two daughters. Hastings was charged by Burke with "injustice and treachery against the faith of nations". Edmund Burke, a member of the Parliament in the House of Commons with the Whig Party, called Hastings a criminal. According to Burke, Hastings was a robber. He stole, plundered, oppressed, and extorted. Burke said that Bengal was ruled by the Company without any checks and balances. The English East India Company was not a British nation. Hastings had corrupted his hands with bribes. He was involved in oppression and tyranny instead of legal government.

Burke, in his speech which took four days, said, "I impeach, therefore, Warren Hastings, Esquire of High Crimes and Misdemeanors".[32] In addition to the allegations of the betrayal of the British parliamentary trust and dishonoring of the British national character, Burke further goes on to say,

> I impeach him in the name of the people of India, whose laws, rights and liberties he has subverted, whose properties he has destroyed, whose country he has laid waste. I impeach him in the name and by virtue of those eternal laws of justice which he has violated. I impeach him in the name of human nature itself, which he has cruelly outraged, injured and oppressed, in both sexes, in every age, rank, situation, and condition of life.[33]

Burke was of the view that the Company rule did nothing other than the pillage of India's assets in the name of trade. Every gain of the Company was the loss of

India. Burke further describes the worst kind of humiliation of Bengali women who were dragged out naked by the Company's tax collectors in front of the mob that stunned everybody who stood there. Loud and horrifying screaming was heard. After Burke, the next prosecutor Richard Brinsley Sheridan rose to speak and he took another four days of hearing. He explained at length the moral darkness of Hastings for four days. His speech was so emotional that the whole house rose to a tumult of applause.

Other than the natural law, the rest of the allegations were just scandalous. It appeared the Parliament had picked up the wrong person for an impeachment. Previously, Burke had bailed out Lord Clive, who was dishonest, deceitful, and a real plunderer, from Parliamentary impeachment. Lord Clive had despised the Indians. In contrast to that, Hastings respected the Indians and ordered the Company officials to deal with them with respect and dignity. Hastings also introduced reforms in the operation of the Company and removed injustices in its operation. The impeachment was at the behest of his rival Francis, who hated Hastings. After recovering from his wound that was caused by his duel with Hastings, Francis returned to London in October 1780. Francis' passion for hate was so great against Hastings that he used his money that he had plundered from India for lobbying in the Parliament to disgrace Hastings. In February 1782, he was lucky to find Edmund Burke of the Whig Party who gave him a sympathetic ear. Before this, Burke was a great admirer of Hastings.

Burke had never been to India. However, some members of his family had lost money in unwise speculation in the English East India Company. Burke and Francis started working together digging out the Select Committee reports about the malfunctioning of the Company. They were trying to find out a justification for initiating impeachment proceedings against Hastings. By April 1782, Francis had prepared a list of 22 significant charges against Hastings and handed it over to Burke. Burke brought this list of charges to the Parliament. Burke and Francis worked for five years on this wicked campaign against Hastings and, in May 1787, convinced the Parliament that there was sufficient evidence for the impeachment of Hastings.

On May 21, 1787, Hastings was arrested by the sergeant at arms and brought to the House of Lords to hear the charges against him. During the 1780s when the Company's forces suffered defeats at the hands of the Marathas and Tipu Sultan, it was felt that the Company was being driven out of India. Hastings immediately raised money to fight for the Company's survivor in Madras and Calcutta. Hastings forcefully and illegally extracted the money from the nawab of Lucknow, Asaf-ud-Daula, and the begum of Oudh. Hastings also twisted the arms of the raja of Benares, Chait Singh, which led to an uprising against him which he survived narrowly. The diwan of the Nawab of Bengal, Nandakumar, had forged the fake documents of Hastings' corruption and handed them over to Francis. Nandakumar was charged with forgery and sentenced to death by the Calcutta chief justice, Sir Elija Impey, who was a schoolfriend of Hastings. The charge of forgery was a trivial offense in India.

Hastings was honest to the people of Bengal and wanted to ensure that justice was done for them. He campaigned against the malpractices of the Company in plundering and destroying the economy of Bengal. The people of Bengal regarded him as the champion of justice. In Bengal, Hastings was the most popular of all the Company's officials in India. The Articles of Impeachment influenced by Francis were full of fantasies and distortions and lacked legal substance. In his defense for several weeks, Hastings pointed out multiple errors of basic facts in the confused narrative of the prosecutors. Hastings was tried for seven years, was found not guilty, and was released on April 23, 1795.

In 1786, General Lord Charles Cornwallis was appointed as governor-general of British India. According to Pitt's Act of 1784, the government in matters of war, diplomacy, and revenue would vest in the governor-general who could overrule the councils. Now the aspects of a powerless governor like Warren Hastings vanished. Over the government of India, a body of "Commissioners for the Affairs of India" was established in London by Pitt. This body, known as the board of control, was presided over by the secretary of state. The strongest governor-general Dalhousie termed it "the board of interference". Before his assignment to India, Lord Cornwallis had served in North America. Lord Cornwallis was a military general who was defeated by the American forces led by George Washington at Yorktown, Virginia, and surrendered the 13 American colonies of the British Empire to him. Cornwallis wanted to make sure that the same was not to be repeated in India.

In August 1786, Cornwallis arrived in Calcutta to reform the land revenue system of Bengal and to maintain peace with the local rulers. The financial position of Bengal was good, and Cornwallis reported to London that Bengal's revenues exceeded the expenditure by £2 million. The major sources of revenue were from sugar, rice, opium, and indigo crops. After covering the deficit elsewhere, it resulted in a net saving of £1.3[34] million which will be used for the purchase of export goods that would be sold in London at £2.4 million. Now the Company was doing a profitable business.

Trade in Bengal flourished, and exports surged fivefold reaching the mark of £5 million. The role of Bengal's textiles such as cotton products, muslins, and silk was important in that they alone then fetched Rs. 28 million. The tea from China played a key role. The tea sales doubled to 20 million pounds. The supply of goods from Bengal exceeded the demand which needed more efforts to explore new markets for the sale of Bengal goods. Now there was no shortage of bullion as Calcutta Mint was annually minting Rs. 2.5 million coins. The provinces of Bengal, Bihar, and Orissa were the richest in the region. Now the Company earmarked an amount of £3 million per annum for maintaining a strong army. The strength of the Bengal army rose from 2,900 in 1757 to 50,000 when Cornwallis arrived in India in 1786. Now the troopers were well paid. Fort Williams in Calcutta was well equipped with arms and ammunition. The Company now felt comfortable to confront Tipu Sultan to take revenge for the 12 years earlier defeat at Pollilur.

In 1783, Haider Ali of Mysore died of a tumor on his back and 33 years old, 5 feet and 7 inches in height, Tipu Sultan succeeded him. On his deathbed, Haider Ali wrote a note of advice for his son Tipu Sultan that pertained to the mechanism of governance. Haider Ali said that the Company had become so powerful that the entire resources of India would not be sufficient to expel them from Indian soil.

> You have to weaken them by dividing the European nations and putting them against each other and this you can do with the help of the French. Haider advised his son that the valor can help them to reach the throne but it is not enough to keep it. It requires the winning of the love of the people.

Tipu Sultan was a competent commander who believed in modern technology and arms which he was capable of acquiring from the Europeans. He imported industrial technology from French engineers to run his machinery. He got silkworm eggs and established sericulture in Mysore. He promoted agriculture in his territory by introducing irrigation and building dams. He established a trading company with its own ships and factories. The commercial activities dealt with sandalwood, silk, spices, coconut, rice, sulfur, and elephants. He established 30 trading centers in Mysore as well as in other places like Kutch, Pondicherry, and Hyderabad. He was the fiercest and behemoth general who defeated the British many times, first at Pollilur; then in 1782 he defeated the British army led by Colonel John Braithwaite just outside Tanjore and then a year later, and before his succession he destroyed a British column on the banks of Coleroon river. Tipu was a big threat to the British. The only way for the British to win against him was to engage the local traitors through conspiracies against Tipu.

The trading centers were financed through his revenue department, and the people were encouraged to invest in the trading centers at a fixed rate of return. Other factories were established at Muscat and other places across the Persian Gulf. He requested the Ottoman Empire to grant him a place at Basra which he would make his overseas base for his vessels, writes Habib.[35] In order to win the people, he protected the Hindus in his empire by granting them land and gifts for the construction of temples. In spite of being a military general, a statesman, he was an intellectual and maintained his own library with a collection of 2,000 volumes in different languages.

Cornwallis made land settlements in the light of instructions from London, but the task of maintaining peace with the local rulers became different when he went to war with Tipu Sultan. Nana Farnavis, Scindia, Holkar, and the nizam were wary of Tipu Sultan's policy of maintaining his hegemony in southern India. Tipu was at war with the Maratha Peshwa and the nizam of Hyderabad. Consequently, the group made an alliance against Tipu Sultan and asked the British to partake in their alliance. Cornwallis, determined with the mission of maintaining peace in the region, reluctonedto join them.

To ensure sustained revenues, Cornwallis introduced land and taxation reforms. The basic principle of the land settlement was that the government had the right to demand a proportion of agricultural produce. The land settlement administration had been centralized with the European collectors being the figurehead, and the revenue was collected by a middleman called zamindar, who received some commission on the collected revenue. The system was engulfed with abuses and corruption. To correct it, Cornwallis had to make his own decision that would revamp the land revenue system.

Cornwallis had studied the revenue collection system of Akbar and restored his system of districts managed by the revenue collectors who assessed and collected the land revenue. The revenue collectors worked under the supervision of a central board. After two years of annual assessments, the system was promulgated for a period of ten years settlement in 1790 and the same was confirmed as the Permanent Settlement in 1793 which was approved by the home office in London. The new system confirmed the role of the zamindars of the province who were vested with the tenure of ownership of the land accompanied by unlimited powers which usurped the rights of sub-tenants and the cultivators. The zamindars enjoyed security over land as long as they paid the revenues punctually. In case of default, the land would be taken back and sold out to another zamindar.[36]

The new regulation, in case of default of payment, authorized the forced sale and detachment. In case of a shortage of revenue, the estates were auctioned for sale to get additional revenue. As a result of the forced auction, the previous landowners were driven into poverty. As a result of the harsh tax laws, the big estates split up and led to nearly 50% of land that changed hands. An unequal agrarian society was created which led to poverty. At the cost of rural poverty, the Company became rich due to an increase in tax revenue. With the transfer of land, a new group of landholders was created as Bengali bhadralok, the upper middle class such as the families of Tagores, the Debs, and the Mullicks who became influential in getting a mid-level public office in Calcutta as well as the control over agricultural production and trade. They advanced loans to the Company at the interest rate of 10–12%. These loans helped the Company finance its army and the purchase of arms, ammunition, and other auxiliary services such as horses, elephants, and bullocks. Due to an increase in tax revenue and the credit facilities from the Indian moneylenders and financiers, the Company became strong and had an edge over the local rulers. The biggest local firms such as Lala Kashmiri Mal, Ramchand-Gopalchand Shahu, and Gopaldas-Manohardes, based in Patna and Benares, performed financial services, including the military-remittances in Bombay, Surat, and Mysore.[37] Gopaldas later replaced Jagat Seth as the state banker. This generated a lot of surpluses which were used as collateral against the large loans from the sahukaras (moneylenders). Bengal produced an annual surplus of Rs. 25 million, while Scindia just managed Rs. 1.2 million from his territory in Malwa.

Later, a district officer appeared before the select committee of the House of Commons, where he testified that the effect of these reforms was disastrous for the countryside. The families whose land was forcefully auctioned compelling them to lose their legal rights considered the sale transaction as unjust, and it became a source of unrest in the countryside, as it had created a situation of do or die for the deprived families. In Cornwallis' code of civil and criminal justice, the Muslim criminal law was followed in a less restrictive way, and this formed the basis of all the future British procedures in Bengal.

The industrial labors were protected under the Factory Acts in India. Weaving activities in India were not carried out in cotton mills but in village cottage industries. The inspectors of the cottage industries had unlimited powers over the workers with physical punishments if they absconded, and the workers' wages were as low as Rs. 7[38] a month, and they were living from hand to mouth, writes Dunbar. In addition, the workers were being taxed by the zamindars which Cornwallis later abolished.

In addition to the Triple Alliance of the Marathas, the nizam of Hyderabad, and the Company against Tipu, Tipu added to his list another enemy by breaking off relationship with the Mughal emperor Shah Alam. Tipu ordered that in the Friday sermon, the khutba should be read in his name rather than the Mughal emperor's. Tipu Sultan argued that Shah Alam was on the payroll of an infidel, Scindia, where he was receiving a monthly salary of Rs. 15,000; therefore, his name was not justified to be read in the Friday sermon and it was in fact a sin to do so. In December 1789, Tipu, after conquering northern Malabar and Cochin, now attacked the raja of Travancore in the south to make him accept his allegiance. The raja had made fortifications for his defense called Travancore Lines. The raja enjoyed the protection of the Company through a defense pact. By attacking Travancore, Tipu provoked Cornwallis. On December 29, 1789, Tipu brought his artillery and destroyed the Travancore defenses, and his soldiers massacred the raja's troops. Now Tipu was at war on four fronts: the Marathas, the nizam of Hyderabad, the raja of Travancore, and the English East India Company.

In 1790, Cornwallis held a meeting of the select committee in the council hall of the Company in Calcutta, writes Jeddy.[39] Cornwallis informed the audience that it was time to end the state of no-war-no-peace between the Company and Tipu.

> As of to-date, the Mughal emperor and other native rulers are under our thumb. This person in the name of Tipu Sultan who, with his father, had raised a big empire of their own. He is a behemoth fighter who had defeated the British many times, and now after defeating the Marathas, the Nizam of Hyderabad, and the Raja of Travancore, he asked the Mughal Emperor in Delhi to grant him the title of a king. Later, he approached the Caliph of Ottoman empire in Turkey and in doing so he had in fact struck the root of the Company's raison d'être. He had established the trading links with the Middle Eastern countries. He had established the factories throughout his state and now the goods imported from England were no longer needed here. He had brought silkworm from China and starting

the manufacturing of silk cloth, thus eliminated the demand for British silk over here. He had established good relations with our rival France and brought the French shipwrights to build his strong navy to confront us in the sea.

George Powney, the Company's representative in Travancore, informed the select committee that the Dutch had built two forts on the coast of Cochin, named Ayicotta and Cranganore, and that when their business was not profitable, they left. They now belong to Cochin, an ally of Tipu Sultan. "Travancore, an ally of ours, also claims the right to those forts. If there is a war, Cochin would be supported by Tipu Sultan and we would support Travancore". The British prohibited the raja of Travancore from buying these forts. Cornwallis said that officially

> we would not withdraw the objections but Powney should secretly convey the Raja of Travancore to go ahead and this would provoke Tipu and he would attack Travancore and this would provide the British with a casus-belli to attack Tipu under our defense treaty with Travancore. In case of Tipu's attack, we, with the help of allies, will attack Mysore from many directions.

On the other hand, Tipu addressed his army generals at his camp on the border between Travancore and Mysore. Tipu explained his disappointment over the purchase of the two forts of Ayicotta and Cranganore by the raja of Travancore when these forts legally belonged to Cochin.

> We had invited him to come and give justification for his claim, but the Raja of Travancore ignored our request. Probably he was incited by the Company. The Company had imposed restrictions on him not to buy these forts. Lally, the commander of the French forces said that there is a saying in the French: perfide Albion, which means perfidious England. The British always say one thing and do just the opposite. Tipu said, anyhow, as a principle, we have to defend Cochin fighting for its legal rights.

When Tipu attacked Travancore, Cornwallis informed the governors of Madras and Bombay that Tipu had fallen into their trap. The raja of Travancore fled to Vypin and sought the protection of the Company's detachment. Cornwallis said that if they did not attack Mysore then Tipu would overrun Travancore. Cornwallis informed General Meadow, the governor of Madras and commander of the English army during the Third Anglo-Mysore War, that "we do not want a protracted war as it will be more expensive and our London backstopping persons will be angry with us". Meadow said that they want to have a cake and eat it too. "They want us to bring the wealth of India to London and at the same time they ask us to treat the natives with respect and dignity. Both of these conflict with each other". Cornwallis said, "I want to send good news to London and that's it".

The Third Anglo-Mysore War began. In early December 1790, Tipu Sultan reached Trichinopoly and, after evading the Company army, marched on the coast between Madras and Pondicherry and on its way destroyed and burnt the towns and villages. The temple town of Tiruvannamalai was plundered and destroyed. Tipu was marching at an imaginable speed which the Company forces could not match. Cornwallis did not want Tipu to be better than the British. Cornwallis, who was defeated by George Washington, decided to confront Tipu by himself. In early February 1791, Cornwallis left Madras with an army of 19,000 men. Tipu's small force near Bangalore led by Bahadur Khan, the khalildar of Bangalore, was not sufficient to defend against the big army of Cornwallis. However, Bahadur Khan fought so bravely that he won the admiration of Cornwallis. Colonel Floyd asked Bahadur Khan to surrender the city of Bangalore without bloodshed, Bahadur Khan replied, "over my dead body". However, the Company got the services of Hindu accountant Krishna Rao and connived with him to fix a pay day for the soldiers. When many of the soldiers were away to get their salary payments, Krishna informed the Company that the soldiers were away and now a surprise attack could be launched. Based on this information, an attack on the citadel of Bangalore was launched. In spite of the fact that the majority of the soldiers had gone to get their pay, Bahadur Khan with a few soldiers left with him fought gallantly and got martyrdom at the gate of the citadel. Cornwallis was impressed with his courage and bravery and admired him as a good fighter. On March 21, Cornwallis seized Tipu's city of Bangalore and made it a base for a further advance toward the capital of Tipu, Srirangapatnam. Cornwallis sent messages to the nizam of Hyderabad and the Marathas to keep up the pressure on Tipu in their respective sectors. Here, the Company's ally, Mir Alam of Hyderabad, joined Cornwallis with a force of 18,000 Mughal cavalries.

By May, the united forces of the alliance entered Tipu's territory. Here, Tipu laid waste the fields and villages on the path of the combined forces of the alliance, and nothing was left for the supply line of Cornwallis. When the combined forces reached the capital of Tipu, Srirangapatnam, 10,000 Company's transport bullocks died and the rest unfed were unable to carry the loads. Now the soldiers had to carry the load. On May 24, Cornwallis after a brief engagement with Tipu retreated to Bangalore. While retreating, Cornwallis was joined by 2,000 Maratha cavalry men and after this a big supply train reached. Now the combined forces of the Company, Hyderabad, and the Marathas marched toward Bangalore.

The Company was very active in recruiting sleuths in Tipu's army. These sleuths were supplying information to the Company about the movement and strength of Tipu's army. Based on the sleuths' information, the English were modifying their plans and Tipu had to move from one place to another. On January 26, 1792, Cornwallis with 22,000 Company's troops accompanied by

12,000 Marathas and 18,000 Hyderabadis left Bangalore to humble Tipu Sultan.[40] Tipu Sultan had 50,000 soldiers and cavalry troopers. Tipu was very careful and stayed within the fortress of Srirangapatnam which was built with the help of French engineers. This fortress was a big challenge for Cornwallis. Tipu sent his eldest son Fateh Haider to confront the contingent of 18,000 Hyderabadi troops led by General Farid-ud-Din. Fateh Haider defeated General Farid-ud-Din. On February 5, 1792, the three combined forces stood in front of the walls of the Srirangapatnam fortress. Cornwallis immediately attacked the fortress. Tipu was surprised at the sudden attack by Cornwallis while he was gathering his forces. The English had penetrated Tipu's army through their hired sleuths. Tipu's Ahmadi battalion of 10,000 had deserted him and were now willing to fight from the other side. Tipu fought bravely for two hours and then retreated into the walls of the fortress. Colonel Floyd was injured and defaced for the rest of his life. Now Cornwallis launched a second attack on the fortress. Soon Tipu's palace, the beautiful Lal Bagh, the Red Garden, was captured by Cornwallis. The palace was converted into a hospital to treat the wounded soldiers.

Next day Tipu tried to fight back, but his soldiers started deserting him. Now Tipu was not able to fight further and sent a message to Cornwallis for negotiation of a treaty. On February 22, 1792, Cornwallis informed his officers that he had received a message from Tipu Sultan through two of his ministers, Mir Sadiq and Purniah, and both had been secretly collaborating with the Company. They had asked for the terms of the agreement. Cornwallis was holding both positions of the governor-general and the commander-in-chief. Cornwallis asked them to go back to their Master and tell him that no terms will be discussed until the personnel of the Coimbatore garrison which he had captured were first sent here. Within an hour Lieutenants Nash and Chalmers came and informed that the rest of the officers were well and ready to be released. General Meadow committed suicide in his camp as he was depressed with his failure in the campaigns and that Tipu was not captured.

On February 24, Tipu held a meeting in the Dewan-e-Khas of the Seringapatam palace of his ministers and generals, wherein he explained the terms received from Cornwallis. In case of non-acceptance of these terms, the war would continue. Tipu was demanded to pay Rs. 1,00,60,000 as the first instalment of the indemnity, hand over his two sons as hostages to guarantee the payment of remaining instalments and surrender half of his territory. The territory will be based on the revenue receipts rather than the area. Now Tipu sought advice from his ministers and the generals. Mir Sadiq said that as there was no chance of winning the battle, it was better to surrender to save the land from destruction. Another minister Purnia, when asked by Tipu, seconded the advice of Mir Sadiq. Both Mir Sadiq and Purniah were British sleuths and were secretly collaborating with the Company while staying in the cabinet of Tipu. Then Tipu said that last night he had sent a messenger to the Maratha general Parashuram Bhau, in which he told him that he was not his enemy. "The real enemy of the whole of Hindustan was the British

Company. If we were not to unite against them, they will eat us one by one". The Maratha general's response was negative. "Purniah, you go and tell them that tomorrow I will be sending my two sons who must be treated with dignity and the first instalment of the indemnity".

The allies brought Tipu Sultan to terms. Cornwallis accepted the peace treaty with severe terms. According to the treaty, Tipu was to surrender half of his empire with the payment of an indemnity of Rs. 30 million. Tipu was to release all the prisoners of war and hand over his two elder sons as a hostage to ensure full payment. The territories next to the Marathas were given to Peshwa. The Marathas got the district of Dharwar which belonged to them before it was taken by Haider Ali. The territories of Koppal, Ganjikottah, and Cuddapah were given to the nizam of Hyderabad. The Company got the territories in the Eastern Ghats as well as the territories in Coorg and the spice-rich Malabar. The Company appropriated the districts of Dindigul, Malabar, and Baramahal, which were the richest in terms of revenue. Thus, the territories captured were shared by the allies.

The treaty was finally signed, and two sons of Tipu Sultan named Abdul Khaliq, who was eight years old, and the second, five-year-old Muizuddin, were handed over to Cornwallis on March 18, 1792. Cornwallis received the kids with due protocols and got them seated on his left and right. Both the boys were taken to Madras. The boys were handed over back to Tipu when he had made the final payment of indemnity. Now after handling Tipu Sultan, Cornwallis asked the allies to sign a peace treaty. The nizam of Hyderabad immediately agreed because he had feared the attack of the Marathas. The Marathas refused to agree on a peace treaty because they were planning to attack Hyderabad. Now the land settlement of Bengal was the major issue for Cornwallis to solve.

A few days later, Cornwallis said, "hell with the principles", and sent Kennaway to meet the vakils of Mysore, and tell them that "we had missed the territory of Coorg which we want to extract from Mysore. The same should be ceded to us". Tipu Sultan already knew about perfidious England. Tipu had heard that Cornwallis was a man of integrity and principle and now he was convinced that he was truly perfidious. Tipu called a meeting of the ministers and generals on March 2, 1792, to discuss the new demand by Cornwallis. When Tipu asked Mir Sadiq and Purniah, both supported the British demand on the ground that they were not in a position to fight with them. Tipu said he would prefer to die rather than give up his right. He will eat the food of the poorest people and will take two meals a day and will sit and sleep on the ground until he gets the strength to take revenge for the defeat and drive out the evil-minded and corrupt foreigners from the soil of India.

Tipu Sultan was true to his oath, but perfidious Cornwallis broke his oath. Cornwallis threw the mask of the caretaker father of the two eight-year-old and five-year-old princes and made them prisoners. The coward Cornwallis who had suffered a shameful defeat at Yorktown and surrendered the 13 British colonies to George Washington was now coercing the infant helpless princes to surrender their territories to the British Allies. Cornwallis held a meeting near the British camp. Captain Kennaway, a British resident at Hyderabad, was in charge of this drama. Kennaway before the meeting had threatened the infant princes to do what they were told to do. If they refused to do so, they would be punished. Kennaway did some rehearsal of this drama. When the guests arrived and were seated, the two infant horrified princes, now prisoners, were brought before the audience, along with their vakil Ghulam Ali Khan. The princes were ordered by Cornwallis to personally present the surrender documents to the vakils of the Marathas and the nizam of Hyderabad. The infant princes were shocked to hear this. The elder prince, 8-year-old Abdul Khaliq, spoke for himself and on behalf of his younger, 5-year-old brother Moizuddin, and said that he could present the documents to the British but not to the vakils of the Marathas and the nizam of Hyderabad. Cornwallis said that they were the British allies and he had to do what he was told to.

When Captain Kennaway translated Cornwallis's orders into Urdu, the infant princes became more hostile. The princes were given the documents that were prepared by Kennaway. Kennaway then beckoned the infant princes to the vakils of Marathas and the nizam of Hyderabad. The infant princes threw the papers on the faces of the vakils of the Marathas and the nizam of Hyderabad and said, "tell your Master that they have nothing to be proud of". Abdul Khaliq said to the vakils that "today you have got the land back that you lost to our grandfather and father who could even take it back from you now if the British are not on your side". When Kennaway translated these words to Cornwallis, he said, "they are Tiger's cubs. Are not they?" Cornwallis said, "had they been the English kids instead of the natives, we would have admired their high spirits".

This was the end of the Third Anglo-Mysore War. Tipu was left with half of his state. Tipu started building up his state by picking up the pieces. There was a fire inside him about getting the perfidious British out of his soil. Tipu again wrote to the Maratha leader Haripant Phadke that the English were their common enemies and in order to circumvent their looting, it had become inevitable that they must get united together as natives. Unfortunately, his request was again rejected by the Marathas. However, Tipu's thinking became true when after 25 years, in 1817, the Marathas' power was shattered by the British at the battle of Kirkee. Under Cornwallis the Indians holding senior positions in the service of the company were removed. Non-Europeans were being treated disdainfully.

Tipu got engaged in trade with countries from China to the Persian Gulf and earned enough money to pay ransom for his princes. The princes remained with the British for more than two years. Every effort of the British to convert the young princes to Christianity failed to make an iota of change in their Islamic conviction. The British realized that holding the princes any longer would serve no purpose. The British sent them back escorted by Captain Doveton, who was to be imposed on Mysore as a resident representative. On March 29, 1794, Tipu Sultan received the princes at Devanahalli.

Captain Doveton met Tipu Sultan at the time of delivery of the princes and informed him that the former governor-general Lord Cornwallis had returned to London and in his place a new governor-general, Sir John Shore, has been appointed. Lord Cornwallis left a message for Tipu that in order to maintain better communications between the Company and Mysore, it would be important for the British to appoint a resident in his court to facilitate communications. Sir John Shore, the new governor-general, was also of the same opinion. Tipu Sultan replied, "thanks for the Company's gesture, but we feel that, at this point in time, there was no need of any representative here". The disappointed representative Doveton suggested Tipu to appoint his Vakil instead at Calcutta or Madras to keep him informed about the affairs of the Company. This was also not needed at this time. "However, tell your Governor-General that if we ever felt a need for a British resident, we would certainly write to him". Sir John Shore wrote many letters to Tipu Sultan which he diplomatically rejected. Sir John Shore was pissed off by the behavior of Tipu Sultan. The British also heard that Tipu Sultan had written a letter to Paris urging for an offense and defense alliance between them. This alerted the British as the French had already helped the American colonial army to drive the British out of America. Governor-General Sir John Shore wrote a letter to the governor of Madras Lord Hobart to get the army ready for a final war with Tipu Sultan.

On June 1, 1793, at the Battle of Lakheri, Scindia defeated his rival Tukoji Holkar. When the news of the defeat reached the blind Shah Alam in Delhi, he commented that the power of the Marathas will soon be destroyed. In 1793, Maratha leader Mahadji Rao Scindia died and he was succeeded by his 15-year-old nephew Daulat Rao. This was a big loss to the Marathas. In 1794, Marathas invaded Hyderabad. The nizam of Hyderabad Ali Khan Asaf Jah entered into an alliance with the British, under which two British battalions paid by the nizam were stationed in his realm. Asaf Jah appealed to the governor-general, Sir John Shore, for help against the Marathas. Under the Act of 1784, the governor-general was bound to stay neutral which he did. The governor-general did not allow Asaf Jah to use the Company's two battalions that were stationed in his dominion. In 1795, Asaf Jah was defeated at Khanda.

After the humiliating defeat, Asaf Jah now turned to the French associated with his army led by Gascon Francois de Raymond. Along with the French, Asaf Jah wanted to make an alliance with Tipu Sultan. The British ministers and the company's directors in London were least concerned with the politics of India. The British management was just concerned with the possessions of the company and the trading business. The British management strictly relayed the policy of noninterference in Indian politics to the governor-general, including non-expansion of territories and war only in self-defense. The peace in the subcontinent was in the best interests of the British.

Tipu tried to get help from the French, Afghans, and Turkish, but the traitors in his court and the British sleuths spread throughout Asia, Central Asia, and the Middle East blocked his efforts. Tipu Sultan sent a message to Shah Zaman of Afghanistan through the governor of Oudh. The governor was scared of the Afghan raiders, and instead of delivering the message to Zaman Shah, he went to Calcutta and delivered the message to the Company and sought the Company's help against Tipu. Tipu wrote to the caliph of the Ottoman Empire for joining in jihad against the infidels, but this message was intercepted by the British ambassador at the Turkish court. It did not reach the caliph. The British ambassador quietly destroyed it. Tipu also requested the French for aid via Mauritius. The French governor of Mauritius, Anne Joseph Hypolite Malartic, was very anxious to help Tipu and tried to recruit an army that would be placed under the command of Tipu Sultan. Though Malartic could not get many recruits, his proclamation of supporting Tipu was intercepted by the British sleuths and sent to London and to the new governor-general of India, Lord Richard Wellesley. When the proclamation of Malartic reached Wellesley, he said that "Tipu must be destroyed".[41]

In December 1797, Tipu sent an emissary to seek Napoleon Bonaparte's help against the Company. When the emissary arrived in Paris in April 1798, Napoleon was already in search of an opportunity to sail his 194 ships with 19,000 men on board, out of Toulon and across the Mediterranean to Egypt. From Egypt he was planning to invade India via Suez. From Cairo, Napoleon sent a letter to Tipu

> that in response to your desire for help against the Company, I would let you know that that I am already on the borders of the Red Sea, with a big invincible army that can help you to drive the British out of India. Please send an emissary to Suez or Cairo with whom I could share my plan of action.

On 17 May, Napoleon's fleet sailed out of Toulon toward Alexandria.

In 1798, 37-year-old Earl of Mornington, later known as Lord Richard Wellesley, a friend of Prime Minister William Pitt, was appointed the governor-general of British India. Lord Wellesley well understood the ground realities of the Indian subcontinent because he had served on the board of the company for five years. His two capable advisors were his brothers Arthur and Henry Wellesley. On his way to Calcutta, Wellesley stopped at Madras and saw the worst conditions that were as a result of misrule and non-performance of the nawab and the company's servants alike. It took him three years to fix the administrative problems. As far as Oudh was concerned, it was not fairly handled.

When Lord Wellesley became the governor-general in 1798, Napoleon Bonaparte was in Egypt defending the French trade interests and was ambitious to invade India, and this was a major threat to the British interests in India. On August 1, in the Battle of Nile, the French fleet was destroyed by Nelson in Aboukir Bay, and Bonaparte abandoned his army in Egypt in 1799, but he did not abandon his ambition of invading India. At the same time another French group sailed from the Ile de France (Mauritius) and reached the court of the great fighter and ruler Tipu Sultan. To counter the French threats in the region, English East India started building up regional alliances. First, a message was sent to the company's representative in Persia with instructions to approach the Persian court and seek their cooperation. About three lakhs of rupees were sent to the representative to grease the palm of the Persians concerned to get the job done. Wellesley also came to know that the Marathas, the nizam of Hyderabad, and Tipu Sultan of Mysore were served by the French mercenaries. Wellesley's first target was Tipu Sultan who was seeking foreign aid from Afghanistan, Turkey, and France. Wellesley wanted to attack Tipu Sultan before he could get any foreign aid, and in this connection, he instructed General Harris, the commander-in-chief at Madras, to assemble the armies of the allies for war against Tipu Sultan. Wellesley also foiled the attempt of the French troops from their base at Mauritius that were coming to help Tipu Sultan. Lord Wellesley prepared his plan of war and sent to Dundas, the president of the Board of Control in London.

The biggest threat to the British in the Indian subcontinent was Tipu Sultan. His representatives were busy negotiating a secret agreement at Versailles, though officially not discovered. However, Muhammad Ali, who became the nawab of Carnatic in 1795n was secretly in touch with Mysore against the English East India Company. The threat of the attack of the French forces led by Perron and de Raymond on the British interests in the Indian subcontinent was also felt. Lord Wellesley was the first to strike French interests in Mauritius. On March 25, 1798, 43-year-old Raymond was found dead. The rumor was that Raymond was poisoned by the Company's sleuths. The death of Raymond made Major Kirkpatrick's job easy.

One of the nizam ministers, Mir Alam, visited Calcutta and observed the headquarter of the Company which was well equipped with a big force and arms and ammunition. He relayed to the court of the Nizam that the rising power of the Company was unstoppable. It was argued in the court of the Nizam, that for the safety of Hyderabad, it was essential that an alliance with the British be made. Hyderabad was surrounded by two powerful neighbors: Tipu Sultan of Mysore to the south and the Marathas in Pune in the west. The nizam of Hyderabad, the Marathas, and Tipu Sultan had agreed to get united against the foreigners on their soil. Kirkpatrick got an appointment with the nizam. On the appointed day, Kirkpatrick did not go alone but took 4,000 troops along and surrounded the palace. The troops reached Hyderabad from Guntur and were led by Colonel Roberts. Kirkpatrick asked the frightened Nizam to sign on the dotted line. On the basis of that paper, Tipu's vakils and 14,000 French troops led by de Raymond were made to leave Hyderabad. The 14,000 French troops were replaced by 6,000 company's troops at Hyderabad. In return the nizam would pay the Company an annual subsidy of £41,710.[42] This was done through the services of James Achilles Kirkpatrick, the British resident at Hyderabad, who was the younger brother of the Military Secretary to Wellesley, Major William Kirkpatrick.

Wellesley, on November 4, 1798, wrote to Tipu Sultan to renounce the alliance that he had made with the French, dismiss the French troops, and replace them with the British troops and to reduce his field army, accept Major Doveton as the British Resident at his court, and cede the only remaining maritime province of Malabar. Tipu Sultan defied. Wellesley finalized his plan of attack and sent an amount of Rs. 10 million, then equivalent to £1 million, to Bombay and Madras. This money was raised on the Calcutta money market, and more money came from London. Wellesley wrote to the British Resident in Pune, William Palmer, to get the Marathas to break off their relations with Mysore and join the war against Tipu. The Marathas saw the increasing influence of the British. However, the Marathas joined the Company against Tipu Sultan and promised Palmer to send 25,000 Maratha troops to the Company which never reached at the time of action. The nizam of Hyderabad was also asked to send his troops to the Company as per agreement reached between him and Kirkpatrick.

According to Wellesley's plan of war, if Tipu surrenders immediately, then the terms will be according to Plan-A, which included the surrender of his remaining coastal province of Malabar, a heavy indemnity, and the reduction in his field army. If Tipu surrenders when the British and the forces of the native traitors reach the gates of Srirangapatnam, then the terms will be according to Plan-B, which, in addition to the terms of Plan-A, included the surrender of half of his remaining territory, double the indemnity, and the surrender of his sons as hostages. "In case, he needs the relaxation of the terms then I would ask him to negotiate with you and you can inform him, these terms can only be relaxed by the Governor-General". In this way Tipu will remain confused. General Stuart Franky thought that Tipu would not accept these terms. Wellesley laughed and said he did not want him to. These terms would just result in a casus belli for an attack on Mysore.

Wellesley now used a spin control strategy against Tipu Sultan, depicting him as a tyrant and arrogant enemy, while in reality, Tipu was loved by his people, both by the Hindus and by the Muslims. On December 25, 1798, on Christmas Day, Wellesley left Calcutta for Madras to control the war affairs. Wellesley arrived in Madras on December 31, 1798, and was greeted by the governor of Madras, Edward Clive, the son of Robert Clive, the victor of Plassey. Wellesley did not like Robert Clive as his assets of talent, knowledge, habits of business, and firmness did not match the requirement of the current situation. Anyhow, Wellesley started working out the details of the plan of war without involving Edward Clive.

Wellesley declared war against Tipu Sultan in February 1799. On February 3, 1799, General Harris mobilized his forces to the siege of Srirangapatnam. The governor-general provided a complete plan of action and ordered that there would be no negotiations until the troops stood in front of the walls of Srirangapatnam. On February 19, 1799, the four battalions of the Company at Hyderabad under the command of Colonel James Dalrymple, accompanied by four Hyderabadi battalions and more than 10,000 Hyderabadi cavalry, joined

General Harris' forces. On March 5, the armies with the supply train crossed into the territory of Mysore. The armies were moving very slowly, at a speed of five miles a day, toward Srirangapatnam. Tipu's strength was reduced due to the loss of half of his territory in 1792. Because of his limited strength, Tipu decided that all of his forces should be concentrated within the fort of Srirangapatnam.

Tipu tried to block the Bombay army of the Company as it passed through the mountains from Coorg. The Bombay army was expected at Periapatam. Tipu wanted to finish the Bombay force at Periapatam and then turn to the British army that was coming from the Baramahal side. Tipu appointed Mohammad Reza as in-charge of this operation and ordered him to do his best not to let the British forces pass beyond Periapatam. On March 6, the Bombay army camped outside the village of Periapatam near the border with Coorg. Here, Colonel Montressor was surprised to see the forces of Tipu. Colonel Montressor found the Bombay forces in trouble and immediately sought reinforcement from General Stuart. General Stuart replied, "hold on as long as you can and by tomorrow, I will be with you with reinforcement." Had Tipu's forces attacked at night, they would have annihilated the Company's Bombay troops? But Tipu's forces attacked at dawn, when they came to know that Montressor's forces are being reinforced during the day. Montressor's troops held the ground in the hope of reinforcements from General Stuart. Tipu's forces, not being matched with the reinforced British forces, decided to withdraw.

On March 16, 1799, Tipu camped near Chennapatna, between Bangalore and Srirangapatnam, to block the second British force that was coming via Bangalore. On March 14, the Company's forces led by General Harris had bypassed Bangalore, and on its way had taken several forts. These forces were heading toward Srirangapatnam. There were three routes leading to Srirangapatnam. Tipu decided to be on the central route and from there to watch the southern route via Kankanhalli and the northern route through Savandurga. The British agents in Tipu's court were listening for their British master. Qamaruddin reported that his men brought the information that the British were taking the Kankahalli route. Tipu said that if it is true then we will move to Malvalli. Tipu Sultan sent Qamaruddin on a reconnaissance mission of finding the enemy's strength in the area. Soon another officer who came back from a reconnaissance mission at Kankanhalli reported that one brigade of the British army was heading toward the village. Tipu was surprised that the Company's forces are coming with just one brigade. He decided to finish this small army and then confront the big force. Now Tipu asked his minister Purniah (a British agent in Tipu's court) to call Qamaruddin back.

On March 23, Harris standing on a small hill near Malvalli, about eight miles west of the Maddur River, was watching the advance of the Mysore army. When General Harris saw a small army of Tipu advancing toward them, he expressed satisfaction to the British informer in the army of Tipu who told him that "our force was just one Brigade, that is why he decided to attack. Had he known that there was a big Company's army, he would have not decided to attack us. Our informers in his army had in fact trapped Tipu".

General Harris told Colonel Arthur Wellesley, brother of Governor-General Wellesley, that he was expecting Brigadier Baird and Major Gowdie anon, and when they were here, "then you had to attack from your concealed position with your Hyderabadi contingent". Before orders by General Harris, someone attacked the advance party of Tipu and forced them to Seringapatam fort. On April 5, Harris' forces reached Seringapatam. On April 6, Arthur Wellesley attacked Sultanpet Tope at night with 13 Company soldiers who were captured and tortured to death by Tipu's forces. This meant the Tiger was still dangerous. On April 7, General Harris camped west of Sultanpet Tope. Now the siege of Seringapatam fort started.

The British not only wanted the surrender by Tipu but they wanted to destroy him forever. The British tried to assassinate him but he was well guarded and loved by his people and nobody dared to do that. On May 2, 1799, Tipu Sultan addressed his army that the British had attacked us without any reason.

> Both Governor General Lord Wellesley and his Commander-in-Chief, General Harris had given me vague answers for the reasons of the attack. Now General Harris sent me the terms for peace which included: 1) the dismissal of all of the French people in our service; the payment of Rs. One crore (Rs. 10 million); the surrender of half of our remaining territory, meaning the surrender of maritime province of Malabar so that we are cut off from the sea and all contacts with other Muslim countries and our friendly ally, the French; surrender of our four sons and four leading generals as hostages; and finally, the acceptance of the British Resident at our court.

All the people decided to fight the foreign invaders till the end, with the exception of the two British agents in his court, Mir Sadiq and Purniah. Finally, Tipu spurned the views of Mir Sadiq and Purniah and decided to fight till the end rather than accepting the harsh and humiliating terms.

Now the traitor Mir Sadiq, with his face covered by the scarf, in the company of McLeod, an intelligence officer with General Harris, enters the tent of General Harris and unmasks himself by taking off the scarf from his face. The traitor Mir Sadiq explained to General Harris that he himself and Purniah had convinced Tipu to accept the terms but he had a strange idea in his mind that he would become a martyr and thus would live in the hearts of the people of the future generation. General Harris said that he wanted to embrace martyrdom rather than their sovereignty.

Mir Sadiq, the British's tail-wagger, said that Tipu wanted to fight in the forefront.

> If you storm the fort from the Mehtab Bagh side, you will enter through the Water Gate. When he learns of the fighting, he will rush to that place

to encourage the fighters. The tail-wagger further said that he would ask his subordinate, Mir Nadeem, who is in charge of the inner citadel to close it and not to open it at any cost. Tipu will then be trapped between the citadel and the Water Gate. Now the intelligence officer, McLeod raised another issue and that was about the former employee of the Company Syed Ghaffar who deserted us. We had written to Ghaffar, that everything will be forgotten and forgiven if he comes back to us and he will so get pension. But Syed Ghaffar spurned our offer. Can you get him transferred from the key position he is holding now, to somewhat an unimportant position? Mir Sadiq boasted, just no problem. If you write a letter to Ghaffar telling him that you were to attack such and such posts, and I will manage this letter to fall in the hands of Tipu. Tipu then would suspect him and may remove him.

General Harris said that

we had already tried one trick seven years earlier when we captured Bangalore. We had hired the services of a Hindu accountant Krishna Rao who had managed to disperse the soldiers from the fort on the pretext of payment of salary and then informed the date and time when the soldiers were away from the fort and asked us it was the time to attack the fort. This scheme worked well and we had captured Bangalore. General Harris asked Mir Sadiq, can we do something like that here again. Mir Sadiq said, just no problem, he is in charge of the Finance Department and he would ask the commander to send his men to collect their salary payment which was in arrears for two months. Just let me know the date and time and then he would schedule the activity. General Harris said that Major McLeod would let you know a few hours before the attack. Then General Harris asked McLeod to escort Mir Sadiq out of the Company's area and then come back for further discussion. Mir Sadiq, the tailwagger, covered his face with a scarf and accompanied McLeod for an exit. Mir Sadiq told McLeod that he had expected a jagir as a reward for his service to the Company. General Harris also said that Qamaruddin Khan also expected something like that. These are disgusting people. I have no respect for them.

On May 4, 1799, Brigadier David Baird addressed his men who had assembled in a ford in the River Cauvery (Kaveri) just near the walls of the Srirangapatnam fort. Boys, Tipu's fort is full of gold and this was an opportunity to get that and retire rich in England. "The boys yelled Huzzah! Huzzah! You must not stop until Tipu Sultan has fallen". Sergeant Graham planted the flag at the highest point in the base of the stones. While he was picking up another stone to strengthen the base of flag, he was hit in the head and was dead. The other boys were ready to hit the fort to get the promised gold.

On May 4, Tipu accompanied by Raja Khan just returned from a quick inspection of the ramparts of the fort and asked for breakfast. The breakfast was ready and he picked a mango from the basket and started cutting it and he was about to take a bite when another servant entered the room and said that a person in the name of Sher Dil Khan wanted to meet him. Tipu sent Raja Khan out to see who he was. Raja Khan told Tipu that he was Sher Dil Khan who was a chowkidar of Muhammad's outpost. Sher Dil Khan was seriously wounded and said that the soldiers were withdrawn just before the attack of enemy. And after the attack, the enemy took over the outpost. When Sher Dil Khan appeared before Tipu, he said he was a son of Bahadur Khan who embraced martyrdom at Bangalore seven years ago. He was defaced with blood and gunpowder and was not recognizable. Sher Dil Khan informed that the soldiers were withdrawn under

> your orders to receive the salary payments. A few who were left at the post were all killed. I also fell and I was unconscious and the enemy passed over the bodies. When I became conscious, I crawled and managed to get to you.

Tipu Sultan said he did not order the withdrawal of the soldiers. Who else ordered it? Sher Dil Khan said that Mir Sadiq ordered the withdrawal of the soldiers under his name. Tipu said withdrawing the soldiers was a treachery. Sher Dil Khan further told Tipu that the soldiers who went to get salary were told there was no money. The soldiers became angry.

Now another servant came in to inform Tipu that a French Commander Musa Seeboo [Monsieur Chapuis] wanted to see him. The French Commander entered the room and informed Tipu that a big army of English had already entered through the breach near Mehtab Bagh. Chapuis further said that "the whole trouble is because of us. To save the city you can surrender us to them". Tipu said even if his entire dominion was plundered and destroyed, he would never ever surrender his French friends to their common enemy. "However, if you want to go on your own, he would not stop you". Chapuis said, Nawab Sahib, "as long as you can resist, we would be proud to be with you in this fight". Now another news came that Mehtab Bagh had fallen. Tipu said, "where is Syed Ghaffar?" Another wounded soldier entered and said that Ghaffar Syed received his orders to leave Mehtab Bagh and report to another post in the rear. Mir Nadeem took his place. Nadeem asked the soldiers to go and spend a few hours with their family and there were a few soldiers left. Tipu said

> we did not issue any such order. Yesterday Mir Sadiq produced a letter addressed to him from the Company officer asking him to prove your collusion with them. We suspected it was a forgery. When the enemy attacked Mehtab Bagh, Mir Nadeem immediately planted the flag of surrender. When Ghaffar Syed heard this, he rushed back, knowing that he was defying your orders, when he reached Mehtab Bagh was taken over by the

enemy. Ghaffar gathered a few soldiers left and started fighting with the enemy and was killed.

Now Tipu Sultan, Raja Khan, and Sher Dil Khan got their horses and went to the Water Gate where the battle was going on. As they got near the Water Gate, they saw many wounded men who were leaving the other way. When Tipu arrived, they turned back to Tipu. Tipu dismounts from his horse and leads his men toward the low-roofed, tunnel-like passage of the gateway. Raja Khan told Tipu he had heard the English men were already inside the fort.

> When we meet them, you identify yourself and ask them to take you to their commander. Tipu responded angrily; how dare you suggest like that. You do not remember the event of Kerbla. The human spirit is more powerful than the flesh. This is what the martyrs of Kerbla have taught us. The British intrigues had prevented us from awarding the title of Padshah by the Mughal emperor. But they cannot prevent us from winning the title of martyrdom. It is our belief that it is better to live one day as a free and fearless tiger rather than a thousand years as a fearing jackal.

The men who followed their leader shouted: "Narre takbir, Allah ho Akbar" and rushed into the dark passage. Their arrival raised the morale of the remaining defenders. Proud of the presence of their leader, no soldier yielded. One by one the soldiers were falling, and Tipu Sultan received two bayonet wounds, one in the left shoulder and the other in his chest, and lost enough blood. He threw his empty pistol and took his sword in hand and laid a heap of enemy bodies before him. Then an English officer fired his pistol at Tipu which hit him in the head and he fell. Raja Khan immediately covers the body of Tipu with his own body to save him from the further English bayonet attack. Sher Dil Khan also fell near Raja Khan. The victorious British ran in joy to celebrate the victory. The English soldiers immediately started plundering the nearby houses and raping and disgracing the women.

Tipu Sultan was unconscious. Raja Khan and Sher Dil Khan carried him to the palace and asked to open the door. The soldier at the gate refused to open the gate of the palace. Raja Khan said this is Tipu Sultan. The soldier at the gate said no matter who he is, they are not allowed to open the gate. Raja Khan asked, "whose men are you? We are men of Mir Nadeem". Raja Khan and Sher Dil Khan understood the situation and carried the body of Tipu Sultan and placed it under a tree and went to make other arrangements. Tipu lay unconscious with a strong grip on his sword and his finger firmly locked to the hilt of the sword, even though he was unconscious. In the meantime, three British soldiers came and saw a body which they assumed was a dead body. They did not know that this was the body of Tipu Sultan. They came close to the body of Tipu Sultan and tried to unlock his fingers which were firmly held to the hilt of the sword. While they are unlocking his fingers, Tipu opens his eyes and stood up, and one of the English soldiers said, "oh, the dead is back in life". Tipu waved his sword and cut the leg of one soldier and cut the second one and both fell. The third retreated and Tipu who had lost a lot of blood finally fell and expired.

Now Raja Khan and Sher Dil Khan carried the body of Tipu Sultan and found a breach in the wall through a dark tunnel. Brigadier Baird along with a group of soldiers entered the palace. Baird met the princes, Abdul Khalique and Moizuddin. The princes introduced themselves and Baird was surprised at their English conversation and asked where they learned such good English. Prince Abdul Khalique responded that they were taken as prisoners to Madras by Lord Cornwallis and stayed there more than two years and learnt the English language in Madras. Baird now asked Abdul Khalique, "where is your father, Tipu?" Abdul Khalique replied that they did not see him since the morning. Baird fixed the edge of the sword at the throat of Abdul Khalique, "tell me about your father, otherwise I am going to kill you". Abdul Khalique said, "we are unarmed and you can kill us, if you wish. My father does not hide in the palace like the women". Baird thought they are really the Tiger's cubs. Then Baird pulled his sword and was about to strike, but he was stopped by Major Monteath, who said, "Sir, he is a boy and he is unarmed".

Baird slipped his sword into its scabbard and decided that they would search the palace.

> To do so you will have to kill us first. In that case, I would order every man, woman and child in the palace to take up the arms whatever available and to resist you. Our mothers, sisters would prefer death than disgrace. Now Raja Khan appears and Abdul Khaliq asked him where is my father. He was wounded and unconscious and I had left him in the postern gate of the citadel.

Baird asked where the postern gate was. Raja replied "we must have a lantern to go there". Abdul Khaliq ordered a lantern and then Raja Khan led to the postern gate and said here he was. Baird took the lantern and got close to the body of Tipu Sultan. Baird said, "is this really him"? Monteath recognized him as Tipu Sultan, because he was his prisoner and had met him by face. Baird ordered to put his body in the palanquin and take it to the treasury and an English soldier just stayed as a guard. At midnight of May 4/5, 1799, Major Monteath visited and asked the Sentry (guard), "has anyone visited this place"? The guard said, "yes sir, one English man named Welden who wanted to see the face of Tipu Sultan, has just gone". Monteath told the guard that he had not given permission to Weldon to visit the body of Tipu Sultan. When Monteath reached, Weldon was just looking at his face with a penknife in hand. Monteath asked Weldon "what you are doing here with penknife". Weldon replied he wanted to cut his ear or nose as a souvenir. Monteath told him, "get out of here".

On May 5, 1799, General Harris held a meeting at Tipu Sultan's Darya Daulat Bagh Palace in Srirangapatnam, where, against the protest of Baird, and on the recommendation of Monteath, it was decided to give Tipu a state burial. On May 4, Tipu's follower, Sher Dil Khan was able to manage an audience with Mir Sadiq on the pretext of a message that he supposedly carried from an English general. Mir Sadiq asked what was the message, he pulled the message from his shirt in the form of a dagger and grabbed Mir Sadiq, the traitor, the tail-wagger of the British, and killed him right there and he himself also fell due to the loss of blood because he was seriously wounded by the English soldiers. The body of the traitor Mir Sadiq was taken by the people and was thrown on dunghill. At night the body was eaten by the jackals, and in the morning, it was not recognizable. The people were celebrating in the streets, the killing of Mir Sadiq, the traitor who was the finance minister of Tipu.

Finally, General Harris ordered the implementation of the state burial arrangements for Tipu Sultan at the expense of the state of Mysore with a salute of 40 guns fired at one-minute intervals. This will send a positive message to the natives. The mourning crowds stood on both sides of the road through which Tipu Sultan's funeral procession passed direct to the white onion-domed tomb of Haider Ali in the Lal Bagh, where he was buried by the side of his father. Some Mourners were beating their head with the palm of their hands and some were lamenting the martyrdom of Tipu Sultan. The British soldiers with fixed bayonets stood alert to avoid any disorder.

On May 20, 1799, Governor-General Lord Wellesley celebrated the victory over Tipu Sultan at a dinner held at the governor-general's banquet hall in Calcutta. Now the British got a firm and permanent hold over India. Tipu fought like a lion and kept the British engaged for three months. After three months Srirangapatam fell to the British, and Tipu was killed in the heroic defense of his capital and sacrificed his life to protect the soil he was born in. Tipu Sultan was an intrepid, genius and a true devoted Muslim who wanted to expel the British from the Indian subcontinent. The booty that was collected from the possessions of Tipu was worth £2 million of gold plate, jewelry, palanquins, arms and armors, silks, and shawls. The most important was Tipu's gold throne, inlaid with precious pearls, diamonds, bejeweled tiger head finials, and other precious decorative stuff. Instead of sending the whole throne to England, the avarice prize agents cut it into pieces and thus destroyed the great wonders of India. This was the looting of Srirangapatnam. After the death of Tipu Sultan, his sons were sent to exile in the fort of Vellore in the state of Tamil Nadu, and Mysore came under the Hindus rule. A number of districts were annexed by the Portuguese Goa and Hindu Cochin. The French still held a small settlement at Mahe. Mysore, Hyderabad, Oudh, Carnatic, Tanjore in Tamil Nadu (1801), and Arcot state, Rohilkhand, Doab (1801) in the northwest frontier of Bengal, had become subordinate of the British empire.

Beyond the Sutlej River in Punjab, by the end of the eighteenth century, the Khalsa movement was led by Ranjit Singh, the soldier, and the statesman. The Sikh religion was preached by its founder Guru Nanak, in the fifteenth century who believed in one God, the Creator. The pool and temple at Amritsar served as the center of the Sikh community where a big religious book called Adi Granth composed by Guru Nanak was placed for prayer. Mughal emperor Aurangzeb's action against the Sikh community transformed them into a military force called Khalsa.

The Sikhs made many unsuccessful attempts against the Muslims during the first half of the eighteenth century. During the period 1756 through 1758, the Sikhs took Lahore under the leadership of Jassa Singh, a carpenter, and minted rupees with the inscription of "Coined by the grace of the Khalsa in the country of Ahmad conquered by Jassa the Kalal, writes Dunbar".[43] In 1763, the Sikhs captured the fortress of Sirhind from the governor of Ahmad Shah Duranni, the victor of Panipat. Ahmad Shah decided to reconcile with the Sikhs and appointed Amar Singh of Patiala as his military commander in Sind with the title of maharaja. However, the Sikh confederacies got united against the invasion of Punjab by Timur Shah, Ahmad Shah's son and successor. By 1785, the Sikhs had ruled the territories between the Jhelum and the Sutlej and received exactions up to Delhi. The Sikhs were good fighters but had no organized government.

Ranjit Singh born in 1780 and the son of a Sikh leader possessed the qualities of a soldier, courage, endurance, a fine swordsman, and a statesman. However, he was a short man with a massive forehead, defaced by smallpox and blind by one eye. He became the lion of Punjab and controlled the irritating chiefs of his court. Ranjit Singh did not pay much attention to his civil government. The Sikh rule severely squeezed the Muslim and Hindu peasants through extortions. The revenue officer, vested with the power of the district judge, had the objective of maximizing the cultivation without the welfare of the peasant. Custom duties and indirect taxes were levied on each product of use. The government had an organized system of massacre and pillage. The center and the south were ruled equitably, but the justice in the North-West Frontier and the Muslim tribal areas was a typical example of the portable gallows of the Italian mercenary general Avitabile, who succeeded Hary Singh Nalwa as the governor of Peshawar under Ranjit Singh.

In 1800, Captain John Malcolm, an envoy of the English East India Company, visited Tehran to build an alliance against the French. Through the weapons of bribery and long negotiations, John Malcolm was able to sign two treaties with Persia which were ratified in January 1801. One of these two treaties was about the trade, and the second one called for working together to resist the French attack on India. But this clause of the treaty became ineffective in that the British had already made Napoleon Bonaparte humble by defeating his navy in Egypt. If the king of Afghanistan wanted to attack India, then Persia would attack Afghanistan to destroy his realm and make him humble. In return the British would provide aid to Persia.

In April 1802, the British carried out a reconnaissance survey of the landscape of India which lasted for 60 years. The survey included a complete map of India, borders, distances, and heights of the Himalaya peaks, including Mount Everest, identification of military resources, gold mines, ancient Indian languages and cultures, and dug Mohenjo-Daro, the old civilization of the Indus Valley. The survey provided raison d'être for the British rule of the Indian subcontinent for centuries. According to Harari, in September 1783, William Jones[44] arrived in India as a judge of the Supreme Court of Bengal. Jones researched the local languages and studied Sanskrit and compared it with the European languages. The British believed that in order to rule their subject they must know their languages and culture. All the British officers who were deputed to India were supposed to spend three years in a Calcutta college where they learned regional languages such as Sanskrit, Urdu, Persian, Tamil, Bengali, and the Indian culture alongside English law, mathematics, economics, and geography. This helped the British to understand their empire well. Without complete knowledge of the Indian subcontinent, it was not possible for a few British officers to exploit and rule about 300 million of Indian people for two centuries.

After the death of Nana Farnavis, a great Maratha statesman and prime minister, on March 13, 1800, Lord Wellesley decided to break up the Maratha Confederacy just by sitting at Calcutta. The Marathas possessed the territories of central India from Orissa in the east to Baroda in the west ruled by a group of four chiefs of Marathas, namely Peshwa Baji Rao II, Scindia, Holkar, and the Raja of Berar. Bhonsla, Scindia, and the Holkars were fighting for the control of Pune. First, the Peshwa Baji Rao with his capital at Pune came under the protection of the British and ceded the territories of Tapti and Nerbudda to the British. According to Holkar, Baji Rao had sold the Maratha power to the British. Now the British would give the same blow to the Marathas that they did to Tipu Sultan. The Maratha chiefs, with the exception of Baroda, got united and considered their independence as a matter of life and death struggle against the British. Wellesley also made his best efforts to circumvent the unification of the warring Maratha armies. He was successful in keeping Scindia and Holkar separate.

Wellesley now started preparation to capture the Mughal Empire. In July, Wellesley sent Scindia an ultimatum to withdraw his forces to north of Narmada or face the consequences. Instead, Daulat Rao Scindia, like Tipu, started making preparation for a war with the Company. On August 1, 1803, he removed the British Resident Lieutenant Colonel John Ulrich Collins. When this news reached Calcutta, Wellesley declared war and ordered attacks on four fronts, including the two minor attacks on the coasts of Orissa and Gujarat and the major two attacks on the entire Deccan and all of India. On August 4, 1803, Scindia declared war. On August 6, 1803, Major General Arthur Wellesley marched with his 40,000 troops heading to the north toward the fortress of Ahmadnagar. On August 11, Wellesley captured the fort by bribing the French and the Arab mercenaries. Inside the fort, he found a large quantity of gunpowder and Scindia's treasures and food supplies. Arthur Wellesley garrisoned here and made it a base for further advancement.

Scindia and Bhonsla got their armies together and moved to plunder the nizam's territories around Aurangabad and thus compelled Arthur Wellesley to get out of his fortification to help his ally, the nizam, and in this effort they were successful. Arthur Wellesley left a large garrison behind to defend Ahmadnagar. On September 23, the two armies appeared on the plain to the north of the Ajanta pass. On September 23, 1803, Arthur Wellesley's forces met the 50,000 Maratha forces next to the fortified village of Assaye. Wellesley divided his force into two parts, one led by his deputy Colonel Stevenson heading to the west and he himself led about 5,000 men which included Madrasi soldiers and Highlanders. Wellesley crossed the Khelna River ford without getting the powder wet. The battle was the fiercest. Scindia's heavy field guns surprised Wellesley. Wellesley's two horses were shot, and several of his immediate staff were killed. Wellesley himself narrowly escaped a shot fired at him.

The Madrasi soldiers in the center and the Highlanders in the left wing of Wellesley's front line were the main targets. Wellesley's infantry continued the advance through the smoke. When the British infantry passed by many of the Marathas' dead around the cannon, they suddenly rose and started firing upon the rear of the British troops. Now Wellesley personally led a cavalry charge against the enemy when his second horse was shot dead. Now a final effort was made in the village fort. The Marathas were driven back over the Juah leaving behind 98 guns which fell into the hands of the British. The casualties on both sides were shocking. The Marathas lost 6,000 men and Wellesley lost 1,584 men who were buried on the plains of Assaye. Wellesley got a complete victory.

In the north, the commander-in-chief, General Lake, was rapidly advancing on the Mughal capital. On August 7, 60-year-old Lake, the loser of the American War of Independence, left Kanpur, heading west toward Scindia's French commander-in-chief's, General Pierre Perron's, fortress at Aligarh. Lake led his army of 10,000 men. On August 29, Lake's army crossed into Marathas' territory advancing toward the strongest fortress of Aligarh with strong corner towers and a deep moat. When Lake reached the Agra fortress, Perron withdrew and told his men that he was going to get reinforcements from Delhi and Agra and asked his deputy, Colonel Pedron, to keep his reputation as a French and not to let the British enter the fort and do his best to expel them. Colonel Pedron and many of his French mercenaries were happy to surrender to the British if they were given safe passage to their home. But Scindia's Rajput and Maratha officers refused to drop their weapons and went inside the wall to take their defensive positions. They imprisoned Colonel Pedron and selected their own Maratha commander and decided to fight till death.

Lake offered a lot of money to the soldiers to vacate the fortress, but they refused. On September 4, Lake attacked the main gate of the fortress. An Irish deserter from Scindia's army, Lieutenant Lucan offered help to lead the attacking party under the supervision of Lake's deputy, Colonel Monson. In the fight at the main gate, Monson was wounded and four of his officers were killed by the Maratha defenders. Finally, one door got open with the cannon fire and the Company soldiers went inside and were confronted by the Rajputs. Soon 2,000 men of the garrison were killed, and many of the Maratha soldiers escaped by swimming in the moat. The Company's soldiers got in and took possession of the fortress of Aligarh.

On September 1, 1803, the Qutub Minar, built by Qutub-ud-Din Aibak in 1193, a symbol of the establishment of Muslim rule in India after defeating the last Hindu ruler of India, was hit by the earthquake and partly damaged which Shah Alam, considered it a bad omen. When Perron surrendered to the Company and got a safe passage for himself and his family to Calcutta, Shah Alam thought that as the Company is now rising in power and it is now the right time to negotiate with them. Shah Alam asked Sayed Reza Khan to get in touch with Lord Lake. Shah Alam remembered that Hastings had cut off the payment of promised revenue from Bengal due to him under the terms of the Treaty of Allahabad. Now he wanted to have written assurances from the Company for the payment of allowances due to him before he submits to the Company.

Perron, who defected to the British, was replaced by Lieutenant Colonel Louis Bourquien in the Red Fort. Scindia's troops were at his disposal to take revenge for the massacre of their men at Aligarh. When the news came that Lake after leaving Aligarh through Agra wanted to capture Delhi, Bourquien alerted his army. Bourquien with his army of 19,000 crossed the Yamuna River from the ghats under the Red Fort over to Shahdara and waited for Lake. On September 10, Lake camped north of Akbar's tomb in Sikandra.

Two months later, Wellesley defeated Bhonsla at Argaon and ended the campaign in Deccan. Bhonsla signed a subsidiary treaty with the British. Lake was successful in Upper India and took Delhi and Agra. By the end of October 1803, Scindia's forces were completely destroyed at Laswari. In December, Scindia surrendered many territories to the Company but did not sign a subsidiary treaty. With the fall of Delhi, Emperor Shah Alam, old and blind prisoner of cruel Scindia and later of French for many years, finally came under the protection of the British. The governor-general gave full respect to Shah Alam, due to the emperors of India. Lake's forces stopped at the bank of the Hindan River for breakfast. While the soldiers were busy making parathas for their breakfast, there was a thunder of heavy artillery which resulted in a massacre. The terrified Company soldiers scattered. The Marathas stayed in their defensive position on the mound and did not advance. This gave time to Lake to organize his army.

To trap the Maratha army, Lake ordered his infantry to fall back between the two cavalry units which were hidden behind the tall grass, and this encouraged the Maratha to advance for an attack which they did. When the Marathas came forward, the Company's infantry turned back and attacked the Marathas and drove them to the River Yamuna and hundreds of them perished while crossing the river. Lake's infantry returned to the field to pick up their wounded soldiers. Five French Commanders surrendered. However, Lake admired the Maratha soldiers who were really heroes who gave their best. The Battle of Delhi was the last battle in Asia between the two rival European nations, the British and the French. This was the end of the war in India, and it also decided the future destiny of India. The Marathas were the last powerful force in India that had the capability of driving the British out of India. After the wars of Assaye and Delhi, the Company was now unstoppable by the natives. The other battles were expected until Scindia and Holkar surrendered. About 600 civil employees of the Company with the support of 155,000 soldiers would now rule India as the British Raj. Shah Abdul Aziz, imam of Delhi Mosque, said that India had gone out of their hands. In 1803, Imam said that "India is no longer Dar ul-Islam". The British were now complete masters of India, and the British supremacy was established that ruled India for another 144 years until its independence in August 1947.

After the defeat of the Marathas, Emperor Shah Alam congratulated the commander-in-chief and said he was looking forward to receiving the general. On September 15, 1803, the general camped on the banks of Yamuna and sent Sayed Reza Khan, a Company's representative at the court of the emperor, to make a humble request for the audience and asked for sending the boats to cross the river. The emperor immediately sent the boats and General Lake crossed the Yamuna and camped at the old fort, Purana Qila. Now, Sayed Reza presented the letter to the emperor from the governor-general expressing good wishes and relationships. On September 16, Crown Prince Akbar Shah came to the camp of Lake at Purana Qila and as a part of a ceremony, Prince mounted on his elephant and the cavalcade was formed. The distance to the palace from Purana Qila was four miles, and Lake arrived at the palace at sunset.

Lake bowed before the blind Emperor and then talked to him through his deputy, Colonel Sir David Ochterlony, who lived in India for a long period of time and spoke Urdu and Persian. Ochterlony read to Shah Alam the letter from the governor-general, Lord Wellesley, who described himself as "the happy instrument of your Majesty's restoration to a state of dignity and tranquility, under the power of the British Crown, writes Dalrymple".[45] In response, the emperor appreciated the Company and gave gifts of rich robes to both men and gave the title of Nawab Samsam al Daula, Khan Dauran Khan, to General Lake. The Colonel Ochterlony also received the title of Nasir al-Daula, Muzaffar Jang.[46] Governor-General Wellesley announced a gift of Rs. 600,000 to Shah Alam's immediate expenses and also pledged Rs. 64,000 per month to cover the costs of the servants of the Imperial Household, the princes, and the courtiers.

Now Lake returned to Agra fort to clear the resistance from the remaining Marathas. Ochterlony was now appointed the Company's Resident and took up his residence in the old Mughal building which was once the library of Sufi Prince Dara Shukoh, the eldest son of Shah Jahan. Hospital and the residences for the army were set up near the Kashmiri Gate. Qamar al-Din's compound near the Ajmeri Gate became the Customs House. After Scindia's defeat, Bhonsla, raja of Berar, ceded Orissa and came under British control. Holkars who ruled central India were the next to deal with. Holkars had gathered a big force and were engaged in unjust and cruel extortion of the people of Rajputana. Holkar got three British men who were in his service murdered. In April 1804, Wellesley defeated the Holkars. Lord Wellesley pursued the policy of the company which led to heavy expenses and imperial responsibilities which the directors at London rejected. Other criticism of Wellesley was favoritism in the employment of his brothers, Henry and Arthur. After his return to England in 1805, Wellesley was impeached, but the proceedings did not reach logical conclusions. His successor reversed Lord Wellesley's policies of Indian's subordination.

Cornwallis, aged, flaccid, infirm, returned to India to die in two months. The subsidiary treaty with Jaipur was renounced, and every effort was made to bring peace with the Maratha families of Scindia and Holkar, and Nawab Amir Khan, a Pushtun by origin, who became the first ruler of Tonk, now Rajasthan in 1806. Amir Khan was allowed to pillage outside the realm of the Company, and likewise the Holkars were still free in raiding on the Sutlej and throughout Rajputana, writes Woodward.[47] The Maratha war was speedily brought to an end.

After the death of Cornwallis, Sir George Barlow, who became the acting governor-general, signed a treaty with Scindia in 1805, wherein the territory was restored to the prince. Scindia also held the Company obligated not to make engagements with the Rajput states against the Marathas. On the financial side, Barlow turned the fiscal deficit into a surplus. The directors of the company were happy, and they recommended Barlow to stay as the governor-general. Barlow showed some reluctance and then finally the board appointed the earl of Minto who came to India in 1807 to carry on the policy of noninterference in Indian affairs.

Minto assessed the situation and later recommended to authorities in London that a policy of strict neutrality in India could not be possible. According to Dunbar, in 1813, based on the Fifth Report of the House of Commons committee, the Charter Act was passed,[48] which renewed the Company's control of the Indian territories and revenues for the next 20 years and abolished its trade monopoly with the exception of tea trade with China. The Christian religious leaders were allowed to go to India to preach to the natives with the knowledge of Christianity. The Catholic Church already existed in India when the Portuguese missionaries arrived in the east in 1500. The British government pursued a policy of noninterference in the religions of the Indian subcontinent.

The abolition of the trade monopoly and the arrival of many European traders in India created political problems for the Company. However, the natives were in favor of free trade, and this did not affect the political relationships between the natives and the Company. In 1809, according to the treaty of Amritsar, the supremacy of Sikh power led by Ranjit Singh beyond the Sutlej was acknowledged. An agreement was signed with the Mirs of Sind for not allowing the French on their territory.[49] Major Alexander Walker had amicably settled the affairs of the state of Baroda, a subsidiary of the company brought by Lord Wellesley through a treaty. The tribes of Marathas, Scindia, Holkar, and Berar enjoyed their freedom and independence through their treaties with the Company.

The French asked the Alexander of Russia to form an alliance for a joint expedition to India through Turkey and Persia. The British governor-general, Lord Minto, was prepared to meet this challenge through alliances with the states which were the target of the potential French-Russian invasions. Lord Minto signed a treaty with Ranjit Singh who ruled Punjab and an ambassador from England tried an alliance with Persia which did not work. Napoleon attacked his own ally and met disaster on the steppes of Russia, and in a few years later he lost his empire and the threat to the British in the region disappeared for a while.

In 1811, Fateh Khan, a wazir in the government of King Mahmud of Afghanistan, with the support of Ranjit Singh, a powerful man of Punjab, invaded Kashmir which was ruled by Atta Mohammad Khan. Ranjit Singh was expecting the governorship of Kashmir. However, Kashmir was given to another brother of the Wazir, Mohammad Azim Khan. Ranjit Singh was disappointed and decided that in future he would never work as a vassal of the Shah of Afghanistan. After the death of Fateh Khan, his brothers fought for power and engaged in fratricide, treachery, and confusion. Taking advantage of this situation, the Sikh leader Ranjeet Singh annexed Kashmir in 1819, writes Ewans.[50] Later Ranjeet Singh defeated the Durrani army near Attock and stretched his territory across the Indus River and took Peshawar. Ranjeet Singh signed an agreement with the British in 1809, and he remained a friend and an ally of the British until his death in 1839.

When Minto left India in 1813, Ranjit Singh transformed Punjab into his strong kingdom in alliance with the Company. By 1823, Ranjit Singh had annexed the Muslim provinces of Kashmir, Multan, and Peshawar. During the next ten years, the Marathas had extinguished and the Khalsa rose to a great state that was independent of the British. As Ranjit Singh rose to control the confederacies of the Sikhs, he wanted to have a strong well-trained and -equipped Sikh army organized on the lines of the British army led by Lake in 1805. His infantry of Sikhs and Hindus was trained by the British deserters and other Europeans. His artillery force was trained by an Irishman supported by the two French generals who served under Napoleon Bonaparte.

In 1813, earl of Moira, Lord Warren Hastings, became the governor-general. Before leaving for India, he had the views in which he had denounced the war against Mysore. In his views the British government in India was based on injustice and established by force. He thought that the British government in India should restore peace and security in the region and take the advantage of the trade. When Governor-general Hastings arrived in Calcutta, he found out there was no peace in the country. The Peshwa was friendly only under his role as a subsidiary of the company. The Maratha chiefs were very hostile. Their armies were financed through the extortions of the neighbors. Outside the Company's territory, the forces of the Marathas and Amir Khan tortured and pillaged throughout Rajputana and Bhopal.

Within a period of four months after the arrival of Hastings in India, he found around him all the elements of war. His preconceived policy of noninterference in the affairs of India remained just a thought. Hastings was to complete the work that was left by Wellesley, writes Woodward.[51] In February 1814, Hastings converted to the policy of Wellesley to make the British government as supreme with all the states as their vassals, and this was not possible without war.

The subjects of Nawab of Oudh were under British protection through the Treaty of 1801. The war broke out against the Gurkha state of Nepal. The Rajput ruler of the Gurkha kingdom conquered the neighboring territories. The Gurkhas were big fighters. The Gurkha Hindu kingdom envied the fertile land of India but could not do anything against Ranjit Sing. In 1814, the Gurkha forces captured two districts of Bengal which were under dispute. The new governor-general had to resort to a war with Nepal. This was the first mountain warfare that the British were experiencing in the region. After six months of continuous defeats, General Sir David Ochterlony forced the Nepalese forces to terms and a peace treaty was signed in 1816 at Sagauli under which the Nepalese gave back the two districts of Bengal which they had occupied before the war and in addition Kumaon and the Himalayan hill station Naini Tal were ceded. Simla pahar was also acquired by the Company after the war, which became the summer capital in 1831. After the treaty, Nepal became an ally of the British with the contribution of Gurkha brigade to the service of the Queen.

In 1816, Hastings signed treaties with 20 Rajput states. Scindia resisted the treaty signed with the Muslim state of Bhopal. The ruler of Nagpur, Appa Sahib Bhonsla, nullified the subsidiary alliance signed with the British when the latter were in war with the Marathas. The Maratha power with the Peshwa rested at Pune and with recalcitrant Scindia at Gwalior. Scindia was an independent prince not bound to the British through any agreement, while the Peshwa was a subsidiary ally of the English East India Company. Peshwa's advisor Trimbakji Danglia was involved in the murder of the Brahman envoy Gangadhar Sastri, who was sent to Pune in 1816 from Baroda. Maharaja Gaekwar of Baroda was an ally of the British. The British took up the matter for their ally. In June 1817, the British compelled the Maratha general Baji Rao to sign an agreement which went far beyond the treaty of Bassein. Under the treaty of Pune, Baji Rao renounced his leadership of the Maratha confederacy, recognized the independence of Baroda, denounced Trimbakji for the murder of Gangadhar Sastri, and transferred his battalions to the company's subsidiary contingent.

In the last quarter of 1817, the two British armies led by Hastings and Sir Thomas Hislop with a total force of 113,000 men including 13,000 Europeans with 300 guns humbled another irregular militant group of Pindaris who were supported by the Maratha states of Pune, Indore, and Nagpur. Pindaris' raiding activities triggered miseries from Rajputana to Orissa. By the end of January 1818, the Pindaris were destroyed.

In 1817, the Peshwa, through an alliance with Indore and Nagpur, revolted. Now the governor-general was in war with the whole Maratha confederacy who were leaderless after the death of Holkar in 1811. The British crushed the revolt. The office of the Peshwa was abolished and his dominion was annexed to the

Bombay presidency. The Peshwa himself was made prisoner. The infant princes were placed in power at Indore and Nagpur under the control of the British. Their territories were not annexed. Rajputana was taken under British protection. The Peshwa was replaced by the Raja of Sattara, a direct descendant of the great Sivaji. The Maratha power was broken and central India was relieved of the raids and this completed the task left of Wellesley.

Hastings marched toward Gwalior, Scindia capitulated, and, on November 5, signed a treaty of Gwalior dictated by Sir John Malcolm, and accepted the military occupation of his country. At the same time, Baji Rao of the Maratha Empire reneged and tried to get himself free of the British. The Marathas forces were defeated three times by Colonel Burr's forces and Baji Rao surrendered in June 1818. Appa Sahib, ruler of Berar, and Holkars were defeated by the British. On April 9, 1819, when Hastings took the fort of Asirgharh, the Maratha war was over. By 1819, the whole of India, except for the Punjab and Sind, was directly and indirectly under British rule.

Hastings left India in 1823, and a new era of peace, prosperity and wealth started in the Indian subcontinent. However, the political liberty in the subcontinent was not clear as yet. When the supremacy of the British had been established over the vast territories of the subcontinent, it was hoped that the character of the Indian subjects would improve to such an extent that they would be able to govern and protect themselves.

Hastings was succeeded by Lord Amherst who had to follow the policy of annexation. The kingdom of Ava, that ruled Burma, had taken arms against the British. The war with Burma (Myanmar) was looming. The Burmese king, in 1818, had asked Hastings to cede one half of Bengal to his kingdom. In 1823, the king of Burma attacked and seized a small island which was in the possession of the Company. The king attacked the mountain ranges of Cachar, a state in Assam, and this conquest threatened the territory of the Company. Cachar was brought under the British protection. Governor-General Lord Amherst declared war in 1824 and dispatched three armies: one against Rangoon by sea; the second against Assam by river; and the third against Arakan by land. The Burmese were defeated and lost Assam in Bengal, coastal districts of Arakan and Tenasserim.[52] However, Burma retained the valley of Irrawaddi intact. Finally, the Burmese signed a treaty of 1826 giving up its lower provinces to the Company and relinquishing its hold on Upper Assam. Later the Company took the control of the whole Assam valley.

Lord Amherst was succeeded by Lord William Bentinck (1828–35), who maintained peace in India. He was concerned with the welfare of the people and abolished cruel rites. Free from the fear of war, he devoted his time to the wellbeing of the Indian people. When the raja of Mysore was not performing to the satisfaction of the people, Lord Bentinck removed him and took the administration of Mysore into the British hands. No annexation took place. On the wishes of the people the Coorg district of Mysore was admitted to the Empire. The governor-general introduced many reforms, including the abolition of Suttee, or immolation of Hindu widows on the funeral pile of their husbands.

Russia was now interested in its expansion in Asia. By 1834, the Russians reached out the court of Persia to influence them to attack Afghanistan. The British strategically were concerned to have a buffer state between Russia and India. The then British foreign secretary, Lord Palmerston, had received the information that the shah of Persia with Russian support wanted to encroach upon Afghanistan, and if it was successful then the Russians would be on the borders of British India. British considered it a great threat to its security in the Indian subcontinent. Though it was not true as Afghanistan was not the buffer state between British India and Russia. The buffer zone then between British India and Afghanistan was Punjab and Sind. Ranjit Singh had taken Peshawar in 1823 and was an ally of the British. Thus, North West Frontier, Punjab, and Sind became the buffer zone between British India and Afghanistan.

The British thinking now changed with a change in leadership in London when Palmerston became the foreign minister in the cabinet of Lord Melbourne and Auckland became the governor-general of British India. Now the focus of British policy was more on Russia than on France. When Auckland arrived in India, he was overwhelmed with the apprehension of the Russian designs in India and Afghanistan. In 1837, Dost Mohammad Khan was the ruler of Afghanistan who was not happy with the British as they were not helping him against Ranjit Singh, who was a friend and an ally of the British. Therefore, Foreign Secretary Palmerston and Governor-general of British India Auckland decided to get Amir Dost Mohammad replaced by their protégé Shah Shuja, who had lost his throne to Dost Mohammad in 1834. This was the first attempt of a regime change in Afghanistan. The British sleuth Mohan Lal was in Kabul working for the British Government. The Barikzai brothers did not like Shah Shuja.

Lord Bentinck's successor Lord Auckland (1836–41) stopped the internal progress as he became more concerned about securing the borders on the North-West of British India. There were three nations that held the peace of North-West India: Punjab ruled by Sikhs, the lower Indus Valley by the Sind tribes, the mountains by the Afghans. The Sikhs with a strong army controlled the path from the Ganges valley to Kabul and Sind blocked the southern way of Quetta and Kandahar. The Russians' move to Central Asia alarmed the British. The British now resolved to resist the Russian advance into Afghanistan by taking the control of Afghanistan's politics.

In 1837, the new governor-general, Auckland, prepared a plan to replace Dost Mohammad by Shah Shuja to have the British influence in Afghanistan's affairs. Through British help, Shuja ascended to the throne on August 7, 1839, as a puppet ruler of Afghanistan. The British controlled the foreign affairs, defense, and tribal affairs, and Shuja only handled the civil administration. Shuja was assassinated in April 1842. The British fought three wars with Afghanistan. The British lost the first Anglo-Afghan War of 1841 when the entire British army and families were killed except for one person named Dr. Byrton, who managed to reach Jalalabad. The British ambassador McNaughton was killed by Mohammad Akbar, the son of the deposed Afghan ruler, Dost Mohammad, and the headless body of the British ambassador was displayed in the streets of Kabul. The first war cost the British between £17 million and 20 million[53] in addition to the loss of 15,000–20,000 soldiers and numerous civilians, writes Ewans. British also lost the Second Anglo-Afghan War fought in July 1880 at Maiwand, where 1,000 British troops were killed. The Third Anglo-Afghan War was fought on three fronts of the northern through Khyber Pass, the central through Paiwan Kotal Pass, and the southern through Bolan Pass, and this war ended without any consequential result. On November 12, 1893, the famous Durand Agreement was reached between the British and Amir Abdur Rahman. In addition to the territories colored and specified in the map, Abdur Rahman also gave up all claims to Swat, Bajaur, and Chitral but was permitted to keep Asmar in Kunar province of Afghanistan. Finally, Afghanistan got its sovereignty back from the British on August 8, 1919, under the Treaty of Rawalpindi.

In 1844, Ellenborough was replaced by Lord Hardinge. In 1843, Sir Charles Napier conquered Sind from the Mirs, as it was strategically important for communications between the Company and Afghanistan. On December 12, 1845, the Sikh forces led by Lal Singh and Tej Singh crossed the borders and the first Anglo-Sikh War began at Sobraon. The British prevailed and entered Lahore on February 10, 1846, but did not annex it. However, the Khalsa army was reduced. The British took Kashmir from the Sikhs in lieu of war indemnity. Lord Hardinge was replaced by Lord Dalhousie, also known as James Ramsay, as the governor-general of India in January 1848. On January 13, 1849, the Second Anglo-Sikh War broke at Chilianwala. On February 21, 1849, the British victory at the battle of Gujarat ended the war and on March 29, 1849, Punjab was annexed to the company and the Koh-i-noor diamond was surrendered to the queen of England. The annexation of Punjab inherited the problem of the North-West Frontier's Pathan tribes with whom no Indian government was ever concerned. Now the British had to handle them.

In 1852, the second Burmese war broke out because of the grievances of the British and Indian traders at Rangoon (Yangon). Lord Dalhousie wanted to maintain peace, but the refusal of all the parties led to a war. Lord Dalhousie ensured adequate medical and supply arrangements. The small war ended in a month when the Rangoon temple was attacked and the province of Pegu was annexed. British India occupied the lower valley of Irrawaddi, a very important port of Burma and annexed it. The peace led to the development of industry, wealth, and population of the coastline of Burma. Burma was included as a province of India. Lord Dalhousie returned to England in 1856 and died four years later. In India, 36-year-old Lord Dalhousie built miles of the railroad in the country and the telegraph wires linked Calcutta with Peshawar. He introduced a postal service, issued the first adhesive stamps, and opened a number of post offices, organized medical services, and started the restoration of the ancient monuments. He also emphasized education for all. His reforms put the country on the path of systematic governance in all spheres of life. In February 1856, despite opposition from Lord Dalhousie, Oudh was annexed to the British territory. Dalhousie wanted to develop Oudh on the lines of Punjab.

Early in 1857, alerts were received by the new governor-general, Lord Canning (1856–62), about the crisis looming. Canning, without realizing the ground realities, assumed that the people would be happy by getting their freedom from the misrule of the king of Oudh. Moreover, he thought that a single battalion and a battery were sufficient to maintain law and order in the new province of Oudh. There were certain predictions of the downfall of the empire after ruling for a century since the British victory over the nawab of Bengal and his French allies at the battle of Plassey in 1757. There were intrigues at work among local people and politicians. There was unrest among the influential people who lost their power and authority. Upper India was hostile to the British. In Delhi, the last of the Temurids, Bahadar Shah II, had lost the title of emperor and his sovereignty. The Muslims were of the view that the imperial power was directed against them. The son of Peshwa, Nana Sahib, who was dispossessed and living in seclusion near Cawnpore, was also resentful. The widowed rani of the Maratha house of Jhansi was resentful of annexation of her state. The Company's defense depended on its military force. Oudh provided 40,000 men. The army of Bengal had become inefficient. Discipline disappeared.

There were many causes of the Mutiny of Meerut as the British called it, while the native called it a War of Independence or Quit India Movement. Lord Dalhousie's policies of abolishing the direct line of succession to the throne and interference in the customs and traditions of the Oriental races contributed to the feelings of discontent among the Indian rulers. The nawab of Oudh was removed on the charges of bad governance. These actions led to the discontentment of the dispossessed rulers like nawab of Oudh, the raja of Mysore, and Nana Sahib, the adopted son of the last Peshwa who then became anti-British. Indian society was passing through a quick change. In Oudh, both the Hindu and Muslim communities were part of the uprising. In January 1857, it was rumored that the new Enfield rifle cartridges had been greased with the fat of pig and cow which adversely affected the religious purity of the sepoys. This rumor was spread like wildfire throughout India. This was the most dangerous charge that led to the rebellion by the sepoys in March and April 1857 who disobeyed their officers. On May 10, 1857, the native troops at Meerut mutinied over the religious issue and marched to Delhi. John Lawrence sent a brigade of British and Indian troops from Punjab and attacked Delhi. Sikh regiment did not take part in the Mutiny and remained loyal to the British. Bombay, Madras, Lower Bengal, and Rajputana remained quiet, and the nizam did not move either.

On June 27, the rebel forces led by Nana Sahib besieged Kanpur and Hugh Wheeler, the commander of the British garrison, surrendered in return for a safe passage and many British men and women were killed. The British forces, consisting of Sikhs, Gurkhas, and men from Jammu led by John Nicholson, recovered Delhi on September 20 and the Mughal emperor Bahadur Shah Zafar was captured and made a prisoner while his sons were shot dead. The last of the Temurids was exiled till his death. Like Kanpur, the residence of Sir Henry Lawrence at Lucknow was sieged. General Havelock fought his way, and then Sir Colin Campbell raised the siege and Lucknow was recovered on November 16. By the end of December 1857, the Mutiny was over with the efforts of Campbell and Sir Huge Rose.

The Mutiny of Meerut by the sepoys shocked London, and it was in fact a death blow to the Company. The British were in trouble against those soldiers of Meerut who were trained by them so well. The immediate effect of the Mutiny of Meerut was the end of the dual control of India by the Crown and the English East India Company. By an Act of 1858, the English East India Company was abolished and India came under the direct control of the Crown and the governor-general got the new title of viceroy. Now the affairs of India were managed by a parliamentary secretary of state with an India office council. The secretary of state was responsible to the parliament. Lord Canning, the last governor-general of the Company, was made the first viceroy of India. This also led to the end of the Mughal Empire by deposing the last Mughal ruler Bahadur Shah Zafar and making him a prisoner.

The proclamation of the sovereignty of the Crown was made at a Darbar held at Allahabad on November 1, 1858. The proclamation said that all the agreements that were made with native princes by the Company will be accepted by the new regime. In January 1877, Queen Victoria became the empress of India by inheriting the dominion of the Mughals. From 1858 through 1919, India was ruled by a civil aristocracy in which the authority was vested in the center and exercised by the executive council or cabinet of the viceroy. Indians were not included in the cabinet. No constitutional arrangement was made to establish contacts between the cabinet and the people. Any government sans the engagement of the people was to fail. India progressed under two viceroys: Lord Lawrence, and Lord Mayo. Lord Mayo was assassinated in 1872 by an Afghan convict, Shir Ali, in the Andaman Islands[54] in the Bay of Bengal, writes Fletcher. Lord Mayo was succeeded by Lord Northbrook. Viceroy Lord Northbrook (1872–76) deposed the Gaekwar of Baroda for mismanagement and disloyalty, but his territory was not annexed. Under the Councils Act of 1861, the viceroy's council could legislate for all the territories under the crown and his council got 12 additional members, including some nonofficials who were Indians. The role of the nonofficial Indian members was just advisory, and they were not allowed to introduce a private bill. In fact, they were not the true representatives. Under the Indian High Courts Act of 1861, the courts of the Crown and the company were merged. Now the Indians could be appointed as judges. All the district officers were mostly British, not Indians. The servants of the British were mostly concerned with the revenue collection activities. The Simon Commission of 1930 spelled out the duties of the servants engaged in different activities. In 1865, a deadly famine occurred in India in which one million people died in Orissa alone. The agriculture was rain-fed. Lord Lawrence, the then viceroy, convinced the secretary of the state about the most important and urgent need of the irrigation work. The irrigation department was established, and within a period of ten years about 10.5 million acres were brought under irrigation, which increased to 31 million acres in 1931. Lord Northbrook resigned and was succeeded by Lord Lytton, who had no knowledge of Asia. With the fall of the government of Disraeli, Lytton's policy disappeared.

In 1889, Maharaja Pratap Singh was ousted and stripped of his power and authority in Kashmir, and the British took the control of Kashmir. From Kashmir the military expeditions were carried out in Hunza and Nagar valleys which had enjoyed an independent status. Both of these valleys were surrounded by mountains which helped the Hunzas and Kanjutis of Nagar to defend themselves. The people of Hunza and Nagar had been engaged in looting the caravans on the Leh-Yarkan route. Both the valleys were suppressed and were placed under the control of local leaders who acted on the advice of the British.

In 1899, with the arrival of Lord Curzon, a new program was started. Curzon withdrew the forces to areas outside the tribal zone and the task of maintenance of order was given to the tribal levies or to the tribes themselves. In 1901, in line with imperial responsibility and military requirements, Lord Curzon divided the province of Punjab by creating a new province known as the North-West Frontier Province under a Chief Commissioner, writes Dunbar.[55] Curzon organized the management of the North-West Frontier Province. Politically it was divided into two zones: an "administered area" which included the districts of Hazara, Peshawar, Kohat, Bannu, and Dera Ismail Khan; and a "free tribal area" lying between the administered border and the Durand Line. The tribes in the free tribal area were placed then in five political agencies, including Wana, Malakand, Khyber, Kurram, and Tochi, managed through the political agents. The tribes in the free tribal area retained complete autonomy and were paid subsidies through the political agents for maintaining peace. Similarly, he divided Bengal into Eastern Bengal and Assam. The people in Bengal protested and resented this division. Lord Curzon returned to England and was replaced by Lord Minto in 1905.

Lord Minto got the impression that the Indians held an inferior status among the subjects of the Crown. The previous viceroys termed the Indians as uncivilized and unimproved people and that the western civilization was superior to the Indian civilizations. The color prejudice and racial superiority were evident in India. Indians had been excluded from high responsible positions in the civil and military services of British India. Indians did get commission in the army as of 1904. The Indians were subordinates of the lowest rank of the British nationals. The noble families of India, which were educated in Western Universities, when they came back to India were barred from the clubs under the British management in their own cities. These conditions bred contempt among the Indians, sowed the seeds of the political awakening, and led to the national movement under the Indian National Congress which was formed in 1885, when 72 delegates representing all communities living in India such as the Hindus, the Muslims, the Parsees, and the Indian Christians assembled at Sanskrit College in Bombay to attend the first session of the Congress. The formation of the Indian National Congress had the unofficial blessing of the viceroy, Lord Dufferin.

On the other hand, the Muslims were disturbed by the introduction of the English as an official language by replacing the Persian. The Muslim education system was inspired by Sir Syed Ahmad Khan, who, in the 1870s, founded the Muslim Anglo-Oriental College in Aligarh. The politics in those days was confined to the English-speaking families of India. Minto had sympathies for the Indian liberal views. Initially, the Muslims supported the Indian national movement. In 1907, when the king addressed the parliament and talked about the Indian constitutional reforms, the Hindu–Muslim unity was broken. The All-India Muslim League was founded in 1906 to safeguard the interests of the Muslims, and now the religious differences became political. In 1907, Bengal opposed the British rule. The Hindus protested against the British rule throughout India and boycotted the British goods, and this protest was fermented by the student community. Later the national movement became violent which started in Bombay and then spread in Bengal. In Calcutta, an assassination attempt was made on the lieutenant-governor as a prelude to the attempts on Minto and Hardinge. Madras had become the center of the violent activities. In April and May 1907, there were serious riots in Lahore and Rawalpindi in Punjab.

The Muslims viewed the partition differently from the Hindus. The Muslims opposed the violent agitation and the boycott of British goods. In 1907, the Muslim peasants in the Mymensingh district rose against their Hindu landlords and creditors. In order to suppress the violence and unrest, the Indian Council Act of 1909 was passed, which was known as Minto-Morley reforms, which was an expansion of the 1861 legislation. According to this act, the official majority in the provincial legislative councils was extinguished and increased the additional members, selected from big landowners, traders, and special Muslim members, of the central legislative council through nonofficial election from the provincial councils. These members had just an advisory role of giving their views only. The governor-general council was controlled by the official majority. This act was not implemented, but it did recognize the representation of the different communities which was resisted by the Hindus during the remaining period of the British rule in India. The secretary of state reluctantly accepted the All-India Muslim League's demand of a Separate Muslim Electorate. Lord Minto left India in November 1910. Minto did his best in uniting the country by giving a gift of the self-government. Lord Minto was succeeded by Lord Hardinge.

In December 1911, during the reign of Lord Hardinge, King George-V and Queen Mary visited India and held their Coronation Darbar at Delhi which was attended by the ruling princes. At the Darbar, in addition to declaring the Indian Army eligible for the Victoria Cross, two important decisions were announced. The first decision was the building of a new capital in Delhi, and the second announcement was to reunite the two Bengals. The Muslims bluntly expressed their opinion of "No bombs, no boons"[56] which spread throughout the country, writes Dunbar.

India contributed to the British in the First World War that began in 1914, and their rewards were not forthcoming. The total number of Indian soldiers who fought for the British overseas was 1,215,318, and 101,439 sacrificed their lives for the British who remained unsung heroes in the British history. Not only that, £146.2 million were contributed by India in cash and kind,[57] the current value of which Shashi Tharoor estimates at more than £50 billion. The Indian soldiers fought for the British to make the world safe for democracy and that democracy was still alien to the Indians. When Muslim Turkey joined Germany, the Muslims of India were caught between the loyalty and the religious allegiance. The Muslims' confidence in the British government had just been shaken by the reunion of Bengal which provided some relief to the Hindus under the Council Act of 1909.

In 1916, the Congress demanded the British to consider self-governing India and announce reforms after the war. For the national cause, the Congress made a coalition with the Muslim League, but this alliance did not go long due to the spread of the religious riots between the Muslims and the Hindus. The British had to handle the war on the one hand and the Hindus' rebellion on the other. During the war, the British agreed to the demand of self-rule in India. Another reason that incensed the Indians was the harsh terms that the victors had imposed on Turkey. Many Muslims from the Punjab who had participated in the British war felt guilty and hurt because of the damage done to Islam. The Allied leaders decided that no non-Turkish area should stay with Turkey. This meant the taking away of the holy city of Mecca from the Turkish. The Muslims from India feared that the holy city of Mecca, after taking it away from the control of Turkey, might be placed in the hands of the infidels. Another reason for unrest in India was the crop failure in 1919 due to no rain in 1918, and this led to famine in the country which caused the influenza epidemic and killed five million people in 1919. After the war, the perfidious British volte-faced and kept the power in their hands through the Montagu-Chelmsford Reforms Act of 1919.

In August 1917, the new secretary of state, Edwin Montagu, announced in the parliament the government's policy on the future of British India, including "the increasing association of Indians in every branch of the administration and the gradual development of self-governing institutions with a view to the progressive realization of responsible government in British India as an integral part of the British Empire".[58] In a country where only 10% of the population could read or write at that time, the goal of a responsible government was a great thing. In this case there would be no democracy but the self-government led by an oligarchy of the Indian middle class until the increase in the education evolved the awareness in the masses.

According to the Montagu-Chelmsford Reforms Act of 1919, in the central legislature, there was an electoral majority over the official members. There was no change in the executive council of the governor-general. The one-man government in the provinces was abolished, the governor was given a small executive council appointed by the Crown, half being Indians; and he selected the ministers responsible to the provincial legislative council which dealt with the subjects transferred to it such as education, health, and local government. The Act also classified the departments of the central and provincial governments. Under this Act, the governor-general, as an overriding safeguard, could veto measures or certify and pass bills in spite of an adverse vote. The governor-general could certify measures and expenditure, withhold consent to central and provincial bills, and, in case of emergency, could rule through ordinances for not more than six months. The governor-general was answerable to the British Parliament through the secretary of state.

The Act of 1919 was the first attempt to get the Indians involved in the administration of the British India, and it laid a foundation for further reforms through the legislation based on the wisdom of the Indians. But the Indians wanted to close the door of the safeguarding restrictions and wanted to open the door of freedom. Both the Muslims and Hindus saw a chink of opportunity in this Act to regain power over the other, and this resulted in communal chaos. The political tension rose and the left-wing got control of the Congress by eliminating the moderate liberals and abandoned the policy of "wait and see" and took direct revolutionary actions. To control the extremists' revolutionary actions, the Government introduced the Anarchical and Revolutionary Crimes Act in 1919 which further aggravated the situation as the new Hindu leader Mohandas Karamchand Gandhi of the Vaisya family of Kathiawar said that this act was "unwarranted and such that no self-respecting people could submit to them".[59]

Gandhi led his nonviolent resistance which was opposed by left-wing extremists. In March and April 1919, riots erupted in Western India where industrialization had taken place and businessmen were making huge profits at the cost of miserable conditions of the labor. The disturbances did occur in the agricultural Punjab, where a mass gathering was held at Amritsar in 1919 and defied General Dyer's orders and in the struggle lost 379 people and 1,200 were wounded. Order was restored, but it shocked the British and in fact it was a rude awakening for them. Now the whole country was in the grip of a state of horror and racial disdain.

Gandhi's principle of nationalism was self-governing within the British Empire, which was in line with the official declaration of Lord Irwin and, afterward, Lord Halifax in 1929. In 1920, Gandhi reached out to the Muslims and formed an alliance with the Khilafat party led by Maulana Mohammad Ali. But within one year this alliance broke due to communal riots and Gandhi's arrest and imprisonment for civil disobedience. The Khilafat party gained support when it organized agitation against the unfair terms imposed on Turkey after the First World War. When Mustafa Kamal Ataturk abolished the Kalifate in 1924, the Khilafat party in India disappeared altogether. When Gandhi realized that his principle of nonviolent passive resistance was not understood by the people, he suspended the civil disobedience movement and confined the Congress to the issues of village industries, suspension of drug traffic, and untouchability. The left-wing extremists did not give any weight to these activities. But Gandhi continuously pursued his mission of nonviolent resistance.

After the Montagu-Chelmsford Act, the Indians were allowed to be part of the administration and granted commission in the army. At the same time the unrest spread in the country. While Gandhi was in prison, his opponent C.R. Das criticized the act and tried to destroy it and they succeeded in forcing the governors of the two provinces to return to a one-man government. Das demanded the dominion status and not complete independence. Das asked for a Round Table Conference to discuss it. Jawaharlal Nehru exhorted the student movement to discuss the social and economic problems of the country. There was chaos in the country. Both the British government and the local politicians were trying to sort out the problems.

In 1927, a statutory commission under Sir John Simon was appointed to report on the working of the 1919 Act and suggest recommendations for future reforms. No Indian was included in the Commission, and they boycotted the commission. Simon commission's findings were later included in the Act of 1935. In 1928, the All-Parties Conference of Indian nationalists appointed a committee under Motilal Nehru with his son Jawaharlal Nehru as secretary. The committee recommended provincial autonomy; joint electorates; and federation with a Dominion status. Due to the split in the conference, the breach between the Muslims and Hindus widened.

Early in 1929, an All-India Muslim Conference was held under Agha Sir Sultan Muhammad Shah, known as Agha Khan. It included the representatives of all Muslim parties of the left and the right. The conference unanimously recommended: complete autonomy in a federal system in the ultimate constitution; separate electorates; in the provinces where the Muslims are in minority, they should have due representation; and the Muslims should have a proper share in the central and provincial cabinets.

By the end of 1929, Viceroy Lord Irwin announced that the Indian political leaders would be consulted to evolve a consensus on future constitutional reforms. However, Lord Irwin denied Gandhi's demand for a Dominion status as it was premature according to the step-by-step movement toward the constitutional reforms. Now the Congress launched an attack on the British government and Gandhi started his campaign in April 1930. Boycott of the British goods, bomb attacks, and mob attack on the police became the strength of the civil disobedience movement. This revolt was from the Hindus only. Maulana Muhammad Ali, who was the president of All-India Muslim Conference in 1930, announced the consensus decision of the Muslims that "We refuse to join Gandhi, because his movement is not a movement for the complete independence of India but for making seventy million Indian Muslims dependents of the Hindu Mahasabha".[60]

In the North-West Frontier Province, the political movement of the Red Shirts was led by Abdul Ghaffar Khan of Utmanzai, a friend of Gandhi. Abdul Ghaffar Khan had an alliance with the Congress party instead of All-India

Muslim League. His idea of independence from the British government was liked by the Congress and they supported it. The movement of Abdul Ghaffar Khan was well organized in that it had threatened to spread it across the tribal borders. Abdul Ghaffar Khan was arrested, and the Red Shirts movement was banned. Under the reforms of 1935, the North-West Frontier Province was given the status of a governor's province.

With the help of the moderate Indians' opinion, Lord Irwin crushed the civil obedience movement and warned the Indian politicians of the danger of advocating defiance of the law and order. In November 1930, a Round Table Conference was held in London which was attended by the three parties of the British Parliament, and the Indian states delegates included the maharaja of Bikaner, Sir Akbar Hyderi from Hyderabad, and Sir Tej Bahadur Sapru from British India, and no member of the Congress was invited. The delegates agreed that the future central and provincial governments of British India should be the parliamentary system of Great Britain.

In February 1931, Gandhi and the Congress Working Committee members were released from the prison. In March 1931, an agreement was reached between Gandhi and the viceroy. According to this agreement, all the prisoners of the movement were released, the emergency ordinances were withdrawn, and the civil disobedience movement was abandoned. Gandhi attended the second session and claimed that he represented every individual of any creed in India and demanded that the responsible central and provincial governments should be established immediately. During the course of the conference, Hindu–Muslim riots erupted in India. British prime minister Ramsay MacDonald warned the Indian politicians to sort out the communal conflicts. If this was not done then the British would be compelled to bring its own scheme for the minority representation. This would be done in the Communal Award of August 1932. Gandhi was frustrated and returned to India and did not attend the third session of the Conference.

The select committee of the British Parliament was formed which invited the delegates from British India, Burma, and the Indian states, and no member of the Congress was included because they had renewed their disobedience movement back home in India which again led to the arrests and the re-imposition of the already withdrawn ordinances. Based on the recommendations of the select committee, the Government of India Bill became law in 1935. The bill was designed to ensure the political unity of the subcontinent with strong central and provincial governments in which British India and the states would combine. The provinces became autonomous, and the rights of the princes over their own territories were preserved. Burma and Aden were separated from India. Aden became a Crown Colony.

The Indians wanted that the status of Dominion should be granted immediately. According to the Statute of Westminster, the Dominion was defined, in 1931, as the right of self-governing colonies to an equal measure of autonomy in external affairs while united in a common allegiance to the Crown, with the right to leave the Commonwealth. The Parliament was supreme over British India. The viceroy of India, as the governor-general, was to preserve the constitution and in case of any danger of a breakdown in the constitution, he was to use ordinance in an emergency situation. The provincial governors were empowered through safeguards to maintain law and order. Like Tej Bahadur Sapru, both the Muslims and the minority parties were of the view that these "safeguards were intended in the interests of the responsible government that we are establishing at the center, and not to strengthen the hands of the British control over us".[61] The relations of the federal government with the British were bound by the treaty and other engagements. The governor-general acted as the federal legislature who represented the Crown, a council of state and a federal assembly, and the elected members from the states. The governor was empowered to choose his cabinet, but in certain circumstances he could refuse to accept their advice.

The provincial administration was transferred to the provinces. The council of nonofficial ministers was appointed by the governor, who himself was nominated by the Crown. The nonofficial ministers were now responsible to the elected provincial legislature. The governor was no longer responsible for the finance of the provinces, and no provincial subjects were reserved with the governor-general. Thus, the dyarchy in the provinces was gone. However, the governor was still vested with the power of issuing ordinances in an emergency. In case of conflict between the central and the provincial law, the central law would prevail. The right to vote was based on property qualifications, and there were separate electorates for the Muslims, the Sikhs, Indian Christians, and Anglo-Indians, and special seats for women, landlords, industry, the universities, and labor.

In July 1936, the implementation of the British India Act of 1935 was started in the provinces. After one year as a result of the election, the provincial governments became autonomous. Gandhi now started the election campaign with the slogan of "vote for Gandhi and the yellow box".[62] In July 1937, the Congress got seven ministries. In Punjab, Sir Sikandar Hayat Khan of the Unionist party won a simple majority and became the chief minister of Punjab by a Unionist government of the Muslims, the Hindus, and the Sikhs. The provinces which had the Congress government did not bother about federation and tried for a constituent assembly under its own auspices and independence, and the Muslims felt ignored and the Hindus' attitude toward the Muslims led to the creation of Pakistan.

The main feature of the British India Act of 1935 was the establishment of a federal government in the subcontinent. Both the Muslim League and the Congress endorsed the principle of the federation. The Congress Working Committee opposed the British control of finance, defense, and foreign affairs and objected to the nominated representatives of the states. The Muslim League strongly objected to the claims of the Congress of representing all Nationalists' opinion. The Muslim League saw the complete Hindu control of the federation at the center. The princely states were to sign an irrevocable instrument of accession to meet the requirement of the federation, but none of them had signed it and remained under the governor-general. Another Hindu fanatical party, known as Mahasabha Party, did not ally with the Congress party, and it opposed the movement of civil disobedience and was hostile to the partition of India between the Hindus and the Muslims. It wanted freedom from the British as Dominion state under the Hindu rule. The All-India Muslim League, under the dynamic and masterful leadership of Muhammad Ali Jinnah, was extremely capable of asserting its influence on the future of the Indian subcontinent. Another party was the Communist Party which had some backing in Kanpur and Bombay but could not produce much of the influence in the politics of the subcontinent.

The actual future of the subcontinent lay between the Congress and the Muslim League. The uncompromising attitude of the Congress since 1936 antagonized the Muslim League, which, after the start of the Second World War, irrevocably pursued the policy of the partition of India and the establishment of Pakistan. In 1933, Chaudry Rahmat Ali, a graduate of Cambridge, originated the word Pakistan, which was announced as the objective of the Muslim League in 1940 to become a reality in 1947. The Muslim League took a firm position that the Muslims were not a minority to be outvoted and controlled by the Hindu majority, but a separate nation; and that their homelands they would govern included those areas in the northwest and the northeast of India in which the Muslims had the majority. According to the population census of 1941: the North-western block had (Punjab, Sind, Baluchistan, North-West Frontier Province): Muslims, 22,653,294; Hindus, 9,005,242; Sikhs, 3,858,269; in a total of 36,493,525. The North-Eastern block (Bengal, Assam) had: Muslims, 36,447,913; Hindus, 29,272,247; Sikhs, 19,745; in a total of 70,511,258.[63] Independent Pakistan would first work as a separate and independent nation in the British Commonwealth of Nations.

There was one towering personality who could carve out a Muslim state out of the Indian subcontinent, and he was Mohammad Ali Jinnah. Jinnah was the most distinguished advocate at the Bombay Bar. Jinnah entered the politics of all Indian nationalism and cooperated with the Congress until he realized that the Congress movement had resulted in a racial prejudice against the Muslim cause. He then stopped cooperating with the Congress. That was a tipping point in his life, and he started uniting the divided Muslims under the umbrella of the Muslim League at the Conference held in 1929. At the conference he expressed his firm resolve for the creation of Pakistan. In 1934, Jinnah was elected president of the Muslim League. He transformed the Muslim League into a big deciding force in the Indian subcontinent and millions of Muslims called him Quaid-i-Azam, great leader. Under his resolute leadership, Pakistan, the land of pure and promise, came into being.

One of the commonalities among the Congress and the Muslim League was the opposition to thrusting India into the Second World War without seeking the opinion of the nationalists. The Muslim League officially disassociated from the British government and refused to accept the offer of any seat by its members on the executive council of the viceroy. Jinnah saw the declaration of civil disobedience movement as a rebellion against the British, and this was also intended in the declaration to force a decision against Pakistan. Jinnah made it clear that any favor to India would be resisted by the Muslim League with full force available at its disposal.

The Congress also resigned in protest from the seven provincial ministries. Congress also refused to join the council of the viceroy when the offer was made in 1940. The Congress saw a chink of opportunity in British's trouble and danger. In spite of the war, Gandhi continued his policy of nonviolent noncooperation. The Ramgarh Session of the Congress held during March 19–20, 1940, passed a resolution calling for *purna swaraj*, the Independence of India, and framing of a constitution by an assembly based on adult suffrage, writes Jaswant Singh.[64]. At the same time, on March 23, 1940, the Muslim League presented a Resolution at Lahore, called Lahore Resolution. This was the first step to the division of India.

On December 7, 1941, Japan attacked Pearl Harbor and the USS *Arizona* was sunk. Now the United States joined the Allies in the war. Consequently, the Second World War came to Asia as the Japanese now focused on India. The Japanese were moving fast. On February 15, 1942, the British commander-in-chief in Singapore, General Percival, surrendered to Japanese general Yamashita. Then Rangoon, Burma (now Myanmar), became vulnerable, and after this India was the next. After the fall of Rangoon, on March 11, 1942, Mr. Winston Churchill announced in the parliament that his coalition government had decided to send Lord Stafford Cripps to India to sort out the political problems to the satisfaction of all parties concerned. The British India Act of 1935 met its failure.

Sir Stafford Cripps arrived in New Delhi on March 23, 1942. Gandhi and Sardar Vallabhbhai Patel suggested that Abul Kalam Azad should meet Cripps on behalf of the Congress. Gandhi believed that as the British were losing the war, Japan was bound to invade India, then why to accept the proposals of Cripps. Gandhi considered Cripps' proposals as "a post-dated cheque on a collapsing bank".[65] Abul Kalam Azad met Cripps several times, and on March 29, 1942, the Congress Working Committee rejected Cripps' proposals. To continue further discussion, Cripps arranged a meeting between the then commander-in-chief, Wavell, Azad, and Nehru. The working committee of the Muslim League saw some drawbacks in it and then rejected the Cripps Plan. According to the plan, there was to be a new Indian Union constituting a Dominion of the British Commonwealth with allegiance to the Crown. An elected body of All India was to assemble and frame a new constitution. It was expected that all the parties would now cooperate in the world war.

Gandhi was released from jail on May 6, 1944. On July 17, 1944, he wrote a letter in the Gujarati language to Jinnah expressing his desire to meet him and also hoped that Jinnah would not disappoint him. Jinnah wrote back to Gandhi in English, explaining that this was the language for clear expression of his views. Jinnah informed Gandhi that he was going to Kashmir and he could visit him at his residence in Bombay after his return from Kashmir in the middle of August 1944. Gandhi wrote another letter to Jinnah, and it was intercepted by the British India Government, but its contents were delivered to Jinnah. Jinnah responded that Gandhi first must agree to the Muslim League's demand for Pakistan and then write to him. Talks between Jinnah and Gandhi started on September 9, 1944, at Jinnah's residence at 10, Mount Pleasant Road, Bombay. The talks continued for 18 days. Both the men met, shook hands, and embraced each other. But that was all. There was no agreement, but both agreed to continue the talks. When Gandhi was asked what he had brought from Jinnah, he responded, "only flowers". Gandhi–Jinnah talks ended without any result. Wavell, the British commander-in-chief, commented on this meeting, "The two great mountains have met and not even a ridiculous mouse has emerged. Jinnah had to keep on telling Gandhi he was talking nonsense which was true and he did so rudely".[66]

Gandhi demanded immediate independence and the British rule to be replaced by a national government where all the parties will unite. Jinnah immediately reacted to the idea of the national government and said that he would accept no compromise and according to him the only solution was the independence of India into independent zones. The British proposals were insufficient to protect the rights of the minorities under the Hindu rule. Cripps' mission failed. After the departure of Cripps, Gandhi started a mass movement on a large scale. Japan could not attack India due to the start of the monsoon.

In 1945, the Allied forces got victory. When the war was over, Churchill restarted the negotiations for the settlement of the political issues of the Indian subcontinent. British aim was to withdraw all control from British India. Now the British wanted to form an executive council of the members drawn from all the parties to develop a consensus for establishing a constitution building body, which was rejected by the Muslim League and the conference failed.

In the general elections of 1945, the Attlee Socialist government came into power. In March 1946, negotiations with the Indian parties restarted through a cabinet mission again led by Cripps. The aim was the establishment of a self-government through transfer of control of the machinery of the state to the Indian authority. The situation again was not plausible. The Congress demanded one constituent assembly for a single unit of the subcontinent; the Muslim League stood for their own independent, autonomous, and self-governing state of 90,000,000 Muslims where they are predominated; and 5,000,000 Sikhs demanded special treatment like the Muslims. The Mission advanced a proposal of constituent assembly with three separate groups controlling their affairs with the exception of the All-India Union subjects of defense, foreign affairs, and communications. To begin with, a coalition government would have to be formed.

The Cabinet Mission failed. In July 1946, Cripps reported in the House of Commons that the only hope of peaceful transfer of sovereignty was to offer the Indians complete and unqualified independence irrespective of being in or out of the British Commonwealth. The Mission had observed one change in India, and that was, unlike in the past, this time they had trust in the sincerity of the British Government and there was willingness to cooperate to solve the problem. Before the end of July, the Muslim League had withdrawn from the proposal as in it there was dangerous ambiguity. The constituent assembly that met in December was not representative.

On February 20, 1947, the prime minister was determined to hand over the power to the Indians under the constitution approved by all the parties. But unfortunately, there did not exist any Indian constitution as yet and there was no hope that it will ever emerge. This state of affairs, if procrastinated, would lead to a dangerous situation. Now the Majesty's government made it clear that the necessary steps would be taken to hand over the sovereignty to the responsible Indians by a date not later than June 1948. The British government decided to send Lord Mountbatten to finalize the final phase of transfer of power to the responsible Indians.

Soon after his arrival, Viceroy Lord Mountbatten first met Gandhi on April 1, 1947, to acquaint himself with the situation of the subcontinent. Gandhi played a perfidious game in which he suggested to the viceroy that he fully supports the appointment of Mohammad Ali Jinnah as the prime minister of the Central Interim Government of a United India that would work under the Viceroy.[67] Then the Congress with its majority in the house would solve the rest of the problems. Mountbatten was smart enough to understand a wily Gandhi. Next day Mountbatten met Pandit Nehru and Maulana Azad to discuss the matters. Next, Mountbatten was to meet the person who held the key to the solution of the subcontinent, and he was Mohammad Ali Jinnah. Jinnah respected Mountbatten but did not agree with him on any terms of understanding. Jinnah informed that he was the sole spokesman for the Muslims and whatever he decided it would be implemented. There was no Muslim League without Mohammad Ali Jinnah. But that was not the case with Congress.

On June 3, the British prime minister announced the intention of the government of bringing a bill to transfer the power of a Dominion status to "one or two successor authorities" and this transfer would take place by the middle of August 1947. The announcement was received in India with mixed feelings. The Muslims expressed their opinion in their majority areas that the agreement had been reached for the partition of the subcontinent. On July 4, 1947, Liaquat Ali Khan wrote a letter to Lord Mountbatten in which he conveyed that Jinnah had made up his mind and requested Mountbatten to recommend his name to the king for the appointment of the governor-general of Pakistan. It was also hoped that Mountbatten would remain as governor-general of India. Jinnah's announcement for the position of governor-general of Pakistan had put the viceroy in an awkward position. In spite of the fact that Mountbatten and his private secretary Sir Eric Mieville[68] had asked Liaquat Ali Khan in early June to request Jinnah to nominate the governor-general of Pakistan as soon as possible, Jinnah had never agreed to have a common governor-general. On the other hand, Mountbatten wanted to be simultaneously the constitutional governor-general of two countries. Mountbatten had also asked Jinnah to restrain the Muslim League press from reporting the fact that the Indians would be having a European governor-general and Pakistan was to have its own national governor-general. Jinnah promised to do that. But *Dawn* had done which it should have not done. Jinnah told Mountbatten that *Dawn* had not broken the undertaking that I took until the Congress press had attacked Jinnah by mentioning that in the first place Jinnah had agreed to a common governor-general and then reneged on his promise.

On July 24, 1947, Jinnah, in a meeting with Lord Ismay, had cleared the position of the Muslim League press, and before leaving the meeting, Jinnah put his hand on the shoulder of Lord Ismay and said, "I beg you to assure the viceroy that I am his friend and yours for now and always. I beg that he should judge me by deeds and not by words".[69] The Indian Independence Bill passed its third reading in the House of Commons on July 16. British India was to be divided into two independent Dominions of India and Pakistan, each under a governor-general to take effect on August 15, 1947, as advised by the viceroy. The Act indicated their respective territories, subject to a referendum in North-West Frontier Province (NWFP) and Sylhet in Assam, and the referendum results in both of these places were in favor of Pakistan. A commission was set up to determine the boundaries in the Punjab and Bengal-Assam. The princes were retained with the British government and were reassured that the pledges in their treaties with the crown would remain inviolate and inviolable. However, the princes had the option of their accession to either of the two Dominions.

Lord Mountbatten, as a representative of the Crown, had set up a state department, whereby the future Dominions could approach and negotiate with the rulers of the states for their accession. Pakistan was to talk to the rulers of the states of Hyderabad and Jammu and Kashmir, then ruled by a Hindu ruler of Jammu and 80% of the population was Muslim. Neither Hyderabad nor Jammu and Kashmir made accession within the stipulated period. Before the transfer of power took place, in mid-July, Lord Mountbatten had set up a caretaker government in which the portfolios were distributed to the Congress and the Muslim League. Nehru of the Congress was given the charge of External Affairs and Commonwealth Relations, and from Pakistan, Liaquat Ali Khan got the portfolio of Finance. Later both Nehru and Liaquat Ali Khan became the prime minister of India and Pakistan respectively.

Now another important task before Lord Mountbatten was the issue of the settlement of the boundaries between India and Pakistan. Bengal, which at different times included Bihar, Orissa Assam, and Agra, was partitioned. Punjab was divided into two parts. In Punjab interim governments were formed. On June 23, the Legislative Assembly met in two parts of Punjab; West Punjab decided for Pakistan and East Punjab decided for India. A few days later, the composition of the two boundary commissions was announced with the task of settlement of the boundaries before August 15. The terms of reference for the commission of Punjab were: "To demarcate the boundaries of the two parts of Punjab on the basis of ascertaining the majority areas of Muslims and non-Muslims. In so doing they will also take into account other factors".[70]

Sir Cyril John Radcliffe was appointed the chairman over the two commissions. Radcliffe was recommended to Lord Mountbatten by Lord Listowel,[71] who considered him a man of integrity, legal reputation, and wide experience. But India was a totally alien land for Radcliffe, who had neither visited India before, nor had knowledge of India's geography of land, culture, or languages. On the suggestion of Jinnah, Radcliffe was asked to be the chairman of both commissions: one for the East of India and the other for the West. Lord Mountbatten immediately accepted Jinnah's idea that one chairman for both commissions could make adjustments of gains and losses between the two borders. Nehru had opposed one chairman for two commissions and recommended that both the commissions should have a separate chairman and four other members, two nominated by the Muslim League and two nominated by the Congress, who must be judicial experts and then each commission should select their own chairman. In fact, Jinnah had asked that the commission be composed of three impartial non-Indians appointed on the recommendations of the United Nations, but the secretary of state, Lord Listowel, did not approve this suggestion. The suggestion of the United Nations was also opposed by Nehru. Though, initially, Mountbatten agreed with Jinnah but later volte-faced his decision on the objections of Nehru. There was a common belief in India that Radcliffe would award whatever is dictated to him by Lord Mountbatten. According to Radcliffe's private secretary, Christopher Beaumont, Mountbatten had persuaded Radcliffe to change the Punjab borderline by awarding the Tehsil of Ferozepur to India. This clearly leads to the question of the Commission's impartiality.[72] The report was considered the chairman's report to the viceroy and the members of the commission were nowhere in the report. One of the members, Justice Munir Ahmad, objected to the report, and later this report was considered as the Commission's report through an amendment in the India Independence Bill. The terms of reference, of the Boundary Commission, were set out by Mountbatten. Nehru also suggested that the Boundary commission be tasked to demarcate the boundaries of the two parts of Bengal after ascertaining the contiguous majority areas of the Muslims and the non-Muslims. Mountbatten again accepted this proposal. In Bengal the important question was about Calcutta with a population of 2,500,000 and its inclusion in one or the other Dominion. Finally, it was allotted to the Dominion of India.

On August 7, 1947, Mohammad Ali Jinnah flew from Delhi to Karachi accompanied by Ahsan, the Naval ADC, and Miss Jinnah in Mountbatten's white Dakota. Before leaving the house, Jinnah gave Hector Bolitho, a cane basket full of documents to be taken to the aircraft. Before takeoff, Jinnah went out to be photographed and did not speak a word. When the aircraft taxied, Mohammad Ali Jinnah remarked, "That is the end of that", meaning the end of the struggle on Indian soil. Jinnah was dressed in a white sherwani and his Jinnah cap. He had a big bundle of the newspapers which he started reading immediately on boarding the plane and continued throughout the duration of flight time of four hours and just spoke once, and said, "Would you like to read these?" The plane arrived Karachi in the evening, and while flying over Mauripur, Jinnah looked down and saw thousands of people waiting to receive him. He was the first one to come out of the plane followed by Miss Jinnah. All the big Muslim personalities were waiting for him; he shook hands with some of them and got into the car. Thousands of people cheered, "Pakistan Zindabad", "Quaid-i-Azam Zindabad". He entered the Government House for the first time. After three days, he changed his apartment from the left to the right of the Government house. Now he was never to return to India. On August 8, Patel said in the Constituent Assembly in Delhi that the "Muslims had their historical and religious places here, what they can do in Pakistan? It will not be long before they return". Later, Nehru also said, "Let us see how long they remain separate". Whatever the words of Patel and Nehru were, Pakistan was created to live, not to return.

Jinnah arrived in Karachi, the new capital of a new nation, Pakistan. The situation in Pakistan's capital is well explained by Major General Syed Shahid Hamid, military secretary to the governor-general. He wrote:

> Karachi is in a festive mood but there is inadequate accommodation for the hundreds of correspondents and visitors who had gathered to see the state of Pakistan being born. Colonel Majid Malik, then Director of Public Relations in General Head Quarters, India, is now the Principal Information Officer to the Government of Pakistan; he is being greatly harassed. All the correspondents expect the impossible. There is no Government of Pakistan but is being created overnight. There are no government offices, no Ministries, no furniture or stationery. Typewriters are a luxury. It is utter chaos. The Viceroy expected that by August 13, Karachi would emerge as a fully-fledged working state capital and would be in a position to receive him, as the King's representative.

The first function was the banquet at the governor-general's house where some 50 guests were invited. Quaid-i-Azam made a short speech and for the first time proposed a toast to His Majesty the King. Mountbatten, after expressing the wishes of the king, engaged in a long speech. Quaid-i-Azam called his ADC and told him to tell Mountbatten to go home and that he has had enough of him. The poor ADC did not know what to do. He came to General Shahid Hamid, who told him go and tell Mountbatten exactly what the Quaid had said. To give him a moral support General Shahid Hamid accompanied him. ADC and Shahid Hamid went to Mountbatten and relayed the message verbatim. He was taken aback and said, "Of course I should have realized how late it was and that Mr. Jinnah was getting tired. He walked up to Quaid-i-Azam, apologized and left. What a day it had been".

Radcliffe's awards were ready on August 12, 1947, well before handing over the power to Pakistan on August 14, 1947. But Mountbatten advised Radcliffe to hold it until August 13, 1947. Lord Mountbatten visited Karachi on August 14 to inaugurate the Dominion of Pakistan. Pakistan came into being on August 14, 1947, and India on August 15, 1947. Both of these two new independent countries did not know where their borders are stretched to and where was the line between the Muslims and the Hindus. Mountbatten's commander-in-chief, Auchinleck,[73] advised him that the delay in Award which was already available would result in chaos and harmful consequences. Mountbatten did not bother again. Radcliffe refused to delay the Award and submitted it on August 12, 1947, as he wanted to escape from India. Mountbatten decided not to release it until August 16, 1947, when he discussed it with the Pakistani and Indian leaders. However, Mountbatten had shared it with Nehru much earlier and did not let Jinnah know about it. The Award was published in the Gazette on August 17, 1947. After the partition of India, Nehru remarked that "the partition was temporary and Pakistan was bound to come back to us".[74] Gandhi had agreed on the partition during his meeting with Jinnah in 1944, and now on March 3, 1947, Gandhi volte-faced, "If the Congress wishes to accept partition, it will be over my dead body". According to Abul Kalam Azad, after meeting Mountbatten, Gandhi volte-faced.

In Punjab the situation was different in that the politicians raised the question about what is meant by "other factors". The Sikhs demanded a new homeland for them in the name of Sikhistan to restore the tradition of Khalsa. Punjab had one of the best canal systems of irrigation which brought great desert areas under irrigation that led to the production of wheat, cotton, and other crops. Now the big canal system had to be disrupted and the commission had to decide the division of the irrigation system, electric power transmission, and rail and road communications. The Radcliffe award was announced on August 17, 1947, two days after the transfer of the power to the two Dominions. Now the Sikhs struck and killed hundreds of thousands of men, women, and children. The Muslim refugees fled to West Punjab and Sikhs and Hindus to East Punjab. After June 30, the Indian Army had become disorganized due to the redistribution between the two Dominions by August 15, 1947, and after that date the British troops could not be used in aid of the civil power.

By July 21, the Union Constitution Committee of the Congress presented to the Constituent Assembly the first draft of the Constitution for the future federation which would be a sovereign independent republic under a President with two houses of Parliament, a Council of State, and a House of the People elected by adult suffrage. For Pakistan, Lord Mountbatten remained the governor-general, until the Independence Day of August 14, 1947. Lord Mountain said that he had picked up the date of partition as August 15 because it was the second anniversary of Japan's surrender. In Pakistan every department of the new government had to be established, and Karachi became its capital with millions of refugees. Dacca became the capital of East Pakistan. The distance from Karachi to Dacca was 1,400 miles and airline, radio communication was impossible and Dacca remained isolated. The inflexible will, dauntless spirit, and dynamic energy of a 70-year-old leader, Mohammad Ali Jinnah, could have turned the Dominion into a prosperous Pakistan.

At the time of partition, India had her economic assets of coalfields, iron and steel centers, and cotton and jute mills. Pakistan was self-sufficient in foodstuff and her products of jute and cotton, but it was industrially undeveloped and did not have coal and textile factories. Just like Punjab, tragic communal violence erupted in Kashmir in September 1947 which led to a civil war between the two Dominions. The British Empire remained in India from 1613–14, when it first established a trading post at Surat and the first factory at Masulipatnam, until August 15, 1947, when the Indian subcontinent was divided into two independent nations. When the British left the Indian subcontinent in August 1947, India, once the richest region of the world, was driven to a third-world underdeveloped country with 90% of its population living below the poverty line. Bengal, which was the richest place in the region at the time of the arrival of the British, became the victim of British's merciless pillage and was left behind as a waste land. Imperialism won and the humanity lost. No remorse, no compensation! (see Figure 7.1).

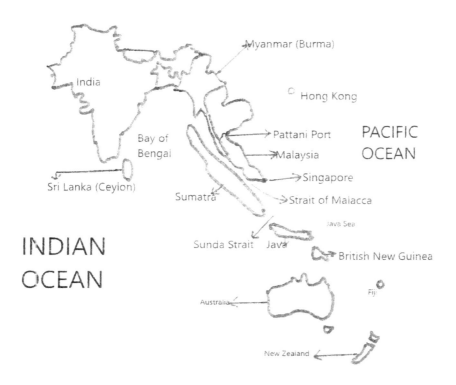

FIGURE 7.1 British colonies in Asia and Australasia

Notes

1. Dalrymple, "The Anarchy, The Relentless Rise of the East India Company", pp. 3–4.
2. Ibid., p. 6.
3. Wright, p. 37.
4. Dalrymple, p. 12.
5. Dunbar, p. 61.
6. Wright, p. 44.
7. Ibid., pp.47–48.
8. Ibid., p. 54.
9. Dalrymple, p. 14.
10. Wright, p. 78.
11. Ibid., p. 82.
12. Ibid., p. 83.
13. Dalrymple, p. 20.
14. Dunbar, p. 65.
15. Dalrymple, p. 15.
16. Wright, p. 263.
17. Dunbar, p. 66.
18. Dalrymple, p. 36.
19. Dunbar, p. 49.
20. Dalrymple, p. 39.
21. Dunbar, p. 49.
22. Dalrymple, p. 42.
23. Ibid., p. 44.
24. Dunbar, p. 73.
25. Dalrymple, p. xvii.
26. Harari, "Sapiens, A Brief History of Humankind", p. 337.
27. Dalrymple, p. 228.
28. Ibid., p. 229.
29. Ibid., p. 234.
30. Ibid., p. 248.
31. Ibid., p. 307.
32. Ibid, p. 309.
33. Ibid.
34. Ibid., p. 315.
35. Habib, "Confronting Colonialism, Resistance and Modernization under Haider Ali and Tipu Sultan", p. xxxi.
36. Dalrymple, p. 328.
37. Ibid., p. 329.
38. Dunbar, p. 109.
39. Jeddy, "Tipu Sultan, the Making of the Man and the Martyr", p. 183.
40. Dalrymple, p. 324.
41. Jeddy, p. 247.
42. Dalrymple, p. 342.
43. Dunbar, p. 121.
44. Harari, "Sapiens, A Brief History of Humankind", p. 334.
45. Dalrymple, p. 385.
46. Ibid, p. 385.
47. Woodward, p. 312.
48. Dunbar, p. 119.
49. Ibid., p. 120.
50. Ewans, p. 32.
51. Woodward, p. 313.

52 Ibid., p. 317.
53 Ewans, p. 52.
54 Fletcher, p. 127.
55 Dunbar, p. 163.
56 Ibid., p.172.
57 Tharoor, "An Era of Darkness, the British Empire in India", p. 88.
58 Dunbar, p. 173.
59 Ibid., p. 175.
60 Ibid., p. 181.
61 Ibid., p. 184.
62 Ibid., p.186.
63 Ibid., p. 216, footnote number 121.
64 Singh, "Jinnah, India-Partition, Independence", p. 284.
65 Ibid., p. 295.
66 Ibid., pp. 542–543.
67 Jaswant Singh, pp. 434–435.
68 Ibid., p. 462.
69 Ibid., pp. 462–463.
70 Dunbar, p. 207; Report of the Boundary Commission, Legislative Department (Reforms) Notification, New Delhi, August 17, 1947.
71 Singh, p. 439.
72 Ibid., pp. 444–445.
73 Ibid., p. 447.
74 Ibid., p. 458.

Bibliography

Dalrymple, William, *The Anarchy, The Relentless Rise of the East India Company*, Bloomsbury Publishing, 50 Bedford Square, London, UK, 2019.

Dunbar, George Sir, *India and the Passing of Empire*, Ivor Nicholson & Watson Ltd., 26 Manchester Square, London, UK, 1951.

Ewans, Martin, *Afghanistan, A New History*, Curzon Press, Richmond Surrey, UK, 2001.

Fletcher, Arnold, *Afghanistan*, Cornell University Press, Ithaca, New York, USA, 1966.

Habib, Irfan, (ed.), *Resistance and Modernization under Haider Ali and Tipu Sultan*, Tulika Books, 35 A/1 Shahpur Jat, New Delhi, India, 1999.

Harari, Yuval Noah, *Sapiens: A Brief History of Humankind*, Vintage Books, 20 Vauxhall Bridge Road, London, UK, 2011.

Jeddy, B.A., *Tipu Sultan, the Making of the Man and the Martyr.*, Syed and Syed Publishers, 6 Thakurdas Building, M.A. Jinnah Road, Karachi, Pakistan, 1995.

Singh, Jaswant, *Jinnah India-Partition, Independence*, Rupa-Co, New Delhi, India, 2009.

Tharoor, Shashi, *An Era of Darkness-The British Empire in India*, Alpha Book Company, 7/16 Ansari Road, Darya Ganj, New Delhi, India, 2016.

Woodward, William Harrison, *A Short History of the Expansion of the British Empire, 1500–1902*, Second Edition, Cambridge University Press, London, UK, 1902.

Wright, Arnold, *Early English Adventurers in the East*, Sang-e-Meel Publications, Lahore, Pakistan, 2000.

INDEX

Abbasid dynasty 39–41, 43
Abdul Aziz (Muslim governor of Sevilla) 22–23, 25–27, 30–31, 33–36
Abdul Malik bin Qatan al-Fihri (governor general of Cordoba) 38
Abdul Rahman bin Abdullah al-Ghafiqi (governor general of Cordoba) 36
Abdul Rahman bin Mu'awiya bin Hisham, Amir of al-Andalus 39
Abu'l Hassan, Amir of Granada 50
Acadia 123–25, 138
Acheen, Sumatra 150–51
Aden 83, 93, 95–96, 145, 213
Afonso De Albuquerque, Portuguese general 92–98, 100
Afghanistan 185–86, 196, 204–05
Africa 5, 9–10, 12–13, 16, 22, 24, 31, 33–35, 45, 48–50, 51, 66, 68, 70, 77, 80, 83–84, 86, 90, 92, 100–01, 103, 109, 120, 128–29, 142, 144–45, 149
Afriqia 10, 38–39
Agra 101, 152–54, 170, 197–98, 199, 219
Ahmad ibn Majid, Arab navigator, 86
Al-Andalus 11, 30, 35–36, 38, 39–44, 46–49, 51, 65, 83
Alcabala, Castilian sales tax 55, 66
Alcala de Henares (place of Table of Solomon) 21
Alcazar, of Toledo 21, 47, 72
Aleppo 83
Alexandria 6, 28, 48, 83, 185
Algeciras 12–13, 17, 22
Algeria 10, 21, 66
Alhambra 50–51
Almeria 44, 48–49
Almohads 49
Almoravids 48–49
Al-Muqtadir, Amir of Zaragoza 47
Amboina, massacre of 110–11, 113–15, 153
Americas: North America 122, 124, 126–27, 129, 131–33, 136–39, 175; Central America 63; South America 4, 63, 67–68, 89, 103
Amherst, Lord 126, 138, 203
Amsterdam 107–09, 116, 120
Antwerp 69–70, 75, 90, 101, 104
Anwaruddin, Nawab of Arcot 127
Aqsa Mosque, in Jerusalem 32, 42
Aragon 5, 30, 45, 49–51, 55, 59, 65–66, 76, 78–79
Arcot 127, 161–62, 172, 194
Arctic Ocean 106
Arian 6
Arius, Presbyter of Alexandria 6
Arianism 6
Arkansas 125
Armengol-IV, Aragonese Count, of Urgel 47
Asaf-ud-Daula, Nawab of Bengal 174
Auckland, Lord, British governor general of India 204
Aungier, Gerald, British governor of Bombay 154
Australia 140–42
Aztec 64–65

228 Index

Badajoz, province 43, 47–48
Baetica 9, 17, 23
Bahamas 57, 64
baladiyyun (Arab settlers in al-Andalus) 38, 40, 42
Ball, George, English commander 110
Baltic 107
Banda, islands 110–11, 113, 115, 117–19, 150
Bandar Abbas 102
Bangalore 171, 180–81, 188, 190–91
Bantam, Java Island 102, 107, 108–09, 110–12, 117, 151–52
Barbados 78, 146
Barcelona 5, 29–30, 41–42, 45, 59, 71, 77
Barlow, George Sir, 200
Battle of: Alcazarquivir 72; Alarcos 49; First Anglo-Afghan 204; Second Anglo-Afghan at Maiwand 205; Third Anglo-Afghan 205; First Anglo-Burmese 203; Second Anglo-Burmese 205; First Anglo-Dutch 117; First Anglo-Mysore at Pollilur 171–72, 175–76; Second Anglo-Mysore 128; Third Anglo-Mysore 179–80, 183; First Anglo-Nepalese (Gurkha) 202; First Anglo-Powhatans 133–34; Second Anglo-Powhatans 135; First Anglo-Sikh at Sobraon 205; Second Anglo-Sikh at Chilianwala 205; Assaye 197, 199; Sikh-Afghan near Attock 201; at Barbate 13–16, 20; Buxar 164, 169, 171; Ecija 16–17, 20; Delhi 158, 198–99, 206; Guadalete 13, 35, 44; Guinea 84; Jerez de la Frontera 14; Kirkee 183; Lakheri 184; Las Navas de Tolosa 49; Lepanto 71, 74; Merida 23–25, 27; Moussais-la-Bataille 37; Third Panipat 169, 195; Tel el Kebir 145; Ucles 49; Wandiwash 127, 164; Yorktown 135, 175, 182; Zallaqa 48
Bengal 97, 103, 117–18, 126, 153–55, 157, 159, 161–70, 173–75, 177–78, 182, 194, 196, 198, 202–03, 206–07, 208–10, 219–20, 223
Bentinck, Lord William 203
Beja (in Portugal) 23, 25, 82
Belgium 70, 72
Bermuda 134
Berbers 9, 11, 13, 21, 28, 35–39, 44–46, 48, 83
Bijapur 93–94, 155–156, 160
Boabdil, last ruler of Granada 50–51
Bobastro, castle in Malaga 43
Bolivia 67, 70, 75

Bombay 126, 145, 154–55, 160, 167, 169, 170, 177, 179, 187–88, 203, 206, 209, 215, 217
Boston 66, 124
Brazil 68, 70, 72, 77, 89, 97, 101, 103, 116, 130, 149
Bukhara 32
Burgundy, southeast of Paris 36, 38, 65, 68, 82
Burgos 49, 55, 62, 69, 75

Cabot, John, explorer of New England 129
Cadiz, province 13–14, 22, 27, 38, 56, 60, 62–63, 68, 70, 72–73, 74, 90, 100, 131
Calicut 87–90, 92–93, 96
California 72, 130, 145
Calatayud (quarters of the Jew) 35
Calcutta 126, 155, 160, 162–63, 167, 168, 170, 172, 174–75, 177–78, 184–87, 194, 196, 198, 201, 205, 209, 220
Caliph Abdul Malik bin Marwan 9
Caliph al-Waleed bin Abdul Malik 10–11, 21, 27–29, 31–32, 42
Caliph Hisham 36, 39, 45–46
Caliph Sulayman bin Abdul Malik 31–35
Cambodia 115, 119, 151
Canada 122, 124–26, 135, 138–40, 142
Canning, Lord 206–07
Cape of Good Hope 86, 141–42, 160
Carcassonne, in the southwestern France 36, 38
Caribbean (islands) 58–67, 69–80, 120, 132, 133, 135
Carnatic 126–28, 156–57, 159–62, 164, 169, 171–72, 186, 194
Carpentier, Peter De, Dutch General 114, 116
Carteya 12
Castile 30, 45–47, 49–51, 55, 59, 65–66, 68–70, 76–77, 79, 82
Catalonia, region in northeast Spain 9, 46, 76–79
Catherine, Queen of Portugal 97, 154
Cerdanya, Spain 36
Ceuta 10–11, 22, 31, 82–84, 100
Ceylon 91, 94, 97, 114, 118, 142, 143
Chanda Sahib 126–27, 161–62
Charlemagne 41–42
Charles Martel, Duke and Prince of France 37, 38
Chesapeake Bay 132, 135
Child, Sir John, British commander-in-Chief of Indian army 155
Chile 130, 146

China 56–57, 67–68, 70, 72, 88, 96–97, 103, 109, 112, 117–19, 145–46, 151–52, 175, 178, 183, 200
Church of San Acisclo 17, 19
Clive, Robert 127–28, 162–65, 167–68, 174, 187
Cochin, in Kerala state 89–93, 95–97, 112, 116, 118, 178, 179, 194
Coen, Jan Pieterson, of the Dutch governor team 110, 112–15, 119
Columbia 64, 135–36, 139, 140
Compagnie van Verre 107
Congo 3, 85, 103, 144
Constantinople 5, 6, 83
Consulado 55–56
Cordoba 5, 12–13, 16–22, 27, 32, 35–47, 49–50
Cornelis Dedel, Dutch commander 111
Corneliszoon van Neck, Jacob, commander of Dutch company 107, 149
Cornwallis, Lord Charles 175
Cripps, Lord Stafford 216–17
Christopher Columbus 56–63, 80, 88, 130, 135
Colbert, Minister of Louis XIV 122
Colorado 124, 146
Columbia 64, 135–36, 139–40
Compagnie des Indes Orientales 122, 160
Comte de Lally, French commander in India 127
Connecticut 133
Coote, Sir Eyre, English commander in India 127, 164, 172–73
Cordillera (gold mine) 63
Cruzada 66, 75
Cuba 57–59, 61, 64, 67, 70, 77, 80, 128, 129
Cuenca 41, 49, 69
Curzon, Lord 208
Cyprus 72

D. Francisco de Almeida 91
Dakota 124, 220
Dale, Sir Thomas, English commander 112, 134
Dalhousie, Lord 205–06
Damascus 10–11, 15–16, 21, 28–36, 38–39, 42–43
Daula, Siraj-ud 162–63
Deccan 93, 126–27, 153, 155–57, 162, 195, 198
Delaware 131, 133, 135
dhimmis (protected people) 35
Diu, India 92, 98–100, 153

Dome of the Rock 9, 32
Dominica 129, 132, 146
Dominican Republic 60–61, 67
Dorchester Company (British) 123
Drake, Francis (British Admiral) 71, 73, 129, 131, 148
Drake Roger, Governor of Fort William, Calcutta 159
Duke Odo, of Acquitaine 36–37
Duke Sacarus 23–24
Dupleix, Joseph Francois, French commander in India 126–27, 159–62
Durand agreement 205, 208
Durrani, Ahmad Shah (Afghan ruler) 169, 201
Dutch West Indies Company 119–20

East Africa 90–92, 144–45
Eastern Archipelago 106, 109, 112, 114
Ecija (Spain) 16–17, 20, 41
Egilona (Daughter of King Roderic) 33–34
Egypt 28, 31, 39–40, 43, 49, 72, 83–84, 92, 95, 142, 145, 185, 195
Elizabeth, Queen 149
Elvira (see Granada) 17, 25
Emperor Aurangzeb 155–57, 195; Bahadur Shah Zafar 206; Constantine 6; Diocletian 5; Jahangir 152–53; Shah Alam 164–65, 169, 178, 184, 198–99; Mohammad Shah 157–58; Shah, Nadir Afshar 158
English East India Company 101, 110, 117, 126–28, 143, 145, 149, 152, 155–57, 159–64, 166–67, 169–70, 173–74, 178, 186, 202, 207
Excusado 75
Eyre, Sir Chales 155

Fajj Tariq (Pass of Tariq) 21
Farnavis, Nana 170–72, 176, 196, 206
Ferghana 32
Finland 107
Flanders 55, 69, 73–75, 79, 85
Florida 57, 61, 64, 122, 124, 128–29, 132, 135
Florinda, daughter of Julian 10
Fort: Agra 197, 199; Alcala de Guadaira 22; Aligarh 197–98; Arcot 127, 162, 172; Ayicotta 179; Carmona 22–23, 40; Chartres 124; Cranganore 179; Dhaka Red 155; Duquesne 125–26; Frontenac 124, 126; Louisburg 124, 125–27; Niagara 124; Orihuela 12, 25–27; Oswego, on Lake Ontario

125–26; Quebec 125–26, 132–33; Delhi Red 157, 198; Sirhind 195; St. David 127; St. George 85, 126–27, 154, 161; Ticonderoga 126; William Henry 126; Srirangapatnam 169, 172, 181, 187–88, 190
France 5, 30, 36–38, 43, 50, 55, 65–69, 71–74, 77–80, 103, 107, 122–24, 126–28, 133, 137, 138, 141, 143, 154, 161, 173, 179, 185–86
Francis, Philip 168
Francisco Albuquerque 90, 92–98, 100
Francisco de Almeida, first Portuguese viceroy in India 91, 97
Francisco de Bobadilla 63

Galicia 5, 45, 47
Galle, harbor, Sri Lanka 117, 118
Gambia 144
Gandhi, Mohandas Karamchand 211–14, 216–18, 222
Genoa 65, 69, 70, 74, 83
George Earl of Cumberland 149
Georgia 124, 135
Germany 50, 65–66, 71–72, 74, 145, 210
Ghana 84
Gibraltar 5, 10, 12, 40, 83, 124
Giralda tower 49, 70
Girona, (Gerona) Spain 41
Goa 93–99, 101–03, 109, 113, 118, 119
Golconda, a state of Deccan 153, 156
Granada 16–17, 25, 40, 42, 49–51, 55, 63, 65, 69, 136
Greek, colonies 2
Guadalajara (Hijara) 20–21, 29, 41
Guadeloupe 60, 62, 79, 128
Guiana 143
Guinea 84–85, 103, 129, 144, 146, 149
Gulf of Mexico 124

Haider Ali, ruler of Mysore 128, 165, 169–73, 176, 181, 182
Haiti, (see La Navidad) 59–61, 67
Hansh bin Abdullah (Muslim governor of Zaragoza) 29
Hardinge, Lord 205
Hastings, Lord Warren 165, 167, 168
Hawkins, John 71, 129
Henry the Navigator, prince 83
Hercules 11
Hermandad 55
Hispania 5–8, 13, 23, 30, 49
Holy Prophet, Peace Be Upon Him 10–11, 22, 37–39, 48, 97

Honduras 63, 143
Hong Kong 145
Hooghli, British factory at, 117–18, 154–55, 162
Hormuz 92–93, 96, 102, 103
Huesca 29, 49
Hujjaj bin Yusuf (Governor of Iraq) 32
Hyderabad, India 127, 156, 160–62, 171, 176, 178, 180, 181–84, 186, 187, 189, 194, 213, 219

Iberian Peninsula 5, 7, 25
Ibn-Rushd known as Averroes, a philosopher 49
Inca Empire 65
India 41, 57, 60, 72, 83, 88–93, 95–104, 106–08, 110, 112–14, 117–19, 124–28, 138, 142, 143, 145, 148, 152–60, 162–70, 172–79, 182–86, 194–96, 198–224
Indonesia 72, 101, 107–08, 110, 117–19, 148
Irwin, Lord 211–13
Isabella, Queen 56–57, 60–63
Ismay, Lord 219
Israel 10
Italy 38, 50, 56, 65–66, 68–72, 74, 77, 85, 153

Jabal-i-Tariq 12
Jaen, Province 17, 20, 25, 41, 49
Jafar, Mir 163–64, 172
Jagat Seths, bankers 156–57, 177
Jakarta, then known as Batavia in eastern Archipelago 112–14, 116
Jamaica 61, 63, 73, 78, 129, 146
Jamestown 132–35
Japan 57, 70, 99, 109, 112, 115–16, 119, 145, 151–52, 216–17, 222
Java 107, 108, 117, 119, 130, 145, 151
Jerusalem 5, 7, 28, 32, 42, 56, 97
Jews 7–9, 12, 17, 19, 20–21, 23, 25, 35, 41, 44, 48, 51, 85
Jinnah, Mohammad Ali 215–23
Jizya 16, 20–21, 23, 29, 48, 156
John Law 123, 125, 206
Jordan 35
Jourdain, (English commander) 110–11, 114
Julian, Governor of Ceuta 10–13 15, 17, 22
Julius Caesar 23

Kabul 156, 158, 204, 205
Kandahar 83, 204
Kasim, Mir 164

Index

Kentucky 136
Kenya 87
Khalid bin al-Waleed, Muslim General 35
Khan, Abdur Rahman, Emir of Afghanistan 205
Khan, Dost Mohammad, Ruler of Afghanistan 204–05
Khan, Sher Dil, killer of the traitor Mir Sadiq 191–9
Kharaj (a tax on land paid by the Muslims and non-Muslims) 38, 44, 66
Khorasan 32, 158
Khubilai Khan 58
Khwarezm 32
King: Afonso-I of Portugal 82; Alfonso-II of Asturias 42; Afonso-V of Portugal 84; Agila 6; Akhila 9; Alfonso-VI of Leon 47–49; Alfonso-III of Castile 49; Athanagild 6; Charles-II of Spain 78; Charles II of England 154; Chintila 8; Duarte of Portugal 84; Egica 9; Erwig 8–9; Ferdinand-I of Castile and Leon 47; Ferdinand of Aragon 50; Fernando-III of Spain 50; Francis-I of France 55; Garcia of Galicia 47; George V of England 209; Gundemar 7; Henry-VII of England 129; Herod-I Agrippa 5; of Holland 111; of Jakarta 113; James-I of England 131; Joao-IV of Portugal 77; John of Portugal 56; John-II 85; John-II 97; Leovigild 6; Liuva 6; Louis XIII, of France 77; Louis XIV 78; Louis XV 123; Luitprand of Italian Lambard 38; Mahmud of Afghanistan 201; Manuel-I 85; Philip-II 68; Philip-III 76; Philip-IV 76; Reccared (Visigoth) 6; Reccared-II 8; Reccesuinth 8; Roderic 9; Saif-ud-Din, of Hormuz 96; Sebastian of Portugal 72; Sisebut 7; Shah Shuja of Afghanistan 204; Theudis (Gothic) 20; Turan Shah of Hormuz 96; Wamba 8; Witteric 7; Witiza 9
Koh-i-Noor, diamond 158

La Isabella (in Dominican Republic) 60–62
La Navidad (see Haiti)
La Salle, French Commander 125
Lake: Champlain 124, 126; Erie 124–25; Huron 125; Michigan 125; Ontario 125; Superior 122, 125, 140
Lawrence, Lord 207
Lebanon 10
Leon, Spain 30, 45, 47–48, 82

Lancaster, James, governor and general of the English Company 149
Lerida 29
Libya 9–10, 21
Lisbon 27, 56, 69, 72, 77, 82–86, 88–92, 97, 100–02, 104
Lodhi, Sher Khan, of Bijapur 160
London Company 123
Louisiana 123–26
Louisburg 124–27
Lusitania, province in Spain 23
Luxembourg 72
Lyon, France 36, 38, 12
Lytton, Lord 208

Madagascar 92, 107, 126, 141, 149, 150, 160
Madras 124–28, 154, 157, 159–65, 167, 169–74, 179–80, 182, 184–87, 193, 197, 206, 209
Madrid 20, 69, 78
Maghreb 9–10, 30–31, 34, 39–40
Maimonides, a court Physician 49
Maine 124, 133–34
Makran (in Pakistan) 32
Malabar coast 87–90, 95, 118, 178, 182, 187, 189
Malacca 91, 93–96, 99, 106, 109, 112, 117–19, 145, 150
Malaga, Province in Spain 17, 21, 25, 42, 43
Malay Peninsula 114, 145
Malaysia 119
Maldives 91, 118
Malta 74, 142–43
Manila 68, 70–71, 77, 119
Manitoba 124, 139
Maoris, tribes of New Zealand 141
Marathas 126–27, 156–58, 162, 169, 170–74, 178, 180–84, 186–87, 196–203
Marco Polo 57, 68, 85, 88
Maryland 132–33, 135, 137–38
Martinique 79, 128
Marwan bin Muhammad bin Marwan, Amir of Armenia, and Azerbaijan (Marwan II) 39
Mary, Queen (of England) 68, 209
Masmuda bin Tumart, leader of Almohads 49
Massachusetts Company 123
Massachusetts 134
Masulipatnam, 118, 127, 153, 155, 223
Mauretania 10
Mauritius 107, 126, 143, 185–86
Maurontus, duke of Marseille 37, 38

Mayo, Lord 207
Medina 42, 96, 97
Meri, dhow 90
Merida (city in Spain) 23–25, 43
Mesta (an association of the Spanish sheep herdsmen) 55–56
Mexico 61, 64–68, 70, 75, 119, 124–25, 129, 130, 133, 145–46, 152
Miami 124
Michelborne, Sir Edward, 151
Middle East 72, 80, 93, 153, 178, 184
Minorca 124
Minto, Earl of 200
Minto-Morley reforms 209
Mississippi 123–25, 128
Mississippi Company 123
Missouri 125
Moluccas, province of Indonesia 101, 110, 112–15, 119
Montagu-Chelmsford Act 210, 212
Montreal 122, 124–26, 138
Moors 72, 83, 85, 87
Morocco 9–11, 21, 38, 42, 44, 48, 49, 72, 84, 91, 100, 117
Mosque of Cordoba (built by Abdul Rahman) 42, 45
Mosque of Rufeena (built by governor Abdul Aziz in Sevilla) 33–34, 48
Mountbatten, Lord 218–20, 222
Mount Calpe 11
Mozaffar Jung, the Nizam of Hyderabad 12
Mozambique 86–90, 103
Mudejar (Muslims living under the Christians' rule) 50, 51
Mughit al-Rumi (Muslim warrior in Spain) 12, 17–21, 27, 28, 30–32, 35, 42
Muhammad bin Abbad al-Mu'tamid, ruler of Sevilla 47
Muhammad bin Qasim (conqueror of Sind, Pakistan) 32, 35
Murcia 12, 23, 26, 41, 48, 49
Musa bin Nasyeer 9–11, 13, 16–17, 21–25, 27–35, 49, 191
Mutiny of Meerut 206, 207
Muwalladun (new Muslims) 40, 48
Myanmar 117–18, 203, 216
Mysore 128, 165, 169–72, 176–77, 179–80, 182–84, 186–88, 194, 201–03, 206

Napier, Sir Charles 205
Napoleon, Bonaparte 142, 145, 185, 195, 201
Narbonne, southern France 30, 35–38, 40

Nasrid dynasty 50
Nathaniel Courthope, English commander 111
Navarre 45, 49, 73, 8
Netherlands 65–69, 71–74, 76, 78–80, 107–08, 114, 120, 133, 137
New Brunswick, (see Nova Scotia) 123, 124, 139
New England 122–25, 132–34, 137
Newport, Christopher 131, 133
New Hampshire 133
New Jersey 104, 120, 135
New Orleans 123–24, 128
New South Wales 140–41, 145
New York 66, 104, 120, 125, 133, 135
New Zealand 141
New Zealand Company 14
Nicaea 6
Nicholas de Ovando, Governor of Hispaniola 63
Niger 85, 144
Nimes, in southern France 36, 38
Nizam, of Hyderabad 127, 161–62, 171, 176, 178, 180, 182–84, 186, 187
Noria (waterwheel) 41
Northbrook, Lord 207–08
North Africa 9, 22, 24, 45–46, 48–49, 66, 82, 84, 100
North Carolina 135
Norway 107
Nova Belgia 120
Nova Scotia, (see New Brunswick)

Ohio 124
Ontario 122, 124, 126, 139
Ottawa 139

Pakistan 32, 35, 39, 214–19, 221–23
Palestine 31, 35, 40, 83
Panama 64, 146
Paris 36, 44, 122–23, 128, 164, 184, 185
Patna 153, 155, 177
Patani, port in Malaya peninsula 114–15, 151
Paulo da Gama 85
Pelayo, nephew of King Roderic 35
Pennsylvania 124–25, 135, 137
Peru 61, 64–66, 67, 72, 77, 80
Plymouth 129–30, 133, 148
Pondicherry 126–27, 159–62, 164, 170, 176, 180
Poolo Ai 110–11
Poolo Roon, island 111–12, 114
Priaman, Sumatra 151
Pulicat 117–18

Index

Philippines 68, 70, 72, 76, 78, 80, 119, 130
Poland 107
Pope Gregory 7
Portugal (ancient name Algrave) 23, 25, 27, 30, 41, 45, 49, 56, 68, 71–72, 74, 76–77, 82, 84–85, 87–89, 92–95, 97–99, 101, 103, 107, 110, 114, 129, 138, 142, 144, 148, 154
Powhatans 133–35
Prince: Akhila 9, 12, 14, 16; Olmondo 9, 13, 16; Ardabasto 9, 13, 16
Puerto Rico 64, 67, 80
Pyrenees, hills 5, 36, 38, 42, 78, 79

Qanat (karez) 41
Qayrawan 10–11, 22, 31
Quebec 70, 125–26, 132–33, 138–40
Qutaiba bin Muslim (Governor of Khrorasan) 32, 35

Rabah, a slave of Mughith 19, 28
Radcliffe, Sir Cyril John, Chairman of the boundary commission 220–22
Reconquest of Spain 49
Reaal, Laurence, Dutch governor general 111–12
Repartimientos 64
Rhode Island 133, 135, 142
River: Adyar 159; Columbia 136; Coleroon 176; Creuse 37; Duero 23, 30, 45–47; Ebro 29–30, 50; Garonne 36; Great Fish 86; Guadalete 13, 35; Guadalquivir (also see Shaquanda River) 17, 20, 23, 70; Guadiana 23, 49; James 132–33, 144; Juba 145; Hindan 158; Hudson 120, 132; of the Good Tokens 86; Johore 109; Kortalaiyar 171; Krishna 92, 162; Khelna 197; Maddur 183; Mandavi 93; Nile 145; Orange 142; Ottawa 138; Ozama 63; Potomac 136; Rhone 38; St. Lawrence 124; Shaquanda (see Guadalquivir); Sutlej 194; Tagus 20, 82–83, 85; Thames 131, 149; Umba 145; Vienne 37; Yamuna 198–99; Zaire 85; Zambesi 144
Russia 106

Sadiq, Mir 181, 189–91, 194
Saint James 5
St. Lawrence 70, 123–24, 126, 138
Samarkand 32, 35
San Salvador 57–58
Santiago de Compostela 5, 45
Santo Domingo 61–63, 71, 73, 79, 133

Saracens (nomadic Arabs) 36
Saskatchewan 124
Scindia, Muhadji Rao 156, 170, 172, 177, 184, 196, 198–200, 202, 203
Seram, island 110, 113
Septimania, France 35–37, 42
Sevilla 5, 16, 19, 22–25, 27, 30, 33, 35, 38, 40, 42–43, 47–51, 63–70, 82
Sidonia 13–14, 22, 40, 73
Shahid, Hamid Syed, Major General (Retd), military secretary to the governor general 221
Sierra Leone 116, 129, 144, 148
Simon, Sir John 212
Singh, Maharaja Pratap 208
Sing, Ranjit 194–95, 200–01, 204
Singapore 118, 145, 150
Slavery, African 7, 21, 56, 58, 61, 142, 148
St. Augustine 5, 79, 132, 149
St. Lucia 128, 143
Santo Domingo 61–63, 71, 73, 79, 133
St. Paul 5, 16, 99
St. Vincent 128, 146
Senegal 128, 144
Shah Abdul Aziz, Imam of Delhi Mosque 199
Spain 5–6, 9–13, 15–17, 20–23, 25–36, 40, 43–45, 47, 49–50, 55–56, 58, 61–80, 87, 89, 100, 110, 119, 123–24, 128–29, 131–132, 135–136, 138, 146, 148; capture of Portugal 72
South Africa 86, 141–42, 149
South Carolina 135
Speult, Herman Van, the Dutch Governor 115–16
Steven Coteels, Dutch resident at Amboina 110
Strait of Gibraltar 5, 10, 40
Strait of Malacca 109, 117–18, 150
Subsidio 66
Sulayman Pasha, of Ottomon Empire 95
Sumatra 117–18, 145, 150–51
Sunda Strait 151
Surat 101–03, 115, 118, 152–55, 178, 223
Sweden 104, 107
Switzerland 38, 66
Sydney 140
Syria 10, 35, 39–41, 72, 83

Table Bay, in South Africa 93, 149
Table of Solomon 21, 27–28, 31–33
Tainos 58–60
Taiwan strait 119
Tangier 10–11, 31, 84, 100
Tanzania 90

Tarif bin Talib al-Mu'afire 11, 13
Tariq bin Ziyad 10–17, 20–22, 25, 27–32, 35, 44
Tarragona 9, 30
Tasa 56
Temple of Solomon 7
Tercias reales 66
Tercial (Tarsail) 88
Tobago, islands 128, 143
Thailand 119
The Lusiads, poems 99
Theodomir (governor of Auraiola province) 12–13, 25–27
Timor, island 103, 119
Tipu Sultan 128, 165, 169–73, 175–76, 178–82, 184–87, 189–94, 196
Toledo 6–10, 12, 15–17, 18, 20–21, 25, 27–29, 40–42, 46–49, 51, 69
Toulouse 6, 36
Towerson, Gabriel, English commander of Batavia, 115–16
Treaty of Aix-la-Chapelle, exchange of Madras for Louisburg 127
Treat of Amritsar, 200
Treaty of Mangalore 128
Treaty of Nanking between England and China 145
Treaty of Paris 128, 164
Treaty of Pyrenees 79
Treaty of Sagauli 202
Treaty of St. Germain 123
Treaty of Versailles 128, 186
Treaty of Vervins 73
Treaty of Wadgaon 171
Treaty of Waitangi 141
Treaty of Zamora 82
Trinidad 62–63, 143
Tripoli 28, 66, 71
Tunisia 10, 21
Turkey 10, 72, 83, 92, 178, 186, 201, 210–11

Umayyad 9–10, 32, 34, 38–47
Umayyad mosque in Damascus 32, 42
United States of America 80, 123, 133, 135–36, 139, 145–46

Vasco de Gama 68, 85–86, 88–90, 98, 100
Vasco Nunez de Balboa, discoverer of Panama 64
Venezuela 63
Verenigde Oostindische Compagnie (VOC) 108–10, 113, 116–19, 122, 149
Vermont 133, 137
Virgin Mary 5, 87
Virginia 112, 122–25, 129, 131–35, 137–38, 175
Visigoths 5–6, 11–12, 15, 21, 40–41
Virginia Company 131–35
Voor-Compagnieen 107, 108

Wabash 124
Wadi-ul-Hajara (Valley of Stone) 21
Washington, George 125, 135, 175, 180, 182
Wavell, the British Commander-in-Chief 216–17
Wellesley, Lord Richard, governor general of India 143, 185, 198–200, 202, 203
Wellesley, Arthur, Major General of British army in India 185–87, 189, 194, 196, 197
West Africa 10, 84, 128, 144
West Indies 58, 62, 64, 66–67, 73, 119–20, 124, 128–30, 134, 137, 143–44, 148
William Barents, Dutch naval commander 106
Wisconsin 125
Wybrant van Warwijck, discovery of Mauritius 107–08

Yaha al-Ma'mun, Muslim ruler of Toledo 47
Yusuf Adil Shah, of Ottomon 93–94
Yusuf bin Tashfun, leader of the Almoravids 48

Zaragoza 5, 29–30, 41, 44, 47–49

Printed in the USA
CPSIA information can be obtained
at www.ICGtesting.com
LVHW011143150324
774517LV00041B/1718